CAPITALISM
IN AMERICA

CAPITALISM IN AMERICA

A HISTORY

ALAN GREENSPAN *and*
ADRIAN WOOLDRIDGE

PENGUIN PRESS
New York
2018

PENGUIN PRESS

An imprint of Penguin Random House LLC
375 Hudson Street
New York, New York 10014
penguinrandomhouse.com

LIBRARY OF CONGRESS CATALOGING-IN-PUBLICATION DATA

Names: Greenspan, Alan, 1926- author. | Wooldridge, Adrian, author.
Title: Capitalism in America : a history / Alan Greenspan, Adrian Wooldridge.
Description: New York City : Penguin Press, 2018.
Identifiers: LCCN 2018020397 (print) | LCCN 2018022007 (ebook) |
ISBN 9780735222458 (ebook) | ISBN 9780735222441 (hardback)
Subjects: LCSH: Capitalism—United States—History. | United States—Economic
conditions. | United States—Economic policy. | Economic history. | BISAC:
BUSINESS & ECONOMICS / Economic History. | HISTORY / United States /
General. | BUSINESS & ECONOMICS / Development / Economic
Development.
Classification: LCC HB501 (ebook) | LCC HB501 .G6454 2018 (print) |
DDC 330.973—dc23
LC record available at https://lccn.loc.gov/2018020397

Printed in the United States of America
1   3   5   7   9   10   8   6   4   2

DESIGNED BY AMANDA DEWEY

Greenspan:
For my beloved Andrea

Wooldridge:
For my American-born daughters, Ella and Dora

CONTENTS

———◆———

INTRODUCTION

———◆———

L ET'S START THIS HISTORY with a flight of fancy. Imagine that a version of the World Economic Forum was held in Davos in 1620. The great and the good from across the world are assembled in the Alpine village: Chinese scholars in their silk robes, British adventurers in their doublets and jerkins, Turkish civil servants in their turbans and caftans . . . all edge along the icy paths, frequently tumbling over, or gather in the inns and restaurants, animated by alcohol.

The subject of the conference is an explosive one: who will dominate the world in the coming centuries? Everyone wants to make the case for their corner of the planet. You rush from panel discussion to panel discussion (and then stumble from after-party to after-party) to absorb the Davos wisdom.

The Chinese have a compelling argument. Peking has a population of more than a million at a time when the biggest European cities (London, Paris, Nice) have no more than three hundred thousand. The imperial civil service is selected from an immense country on the basis of the world's most demanding examinations. Chinese scholars have compiled an eleven-thousand-volume encyclopedia. Chinese sailors have built the world's biggest ships.

Others make a good case too. A Turk boasts that the Ottoman Empire, the most important of an arc of Islamic countries extending from Turkey and Arabia to sub-Saharan Africa and Asia, is expanding westward and will soon hold Europe under its sway. A Mughal says that his empire mixes people from every race and religion in a cocktail of creativity. A Spaniard boasts that Spain is sweeping all before it—blessed by the one true Church, it is bringing the rest of Europe under its benign rule and extending its power even to Latin America (where a huge store of gold and silver is funding yet further expansion). A plucky Briton makes the most unlikely case of all. His tiny country has broken with a corrupt and ossified continent and is developing dynamic new institutions: a powerful Parliament, a mighty navy (backed up by a few pirates), and a new species of organization, the chartered corporation, which can trade all over the world.

In all of the arguing in Davos, one region goes unmentioned: North America. The region is nothing more than an empty space on the map—a vast wilderness sitting above Latin America, with its precious metals, and between the Atlantic and Pacific oceans, with their trading routes and treasure troves of fish. The wilderness is populated by aboriginal peoples who have had no contact with the Davos crowd. There are a few Europeans in New England and Virginia—but they report that the life is hard and civilization nonexistent. The entire North American continent produces less wealth than the smallest German principality.

Today the United States is the world's biggest economy: a mere 5 percent of the world's population, it produces a quarter of its GDP expressed in U.S. dollars. America has the world's highest standard of living apart from a handful of much smaller countries such as Qatar and Norway. It also dominates the industries that are inventing the future—intelligent robots, driverless cars, and life-extending drugs.

America's share of the world's patents has increased from 10 percent when Ronald Reagan was elected in 1980 to 20 percent today.

The American economy is as diverse as it is huge. The United States leads the world in a wide range of industries—natural resources as well as information technology, paper, and pulp as well as biotechnology. Many leading economies are dangerously focused on one city: most obviously the United Kingdom but also South Korea and Sweden. The United States has numerous centers of excellence: New York for finance, San Francisco for technology, Houston for energy, and Los Angeles for films.

American capitalism is also the world's most democratic. The United States was the birthplace of the engines of popular capitalism, from mass production to franchising to mutual funds. In many countries capitalism has always been associated with a plutocratic elite. In America, it has been associated with openness and opportunity: making it possible for people who were born in obscurity to rise to the top of society and for ordinary people to enjoy goods and services that were once confined to the elites. R. H. Macy, a former whaling skipper with a tattoo on one of his hands, sold "goods suitable for the millionaire at prices in reach of the millions." Henry Ford, a farmer's son, trumpeted the Model T as "a car for the common man." Amadeo Giannini, an Italian immigrant, founded the Bank of America in order to bring banking to "the little guy." Pierre Omidyar, another immigrant, created an electronic bazaar, eBay, for ordinary people to engage in free exchange.

America's rise to greatness has been marred by numerous disgraces, prime among them the mistreatment of the aboriginal peoples and the enslavement of millions of African Americans. Yet judged against the broad sweep of history, it has been a huge positive. America has not only provided its own citizens with a prosperous life. It has exported prosperity in the form of innovations and ideas. Without America's intervention in the Second World War, Adolf Hitler might well have subdued Europe. Without America's unwavering commitment to the Cold War, Joseph Stalin's progeny might still be in power in Eastern Europe and perhaps much of Asia. Uncle Sam provided the arsenal of democracy that saved the twentieth century from ruin.

This is a remarkable story. But it is also a story with a sting in the tail: today, productivity growth has all but stalled. Tyler Cowen has talked about a "great stagnation." Lawrence Summers has revived Alvin Hansen's phrase, "secular stagnation." Robert Gordon's study of the American economy since the Civil War is called *The Rise and Fall of American Growth*. America is being defeated by China and other rising powers in one industry after another. The number of new companies being created has reached a modern low. The labor market is becoming stickier. Regulations are multiplying.

America has bounced back from previous disappointments. In the 1930s, the country suffered from one of the longest and deepest depressions in history. Then it emerged from the Second World War as by far the world's most powerful economy. In the 1970s, it was plagued by stagflation and bruised by competition with Germany and Japan. In the 1980s and 1990s, it seized the opportunities provided by information technology and globalization to regain its position as the world's most dynamic economy. Whether it can pull off this trick again is still unclear.

This book will tell the most remarkable story of the past four hundred years: how a collection of thirteen colonies in the middle of nowhere transformed itself into the mightiest economy the world has seen. It will also try to use the lessons of history to address the great question of our time: whether the United States will preserve its preeminence or whether its leadership will inevitably pass to other (almost certainly less liberal) powers.

A GREAT AGE FOR BEGINNINGS

Three hundred years ago America was nothing more than a collection of sparsely populated settlements hanging off the edge of the known world—an afterthought to educated minds and a sideshow in great power politics. Though rich in natural resources, it was far away from the centers of civilization; though huge, it was mostly inaccessible. Yet luck smiled on the young country. America owed its birth to a succession of lucky breaks. The rebellion that created the United States might not have gotten off the ground at all if the British establishment had listened to Edmund Burke and pursued a more moderate policy. The rebels were the beneficiaries of a global war between the British and the French. The independence struggle would have faltered if George Washington had not been such a great leader of men. The lucky breaks continued after the country's birth. Thomas Jefferson's purchase of the Louisiana Territory from France in 1803 doubled the size of the country, adding fertile farmland, the Mississippi River, and the port of New Orleans. America bought Florida from Spain in 1821, annexed Texas in 1845 and Oregon in 1846, and with its victory in the Mexican-American War, added California in 1850.

America was lucky in its paternity: it was far better to be the child of the country that produced the first Industrial Revolution and the first parliamentary government than, say, the child of Spain or Belgium. To this day Americans invoke the evils of monarchical tyranny and the virtues of the Revolution. Yet in many ways the American Revolution was only a half revolution: America inherited many of Britain's best traditions, from limited government to the common law to a respect for individual rights that, according to one eminent historian, Alan Macfarlane, stretches back to the thirteenth century.[1] America engaged in a ceaseless exchange of informal knowledge with Britain, importing British immigrants, who frequently brought industrial secrets with them, and sending Americans to visit British factories, steelworks, and exhibitions. It looked to British models for its stock market, commodity exchanges, and patent laws. Divided by a common language, America and Britain are nevertheless united by a common culture.

The luckiest break of all was timing. The United States was born in the age of the Enlightenment, when old verities were being rethought and established institutions remodeled. The country's bloody struggle for independence (1775–83) began a year before the publication of the greatest work of free-market economics ever written, Adam Smith's *The Wealth of Nations* (1776). For most of recorded history, people had acquiesced in, and in some ways embraced, a society that was static and predictable. From the birth of Jesus to about 1820, economic growth amounted to no more than 0.11 percent a year or 11 percent a century, according to Angus Maddison.[2] A young fifteenth-century vassal could look forward to tilling the same plot of his landlord's soil until disease, famine, natural disaster, or violence dispatched him. And the vassal could fully expect that his children and his children's children would till the same plot.

Adam Smith advanced a vision of a dynamic society in which wealth multiplied and opportunities abounded. In doing so, he performed a remarkable intellectual somersault. Until this point, people had generally regarded the pursuit of self-interest as, at best, unseemly, and at worst, sinful. Smith countered that, provided it took place within the constraints of law and morality, the pursuit of self-interest boosts the well-being of the entire nation.

No country has embraced this insight more fully than the one that was born shortly after Adam Smith advanced this argument. The new country was conceived in a revolt against a mercantilist regime that believed that a nation's economic success was measured by the size of its stock of gold, which was, in turn, driven by the extent of positive trade balances fostered by protectionist policies. The U.S. Constitution, written in 1787 and ratified in 1788, established that the entire country was a unified common market with no internal tariffs or taxes on interstate commerce. America was the first country to be born in an age of growth—an age when the essential economic problem was to promote the forces of change rather than to divvy up a fixed set of resources.

The second force shaping America was the Enlightenment's great antagonist, religion, particularly the Protestant religion. More than any other country America was the child of the European Reformation. Whereas the Catholic Church encouraged its members to approach God through the medium of the priest, the Protestant Church encouraged the faithful to approach God through the medium of the Bible. Protestants were supposed to read the Good Book at home and come to their own judgment on religious affairs rather than rely on the authority of their superiors. The Massachusetts Puritans founded schools and universities on a scale unmatched in any other country. A Massachusetts law obliged all heads of households to teach their children to read. "After God has carried us safe to New England, and we had builded our houses, provided necessaries for our livelihood, reared convenient places for God's worship, and settled Civil Government," stated a 1643 letter from Harvard University to England that is the first known example of a university funding letter, "one of the next things we longed for and looked for was to advance learning and perpetuate it to posterity."

America had one more piece of luck in its early years: the Founders realized that the only way to thrive in a mobile world was to establish some fixed points to navigate by. They provided citizens with a set of rights that the government couldn't violate and a

Constitution that kept power in check. The more you opened the way to the rule of the people, the more you had to make sure that the people didn't abuse their power. And the more you opened the door to commercial passions, the more you had to make sure that merchants didn't debase the currency or cheat their customers.

The Founders injected property rights into the country's DNA. Thomas Jefferson's phrase about man's "inalienable right" to "life, liberty and the pursuit of happiness" was a gloss on John Locke's phrase, in his "Second Treatise," about man having "by nature a power" to preserve "his life, liberty and estate, against the injuries and attempts of other men." The Constitution divided power in large part to protect propertied people from the predations of the masses or a dictator. This vigorous protection of property not only encouraged entrepreneurialism at home, because people had a reasonable certainty of keeping their gains, it also encouraged foreign investors to put their money in America on the grounds that they wouldn't see their capital stolen and their contractual rights ignored.

America's passion for protecting property extended to the fruits of their imaginations. The Founding Fathers built patent protection into Article I, Section 8, of the Constitution. America extended intellectual property rights to people who would never have had them in Europe, setting the patent fee at only 5 percent of the amount charged in Britain. It also required inventors to publicize the details of their patents so that innovations could be disseminated even as the right to profit from making them was protected.

The preoccupation with patents points to another advantage: America was born in an age of business. The country was founded by business corporations such as the Virginia Company and the Massachusetts Bay Company: the first American "freemen" were, in fact, company stockholders, and the first "commonwealths" were company general assemblies. Americans were the first people to use the word "businessman" in the modern sense. In the eighteenth century, the English used the term to refer to people who were engaged in public affairs: David Hume described Pericles as a "man of business." In the 1830s, Americans began to use the phrase to refer to people who were engaged in mercantile transactions.[3]

Thereafter Americans reserved the same respect for businesspeople that the British reserved for gentlemen, the French for intellectuals, and the Germans for scholars. America's willingness to "put something heroic into their way of trading," as Alexis de Tocqueville put it, produced a cult of the entrepreneur. Americans were instinctive supporters of Joseph Schumpeter's idea that the real motors of historical change were not workers, as Marx had argued, nor abstract economic forces, as his fellow economists tended to imply, but people who build something out of nothing, inventors like Thomas Edison, who had 1,093 patents, and company builders like Henry Ford, Thomas Watson, and Bill Gates.

America didn't progress in a straight line after the War of Independence. The infant republic was torn between two different visions of the future—Thomas Jefferson's vision of a decentralized agrarian republic of yeomen farmers, and Alexander Hamilton's (astonishingly prescient) vision of an urban republic with industrial mills driving economic growth and a powerful bank irrigating the economy. America was also divided into two strikingly different economies— the capitalist economy of the North and the slave-owning economy of the South. This division became more pronounced over time as the North invested more heavily in machinery and the South invested more heavily in cotton growing and tried to expand the slave system into new territories such as Kansas. The Civil War eventually decided which version of America would emerge—and the United States tirelessly spread its version of a business civilization across the entire continent.

PEOPLE OF PLENTY

America's business civilization took root in a country that enjoyed an abundance of the three great factors of production: capital, land, and labor. America's banking sector expanded from 338 banks with total assets of $160 million in 1818 to 27,864 banks with assets of $27.3 billion in 1914. America also became the world's leading importer of capital, particularly from America's predecessor as the headquarters of capitalism, the United Kingdom. The country's official land area kept growing rapidly in the first half of the nineteenth century, from 864,746 square miles in 1800 to 2,940,042 in 1850. Americans brought 400 million acres of virgin territory under cultivation between the end of the Civil War and the outbreak of the First World War—a quantity of land almost twice the size of Western Europe.

The land contained a vast store of natural resources. America has more miles of navigable rivers than the rest of the world combined. The greatest of these rivers—the Missouri, Ohio, Arkansas, Tennessee, and of course, the mighty Mississippi—flow diagonally rather than perpendicularly, drawing the country together into a natural geographical unit.[4] The Appalachian Mountains, from Pennsylvania to Kentucky to the hills of West Virginia, are filled with coal. Montana is so rich in precious metals that its official nickname is the Treasure State. The Mesabi Range in Minnesota is stuffed full of iron ore. Texas sits on a lake of oil (a lake that is now getting bigger thanks to the invention of fracking). The Midwest is a wheat bowl.

It's easy to see the impact of resource wealth in American history. You can see it in the succession of commodity-driven crazes—most notably the gold rush of 1849 and the oil booms of the early 1900s and 1950s—that have gripped the country. You can see it in giant export industries such as wheat. But one of the most important impacts was invisible: America didn't suffer from the resource constraints that have slowed down growth in other countries. From 1890 to 1905, when America's steel industry was booming, Minnesota's share of the country's iron ore production rose from 6 percent to 51 percent and the domestic price of iron ore fell by half, ensuring that the country's steel magnates were paying significantly less for their raw materials than their British competitors.

America was also a people magnet. Colonial America had one of the highest birthrates in the world thanks to the abundance of land and shortage of labor. Population growth kicked into a still higher gear when America began to suck people from abroad. In the nineteenth century, the population multiplied by a factor of almost fifteen, from 5.3 million to 76 million, a total larger than any European country except Russia. By 1890, 80 percent of New York's citizens were immigrants or the children of immigrants, as were 87 percent of Chicago's.

A striking proportion of America's entrepreneurial heroes were immigrants or the children of immigrants. Alexander Graham Bell and Andrew Carnegie were born in Scotland. Nikola Tesla, the discoverer of AC electricity, was Serbian. George Mitchell, the inventor of fracking and one of the most consequential businessmen of recent decades, was the son of a Greek goatherd.

Having arrived in the country, the settlers were unusually mobile: brought up in countries where land was in short supply, they were seized by a mixture of land lust and wanderlust when they realized that land was abundant. This addiction to mobility survived the creation of a more prosperous civilization: in their *Middletown* studies of a typical town in the Midwest, Muncie, Indiana, Robert and Helen Lynd discovered that Americans became more mobile as time went on, with 35 percent of families moving in 1893–98 and 57 percent in 1920–24. In the decades after 1900, millions of black Americans fled the indentured servitude of sharecropping in the South for booming northern industrial towns such as Detroit and Chicago. (From the 1980s onward this flow was reversed as millions of people of all colors fled the Rust Belt for the booming Sun Belt.)

In the second half of the nineteenth century, the country combined its various advantages—cultural and demographic, political and geographical—to turn itself into the world's most powerful economy. Railroads knitted the country together into the world's biggest single market: by 1905, 14 percent of the world's railway mileage passed through a single American city, Chicago. America produced the world's biggest corporations: U.S. Steel, formed in 1901, the world's first billion-dollar company, employed some 250,000 people. America did more than any other country to transform two new technologies—electricity and the internal combustion engine—into a cornucopia of consumer products: cars and trucks, washing machines and radios.

HOW TO GET RICH

In telling this story, this book will focus on three organizing themes: productivity, creative destruction, and politics. Productivity describes society's ability to get more output from a given input. Creative destruction defines the process that drives productivity growth. Politics deals with the fallout of creative destruction. The first is a technical economic issue. The second is an economic issue that also touches on some of the most profound problems of social philosophy. The third takes us far from the world of charts and numbers into the world of practical politics. Anyone who regards economic history as history with the politics left out is reading the wrong book.

Productivity is the ultimate measure of economic success.[5] The level of productivity determines the average standard of living in a society and distinguishes advanced countries from developing countries. The most commonly used measure of productivity is labor productivity, which is measured by output (value added) per every hour worked (OPH). Two big determinants of the level of labor productivity are the amount of capital (plant and equipment) employed in making things and the number of hours people work, adjusted for their level of education and skills.

In the 1950s, "growth economists," led by Moses Abramovitz and Robert Solow, discovered that the inputs of capital and labor do not fully account for all the growth in GDP. They dubbed the unexplained leftover multifactor productivity (MFP) or, sometimes, total factor productivity. The heart of MFP is innovation. MFP arises mainly from innovations applied to the inputs of capital and labor.

The problem with calculating GDP and MFP over a long period is that the further back you go in time, the more difficult it is to find solid statistics. The U.S. government only began collecting systematic data on national income and product accounts in the 1930s, when it called on the expertise of Simon Kuznets of Stanford University and the National Bureau of Economic Research. For prior data, historians have to rely mainly on the decennial census, which started in the 1790s. Historians supplement official census data with scattered data on industrial production, crops, livestock, and hours worked, but, as Paul David identified, such data were not very accurate before the 1840s. Despite these limitations, a legion of economic historians has, more or less, constructed a useful statistical history of GDP, both nominal and real, for the early years of the republic (see appendix).[6] We draw on that work throughout this book.

CREATIVE DESTRUCTION

Creative destruction is the principal driving force of economic progress, the "perennial gale" that uproots businesses—and lives—but that, in the process, creates a more productive economy. With rare exceptions the only way to increase output per hour is to allocate society's resources to areas where they will produce the highest returns—or, in more formal language, to direct society's gross domestic savings (plus savings borrowed from abroad) to fund cutting-edge technologies and organizations. Creation and destruction are Siamese twins. The process involves displacing previously productive assets and their associated jobs with newer technologies and their jobs. Thus Henry Bessemer's novel steel technology of 1855 displaced previous, more costly steelmaking.

The world owes the idea of creative destruction to Joseph Schumpeter and his great work *Capitalism, Socialism and Democracy* (1942). "The process of creative destruction is the essential fact about capitalism," Schumpeter argued. "It is what capitalism consists in and what every capitalist concern has got to live in." Yet for all his genius, Schumpeter didn't go beyond brilliant metaphors to produce a coherent theory of creative destruction: modern economists have therefore tried to flesh out his ideas and turn metaphors into concepts that acknowledge political realities, which is to say, the world as it really is.

There is no better place to study this perennial gale than late-nineteenth-century America, when the country produced a throng of business titans who reorganized entire industries on a continental stage. It was a time in which the federal government focused overwhelmingly on protecting property rights and enforcing contracts rather than on "taming" the process of creative destruction. Thanks to relentless innovation the unit cost (a proxy for output per hour) of

Bessemer steel fell sharply, reducing its wholesale price from 1867 to 1901 by 83.5 percent. And cheap steel set off a cycle of improvements: steel rails lasted more than ten times longer than wrought-iron rails at only a modest increase in price, allowing more people and products to be carried by rail for less money. A similar cascade of improvements in almost every area of life produced a doubling of living standards in a generation.

The most obvious way to drive creative destruction is to produce more powerful machines. A striking number of the machines that have revolutionized productivity look like improvised contraptions. Cyrus McCormick's threshing machine, described by the London *Times* as a cross between a flying machine and a wheelbarrow,[7] helped to produce a 500 percent increase in output per hour for wheat and a 250 percent increase in output for corn from its invention in 1831 to the end of the nineteenth century. In the process, it helped to displace as much as a quarter of the world's agricultural labor force. In 1800, a farmer working hard with a scythe could harvest only a single acre in a day. By 1890 two men using two horses could cut, rake, and bind twenty acres of wheat in the same time. The sewing machine, which was invented in 1846 and produced in large numbers by the 1870s, increased productivity by more than 500 percent. New tabulating machines meant that the 1890 census was compiled in less than a year, compared with an estimated thirteen years for the 1880 census. Teleprinters, which appeared in 1910, displaced 80 to 90 percent of Morse code operators by 1929.

Better business processes are as important as better machines. Mass production was arguably America's greatest contribution to human productivity. In nineteenth-century Europe, the production of complicated systems such as guns or clocks remained in the hands of individual master craftsmen. In America, Eli Whitney and other innovators broke down the manufacture of the machine into the manufacture of uniform parts. In 1913, Henry Ford added a moving assembly line, which brought the job to the man. America's success in producing better machines and smoother production processes has been recognized by even the crudest intellects. Stalin described America as a "country of machines."[8] Hitler claimed that Nazism was "Fordism plus the Fuhrer."

These big forces are supplemented by more subtle ones. Most important is better information. In recent years we have grown so accustomed to receiving timely information that we treat it like the air we breathe. But for most of human history information has been so costly to acquire that people were often operating in the dark. The Battle of New Orleans, the last major engagement in the War of 1812, which turned Andrew Jackson into a national hero and cost seven hundred British troops their lives, took place two weeks after the war had ended with the Treaty of Ghent.

The *Journal of Commerce,* first published in 1827, became an indispensable source for breaking news on trade by deploying deep water schooners to intercept incoming ships before they docked. Samuel Morse's telegraph, first demonstrated in 1844, reduced the potential time it took to transmit information to seconds. Western Union telegraph communication joined the coasts in 1861 at Fort Laramie, Wyoming. Transcontinental freight and people travel became a reality only a few years later, in 1869. The golden spike was ceremoniously driven in at Promontory Summit, Utah Territory, joining the Union Pacific and Central Pacific rail networks, into which new telegraph lines were added. The opening of the transatlantic cable (after several false starts) in 1866, finally created a transatlantic financial community with traders in New York, San Francisco, and London communicating with each other in real time.

The information revolution has removed all sorts of inefficiencies and uncertainties that used to slow down business transactions.

Retailers can order new products as soon as old ones leave the shelves. Suppliers can keep a constant watch on the supply chain. Instant communication between the retail checkout counter and the factory floor and between shippers and truckers hauling freight reduces delivery times and eliminates the need for keeping large inventories of idle stock.

A second aspect of creative destruction is the reduction in the cost of basic inputs into the economy. Andrew Carnegie and John D. Rockefeller were heroes of creative destruction because, by dint of superior organization and ceaseless innovation, they reduced the cost of the basic economic inputs of steel and energy, respectively, sending ripples of lower prices and more abundant resources through the economy.

A third is the more efficient use of those inputs. In the glory days of America's industrial might, people measured success in terms of the size of factories or the height of skyscrapers. Over time, size has become an ever-weaker proxy for economic vigor: the amount of materials needed to produce a given unit of output has declined in recent decades. The development of integrated circuits has allowed us to cram more functions into sleek electronic boxes. Advances in material science have allowed us to produce lighter cars (per unit of horsepower) and more efficient buildings. By our estimates, the decline in materials used per dollar of real GDP added 0.26 percentage points a year to real GDP growth between 1879 and 2015. That added 40 percent to real GDP by 2015. The annual gains were markedly greater from 1879 to 1899, where effectiveness added 0.52 percentage points a year to real GDP growth. That added 10.6 percent to the level of real GDP in 1899.

An additional aspect of creative destruction is the reduction in transportation costs. Cold-rolled steel sheet is worth more on a car located in a car dealership than rolling off a steel mill in Pittsburgh.

Improved transport accordingly brings two obvious benefits: it allows entrepreneurs to bring the factors of production together more easily and get the fruit of the combination of those factors, the finished products, to the consumers more swiftly. In the early years of the republic, productivity improvements were limited by the speed that horses could run or ships could sail. Improved roads or rigging could only improve productivity a little, since hooves or sails could only go so fast. Productivity increased when steamships replaced sails, not only because steamboats could go faster than sailboats in inland waterways, but also because they could sail upstream as well as downstream. The transcontinental railroad reduced the time it took to transport people and goods across the continent from six months to six days.[9] The addition of local lines gradually plugged a larger proportion of the country's human and physical resources into a national rail line and dramatically increased the flow of people and goods around the country. Motorcars and highways eventually supplanted railway lines because they are more fluid and flexible: they can take goods to your front door rather than just to the local railway station. The miniaturization revolution has reduced transportation costs still further: the computer industry is inherently more global than, say, the concrete industry because it's so easy to move light, precious computer parts from one part of the world to another.

A fifth source of productivity improvement is location. In today's flattened world of global supply chains and instant communications, we tend to forget what was all too evident to our forebears: that clever location can boost productivity. Entrepreneurs made their fortunes simply by building mills next to waterfalls (which provided free power), or by locating their factories near rivers (which provided free transportation), or by the smart layout of their facilities. The same productivity-boosting logic applies to fractions of an inch as it does to yards or miles. In the nineteenth century, entrepreneurs created economic value by building a railroad to bring iron ore from Minnesota's Mesabi Range and coal from West Virginia to the furnaces in Pittsburgh, where they were added together to produce steel. Today they create economic value by fitting ever-smaller silicon chips ever closer together within an integrated circuit in order to produce ever-greater amounts of computing capacity.

THE CUNNING OF HISTORY

In the real world, creative destruction seldom works with the smooth logic of Moore's law. It can take a long time for a new technology to change an economy: the spread of Samuel Morse's telegraph was complicated by the size of the country and the difficulty of the terrain. Though telegraph wires quickly blanketed the East Coast and the more densely inhabited parts of the West Coast, giving people access to almost instant communications, the center of the country remained an information void. In the late 1850s, it still took more than three weeks to convey a message from one coast to the other by a combination of telegraph and stagecoach. Sometimes old technologies can work in tandem with new ones: starting in 1860, the Pony Express, with its riders leaping from one horse to another fresh one, reduced the time it took to get a message across the country to under ten days.[10] The ponies were much more flexible than more advanced methods of transport such as wagons or trains: railroads could ride up steep ravines and negotiate narrow trails.

As the mention of the Pony Express suggests, new technologies can often reinforce old ones. The *Nation* magazine addressed the paradox of the popularity of the horse in the age of steam in October 1872:

Our talk has been for so many years of the railroad and steamboat and telegraphy, as the great "agents of progress," that we
have come almost totally to overlook the fact that our dependence
on the horse has grown almost *pari passu* with our dependence on steam. We have opened up great lines of steam and
communication all over the country, but they have to be fed with
goods and passengers by horses. We have covered the ocean with
great steamers, but they can neither load nor discharge their car-
goes without horses.[11]

For several decades America's equine population grew more than
twice as fast as its human population, from 4.3 million horses and
mules in 1840 to 27.5 million in 1910. That meant that the ratio of
horses and mules to people increased over seventy years of pell-mell
progress from one to every five humans to one to every three.[12] People used horses to drive mills, pull plows, walk alongside canal boats,
herd cattle, fight battles, and above all, carry burdens for short distances. It took the combination of three kinds of power to displace
horses from the heart of the American economy. Steam power replaced horses for long-distance hauling. Electric power replaced
them for urban transport. And "horseless carriages" replaced them
for short hauls.

There is often a significant time lag between the invention of a
new technology and the boost in productivity that it produces. Four
decades after Thomas Edison's spectacular illumination of Lower
Manhattan in 1882, electricity had done little to make the country's
factories more productive. Introducing electricity was not just a matter of plugging factories into the electricity grid. It involved redesigning entire production processes and replacing vertical factories with
horizontal ones to get the best out of the new power source.[13]

Some of the most important improvements in productivity take place without much fuss. Both steelmaking and farming witnessed astonishing improvements long after commentators had given up talking about the "age of steel" or the "agricultural revolution." The oxygen furnaces that replaced open-hearth furnaces after the Second World War (and which as the name suggests used oxygen rather than air) reduced the time taken to produce a batch of steel from eight to nine hours to thirty-five to forty minutes. Between 1920 and 2000, labor requirements per ton of raw steel decreased by a factor of a thousand, from more than 3 worker-hours per metric ton to just 0.003.

Some of the most important improvements are felt in the convenience of everyday life rather than in discrete economic sectors such as "industry" or "agriculture." Herodotus described an Egyptian king who only had six years to live. "Perceiving that his doom was fixed, [he] had lamps . . . lighted every day at eventime . . . and enjoyed himself . . . turning the nights into days, and so living twelve years in the space of six." The spread of electricity from 1900 onward had the same effect on the American population as a whole.[14] Home appliances and convenience foods reduced the time spent on preparing meals, doing the laundry, and cleaning the house from fifty-eight hours a week in 1900 to eighteen hours a week by 1975.[15] The Bureau of Labor Statistics estimated that bar code scanners at checkout counters increased the speed that cashiers could ring up payments by 30 percent and reduced labor requirements of cashiers and baggers by 10 to 15 percent.

THE DOWNSIDE OF CREATIVE DESTRUCTION

The destructive side of creative destruction comes in two distinct forms: the destruction of physical assets as they become surplus to requirements, and the displacement of workers as old jobs are abandoned. To this should be added the problem of uncertainty. The "gale of creative destruction" blows away old certainties along with old forms of doing things: nobody knows which assets will prove to be productive in the future and which will not. New technologies almost always bring speculative bubbles that can pop, sometimes with dangerous consequences.

Partly because people are frightened of change and partly because change produces losers as well as winners, creative destruction is usually greeted by what Max Weber called "a flood of mistrust, sometimes of hatred, above all of moral indignation."[16] The most obvious form of resistance comes from workers who try to defend their obsolescent jobs. Before the Civil War, American workers didn't have much chance to organize because companies were small; elite craft guilds defined the labor market; relations were face-to-face; and strikes were rare. After the Civil War, as big business took off, unskilled workers began to form trade unions to increase their pay and improve their conditions. Battles with bosses sometimes resulted in violence and frequently poisoned class relations.

American unions were much weaker than their European equivalents. They were harried by the courts, which repeatedly ruled that combinations of labor were illegal, and plagued by internal conflicts between skilled and unskilled workers, immigrants and native-born workers, and various regional interest groups. The unions finally achieved significant power in the 1930s with a succession of pro-labor bills. During the long period of prosperity after the Second World War, about a third of America's private-sector workers were unionized, and the unions played an important role in making public policy. Yet America's individualistic tradition remained powerful. The Taft-Hartley Act of 1947 outlawed "closed shops." The southern states were much more antiunion than the northern states. And after the wave of deregulation starting in the 1970s, American trade-union membership went into decline. Trade unions didn't place much of a brake on progress during the long era of managerial capitalism after the Second World War because the United States was reaping the benefits of mass production and maturing technologies, such as electricity. Yet the same trade unions became a powerful constraint on growth when mass production needed to be replaced by flexible production, and managerial capitalism by a more entrepreneurial capitalism.

Resistance can come from business titans as well as labor barons. One of the great paradoxes of creative destruction is that people who profit from it one moment can turn against it the next: worried that their factories will become obsolete or their competitors will produce better products, they do everything they can—from lobbying the government to appealing to the courts—to freeze competition and turn their temporary advantage into a permanent one. In the 1880s, Andrew Hickenlooper, the head of the Cincinnati Gas Company and sometime president of the American Gas Association, conducted a vigorous campaign to defend the "gas meter" against the "dynamo." He bullied the city fathers into refusing to give contracts to electricity companies (or rival gas companies, for that matter) and conducted a propaganda campaign in the press about the dangers of the new technology: wires could deliver death by electric shocks or set cities on fire.[17]

ENTER THE POLITICIANS

America has been better at both the creative and the destructive side of creative destruction than most other countries: it has been better at founding businesses and taking those businesses to scale, but it has also been better at winding down businesses when they fail. The most obvious expression of this is the country's unusual tolerance of bankruptcy. Many of nineteenth-century America's greatest entrepreneurs, including Charles Goodyear, R. H. Macy, and H. J. Heinz, suffered from repeated business failures before finally making it.

America's appetite for creative destruction has many roots. The fact that America is such a big country meant that people were willing to pull up stakes and move on: from its earliest days, the West was littered with ghost towns as people built new towns and then quickly abandoned them. The fact that it is a relatively new country meant that vested interests had less power: there were fewer people, particularly in the West, with established ways of life to defend. In Britain, railroads had to make strange loops to avoid ancient settlements. In America, they could carve a straight line from "Nowhere-in-Particular to Nowhere-at-All," as the London *Times* once put it. America sometimes paid a heavy price, not just aesthetically but also economically, for this attitude, with jerry-built settlements put up with little consideration for the future and abandoned with even less, but at the very least it avoided stagnation.

The country's political system has powerfully reinforced these geographical and cultural advantages. The biggest potential constraint on creative destruction is political resistance. The losers of creative destruction tend to be concentrated while the winners tend to be dispersed. Organizing concentrated people is much easier than organizing dispersed ones. The benefits of creative destruction can take decades to manifest themselves, while the costs are often immediate. Adding to this is the fact that a perennial gale is disconcerting to everyone, winners as well as losers: people have a strong preference for sticking with the familiar rather than embracing change (and explaining to them that you can't preserve the familiar if you can't afford it is hard).

America has been much better than almost every other country at resisting the temptation to interfere with the logic of creative destruction. In most of the world, politicians have made a successful business out of promising the benefits of creative destruction without the costs. Communists have blamed the costs on capitalist greed. Populists have blamed them on sinister vested interests. European-style socialists have taken a more mature approach, admitting that creation and destruction are bound together, but claiming to be able to boost the creative side of creative destruction while eliminating the destructive side through a combination of demand management and wise intervention. The result has usually been disappointing: stagnation, inflation, or some other crisis.

For much of its history the United States was immune from these short-term political pressures. The Founding Fathers did a remarkable job in protecting the economy from political interference by providing citizens with inalienable rights and by constraining political power in various ways. America's economic culture promoted the vigorous virtues of prudence and self-reliance. The gold standard provided such a stable framework for monetary policy that America did without a central bank for seventy-seven years, from 1836 (when Andrew Jackson vetoed a third bank) to 1913. Income tax was nonexistent. Most educated Americans believed in the law of the survival of the fittest.

The Progressive movement challenged some of these long-standing assumptions. Woodrow Wilson introduced a federal income tax in 1913. The New Deal put an end to the era of laissez-faire. The postwar era saw a much more activist government than the government of the 1920s. Dwight Eisenhower embarked on a huge highway-building program. LBJ promised to build the "Great Society."

The shift away from laissez-faire was nevertheless much less dramatic than it was in Europe, let alone in Latin America. The American Constitution has repeatedly kept the government activists in check. The Supreme Court struck down FDR's National Industrial Recovery

Act, which imposed extensive state controls on the economy. Republican congressmen prevented Harry Truman from introducing a national health service after the Second World War. Liberal activists have repeatedly been followed by more conservative successors—FDR by Dwight Eisenhower (by way of Truman), Lyndon Johnson by Richard Nixon, and Jimmy Carter by Ronald Reagan. America's powerful tradition of laissez-faire liberalism also reasserted itself after the Second World War. Friedrich Hayek's *The Road to Serfdom* (1944) was condensed in *Reader's Digest* and read by millions. Milton Friedman became a television star. Ronald Reagan campaigned on the idea that government was the problem rather than the solution.

But can America continue to preserve its comparative advantage in the art of creative destruction? That is looking less certain. The rate of company creation is now at its lowest point since the 1980s. More than three-quarters of America's major economic sectors are witnessing a decline in the level of competition. The dependency ratio is going up as the baby boomers retire. Entitlements are rising inexorably, and by crowding out capital investment, are reducing productivity and economic growth in the process. And America's defenses against populism are weakening every day as professional politicians sell their votes to the highest bidder and voters demand unfiltered democracy to discipline a corrupt system. Donald Trump is the closest thing that America has produced to a Latin American–style populist, promising to keep out foreign competition and forcing companies to offer their workers a "fair" deal.

RESTORING AMERICA'S LOST DYNAMISM

This book will conclude by suggesting some policies that can restore America's fading dynamism. The most important reform would be to follow Sweden in 1991 in reforming entitlements. Sweden addressed its fiscal crisis by shifting from social benefits (entitlements) to a system of defined contributions. In 2017, entitlements claimed more than 14 percent of U.S. GDP, compared with less than 5 percent in 1965, diverting ten percentage points of GDP and economic activity from investment to consumption and swelling America's already worrying budget deficit. In the 2017 Annual Report of the Board of Trustees of the Federal Old-Age and Survivors Insurance and Federal Disability Insurance Trust Funds, the actuaries note that in order to make the system truly actuarially sound, benefit levels need to be reduced by 25 percent indefinitely into the future, or taxation rates need to be raised. A symbol of the political sensitivity of such a diagnosis is the fact that it appears toward the end of a 296-page report.

Close behind in second place is the reform of the financial system: another financial crisis on the scale of 2008 or 1929 would undermine the legitimacy of the entire system, as well as wreak short-term havoc. As we will detail later in this book, all such crises are set off by financial intermediaries' having too little capital in reserve and fostering modern versions of a contagious run on the bank. The nonfinancial sectors of the American economy have historically had equity-to-asset ratios in the range of 40 to 50 percent of assets. Contagious default of firms with such capital balancing is quite rare. Periodic contagious defaults are a regrettable characteristic of financial institutions that have much lower equity-to-asset ratios. The best way to prevent the crisis from recurring is to force banks to hold substantially more capital and collateral. History does not support the contention that such a requirement would significantly constrain lending and economic growth, as is often alleged. Unfortunately, policy makers have chosen a different solution—creating complicated regulations such as the Dodd-Frank Act (2010) that are driven by pressure groups with a wish list of demands rather than being a focused attempt to solve the problem at hand. Dodd-Frank adds yet further to the complexity of a regulatory structure that has been jerry-built over the decades.

Yet whenever America has flirted with national decline in the past—in the 1930s, for example, or the 1970s—it has always grappled with its problems and come back stronger. The underlying vigor of the national economy, and indeed of the national character, has always trumped failures of policy making. In 1940, America's future looked dismal: the country had just been through a decade of economic stagnation and financial turmoil. Yet a decade later the economy was once again firing on all cylinders and America was by far the world's most successful economy.

One way to counter the growing mood of pessimism is to look at Silicon Valley, where entrepreneurs are inventing the future of everything from smartphones to robotics. Another way is to look at the past. Two hundred years ago America's settlers were confronted with problems that make today's problems look quaint: how to make a living out of a vast unforgiving landscape and how to forge a political system that reconciled states' rights with national government, individual initiative with collective responsibility.

The story of how they succeeded is as exhilarating as it is instructive.

One

A COMMERCIAL REPUBLIC: 1776–1860

———◆———

THE TERM "COLONY" CONJURES up images of exploitation and marginalization. Yet Colonial America was in many respects among the most fortunate places on earth, blessed by rich resources and a relatively liberal regime. From 1600 to 1766 the colonies enjoyed the world's fastest growth rate, growing more than twice as fast as the mother country. And by the time they were ready for divorce, Americans were the world's richest people, with an average output per head of $4.71 a day measured in 2017 dollars.[1] Americans were two to three inches taller than Europeans. They were also more fertile, with six to seven births for every woman compared with four to five in Britain, leading Benjamin Franklin to speculate that by the mid-1800s "the greater number of Englishmen will be on this side of the Water." Planted in a huge continent, Americans enjoyed a relative abundance of basic resources of life, land, game, fish, timber, and minerals. Cut off from their colonial master by three thousand miles of ocean, they were also relatively free to do their own thing.

The British colonists failed to reproduce Britain's closed society on the other side of the Atlantic: there were simply too few colonial administrators or Anglican clergymen to impose their will on the natives.[2] In Britain, the learned professions and craftsmen's guilds could crush ideas and regulate competition. In America, they were too weak to get much purchase on society. Colonists were addicted to independence. "They acquire no attachment to place but wandering about seems engrafted in their nature," one observer commented, "and it is weakness incident to it that they should forever imagine the lands further off are still better than those upon which they are already settled."[3]

At the same time the colonies strived for sophistication. The "quality" tried their best to live like English gentry, importing furniture, china, clothes, and tea from the mother country. America was second to none when it came to higher education: by 1800 the new country had dozens of universities, at a time when England only had two. Twenty-nine of the fifty-six delegates to the Continental Congress had college degrees.[4] Educated Americans were as sophisticated as any in the world. They studied the great texts of Western thought—the Greek and Roman classics, the Bible and its various commentaries. They were particularly keen on immersing themselves in British thinkers, giving pride of place to jurists such as William Blackstone and philosophers such as John Locke, but also found some time for the French philosophes. When they finally decided that they needed to form a new country, they created the most impressive constitution the world has seen.

The Constitution addressed the most enduring questions in political philosophy. How can you secure a balance between wisdom and popular participation? How can you balance the rights of individuals against the will of the majority? It also addressed a new set of questions that were provoked by the dissolution of the old, stable world: How do you provide for the needs of commerce and popular power? And how do you provide certain fixed points in a world in flux?

The Constitution turned the United States into something unique in history: a fledgling democratic society that set strict limits on what the majority could do. The majority cannot trample on people's rights to own private property, engage in trade, and keep the fruits of their labor (including their mental labor). This did far more than anything else to guarantee America's future prosperity—far more than conventional economic advantages such as abundant land and raw materials. It encouraged people to engage in trade by reducing the risk that they could have the fruits of their labor stolen from them. The Founders got the details right as well as the architecture. They established the world's biggest single market by banning internal tariffs (something the Europeans didn't get around to until the 1980s). This allowed its industries to grow huge and its regions to specialize. They also extended property rights to the all-important world of ideas.

SCRAPING A LIVING

For all its advantages, the country that was born in the American Revolution was still, to a significant extent, a subsistence economy. Touring the country in 1794 to 1796, Talleyrand, the great French diplomat, was struck by America's backwardness. America is "but in her infancy with regard to manufactures: a few iron works, several glass houses, some tan yards, a considerable number of trifling and imperfect manufactories of kerseymere [a coarse kind of knitting] and, in some places, of cotton . . . point out the feeble efforts that have hitherto been made [to] furnish the country with manufactured articles of daily consumption."[5]

America's financial system was primitive compared with the mother country's. Britain established its national bank in 1694, when it gave the governor and company of the Bank of England a monopoly of issuing banknotes, and introduced the gold standard in 1717, when the master of the mint, Sir Isaac Newton, defined the pound in terms of gold weight (£4.25 per troy ounce). America didn't have any banks whatsoever until the 1780s, when Robert Morris chartered the Bank of North America (1781), Alexander Hamilton established the Bank of New York (1784), and John Hancock and Samuel Adams chartered the Massachusetts Bank (1784). It didn't adopt a clear monetary policy until the 1830s. The Constitution included a clause (Article I, Section 8) granting Congress the right to "coin money" and "regulate the value thereof." The Coinage Act of 1792 defined the U.S. "dollar" primarily in terms of silver rather than gold (a dollar equaled 371.25 grains of silver) but also made room for gold by authorizing gold coins for larger denominations ($2.50 and $10.00) and fixing the value of the dollar at 24.75 grains of pure gold and the ratio of the price of gold to silver at fifteen to one. This ratio proved unsustainable: as the relative market price of silver declined, gold, which was more valuable abroad than at home, was exported in such large quantities that it looked as if America might run out of circulating gold coin. In 1834, the federal government finally cleared up the mess by revising the ratio to sixteen to one and adopting Britain's gold standard.

More than 90 percent of Americans lived in the countryside, either on farms or plantations. Only three cities, Philadelphia, Boston, and New York, had populations of more than 16,000, making them flyspecks compared with London (750,000) or Peking (almost 3 million).[6] Most Americans grew their own food, spun their own cloth, made their own clothes, cobbled their own shoes, and most tiresomely of all, made their own soap and candles from vats of boiled animal fat. They relied on wood for construction and fuel, animals for power, and when manufacturing began to take off, on water to drive their rudimentary mills. Their plows were no more sophisticated than the plows that the ancient Romans had used: branches of trees embellished with bits of iron and strips of cowhide. Their roads were rutted trails littered with rocks and tree stumps: a rainstorm could turn them into seas of mud; a prolonged drought could leave them dusty and dry.

For the most part, life was a slog, hard, relentless, and unforgiving. Farmers could only survive if all members of the family—children as well as adults, women as well as men, old as well as young—pulled their full weight. Slackers were punished or told to make their own way in the world. The most basic daily chores—getting water for a bath or washing clothes or disposing of household waste—were back-breaking and time-consuming. The rhythm of people's days was dictated by the rise and fall of the sun (the main sources of light, candles and whale-oil lamps, were inefficient and expensive). Their idea of speed was defined by "hoof and sail." Travelers had to endure endless inconveniences: they were jogged up and down on horseback, tossed around like sacks of potatoes in stagecoaches, shaken into sickness on boats, or left stranded when horses lost their shoes and stagecoaches lost their axles. Thomas Jefferson had to ford five rivers in order to travel from his home in Monticello, Virginia, to Washington, D.C., for his inauguration in 1801.[7]

Americans were the prisoners of climate. Modern historians, snug in their air-conditioned offices, tend to pooh-pooh Montesquieu's argument, in *The Spirit of the Laws* (1748), that climate is destiny. To George Washington and his contemporaries, it was a statement of the obvious. In the Northeast, the winter could leave people snowed in for months. In the Midwest, tornadoes could wreck communities. In the South, there were only two seasons: hot and hellish. (Slavery was in some ways a horrific response to a basic climatic fact: you could not get free men to harvest labor-intensive crops in the heat and humidity.) The weather was a fickle master as well as an imperious one. A sudden flood could make the roads impassable. A late frost could destroy a crop.

In the early years after the Revolution Americans were also prisoners of a narrow sliver of land on the Eastern Seaboard. They didn't dare to venture inland because the territory was largely an unmapped wilderness controlled by competing European powers and private companies. The wilderness contained all manner of dangers—Native Americans angry at being displaced by white men; bears and wolves eager to taste human flesh; the soldiers and mercenaries of hostile powers. Above all, the wilderness contained emptiness: without accurate maps it was easy to get lost.

Americans were prisoners of ignorance as well as climate: they simply didn't have up-to-date information about what was going on in the world. News about important events could take weeks to travel from one region to another, let alone from Europe to the United States. It took nearly a week for the news of George Washington's death to reach New York. It took over a month for the news that Napoleon was willing to sell "Louisiana" to travel from James Monroe in Paris to Thomas Jefferson in Washington, D.C.

Robert McNamara talked about the "fog of war." In the early decades of the republic, Americans tried to make their living surrounded by the fog of everyday life. They fought battles when the war was already won. They paid over the top for "rare" commodities even when ships loaded with those commodities were about to arrive. This was all the more dangerous because life was so volatile. The flow of imports into the East Coast depended on a small number of ships, which might be disrupted by wars between rival powers or bad weather.

This fog of ignorance applied to the government as well as to ordinary people. During the American Revolution the rebels didn't have the basic information about the country they were freeing. How many people were there? How did they make their living? Were they capable of supporting themselves? The new government was quick to start collecting data on the population: the Constitution included a provision for a decennial census in order to apportion congressional seats, and America conducted its first census soon after its birth, in 1790. The government didn't start collecting data on manufacturing and agriculture until 1840. Paul David of Stanford University labeled the era before 1840 a "statistical dark age."

People's most important economic relationship was with the natural world, particularly with animals, water, and wind. Americans, urban as well as rural, were surrounded by a menagerie of creatures: pigs, sheep, hens, ducks, and horses. Pigs scavenged in the streets. Dogs ran wild. Every house above a hovel had a horse. These animals were small and sinewy compared with today's specimens, adapted to surviving in tough conditions rather than producing the maximum amount of meat, milk, or eggs. In 1800, the average cow probably produced a thousand pounds of milk a year compared with sixteen thousand pounds today.[8] At the same time they were used for a lot more than just food: their hides provided clothes and shoes, their trotters could be turned into glue. "Everything but the squeal" was the rule in these far from sentimental times. Americans as a people were hunters as well as farmers. The great outdoors was full of free food and clothes in the form of elk, deer, and ducks. John Jacob Astor succeeded in amassing America's biggest fortune by trading in the furs of beavers, otters, muskrats, and bears (though he wisely used some of the money he made from hunting in America's great wilderness to buy real estate in Manhattan).

The most important animals by far were horses: indeed, horses were arguably the most important part of the country's capital stock at this time. In 1800, America probably had a million horses and mules. The human-horse combination was as central to economic life as the human-computer combination is to economic life today. Pedigree horses functioned as stores of wealth as well as sources of entertainment: in Virginia and Kentucky, in particular, discussing bloodlines was a commonplace activity.

Americans were fortunate in having a network of rivers and lakes that functioned like watery highways: the Mississippi River in particular was a four-thousand-mile superhighway that linked the South and the Midwest. Goods easily flowed down these highways and across lakes. The settlers harnessed waterpower by building mills next to fast-moving streams, or even better, harnessed a combination of gravity and waterpower by building mills next to waterfalls, such as the falls on the Charles River in Waltham, Massachusetts. Francis Cabot Lowell and a group of Boston merchants even created a company, the Proprietors of the Locks and Canals on the Merrimack River, to control the flow of the river and sell the resulting waterpower to the local mill and factory owners.[9] The watery highways had their limitations, however. Moving things upstream, against the current, particularly a mighty current like the Mississippi's, was often impossible.

Americans were also fortunate in having the great Atlantic Ocean to provide them with both a ready supply of fish and a thoroughfare to the European continent. The New England fishing industry was so successful that no less a figure than Adam Smith described it in *The Wealth of Nations* as "one of the most important, perhaps, in the world."[10] Communities sustained themselves on lobster, oysters, herring, sturgeon, haddock, crabs, and scrod; indeed, the codfish was to Massachusetts what tobacco was to Virginia. The "cradle of American liberty," Faneuil Hall, was the gift of Peter Faneuil, a Boston merchant who had made a fortune selling New England codfish around the world.

The most valuable "watery beast" was not a fish but a mammal:

demand for whale oil was so insatiable that returns in the whaling business in America's leading whaling port, New Bedford, Massachusetts, averaged 14 percent a year from 1817 to 1892, and Gideon Allen & Sons, a whaling syndicate based there, made returns of 60 percent a year during much of the nineteenth century by financing whaling voyages—perhaps the best performance of any firm in American history.[11]

America was as rich in trees as it was in sea life, with some 900 million acres of forest across the continent. English settlers commented on how many more trees there were than in deforested England: pines, oaks, maples, elms, willows, conifers, and many more. A settler in Virginia said that it looked "like a forest standing in water." A settler in Maryland wrote that "we are pretty closely seated together, yet we cannot see our Neighbours House for trees." Settlers looked at America's mass of trees and saw the lineaments of civilized life: furniture for their houses, fuel for their hearths and smithies, masts and hulls for their boats, parts for their machines, false teeth for the toothless.[12]

Walt Whitman held up the ax as a symbol of what divided the Old World from the New. In Europe, the ax was used to chop off the heads of autocrats. In America, it was used to turn the forests into useful objects:[13]

The axe leaps!
The solid forest gives fluid utterances,
They tumble forth, they rise and form,
Hut, tent, landing, survey,
Flail, plough, pick, crowbar, spade,
Shingle, rail, prop, wainscot, jamb, lath, panel, gable. . . .

Americans weren't content to eke a modest living from these natural resources. They developed new ways of squeezing more wealth from their environment. Jacob Perkins invented a machine capable of cutting and heading two hundred thousand nails a day in 1795. The nail machine made it possible to build "balloon frame" houses with a minimum of skill and effort. William Wordsworth made it more useful still when he invented a machine in the 1820s that could cut wood to specifications. By 1829, Americans were consuming 850 million board feet a year, three and a half times the amount of wood per head as the British.[14] Yet even as they transformed the natural world with their ingenuity, they continued to be dependent on it: by 1850, even the most sophisticated machines were made out of wood and employed belts made out of leather.

RIP VAN WINKLE

The War of Independence delivered a shock to America that makes the shock delivered to Britain by leaving the European Union look minor. During the eighteenth century, British America had become more closely enmeshed with the British economy. America imported manufactured goods from the workshop of the world and paid for them with its abundant natural resources, such as fish and wood, and its cash crops, such as tobacco and rice. The growing trade across three thousand miles of ocean was justified by the theory of mercantilism and reinforced by a surging economic struggle between the major European powers.

The war devastated America's fragile economy. Rival armies destroyed towns and homesteads. British warships disrupted trade. More than twenty-five thousand Americans died in battle. The Continental Congress's attempt to finance the war by firing up the printing presses, printing more than $242 million worth of fiat money in the form of continentals, worked well at first, allowing George

Washington to buy food and armaments, but eventually led to hyper-inflation. By 1780, continentals traded at one-fortieth of par (hence the phrase "not worth a continental") and the government was forced to withdraw them from circulation. The new currency thus functioned as a hidden tax on ordinary, and particularly richer, Americans who, having translated their savings into continentals that progressively lost their value, ended up footing the bill for a substantial portion of the cost of the war. (See chart below.)

DISCOUNT ON CONTINENTAL CURRENCY VS. AMOUNT OUTSTANDING
PLOTTED QUARTERLY MAY 1775 – APR 1780

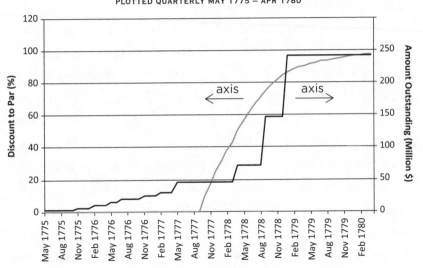

The aftermath of the war did further damage. As it struggled to find a new role in a changed world, America experienced what one historian has called its "greatest economic income slump ever," with a 30 percent decline in national income as reflected in international trade.[15] On top of all that, America had a huge war debt: the new U.S. government, established under the Articles of Confederation, owed $51 million (and the individual states owed another $25 million), yet the government lacked the ability to raise revenue in the form of taxes.

Nonetheless, thanks largely to Alexander Hamilton, America's treasury secretary, the new nation did an astonishingly good job of putting its public finances in order. The U.S. Constitution gave the federal government increased authority to raise revenue through customs fees. This gave Hamilton the wherewithal to establish trust in America's reliability by paying off old loans, particularly to France, and then to use that trust to negotiate new ones.[16]

Within a few years of independence, the American growth streak resumed. In 1819, Washington Irving published a story that captured the spirit of the new country, "Rip Van Winkle," about a man who goes to sleep for twenty years and awakens to find his world utterly transformed. Overall, America galloped ahead in the most important dimensions of economic life—territory, population, and material well-being. Americans quadrupled the size of their territory by purchasing, conquering, annexing, and settling land that had been occupied for millennia by indigenous peoples and subsequently claimed by France, Spain, Britain, and Mexico. In 1803, in the Louisiana Purchase, Thomas Jefferson purchased the entire river basin west of the Mississippi River from Napoleon Bonaparte for $15 million. The purchase, largely funded by Baring Brothers, reflected the recently enhanced credit status of the fledgling United States and turned New Orleans into an American port and the Mississippi into an American river.[17] In 1821, Andrew Jackson engineered the purchase of Florida from Spain. America added Texas (1845), California (1850), and much of today's Southwest to the Union. In 1846, it snuffed out the last British claims to American territory in Oregon.

The country's population increased from 3.9 million at the time of the first census in 1790 to 31.5 million in 1860—growing four times faster than Europe's and six times the world average. From 1815 to 1830, the population of the region west of the Appalachians grew three times as fast as the original thirteen colonies, and

America added a new state every three years. New cities were created to the south and west—Pittsburgh, Cincinnati, and Nashville, to name but three—as regional hubs and people magnets. America's capital stock grew even faster, more than tripling from 1774 to 1799 and increasing sixteenfold between then and the Civil War.[18]

America's real gross domestic product increased by an average of 3.7 percent a year from 1800 to 1850. Income per head increased by 40 percent. "No other nation in that era could match even a single component of this explosive growth," James McPherson noted in *Battle Cry of Freedom*. "The combination of all three made America the *Wunderkind* nation of the nineteenth century."[19] Growth was eventually accompanied by boom-bust cycles. In subsistence societies, economic problems are usually driven by either local conditions or natural forces. In mature economies, by contrast, business activity tends to move in tandem: a gradual but escalating increase in activity is followed by a dramatic collapse that is variously labeled a "crisis" or "panic."

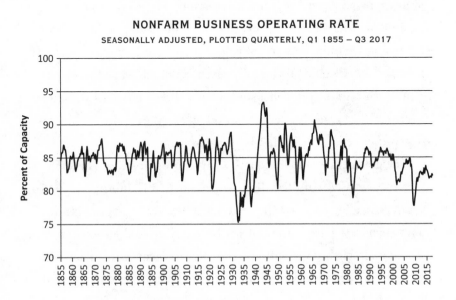

NONFARM BUSINESS OPERATING RATE

SEASONALLY ADJUSTED, PLOTTED QUARTERLY, Q1 1855 – Q3 2017

The panic of 1819 was America's first experience of a financial crisis in peacetime. In August 1818, the Second Bank of the United States began to reject banknotes because it worried that credit was dangerously overextended. Then in October, the U.S. Treasury tightened the credit crunch still further by forcing the bank to transfer $2 million in specie to redeem bonds on the Louisiana Purchase. State banks across the South and West began to call in their loans on heavily mortgaged farms. The value of many farms fell by 50 percent or more. Local banks began foreclosing on farms and transferring the title deeds to the Second Bank of the United States. The price of cotton dropped by 25 percent in a single day in 1819. America did not recover from the subsequent recession until 1821.

This panic set the pattern for a succession of panics in 1837, 1857, 1873, 1884, 1893, 1896, and 1907. The specific causes of each boom-bust cycle varied widely. But the underlying pattern was always the same: expansions gathered pace until they were finally constrained by a "gold ceiling" that limited the supply of credit and forced businesses to retrench. Expansion led to euphoria and euphoria led to overexpansion. Overexpansion led to rising interest rates and rising interest rates to sharp stock market corrections and political furor. As can be seen in the chart on page 41, economic activity between 1855 and 1907 would consistently reach about 85 percent to 87 percent of capacity before collapsing shortly thereafter. This was a far cry from the eighteenth-century world, where the rhythm of life was largely dictated by the change of the seasons.

The gold ceiling was lifted a little in coming decades. The supply of gold increased with the discovery of gold in California in 1848, South Africa in 1886, and the Yukon in 1896. Technological innovations such as the use of cyanide leaching improved the yield of both new and established gold mines. The improvement in financial technology, such as check clearinghouses, increased the amount of credit expansion that could be produced by a given supply of gold. But this was not without its side effects: the expansion in the supply of gold probably helped to produce one of the most severe economic contractions in American history, starting in 1893. Pressure to find a way of preventing such crises engendered the Aldrich-Vreeland Act of 1908, which eventually led to the formation of the Federal Reserve System in 1913, substituting the expendable sovereign credit of the United States for gold specie.

THE CULTURE OF GROWTH

The wunderkind had an unusually open and dynamic culture. The Founding Fathers did a good job of voicing the zeitgeist of the new culture. "A plowman on his legs is higher than a gentleman on his knees," said Benjamin Franklin. "The mass of mankind has not been born with saddles on their backs, nor a favored few booted and spurred ready to ride them," said Jefferson. And the new culture of openness became ever more deeply entrenched over the subsequent decades. Foreign visitors were impressed (or appalled) by America's bourgeois nature. They noted Americans' obsession with business and money. Lady Stuart-Wortley wrote, "No drones are admitted into the great Transatlantic hive." Francis Grund proclaimed, "Labor is essential to their well-being as food and raiment to a European." Tocqueville wrote, "I know of no country, indeed, where wealth has taken a stronger hold on the affections of men." On arriving in Ohio, he exclaimed that "the entire society is a factory." The visitors usually linked this energetic striving-cum-money-grubbing with the fact that, as Frances Trollope put it, "any man's son may become the equal of any other man's son."[20] Slavery, of course, would remain an abominable exception, as we will examine.

This open culture was reinforced by two powerful influences. Protestants valued hard work as a proof of virtue and education as a path to biblical understanding. The philosophes of the Enlightenment questioned the value of hierarchy and authority and encouraged people to rely on their own judgment. For all their differences, these two traditions were both friendly toward creative destruction: they taught Americans to challenge the established order in pursuit of personal betterment and to question received wisdom in pursuit of rational understanding.

Shortage of labor also did its bit. America enjoyed the lowest ratio of people to land in the world. (Indeed, one reason the British found it so difficult to defeat their colonial subjects was that they were so widely scattered: the British could capture the coastal cities with the mighty Royal Navy but lacked the manpower to subdue the countryside, where 95 percent of the people lived.) In Europe, Malthus's warning in his *Essay on the Principle of Population* (1798) that the population would expand faster than the land necessary to support it rang true. In America, it was an absurdity: there weren't enough hands to work the available land.[21] The ratio of people to land remained generous even as America was flooded with immigrants, because the country's territory expanded along with its population: the number of people per square mile fell from 6.1 in 1800 to 4.3 in 1810.

This combination of abundance of resources and scarcity of labor paid rich material dividends. Americans got married early because it was easier to find land to farm, and they bred prodigiously partly because they could and partly because they needed children to farm the land. The median age of the population was sixteen in 1815, with only one person in eight over forty-three years old.[22] For all this general youthfulness, Americans also had a longer life expectancy because diseases found it harder to spread than in Europe's dense cities (the life expectancy was lower in the South because the humidity incubated diseases).

It also paid rich psychological dividends. Shortage of labor changed the balance of power: in Walter McDougall's words, "More than any other people on earth, Americans had the option of saying, 'Take this job and shove it.'"[23] The need to conquer so much space put a premium on organizational skills. The Mormons' Great Trek to Utah was perhaps the best example of this: brilliantly led by Brigham Young, the Saints built their own roads and bridges and even planted crops that could be harvested by the next wave of settlers.[24] At the same time, the availability of so much space took the sting out of the early stages of industrialization. In Europe, the Industrial Revolution was associated with urban overcrowding and "dark Satanic Mills." In the United States, the first shoots of industrialization grew in a green and pleasant land—usually by the side of rivers in small New England towns. In the 1830s, Michel Chevalier, a French economist, remarked that American factories were "new and fresh like an opera scene." In 1837, Harriet Martineau, an Englishwoman, opined that American workers were lucky to "have their dwellings and their occupation fixed in spots where the hills are heaped together, and the waters leap and whirl among rocks."[25]

America quickly took over from Britain as the world's leading factory of entrepreneurs, producing the most patents per capita by 1810, and excelling in industries that were at the heart of the productivity revolution, including steamboats, farm machinery, machine tools, and sewing machines. American entrepreneurs were drawn from every level of society but united by their common assumption that every problem was capable of solution so long as you thought hard enough.

Oliver Evans was the self-educated son of a Delaware farmer. In 1784–85, he built a flour mill outside Philadelphia run by gravity, friction, and waterpower. Grain was moved from the loading bin through the mill's several levels by buckets and leather belts, without human beings doing anything more than guiding and regulating. Both Thomas Jefferson and George Washington installed Evans's mills on their farms and paid him a license fee for doing so. A few years later, he developed one of the first high-pressure steam engines and established a network of machine workshops to produce and repair popular inventions. In 1813, he even predicted a future when people would travel in stagecoaches "moved by steam" and guided by rails from one city to another.

Eli Whitney was a graduate of Yale University. In 1793, he developed a device that reduced the work involved in separating cottonseeds from cotton fiber by a factor of fifty: a roller studded with nails stripped the lint from the seeds by pulling it through a grid that was too narrow to let the seeds pass. The seeds fell into one compartment while a brush swept the lint off the nails and into another. A reasonably competent carpenter could build one in an hour. Frustrated in his attempts to patent his innovation, Whitney then moved on to manufacturing rifles and other weapons for the government.

Samuel Morse was an accomplished painter and professor of fine arts at New York University who was so furious when Congress denied him a commission to paint a historical mural for the Capitol Rotunda that he gave up painting and threw his energies into developing a way of using electromagnetism to send messages down wires. In 1843, Morse persuaded Congress to give him thirty thousand dollars to build a demonstration line from Baltimore to Washington using the new technology. On May 24, 1844, he sent his first message, "What hath God wrought."

Cyrus McCormick and John Deere were both agricultural workers who tinkered on the side. In 1833–34, McCormick invented a mechanical reaper that could harvest more grain than five men working with hand scythes. In 1837, Deere invented a plow with a polished steel moldboard that successfully "scoured" itself as it pushed through the soil. A few years later, the addition of a seat on top of the plow allowed the farmer to ride along rather than walking behind, a veritable Prince of the Prairie. The "plough that broke the plains" was to be comfortable as well as efficient. Isaac Singer was a rogue who ran three households simultaneously and fathered at least twenty-four children. In the 1840s, he invented a sewing machine that did as much as any invention in the nineteenth century to liberate women, reducing the time it took to sew a shirt from fourteen hours and twenty minutes to one hour and sixteen minutes. Charles Goodyear was an obscure storekeeper in New Haven, Connecticut, who had no training whatsoever in chemistry but somehow became convinced that his Maker had chosen him to solve chemical problems that had defeated professional scientists. In 1844, after years of grinding poverty and spells in debtors' prison, he patented a process for using a blend of sulfur, latex, and white lead to "vulcanize" rubber.

A striking number of entrepreneurs combined technical ingenuity with commercial savvy. Deere drummed up demand for his plows by regularly entering them in plowing competitions, and satisfied that demand by creating a national network of "travelers" who sold the plows across the country.[26] McCormick recruited local business-people to act as "agents" to promote his reapers. He pioneered many of the staples of modern business: free trials to whet the appetite, money-back guarantees to assuage doubts, and "educational" ads in farm journals to create a new market.[27] As the price of advertising in other people's papers increased, he even published his own paper, stuffed full of infomercials for his products, the *Farmers' Advance*, which eventually had a circulation of 350,000. "Trying to do business without advertising is like winking at a pretty girl through a pair of green goggles," one of his editors quipped. "You may know what you are doing, but no one else does."[28] Singer and his partner, Edward Clark, solidified their hold over the sewing-machine market with two innovations: long-term installment buying, allowing customers to buy a sewing machine for five dollars down followed by three dollars a month for sixteen months; and guaranteed buybacks of all used sewing machines, whether made by his company or not, in return for money off a new machine. The company then destroyed the trade-ins in order to kill the market in both secondhand machines and spare parts for broken machines.

Entrepreneurs were so productive in part because they had a reasonable confidence that they would enjoy the fruits of their labor. The Patent Act of 1790 turned America into a single intellectual market and gave inventors exclusive rights for fourteen years. The establishment of a patent office in 1836 provided the law with teeth. The office not only escaped the inefficiency and corruption that was common in the government at the time, it succeeded in embodying the new country's faith in innovation. Housed in a Greek temple on F Street in Washington, D.C., it was so full of models of the latest innovations that it became a major tourist attraction. Even Charles Dickens, who was frequently dismissive of the fledgling country, admitted that it was "an extraordinary example of American enterprise and ingenuity."

These pioneering entrepreneurs worked in a world that was being transformed by three productivity-boosting changes. The first was a resource revolution. Writing in 1790, Benjamin Franklin declared that "gold and silver are not the produce of North America, which has no mines."[29] Over the next few decades all that changed. Americans discovered a range of minerals such as iron ore, silver, copper, and of course gold, setting off the gold rush of the 1840s and 1850s. Americans also learned how to harness a widening range of materials to provide them with energy. In 1800, Americans relied on wood for almost all of their energy. Eighty years later, 100 percent had become 57 percent.[30] Americans doubled their coal production by 1813 and trebled it by 1818. They also discovered in Pennsylvania huge deposits of "hard" (anthracite) coal, which produces less smoke and ash than "soft" (bituminous) coal. Coal became such an important source of energy that Freeman Hunt's *Merchants' Magazine* proclaimed in 1854, "Commerce is President of the Nation and Coal her Secretary of State."[31] Just five years later, the United States had a co–Secretary of State with the discovery of oil in Pennsylvania. Coal powered the locomotives and iron smelters. Oil provided kerosene for lighting and lubricants for machines.

Even as they introduced new sources of power, Americans found new ways of getting more out of old sources. The New England textile industry developed clever ways of using a combination of water and gravity to produce power at minimal cost, starting with water-wheels and later adding water turbines.

Americans were particularly successful at making horses more productive. There were clear limits to this. Horses are labor intensive: you have to feed them, groom them, and walk alongside them. They can carry only so much weight. But Americans nevertheless squeezed more out of them. They practiced horse eugenics with an enthusiasm that would have dazzled Francis Galton: by 1900, there was a much wider variety of physical types available than in 1800. They also put horses to work in all sorts of clever ways. Stagecoach companies used four to six horses to pull a "stage" that could be sixty feet or more in length. Stagecoaches could travel as fast as ten miles an hour and provided fairly reliable timetables. The Eastern Stage Company, based in Boston, owned more than a thousand horses and a complex of stables and blacksmith shops as well as a financial interest in a network of stopping places, inns, and hotels.[32] The Pony Express brought industrial-style planning to taming the West: it not only built an express lane of roads and bridges across the country, so that the riders knew where they were going, it also built a network of inns, stables, and way stations, so that they had a supply of fresh horses to ride. At its peak the Pony Express employed over 400 horses, 125 riders, who had to keep detailed time sheets, and a support staff of another 275.[33]

The Pony Express was part of a second change: the transportation revolution.[34] If one great theme of America's first hundred years of life is its relentless geographic expansion as it added new territories, another great theme is temporal contraction, as new modes of transportation reduced the time it took to travel by factors of perhaps a hundred. Before 1815, the only cost-efficient means of carrying freight long distances was by water—in either sailing ships or flat-bottomed boats. It cost as much to transport a ton of goods thirty miles by wagon as it cost to ship it three thousand miles across the ocean.[35] After 1815, Americans improved transportation by three methods: making better use of existing physical resources (basically rivers), harnessing new sources of power such as steam, and adding new transportation routes such as roads, rails, and canals.

In the first few decades of the nineteenth century, hundreds of chartered companies built thousands of miles of turnpikes that offered improved surfaces (thanks to stone, gravel, or wooden planks) in return for a fee.[36] Albert Fishlow estimates that the average annual profit rates of the turnpikes were low, at only 3 to 5 percent, thanks in part to tight government regulation and in part to opportunism on the part of travelers, who cleverly alternated between turnpikes and free roads.[37] Soon the road-building craze was eclipsed by a canal-building craze: by 1850, America boasted 3,700 miles of canals. The cost of moving things by canal was between two and three cents per ton compared with over thirty cents by wagon, because the average horse can pull fifty tons on water compared with only a ton on land.

The canal era was triggered by New York State's construction of the Erie Canal from Albany, New York, on the Hudson River, to Buffalo, New York, on Lake Erie. Constructing such a canal would be an enormous challenge today, let alone in the 1820s: the canal was 363 miles long and cut through swamps and ridges and vaulted over rivers (at Rochester the builders had to construct an 802-foot aqueduct). It took eight years to complete. Yet the canal recouped its cost of construction in tolls in the first year, quickly justifying the Canal Commission's extensive use of eminent domain to force private property holders to sell their land. And its broader economic benefits were huge. The canal cut the costs of shipping goods by 75 percent and the time involved by 67 percent. It settled the battle between Boston, New York, and New Orleans for the position of America's leading port, in favor of New York. It spurred westward expansion: Buffalo became a jumping-off point for the lakes and helped to turn lakeside cities such as Detroit, Cleveland, and Chicago into urban hubs. Canalside towns such as Albany, Syracuse, Rochester, and Buffalo all boomed. It also inspired yet more canal building: Maryland sponsored a canal between the Chesapeake and the Delaware River, and Pennsylvania started to build a canal to Pittsburgh.

Canals eventually linked the Great Lakes into the country's wider transportation system. In 1855, a group of businesspeople, in cahoots with Michigan's leading politicians, built a canal, complete with a set of locks, to link Lake Superior to the lower Great Lakes and provide a way around the twenty-seven-foot-high St. Mary's Falls. The Soo Locks boosted local freight from 14,503 tons in 1855 to 325,357 tons in 1867—an increase of about 30 percent a year. They made it much easier to carry grain from the granaries of the Midwest to the East Coast. They also opened up a two-way industrial trade that grew explosively over the coming decades: ships took Mesabi iron ore to Pittsburgh (where it was turned into steel) and returned loaded with Pennsylvania coal.

For most people, the nineteenth century is associated not with turnpikes or canals but with something more dramatic: the fire-breathing, steam-belching, earth-shaking iron horse. In the 1780s, America possessed a grand total of three steam engines. These were used to pump water—two to keep mines dry and one to provide New York City with water—rather than for locomotion. By 1838, when the Treasury Department produced a report on steam power, the country possessed two thousand steam engines with a collective horsepower of forty thousand. Oliver Evans laid the foundation of the boom by developing a high-pressure steam engine in 1801 and establishing the Pittsburgh Steam Engine Company, in Pittsburgh, Pennsylvania, in 1811.

The most exciting application of steam engines was to transportation. Steam was the first source of power that was entirely under human control: you didn't have to wait for the wind to blow in the right direction or the horse to be broken.[38] The first steam-driven transportation devices were boats rather than trains. America's first paddle-powered steamboat, the *North River*, made its first trip, from New York City to Albany, on August 17, 1807, using a low-pressure engine. By 1838, there were hundreds of steamboats on America's rivers, using high-pressure engines. Steamboats boasted a combination of romance and efficiency: they were majestic to behold with their vast waterwheels on their sides or backs, but they were also extremely efficient. They could move freight upstream as well as downstream. They could cope with powerful currents and even take on the mighty Mississippi. They got faster as the decades passed: the trip from New Orleans to Louisville was cut from twenty-five days in 1817, which was celebrated with much tub-thumping at the time, to eight days in 1826.[39] They reduced the cost of moving freight upstream by 90 percent between 1815 and 1860, and by nearly 40 percent downstream.

Applying the emerging steamboat technology to engines that could travel on land proved frustrating. Oliver Evans suggested creating a railway to connect New York and Philadelphia with "carriages drawn by steam engines" as early as 1813, but nothing came of it. At first, Americans were forced to import engines from the more technologically sophisticated United Kingdom, including the "Stourbridge Lion" in 1829 and the "John Bull" in 1831. But soon they succeeded in producing engines of their own, reengineering British models and adding innovations.

The first U.S. railroad, the Baltimore and Ohio, began operation in 1830, five years after Britain's Stockton and Darlington. Soon the new technology was spreading much faster in America than in Europe: American railway companies found it much easier to acquire rights-of-way than their European equivalents because the country was so empty, and the government gave them free, or cheap, land. America laid down five thousand miles of rail in the 1840s and twenty thousand in the 1850s. By the outbreak of the Civil War, America had more miles of railroad than the United Kingdom, France, and the German states combined. According to Fishlow, the amount of money invested in the railroads was more than five times the amount invested in canals.[40]

The railway boom proceeded in a very American way. There was a lot of creative destruction: railways quickly killed canals because rails could carry fifty times as much freight and didn't freeze over in winter. There was a lot of waste. Many rail barons overbuilt furiously before going spectacularly bust. There was no railroad system but a hodgepodge of rival companies that used different gauges, different-size cars, and even different time zones (though gauge standards and even time-zone standards were sometimes addressed regionally). There was also a lot of hypocrisy: while proclaiming its hostility to subsidies in the form of cash or bonds, the federal government used its vast land holdings in the West to subsidize development. In 1851, for example, the government made a land grant of 3.75 million acres to encourage the creation of the Illinois Central Railroad.[41] The land-grant system worked because it offered railroads the chance of increasing the value of the land by many multiples: building rails in the middle of nowhere might be expensive and risky, but you might end up by turning a piece of nowhere into a part of the global economy.

Historians once confidently asserted that the railroads "opened up" America like nothing else. They were the perfect mode of transport for an economy that relied on moving bulky stuff around the country: mountains of wheat; tons of coke, copper, and ore; oceans of oil; forests of timber. A group of energetic revisionists, led by Robert Fogel and Albert Fishlow, has qualified this view, pointing out, for example, that the railroad was only one of several forms of transport.[42] But for all these qualifications, the railroads nevertheless deserve their garlands. Railroads were significantly more efficient than other forms of transport. They could be built almost anywhere. This meant that they could carve the shortest route rather than having to follow a meandering river, like steamboats, or admit defeat when confronted by high mountains, like canal boats. By river the distance from Pittsburgh to St. Louis was 1,164 miles. By rail it was 612 miles. The Alleghenies, which rose to 2,200 feet, formed an insuperable barrier between Pittsburgh and Cleveland during the canal age. Once a railroad was built, the route between the two cities became one of the most heavily trafficked in the world. On top of all this they offered predictability. They quickly adopted timetables that could predict when trains would arrive down to the minute.[43] Add to that superior speed and you have a winning formula.

That formula improved the productivity of the economy as a whole. Railroads slashed the unit cost of overland transportation: in 1890, the cost of railroad freight was 0.875 cent per ton-mile compared with 24.5 cents per ton-mile for wagon freight, a reduction of 96 percent.[44] Railroads promoted economic specialization because farmers could specialize in crops for which the climate was most suitable and purchase the most efficient agricultural tools. They promoted labor arbitrage: workers could move to places where they got the highest pay for their labor. They even promoted industrial development because trains were resource-hungry beasts—they needed coal for fuel, iron and steel for rails, and rolling stock and skilled workers to run the whole show. Plenty of farmers abandoned the land and turned themselves into firemen, engineers, mechanics, brakemen, switchmen, and conductors.

Above all, they changed the entire tenor of life. When Andrew Jackson arrived in Washington in 1829, he traveled by horse-drawn carriage, moving at the same speed as the Roman emperors. When he left eight years later he traveled in a train, moving at roughly the same speed as today's presidents when they deign to travel by train. Nathaniel Hawthorne captured the speeding up of time and shrinking of space as well as any economic statistics when he wrote that "the whistle of the locomotive" "tells a story of busy men" and "brings the noisy world into the midst of our slumberous peace."[45]

The third revolution was an information revolution. Central to the process of creative destruction is knowledge of what combination of what resources yields maximum gains in living standards. Information-starved Americans recognized the importance of the old adage that in the land of the blind the one-eyed man is king. The *Journal of Commerce*, which started publishing in 1827 to provide information about the flow of imports into the United States, came up with the clever idea of deploying deepwater schooners to intercept incoming ships before they docked. The most important breakthrough in information was, of course, the telegraph. Railway companies installed telegraph lines wherever they went because they

needed to communicate quickly over vast distances in order to prevent trains from crashing into each other. The telegraph revolution
quickly outpaced the railway revolution. Telegraph lines were much
cheaper to construct than railway lines: by 1852, America had twenty-
two thousand miles of telegraph lines compared with eleven thousand miles of tracks. They also had a more dramatic effect: information
that once took weeks to travel from place A to place B now took
seconds.

The invention of the telegraph was a much more revolutionary
change than the invention of the telephone a few decades later. The
telephone (rather like Facebook today) merely improved the quality
of social life by making it easier for people to chat with each other.
The telegraph changed the parameters of economic life—it broke the
link between sending complicated messages and sending physical
objects and radically reduced the time it took to send information.
This was already evident in the early years of the telegraph: data collected in 1851 identified about 70 percent of telegraph traffic as commercial in nature, from checking credit references to "conveying
secrets of the rise and fall of markets."[46]

The telegraph eventually turned America into a single market for
financial information: Chicago was able to open its commodities exchange in 1848 because it enjoyed instant communication with the
East Coast. San Francisco was able to flourish as a commercial city
because it was in close communication with New York. When Leland
Stanford hit the gold spike with his silver hammer, automatically
sending a telegraph signal in two directions, east and west, and triggering bursts of cannon fire in both New York and San Francisco, he
wasn't just engaging in a wonderful display.[47] He was ushering in a
new age of business.

The expansion of the telegraph became global with the opening of
the transatlantic cable on July 28, 1866. Laying a cable across a huge

ocean had inevitably proved difficult—five attempts between 1857 and 1866 had failed because the cable snapped—but it was, nevertheless, worth the effort. Before the cable it had taken about ten days to get a message across the Atlantic by ship—longer if there was severe weather. The cable reduced the time lag for sending a meaningful message to an hour or two, or even less (the first cable could handle about eight words a minute). The cable allowed for an integrated transatlantic financial market based in London, New York, and San Francisco. This market kept up a flow of information that made it possible to adjust supply to demand and thereby improve the allocation of global resources.

A RESTLESS PEOPLE

European visitors were almost always impressed by the *busyness* of the young country: this was a world in motion, with everybody moving hither and thither in pursuit of their fortunes. Frances Trollope talked of a "busy, bustling, industrious population, hacking and hewing their way" into a continent.[48] Tocqueville thought that there was a single underlying logic to all this movement: people were heading westward in pursuit of new territory. In fact, there were two great movements under way.

The first was from the East Coast to the interior. In 1790, the population was clustered along the Atlantic Coast, roughly evenly divided between the North (New England) and the Mid-Atlantic and the South. The American border was effectively the Appalachians, the mountain chain that runs some five hundred miles inland from the Atlantic. By 1850, in the space of a few decades, half of America's 31 million people and half of its thirty states lay beyond the Appalachians.

This vast internal colonization involved every resource that the new republic had to offer. The expansion started with collecting information. Surveying was a national obsession from the earliest days: George Washington, an enthusiastic amateur surveyor, studied the "land as a jeweler inspects a gemstone, with minute attention to its flaws, facets and values."[49] In 1814, the U.S. Army Medical Department began collecting systematic material on weather across the country. In 1847, the Smithsonian Institution began collecting information about minerals. Information was a prelude to settlement. America's various governments, federal, state, and local, actively tried to promote expansion by dredging rivers and streams, building turnpikes and canals, and offering inducements to private companies to move westward. Entrepreneurs also formed partnerships or even corporations to hasten the drive west.

The second movement was from rural to urban areas. The proportion of Americans living in cities increased from 5 percent in 1790 to 20 percent in 1860.[50] The proportion of the labor force engaged in nonagricultural pursuits grew from 26 percent to 47 percent. In 1810, there were only two cities with populations of more than fifty thousand (New York and Philadelphia). By 1860, there were sixteen.

Movement improved productivity. The most powerful boost came from reallocating people from farms to the cities and from agriculture to industry. Despite the fact that American agriculture was the most productive the world had seen, farmworkers could double their incomes, on average, simply by moving from the farm into the city.[51] Movement also brought new productive powers on stream as settlers commanded new resources and linked them, via canals and railways, to older population centers (and thence to the global economy). Movement also boosted a sense of national identity: people increasingly thought of themselves as "Americans" rather than just New Yorkers or Virginians. The first half of the nineteenth century saw the birth of a succession of national societies such as the American Bible Society (1816), the American Education Society (1816), the American Colonization Society (1816), and, most significant for the future history of the country, the American Anti-Slavery Society (1833).

Growth also increased people's standard of living. Until the early nineteenth century, economic growth had been "extensive"—that is, almost the same as population growth. At some point after the War of 1812, economic growth became "intensive"—that is, the economy began to grow faster than the population. Economists estimate that real output per head increased by 1.25 percent a year from 1820 to 1860, compared with 0.24 percent from 1800 to 1820.[52]

This all sounds relatively simple: America was a young republic powered by revolutionary ideals and dedicated to the god of growth. In fact, the story was far from simple: America was divided by two different visions of the good society—one dynamic and the other static; and two different economies—one based on free labor and the other on slavery.

Two

THE TWO AMERICAS

———◆———

T HERE WERE MANY DIFFERENT versions of America in this formative era. In *Albion's Seed* (1989), David Hackett Fischer has identified four distinct British "folkways" that shaped American culture. Puritans shaped the Northeast. They were inveterate moralizers but also successful institution builders. Quakers shaped Pennsylvania and Delaware. They were more egalitarian than their northern counterparts but far less successful at building institutions. Cavaliers shaped Virginia and Maryland and, by extension, the South. They were aristocratic, hierarchical, slave-holding, addicted to horse racing and gambling. Anglican and Anglophile, many were the younger sons of British aristocrats who emigrated so that they could live like the elder sons. The Scotch Irish who laid claim to the frontier were fiercely independent and egalitarian, tough and hard living. They drank super-strong moonshine, or "white lightning," chewed tobacco, and entertained themselves with hunting, cockfighting, and wrestling matches. Trying to tame them was a fool's errand.

Mixed in with these British subcultures were lots of foreign subcultures. America imported millions of slaves from Africa via the

West Indies. The 2010 census revealed that more Americans traced their ancestry back to Germany than any other country, England included: Germans came in three great waves, in the eighteenth century, after 1848, and after 1890, and, because those waves included Protestants, Catholics, and Jews, intermarried with every religious subculture in the country. Part of the success of America's economy lay in its ability to draw on these different traditions—and part of its success lay in its ability to produce one out of many.

HAMILTON VERSUS JEFFERSON

From 1776 to 1865, these multiple divisions were subsumed in a great binary dispute that determined the course of American history: the dispute between industrial modernizers and agrarian slaveholders. This dispute started with a great intellectual argument between Alexander Hamilton, America's first treasury secretary, and Thomas Jefferson, America's first secretary of state and third president. It eventually broadened out into a huge regional argument between the industrial North and the slave-owning South. In February 1861, the "two Americas" became more than a metaphor: the Confederate States of America became a self-proclaimed nation, with its own president (Jefferson Davis) and its own capital (Richmond), a status that it maintained, in its own eyes, for forty-nine months, until early April 1865.

Alexander Hamilton and Thomas Jefferson came from the opposite ends of the social spectrum. Hamilton was "the bastard brat of a Scottish pedlar," as John Adams put it. Jefferson inherited a large estate on his twenty-first birthday, along with the slaves to work it, and married into one of Virginia's richest families. Hamilton was born in Nevis in the West Indies and worked his way through King's

College, New York, as Columbia University was then called (one of the few times he lost his temper in public debate was when John Adams accused him of being "foreign-born"). Jefferson went to the Virginia elite's favorite university, William and Mary. Hamilton saw the world in terms of upward mobility: America needed to make sure that everyone could rise on the basis of their own efforts. Jefferson saw it in terms of noblesse oblige: the planter class had to scour society for natural geniuses who could be given a hand up and a place in the elite.

The disputes had a personal edge. Jefferson took a visceral dislike to Hamilton, and his dislike was amplified over the years by fear and envy. Jefferson regarded himself as the natural leader of the Revolution. He was the product of one of America's great families! He was the author of the great declaration! He was twelve years older than his rival! Yet Hamilton kept accumulating power. He was chosen by Washington as his key aide during the Revolutionary War, ran his most powerful department, the Treasury, and trespassed in every other department, including foreign affairs. Though Washington was a fellow Virginian and patrician, he seemed to prefer Hamilton's company and ideas to Jefferson's. Hamilton was full of elaborate schemes for developing the new country. Jefferson preferred to study his books in Monticello.

Hamilton wanted America to become a commercial republic powered by manufacturing, trade, and cities. Jefferson wanted it to remain a decentralized agrarian republic of yeomen farmers. Hamilton hoped to equip America with all the accoutrements of a commercial republic. Jefferson wanted to preserve America as an agrarian society populated, as he saw it, by public-spirited landowners and independent-minded yeomen. "Cultivators of the earth are the most valuable citizens," he wrote to John Jay in 1785. "They are the most vigorous, the most independent, the most virtuous, and they are tied to their country and wedded to its liberty interests by the most last-ing bonds."[1] America's greatest advantage was that it possessed an "immensity of land courting the industry of the husbandman." Its wisest course of action was to get as many people as possible to im-prove the land.

Both Hamilton and Jefferson were what contemporaries called "natural aristocrats." They were omnivorous readers, fluent writers, brilliant debaters, capable of speaking for hours without a note. Yet of the two, Hamilton was the more impressive. Jefferson thought in terms of the preservation (and improvement) of the old agrarian so-ciety. Hamilton conjured up the future almost from thin air. He not only anticipated the development of an industrial society before America had any industry to speak of, he understood what was needed to bring that commercial society to life: a sound currency ad-ministered by a central bank modeled on the Bank of England; a source of revenue from customs; a single market to encourage the division of labor; an "energetic executive" to enforce the rules of com-merce. He was a natural genius of the caliber of Mozart or Bach.

The argument between these two great men continued on and on, in public and in Washington's Cabinet meetings. Hamilton argued that America's very survival depended on its ability to develop a strong manufacturing sector. A strong manufacturing sector would enable the young country to create a powerful army and to control its own economic destiny. Survival was only the beginning: what made Hamilton's vision so exciting was that it was dynamic rather than static. A commercial republic would become more successful over time—bankers would allocate capital to where it could be most use-fully employed and entrepreneurs would invent new machines. Eco-nomic progress would bring moral progress with it—people who had hitherto been condemned to be tillers of fields and drawers of water would be able to develop their abilities to the full. "When all the different kinds of industry obtain in a community," he wrote, "each individual can find his proper element, and can call into activity the whole vigour of his nature." Hamilton was particularly forceful on this point because, of all the Founding Fathers, including Franklin, he came closest to the ideal of a self-made man.

Born to the purple, Jefferson thought that this was all nonsense. Hamilton's version of economic progress would destroy the American republic just as surely as the barbarians had destroyed Rome. America's survival depended on its ability to preserve civic virtue, he argued, and its ability to preserve civic virtue depended on its ability to promote manly qualities in its population (such as frugality, industry, temperance, and simplicity) and to prevent some people from lording it over others. Hamilton's republic would destroy manly virtues by promoting luxury and destroy independence by promoting the power of employers and stock-jobbers. Industrialization was the road to ruin.

Jefferson complained that "the mobs of great cities add just so much to the support of pure government as sores do to the strength of the human body." (He conveniently forgot that there is no more debilitating "sore" than slavery.) He responded to Hamilton's "Report on the Subject of Manufactures" by trying to strengthen the power of the agricultural interests. "The only corrective of what is corrupt in our present form of government," he wrote to George Mason shortly after the report appeared, "will be the augmentation of the numbers of the lower house, so as to get a more agricultural representation, which may put that interest above that of stock-jobbers."

Jefferson hated Hamilton's method for promoting economic progress just as much as he hated the progress itself: collecting power in the hands of the federal government and imposing control from the center. Hadn't they just fought a revolution against the British to prevent precisely such centralization of power? Americans worried that all rulers were tyrants in the making: hence their enthusiasm for making ambition counteract ambition, as James Madison put it in *Federalist* number 51. They were also intensely jealous of the powers of their local governments.

Jefferson started off with the dice loaded in his favor. America's comparative advantage in 1789 was in agriculture: it had more empty land than any other country and most of its immigrants, from younger sons of British aristocrats to Pomeranian peasants, had farming in the blood. The country's manufacturing industry, by contrast, was confined to household production. Yet Hamilton got the best of both the argument and history. As America's first secretary of the treasury in George Washington's administration, he laid the foundations of the Hamiltonian republic. He produced the clever idea of "implied powers"—namely, that if an act of the federal government is authorized by the Constitution, then so are the initiatives necessary to implement it. The federal government could build lighthouses even if the Constitution did not give it specific permission, since protecting the country's borders is itself a constitutional imperative.

More important, Hamilton succeeded in establishing strong national credit by, first, assuming the state's debts and, second, funding the debt with revenues from tariffs on imported goods, authorized by the Hamilton Tariff of 1789.[2] He also established the first Bank of the United States in 1791 (in Philadelphia, then the nation's capital) with a charter that lasted until 1811. The bank's capitalized reserves facilitated a multiple of additional national credit similar to today's money multiplier.

As America's industrial economy emerged at the turn of the century, Jefferson had second thoughts about his agrarian stance. He began to worry that he was behind the times and that America was beginning to look like Hamilton's commercial economy. In his masterful presidential inaugural address in March 1801, he went a long way to closing the gap with his rival.[3] "Every difference of opinion is not a difference of principle," he said in a passage that should be re-read today. "We are all Republicans, we are all Federalists." Hamilton welcomed the address as "virtually a candid retraction of past misap-prehensions, and a pledge to the community" that the new president would "tread in the steps of his predecessors." Chief Justice Marshall, a Federalist, concluded that Jefferson's remarks were "well judged and conciliatory." James Bayard, a Federalist senator, thought it "in political substance better than *we* expected; and not answerable to the expectations of the partisans of the other side." To Benjamin Rush, the physician and a Jefferson admirer, it was an occasion for thanksgiving. "Old friends who had been separated by party names and a supposed difference of *principle* in politics for many years, shook hands with each other, immediately after reading it, and dis-covered, for the first time, that they had differed in *opinion* about the best means of promoting the interests of their common country."[4]

In his biography of Jefferson, Jon Meacham says that "it is not too much to say that Jefferson used Hamiltonian means to pursue Jef-fersonian ends."[5] Even that ringing conclusion may not go far enough in acknowledging Jefferson's change of mind: having previously been a stickler for what was sanctioned by the 1788 Constitution, as presi-dent, Jefferson exhibited such extraordinary degrees of pragmatism and opportunism that it is difficult to see how Hamilton would have acted differently. This frame of mind was most clearly displayed in the Louisiana Purchase of 1803. In 1800, Napoleon Bonaparte, the emperor of France, seized control of Louisiana from Spain as part of a broader attempt to establish a French empire in North America. But he quickly gave up on his imperial dream, as France's failure to put down a revolt in Saint-Domingue demonstrated how difficult it was to run such a far-flung empire while Britain's determination to defend its empire ramped up the costs of expansion; he decided to sell Louisiana to the United States for $15 million (or three cents an acre). Jefferson did everything he could to make the most of the opportunity, despite bitter opposition from Federalists who argued that it was unconstitutional to acquire any territory. He overruled naysayers who wanted to limit the purchase to the port city of New Orleans and its adjacent coastal lands. He pushed through his purchase despite lack of a constitutional amendment. When he discovered that America didn't have enough money to make the purchase, he relied on America's strong credit rating, which Hamilton had established, to borrow the difference. This was a very different Jefferson from the man who, as Washington's secretary of state, was asked by the president in 1791 for his view on the constitutionality of the national bank and replied that any power not specifically mentioned in the Constitution was reserved for the states, not the federal government. "To take a single step beyond the boundaries thus specially drawn around the powers of Congress, is to take possession of a boundless field of power, no longer susceptible of any definition."

The Louisiana Purchase was one of the most important things that any American president did to promote national development. It hugely increased America's territory, adding fertile and mineral-rich land, as became apparent during the Lewis and Clark Expedition to the West Coast (May 1804–September 1806). It also gave a fillip to the commercial forces that Jefferson had once feared but now encouraged. Jefferson got his just political rewards for his bold pursuit of expansion and innovation. He not only beat Charles Cotesworth Pinckney by 162 electoral votes to 14 when he stood for his second term. He also helped to carry two of his closest allies, James Madison and James Monroe, to the White House as his successors.

James Madison unwisely let the bank charter expire in 1811. But he was soon forced into a rethink. The War of 1812, America's second war with Britain, cost some $158 million at a time when the country had few ways of raising revenues. The U.S. policy of embargoing British goods also cut off one of the country's most important revenue streams, customs fees, while also reducing economic activity. Congress refused to raise taxes. The government initially borrowed heavily in a desperate attempt to finance the war, and then, in 1814, defaulted on its obligations, leaving soldiers and weapons manufacturers going unpaid. In 1816, Madison bowed to reality and created a second national bank with a charter for twenty years. Once again Hamilton had triumphed from beyond the grave.

The pivotal figure in reconciling the agrarian and industrial visions of America was Andrew Jackson. Jackson is hard to like: a brawler and a braggart who unleashed havoc on the Indians as well as the British. He was a product neither of Hamilton's bourgeois world of urban commerce nor of Jefferson's aristocratic world of slave-powered plantations, but of the Scotch Irish frontier culture: his parents were from Tennessee and he was born in South Carolina.

Andrew Jackson was the embodiment of a growing force in American life—popular democracy. In 1824, he lost the presidency to the last great representative of patrician America, John Quincy Adams, who shared his father John Adams's belief that democracies could survive only if they were hedged around with all sorts of restrictions. But Adams won only because the election was thrown into Congress, a point that angry critics kept hammering home during his unhappy stay in the White House, and four years later Jackson triumphed in a populist landslide. He claimed his biggest victories in the new states, which had fewer restrictions on the franchise than the founding states. He also enjoyed enthusiastic support among mechanics, merchants, and artisans, some of whom made the arduous journey to Washington, D.C., to cheer his inauguration.

Jacksonian democracy was intimately connected with another force: hostility to privilege and restrictions. Jackson liked to think of himself as belonging to a historic struggle against privilege that ran back to the Magna Carta and included the Protestant Reformation of the sixteenth century, the English Revolution of the seventeenth, and the American Revolution of the eighteenth. At each stage, the people seized more of what by right belonged to them from those who intended that power remain the monopoly of the few. He railed against "artificial distinctions," such as requiring a charter to form a corporation.

At the same time, Jackson combined populism with something that it is seldom coupled with, fiscal conservatism. He reduced the federal debt to zero for three years in a row for the first and last time in American history, and strongly supported sound money and the gold standard. He thus introduced a powerful new element into America's economic debate—laissez-faire populism.

NORTH VERSUS SOUTH

For its first seven decades as a nation, the United States was divided into two different economies—the capitalist economy of the North and the slave-owning economy of the South. New England was a land of textile mills powered by water, the South a land of plantations powered by slaves. This division became more pronounced over time as the North invested in new machinery and the South invested in more slavery.

The North was the home of Yankee ingenuity, a problem-solving and innovation-generating mind-set that Mark Twain captured perfectly in the person of Hank Morgan in *A Connecticut Yankee in King Arthur's Court* (1889):

"I am an American . . . a Yankee of Yankees—and practical; yes, and nearly barren of sentiment I suppose—or poetry, in other words. My father was a blacksmith, my uncle was a horse doctor; and I was both, along at first. Then I went over to the great arms factory and learned my real trade; learned all there was to it; learned to make everything: guns, revolvers, cannon, boilers, engines, all sorts of labor-saving machinery. Why I could make anything a body wanted—anything in the world, it didn't make any difference what; and if there wasn't any quick new-fangled way to make a thing, I could invent one."

Ninety-three percent of the important inventions patented in the United States between 1790 and 1860 were produced in the free states and nearly half in New England. Yankees applied their ingenuity to everything they touched. Frederic Tudor discovered that New England's ice could be exported at a profit to tropical countries. Nathaniel Wyeth then added that the ice could be packed in sawdust produced by local lumber mills.[6] Arial Bragg, an apprenticed shoemaker in rural Massachusetts, turned his industry upside down by showing how shoes could be ready-made instead of custom-made.[7] A British visitor remarked that "every workman seems to be continually devising some new thing to assist him in his work, there being a strong desire, both with masters and workmen, throughout the New England States, to be 'posted up' in every new improvement."[8] An Argentine visitor put it best: Yankees are "walking workshops."[9]

Though he earned his living as a lawyer, Abraham Lincoln fit this description of a "walking workshop" to a tee. He couldn't see a machine in the street without stopping to find out how it worked: clocks, omnibuses, and paddle wheels were among the machines that never escaped his "observation and analysis," according to his law partner. While serving in the House of Representatives, he patented "a device for buoying vessels over shoals" that consisted of bellows that inflated beneath a ship's waterline in order to lift the ship in shallow water. (A wooden model of the invention that Lincoln commissioned can be seen in the National Museum of American History.) In 1859, he talked about commercializing his idea for a "steam plough" but soon found that he had other more pressing matters on his hands.

In the first half of the nineteenth century, the lion's share of this ingenuity went to the textile industry rather than bellows and steam plows. Northern textile makers turned their region into a spinning and weaving powerhouse by a combination of industrial espionage—stealing the idea for power looms from Britain—and commercial moxie. In 1790, Almy and Brown built a textile mill in Pawtucket, Rhode Island, using designs that a British immigrant, Samuel Slater, "Slater the traitor" to the British, had memorized. (The British had banned immigrants from taking plans of the new looms to the United States, even searching their luggage, but couldn't do anything about feats of memory like Slater's.) In 1815, Francis Cabot Lowell, of the Boston Manufacturing Company, built a new factory in Waltham, Massachusetts, employing more than three hundred people, based on examples that he had seen in Lancashire. The Boston Manufacturing Company proved so successful that it declared a dividend of 17 percent in October 1817 and invested in another mill in 1818.

The power loom enabled factories to weave yarn into cloth under a single roof rather than having to send thread out to be spun in specialized spinning mills, quickly reducing the cost of production by half. The new technology spread rapidly across New England: by 1820, 86 firms were using 1,667 power looms while traditional spinning mills in Philadelphia and Rhode Island were forced to shut up shop.[10] Production boomed from 4 million yards of cotton cloth a year in 1817 to 308 million twenty years later.[11]

As well as importing the idea of the factory from Britain, the Yankees pioneered a new system of production—what Europeans called the "American system of production," and what might better be known as the system of interchangeable parts. In 1798, Eli Whitney was given a gigantic contract for ten thousand muskets from the U.S. government. When it became clear that he could not possibly meet his deadline, he came up with the idea of mass-producing muskets with interchangeable parts. Though his idea was not original—the French had pioneered interchangeable parts for muskets in the 1780s—the Americans took it to a much higher level. In France, the parts were made by craftsmen working with hand tools. In America, the parts were made by semiskilled workers who used specially designed machines that could keep churning out parts indefinitely. The point of the French system was to make handcrafting a bit more efficient. The point of the American system was to replace handcrafting with something new—something that was functional rather than beautiful, and democratic rather than exclusive. Samuel Colt, the inventor of the six-shooter, followed in Whitney's footsteps and, flush with government contracts, established a giant factory in Hartford, Connecticut, in the winter of 1855–56, employing more than a thousand people. The government also established huge armories of its own in Springfield, Massachusetts, and Harpers Ferry, Virginia.

The military drove the mass-production revolution because it needed a large number of identical products and wasn't worried that it might go bankrupt in acquiring them. The idea soon spread to civil society. Francis Pratt and Amos Whitney worked in Colt's armory and applied mass production to machine tools. Eli Terry massproduced inexpensive clocks and made it possible for a busy country to tell the time.[12]

As they spread to the Midwest in search of land, the Yankees revolutionized agriculture as well as industry. For millennia, farmers had broken their backs harvesting corn with scythes. Thanks to McCormick's mechanical reaper they could reap ten acres a day while perched on their behinds. The reaper was the tip of an iceberg: the U.S. Patent Office reported 659 agricultural inventions in the 1850s ranging from plows and threshers through speeders and corn huskers to butter churns and beehives.[13] Farmers were hungry for knowledge. They put on state fairs to display prize animals and new machinery and organized societies to represent their interests and spread "best practice": by 1858, there were 912 of them, all but 137 in the North.[14] Thomas Green Fessenden's *The Complete Farmer and Rural Economist* (1834) was a bestseller. Local entrepreneurs created newspapers and magazines such as the *Western Farmer* (1839) and the *Prairie Farmer* (1841). Horace Greeley's *New York Tribune* was stuffed with articles about animal husbandry and soil conservation, many of them reprinted in local papers such as the *Cleveland Plain Dealer* and the *Chicago Tribune.* In 1860, there were sixty specialized agricultural periodicals with a combined circulation of three hundred thousand.[15]

At the same time, the North created the infrastructure of a modern commercial nation. The Suffolk Bank of Boston performed some of the functions of a central bank for New England, helping to shield the region from the financial chaos that followed the abolition of the Second Bank of the United States in 1836. Under Horace Mann's leadership, the Massachusetts State Board of Education created a modern education system: teacher training colleges, standardized and graded curricula, various levels of rural schools, and secondary schools for older pupils. Schools were "the grand agent for the development or augmentation of national resources," Mann wrote in 1848, "more powerful in the production and gainful employment of the total wealth of a country than all the other things mentioned in the books of political economists."[16]

As the North threw in its lot with industry, the South fell under the sway of King Cotton. In 1793, Eli Whitney, returning to

Savannah from studying at Yale, invented his cotton gin (short for "engine"), which, as we've seen, speeded up the separation of seeds from fiber by a factor of twenty-five. This marked a turning point in American history. Before Whitney's invention, most plantations focused on tobacco, sugar, rice, and indigo. Cotton was a luxury item: high-quality long-staple cotton grew on the Sea Islands just off the coast of Georgia and South Carolina, but didn't grow at any distance from the coast (Sea Island cotton remains a byword for luxury today). Whitney's invention meant that upland cotton, which was much more difficult to harvest than long-staple cotton (the fiber being tightly attached to the seed) but could be grown across the South, could be turned into a cash crop. The production of cotton rose from 5 million pounds in 1793 when the gin was invented to 63 million pounds ten years later.

The gin helped to create one of America's greatest export industries: by 1820, cotton comprised half of America's exports, turning the South into America's most export-oriented region and Southern plantation owners into its most vocal supporters of free trade. It turned out that the South was superbly suited for mass production of the crop, with the right quantity and distribution of rain, the right number of days without frost, and, particularly in the Mississippi Delta, the right sediment-rich soil.[17] Farmers quickly set about improving the crop still further: in 1806, Walter Burling, a Natchez planter, brought a new strain of cottonseeds from Mexico that had larger bolls that could be picked more easily and had a better quality of fiber.[18] Cotton growers published specialized journals such as the *American Cotton Planter* and established agricultural colleges that delivered advice on how best to worship the king.

The cotton growers could also rely on what the *American Cotton Planter* called "the cheapest and most available labor in the world."[19] By 1860, about 4 million of America's 4.5 million African Americans were slaves and almost all of them were owned by Southern planters. Before the rise of King Cotton there was a chance that slavery might have died a natural death, as abolitionists denounced the institution as barbaric and liberals argued that free labor was more efficient than coerced labor. In 1807, the American Congress passed and Thomas Jefferson, a slave owner, signed the Act Prohibiting Importation of Slaves. In 1833–34, abolitionist sentiment was given a further boost by Great Britain's decision to abolish the slave trade across the empire. But the cotton gin gave an ancient evil a new lease on life across the South. We will never know whether slavery might have been abolished peacefully, as happened in the British Empire, were it not for the invention of the cotton gin. But slavery and cotton production certainly advanced in lockstep, as Sven Beckert demonstrates: the proportion of slaves in four typical South Carolina upcountry counties increased from 18.4 percent in 1790 to 39.5 percent in 1820 to 61.1 percent in 1860.

Slavery was at the heart of a productivity revolution: output of cotton in pounds per slave (aged ten to fifty-four) rose by 34 percent a year from 1790 to 1800 and 11 percent a year from 1800 to 1806. Though this rate of growth proved unsustainable, productivity nevertheless rose by a respectable 3.3 percent a year from 1806 right up until the outbreak of the Civil War. Slave owners invested a growing amount of capital in their slaves: by 1861, almost half the total value of the South's capital assets was in the "value of negroes." "To sell cotton in order to buy Negroes—to make more cotton to buy more Negroes, 'ad infinitum,' is the aim and direct tendency of all the operations of the thorough going cotton planter," one Yankee visitor to the cotton kingdom commented in the 1830s, "his whole soul is wrapped up in the pursuit. It is, apparently, the principle by which he 'lives, moves and has his being.'"[20] The spatial distribution of America's black population changed as the cotton industry expanded.

Blacks (including free people who were kidnapped and imprisoned) were forcefully relocated from the North to the South and from the upper South to the lower South. Domestic servants were reallocated to the fields. But such was the ruthless efficiency of the system that demand for slaves outstripped supply: the cost of a young adult male in the New Orleans slave market increased from $520 in 1800 to as much as $1,800 on the eve of the Civil War (see chart below), and Southern newspapers talked of "Negro Fever."

AVERAGE PRICE OF PRIME FIELD HAND IN NEW ORLEANS
1800 – 1860

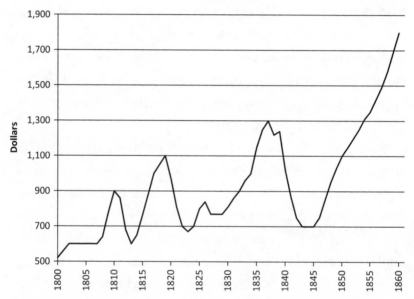

The combination of a new technology (ginning) and portable slave labor meant that the cotton industry could easily be expanded into America's new territories: in 1850, 67 percent of U.S. cotton grew on land that had not been part of the country when Whitney invented his gin.[21] The volume of cotton exported increased exponentially. In 1820, America exported 250,000 bales, worth $22 million. In 1840, it exported 1.5 million bales, worth $64 million. In 1860, on the verge of the Civil War, it exported 3.5 million bales worth $192 million. At the same time, the price of raw cotton, reflecting the sharp decline in the cost of production, plummeted, falling by 86 percent from 1799 to 1845. America was truly a cotton hyperpower, producing three-quarters of the world's cotton, up from just 9 percent in 1801, and providing the matériel for an industry that, according to one estimate in 1862, employed 20 million people worldwide—or one out of every 65 people alive.[22]

This rapidly expanding industry rested on foundations of unfathomable cruelty. Slavery deprived millions of Americans of their basic human right on the basis of their skin color. Disobedient or unproductive slaves were beaten; fugitive slaves were hunted down and tortured; female slaves were raped and abused. As the century wore on, the "lords of the lash" developed more brutal and sophisticated forms of coercion in order to squeeze the maximum amount of labor out of their human chattels.

They used gang labor to make work as machinelike as possible, with slaves performing the same tasks, at the same pace, from dawn to dusk. They divided workers into three groups according to their ability: the first gang, or great gang, consisting of the strongest slaves, the second gang consisting of the teenagers and the elderly, and the third gang consisting of the stragglers. At the McDuffie plantation at planting time, for example, the first group dug small holes seven to ten inches apart, the second group dropped in seeds, and the third group covered the holes with dirt.[23] John Brown, a fugitive slave, remarked on the connection between the price of cotton on the global market and coercion back in Dixie. "When the price rises in the English market the poor slaves immediately feel the effects, for they are harder driven, and the whip is kept more constantly going."[24]

This system of coercion allowed Southern whites to enjoy roughly the same income per head as northern whites despite living in a much more backward economy. It also allowed the Southern elite to live as large as anyone in the country: of the 7,500 Americans with fortunes above $3.3 million (in today's terms) in 1860, 4,500 were in the South.[25] In 1860, the total value of the slave population was somewhere between $2.7 billion and $3.7 billion—more than the country's railroad and manufacturing capital. Slaves constituted anywhere from 37 percent of the taxable wealth in Virginia to 61 percent in Mississippi (see table below).

TAXABLE PROPERTY IN THE CONFEDERACY, BY STATE: 1861

THOUSANDS IN CONFEDERATE $ (EQUIVALENT TO U.S. $)

	TOTAL ASSESSED TAXABLE PROPERTY	ASSESSED VALUE OF SLAVES	SLAVES AS A PERCENTAGE OF TOTAL
TOTAL	4,632,161	2,142,635	46.3
ALABAMA	484,966	261,284	52.8
ARKANSAS	138,442	65,438	47.3
FLORIDA	67,752	38,285	56.5
GEORGIA	633,322	280,477	44.3
LOUISIANA	480,597	187,312	39.0
MISSISSIPPI	471,677	287,765	61.0
NORTH CAROLINA	343,125	197,026	57.4
SOUTH CAROLINA	440,034	244,311	55.5
TENNESSEE	485,339	172,267	35.5
TEXAS	282,077	110,974	39.3
VIRGINIA	794,830	297,496	37.4

Though most slaveholders owned only about ten slaves, an elite group of 339 families owned 250 or more. The largest Delta planter, Stephen Duncan, owned 1,036.[26] The plantation owners were the champion consumers of antebellum America: they built great houses, staffed with armies of domestic servants, and entertained on a lavish scale, much like the British aristocracy.[27]

Southerners weren't the only people to profit from slavery: Dixie was enmeshed in a global cotton economy that stretched from the Mississippi Delta to New York banking houses to European spinning mills and stock exchanges.[28] Several of New York City's leading banks made fortunes in the cotton trade. Brown Brothers provided cotton growers with both financial and logistical services, lending money on future harvests and arranging shipping to Liverpool on its own ships. The Lehman brothers, Henry, Emanuel, and Mayer, started out in business as factors for cotton farmers in Alabama. Mayer shifted the company's business to New York, founding the first New York Cotton Exchange, but he supported the South in the Civil War and personally owned seven slaves. The specter of slavery even haunts financial brands that weren't around at the time: in looking back over its history of acquisitions, Chase Bank discovered that two banks it had acquired, Citizens Bank of Louisiana and the New Orleans Canal Bank, had collateralized over thirteen thousand slaves.[29]

These fortunes were bought at the price of not only the misery of slaves but also the backwardness of the economy in general. Slave owners had little incentive to plug into the national labor market since they were sitting on a supply of bonded laborers. They had little incentive to develop cities or other centers of population: their wealth resided in scattered plantations. And they had even less incentive to invest in education since they didn't want their slaves to get ideas above their stations.

AN UNEQUAL FIGHT

There should never have been any doubt about which version of America would prevail. General William Tecumseh Sherman issued a prophetic warning in a letter to a Southern acquaintance in late 1860:

> The North can make a steam engine, locomotive or railway car; hardly a yard of cloth, or a pair of shoes can you make. You are rushing into war with one of the most powerful, ingeniously mechanical and determined people on earth—right at your doors. You are bound to fail. Only in your spirit and determination are you prepared for war. In all else you are totally unprepared.[30]

The North possessed 70 percent of the country's wealth and 80 percent of its banking assets. Just three northern states—Massachusetts, New York, and Pennsylvania—accounted for 53 percent of the country's manufacturing capital and 54 percent of its manufactured output, according to the 1850s Census of Manufacturing.[31] The North invested in labor-saving devices, in both agriculture and industry. The South invested in slaves. The proportion of the North's population engaged in agriculture declined from 80 percent to 40 percent, while the proportion of the South's same population remained stuck at 80 percent.[32] It also invested more heavily in its human capital: New England was probably the most educated society on earth—95 percent of New Englanders could read and write and 75 percent of five- to nineteen-year-olds were enrolled in school—and the rest of the North was not far behind. No wonder seven-eighths of the 4 million Europeans who immigrated to America from 1815 to 1860 chose to go to the North.

The South could draw only on half the number of potential soldiers as the North. It was also dangerously reliant on cash crops, particularly cotton, that had to be exported outside the region: all the
North had to do was to close the region's land border and blockade its
ports and the economy would be starved of its lifeblood. The chart
below compares the economies of the Union states with those of the
Confederate states from 1800 onward in terms of GDP per head and
share of national GDP. The chart not only shows how much bigger
the Union economy was than the Confederate economy, but also how
long it took for the South to catch up after the Civil War.

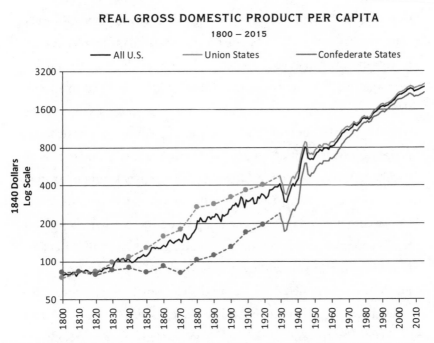

REAL GROSS DOMESTIC PRODUCT PER CAPITA

1800 – 2015

Note: "Union States" include states in the Union at the time of the Civil War and those admitted to the United States thereafter.

Yet the war was hardly a walkover. The North's war machine
didn't tap the full potential of its economy until three years after the

outbreak of the war. And even if the South wasn't as productive as the North, it was no slouch. It sat at the heart of the world's most globalized industry. Moreover, there is no simple relationship between economic power and military power, as North Korea reminds us with alarming frequency. The Southern elite were a martial caste, raised in the saddle and obsessed with "honor." Southerners were much better represented in the higher ranks of the army than northerners: among antebellum American soldiers prominent enough to be chronicled in the *Dictionary of National Biography,* the South contained twice the percentage of the North despite a smaller population.[33]

The South might have lasted longer if it had applied the same genius to economic governance as it did to military affairs. The Confederate Treasury scored a success with its war bonds. In early 1863, the Treasury issued bonds on the Amsterdam market backed by cotton rather than gold. Called "Erlanger Bonds" after the French firm that underwrote the issues, these bonds continued to sustain their value long after it became clear that the South was losing the war in large part because the option to buy cotton gave investors a hedge against war risk.[34] In general, though, it made a mess of both fiscal and monetary policy. Efforts to raise money through taxation were feeble at best: only 6 percent of the $2.3 billion in revenues came from a combination of export and import duties together with a "war tax" on commodities. Both the North and the South printed fiat currency in order to pay soldiers and buy supplies. But the North was much more restrained than the South. The North's "greenbacks" (so called because of their color) still retained about 70 percent of their face value by the end of the war. The Confederacy's currency lost value much more quickly, reducing the army's ability to buy military matériel and unleashing hyper-inflation of up to 9,000 percent (see chart opposite). The Confederacy canceled a significant part of its outstanding money supply in 1864, which temporarily lowered the

CONFEDERATE MONEY STOCK AND PRICE LEVEL
JANUARY 1861 – APRIL 1865

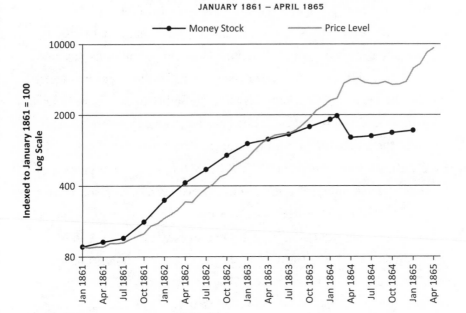

pace of inflation. After the war, the South's money was, of course, completely, rather than just largely, worthless, and Southerners had to resort to barter.

The first large-scale conflict of the industrial era, the Civil War was ruinously costly in blood and treasure for both sides: by recent estimates, somewhere between 650,000 and 850,000 men died, more than the number of Americans killed in every subsequent war and the equivalent, if you adjust for population size, of 5 million people today.[35] Half a million people were wounded. The carnage wasn't confined to humans: the ratio of cattle to humans declined from 749 for every 1,000 people to 509 per 1,000 in 1870, largely due to slaughter in the South.[36] The economic cost of the war amounted to $6.6 billion (in 1860 dollars), nearly 150 percent of the country's GDP in the year before the war broke out, and far more than it would have cost to buy the freedom of every slave in America.

The South inevitably paid the heaviest price. Roughly 13 percent of men of military age died during the war, twice the figure of men born in the free states or territories. More were maimed: in the first year after the war, 1866, Mississippi spent 20 percent of its revenues on artificial limbs.[37] Slave owners lost over $2 billion in capital when their slaves were freed. They also lost the ability to use the gang system of production, which they had perfected over the years, to maximize the production of cotton. Exports, which mostly came from the South, fell from 7 percent of GDP in 1860 to less than 2 percent in 1865.[38] The region even lost one of its greatest hidden resources, its political power. The South didn't have a single Speaker of the House or Senate majority leader for half a century after the Civil War.

In some way, the war prolonged the division between a progressive and a backward economy. The North was invigorated by the exertions of war. Senator John Sherman wrote an almost gloating letter to his brother William Tecumseh Sherman: "The truth is the close of this war with our resources unimpaired gives an elevation, a scope to the ideas of leading capitalists, far higher than anything ever undertaken in this country before. They talk of millions as confidently as formerly of thousands." By contrast, the South was shattered: in 1870, its overall output was only two-thirds of what it had been in 1860 and it was not until 1890 that per capita income returned to its prewar level.[39] The two censuses that bookend the Civil War years, the censuses for 1860 and 1870, reveal just how badly the war affected various sectors of the agricultural economy (see table opposite). Farm values fell by 42 percent. The number of improved acres fell by 13 percent. The "workstock" fell by 42 percent. The number of farms with more than one hundred tilled acres declined by 17 percent, while the number of farms with fewer than fifty tilled acres more than doubled.[40]

FARMS AND FARM OUTPUT IN THE
CONFEDERATE STATES

1870 VALUES AS A PERCENTAGE OF 1860 VALUES

Farms	
Number	*148*
Value	*58*
Improved Acres	87
Workstock	79
Farm Output	
Cotton	*56*
Tobacco	*36*
Wheat	*77*
Corn	*66*
Irish potatoes	*84*
Sweet potatoes	*47*
Rice	*39*
Oats	*111*

The reason for the collapse of southern agriculture was simple and understandable: people who had been forced to work at the master's bidding under slavery gained the freedom to decide how much work they would do. Roger Ransom and Richard Sutch estimate that the withdrawal of former slave labor (ranging from stopping working on the weekends to dropping out of the labor force entirely) was the equivalent of the loss of 28 to 37 percent of the former black labor force. Though the decline was a relatively modest 12.4 percent for males, it was as much as 60 percent for women and even more for children.[41]

The abolition of slavery affected far more than just the

productivity of agriculture. Slavery had underwritten every aspect of southern economic life. Bhu Srinivasan points out that in most agricultural societies the most valuable asset is land. In the slave-owning South, however, slaves were an even more valuable asset because they were portable: you could buy a lifetime's worth of labor and then sell that laboring asset to another part of the region. So mortgaging slaves became the most common way of raising money.[42] In antebellum Louisiana, for example, 88 percent of loans secured by mortgages used slaves as (at least partial) collateral. The Thirteenth Amendment ended this practice at the same time that other forms of capital were vanishing or going into sharp decline. War bonds became worthless. Land prices plummeted.[43]

The South struggled with a peculiar problem: how to adjust to the end of a uniquely terrible but also uniquely effective system of coerced labor. How do you replace "Mr. Lash" with "Mr. Cash"? How do you turn almost 4 million former slaves into wage laborers when those former slaves have never used money, never owned property, and never been taught to read or write? Abolishing the institution of chattel slavery is one thing. Creating a system of free labor is quite another. The problem was made all the more difficult to solve by the pressure of competition from other cotton producers, particularly Egypt and India. In 1870, the South produced only 56 percent as much cotton as it had ten years previously.

In the immediate aftermath of the Emancipation Proclamation, many former slave owners did their best to preserve old wine in new bottles. Yearlong contracts under which freedmen agreed to labor for their "rations and clothing in the usual way" became common across the South. In South Carolina, William Tunro tried to get his former slaves to sign contracts for life. When four of them refused, they were first expelled from the plantation and then hunted down and killed.[44]

Whites also resorted to violence to force freed people back into gang labor.

Plantation owners eventually hit on the system that existed in the gray zone between coerced labor and free labor: sharecropping. Under this system former slaves were allowed to use the master's tools and work the master's lands in return for a share of the crop they had grown. The system was reinforced by coercive laws, extralegal violence, and, above all, crushing debt. Most sharecroppers were locked in a cycle of debt that kept them tied to their land: the only way to pay off what they owed was to increase the amount they planted, but the more they planted, the more they reduced the price of their products and exhausted the soil that provided them with their livelihood. The population grew faster than the economy as a whole after the Civil War. Poor whites were also eventually sucked into the system, further inflaming racial tensions.

The most brutal development after the Civil War was prison labor. Convicts (90 percent of whom were black) were forced to work in some of the region's toughest industries: the railroads, mining, turpentine manufacturing, and, of course, cotton growing. In Georgia, the state sanctioned the creation of three private companies, Penitentiary Company One, Two, and Three, which specialized in hiring out laborers. James Monroe Smith, the owner of Smithsonia, a twenty-thousand-acre plantation in Oglethorpe County, Georgia, which required 1,000 workers to harvest the cotton, was so keen on prison labor that he bought a quarter share in Penitentiary Company Three to guarantee a supply of prisoners.[45] He regularly employed 200 to 300 convicts and in 1895–96 employed as many as 426.[46]

Convicts had no choice but to obey: the price of disobedience was a whipping, a maiming, or even execution. The death rate for convict laborers was astonishing: 11 percent in Mississippi in 1880, 14 percent in Louisiana in 1887, 16 percent in Mississippi in 1887. One southern businessman who leased prison labor summed up the situation with brutal honesty: "Before the war, we owned the negroes. If a man had a good negro he could afford to keep him. . . . But these convicts, we don't own 'em. One dies, get another."[47]

Even with the help of prison labor, industry only made a few advances in the South.[48] In the 1880s, Birmingham, Alabama, located amid coal and iron ore deposits, became the region's most successful iron producer. In the 1890s, mill owners began building mills powered by steam engines. Frank Sprague built America's first electric street railway in Richmond, Virginia, in 1888. Yet progress was patchy. Birmingham churned out cheap pig iron at a time when northern manufacturers were producing steel. Many northern business leaders refused to invest in the South. "I am not interested in any business proposition in any place where it does not snow," declared James J. Hill, the builder of the Great Northern Railway.[49] For the most part, the southern elite continued to try to squeeze as much as it could from agriculture. In 1874, a European visitor, Friedrich Ratzel, was shocked by the contrast between urban life in the South and the rest of the country:

> The general character of Southern cities [is] . . . very different from their Northern and Western counterparts. . . . The commerce of this area is still not connected to any industrial activity to speak of. For that reason, besides the big merchants here there are no big industrialists, no skilled workers, nor a vigorous white working class of any size worth mentioning. The shopkeepers and hand workers cannot make up for the lack of these hefty classes that create civilization and wealth. . . . Therefore . . . this society has an incomplete, half-developed profile like that which one tends to associate with the industry-less large cities of the

predominantly agricultural countries. In this regard New Orleans, Mobile, Savannah, and Charleston look more like Havana and Veracruz than, say, Boston or Portland.[50]

The South also remained culturally different, as the North's attempt to impose equal rights by force ran out of steam. White southerners laboriously erected a system of legal segregation and voter intimidation, outfoxing integrationists at every turn. They not only turned the local wing of the Democratic Party into an instrument of regional resistance, they also established an armed division within the Democratic Party, in the form of the Ku Klux Klan, which was founded in 1866 and which routinely used violence against uppity blacks or liberal whites. Ambitious blacks left for the relative freedom of the North. Immigrants shunned the region: in 1910, only 2 percent of the southern population had been born abroad, compared with 14.7 percent of the country as a whole. It took the New Deal of the 1930s and the Sun Belt boom of the 1980s to turn the South into one of America's great economic dynamos.

Still, even if the Civil War reinforced the division between the progressive North and the backward South, it also settled the biggest division of all, over America's future. The Republicans, who controlled Washington, had a clear vision of what sort of America they wanted—a great industrial nation, powered by factories, spanned by steel rails, sprinkled with schools, and crowned by great cities—and they set about turning that vision into a reality.

In some ways the federal government was pathetically weak: it hardly had any employees and was still unsure about its powers to tax or legislate. In one way, however, it was extraordinarily powerful: thanks to a succession of clever land purchases, it had some two billion acres of land at its disposal, a territory greater than any Western European nation. And it cleverly used this land bank to pay off its debts, modernize its infrastructure, and extend its empire westward. The Homestead Act of 1862 offered 160-acre plots of free land to anyone who could occupy and improve it (making the gift conditional on improvement was quintessentially American). Men who in the Old World might have hoped to acquire a 10- or 20-acre plot over many generations could get their hands on twenty times that by crossing the Atlantic and filing a claim. By the outbreak of the First World War, some 2.5 million claims had been granted.

ONE NATION . . . UNDER CAPITALISM

There were several great moments when America "came together" as a single country. The moment in 1869 when Leland Stanford hammered his silver hammer on the gold spike that joined the Union Pacific to the Central Pacific at Promontory Summit in Utah and thereby joined America's great West to its old East; or the moment in 1986 when workers finally completed the first transcontinental interstate, I-80, from the George Washington Bridge in Manhattan to the western terminus of the San Francisco–Oakland Bay Bridge. None was as important as the moment when the South surrendered to the North in the Civil War and a once-divided country embraced its fate as a fully capitalist republic.

Three

THE TRIUMPH OF
CAPITALISM: 1865–1914

I N THE DECADES BETWEEN the end of the Civil War and the outbreak of World War I, the United States became a recognizably
modern society. In 1864, the country still bore the traces of the
old world of subsistence. Cities contained as many animals as people,
not just horses but also cows, pigs, and chickens. A spark could ignite
an urban conflagration, as happened most spectacularly in Chicago
in 1871, supposedly when a cow kicked over a lantern, because most
buildings were still made of wood. People worked for small family
companies. By 1914, Americans drank Coca-Cola, drove Fords, rode
underground trains, worked in skyscrapers, doffed their hats to "scientific management," shaved with Gillette's disposable razors, lit and
heated their houses with electricity, flew in airplanes, or at least read
about flights, and gabbed on the phone, courtesy of AT&T.

AT&T was one of more than a hundred giant corporations that
established themselves at the heart of the American economy. Fifty-
three of the firms on the Fortune 500 list in 2000 were founded in the
1880s, thirty-nine in the 1890s, and fifty-two in the 1900s. America

established a huge lead over the rest of the world in new industries such as steel, cars, and electricity. It also set the pace in old industries such as agriculture: by the late 1870s America accounted for 30 to 50 percent of the world's trade in grain and 70 to 80 percent of its trade in meat.

At the same time, America became a consumer society with the world's biggest class of dollar millionaires (4,000 by 1914) and its richest workers: Americans enjoyed a per capita income of $346 in 1914, compared with $244 in Britain, $184 in Germany, $153 in France, and $108 in Italy. Companies produced not just products but brands in which consumers could put their trust: Aunt Jemima's pancakes, Kellogg's shredded wheat, Juicy Fruit gum, Pabst Blue Ribbon beer, Quaker Oats. Advertisers sold their brands with a pizzazz that quickly became familiar. Jell-O was "quick and easy." Kellogg's products were a key to healthy living. In 1896, Heinz built a fifty-foot-tall electric pickle in Times Square with twelve hundred lights that listed all of the company's fifty-seven varieties.[1] Consumers were seized by crazes: roller skates in the 1870s, bicycles in the 1890s. The big cities boasted temples of consumption: Wanamaker's in Philadelphia; Macy's, Bloomingdale's, and Lord & Taylor in New York; Filene's in Boston; and, perhaps most impressive of them all, Marshall Field's in Chicago. In 1864, the tallest building in New York City was Trinity Church at Wall Street and Broadway. In 1914, it was America's "cathedral of commerce," the sixty-story Woolworth Building.

This era saw America's takeoff into self-reinforcing growth. After millennia of economic stagnation or near stagnation, the increase in the country's growth rate was inevitably slow and halting at first. For the most part, innovation (multifactor productivity) and unit-cost reduction (output per hour) depend on a complex interaction of new ideas and production processes that can take decades to bear fruit. In the second half of the nineteenth century, the great economic breakthroughs—improved information transfer (the telegraph), the defeat of distance (the railway), and a new source of power (electricity)—were particularly slow because they depended on the construction of networks. But the growth rate finally began to accelerate rapidly in the late nineteenth and early twentieth centuries as new ideas fed on each other, goods circulated more quickly, and regional specialization intensified. The annualized rate of productivity growth rose from an average of 1.4 percent a year in the period 1800 to 1890 to 2 percent or more a year from 1889 to 1899, an increase in the underlying growth rate of two-fifths, and then increased again in the 1920s.

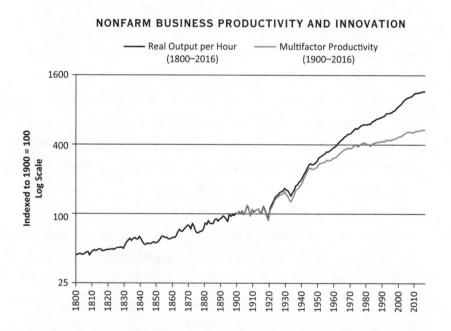

NONFARM BUSINESS PRODUCTIVITY AND INNOVATION

Americans celebrated all this growth far more lustily than Europeans. The Republican Party that held sway for much of the postwar period was unashamedly progrowth and probusiness. In 1864, Congress passed the Act to Encourage Immigration, creating an

Immigration Bureau within the State Department and allocating federal money and federal workers to recruit foreign workers and ease their passage to America. Big companies (particularly railways) and state governments advertised for new citizens across Europe. Even intellectuals, usually the wallflowers at the capitalist ball, joined the chorus. Walt Whitman praised America's "extreme business energy" and its "almost maniacal appetite for wealth." Ralph Waldo Emerson lauded America as "the country of the Future . . . a country of beginnings, of projects, of vast designs and expectations." He traveled the country lecturing on the virtues of self-improvement and commercial progress. "There is more poetry in the rush of a single railroad across the continent," said Joaquin Miller, a western poet, "than in all the gory story of the burning of Troy."[2]

Sometime before the Great War, this brash and thrusting adolescent replaced its aging parent, Great Britain, as the world's leading economy. In one measure after another America accelerated past the old country. In 1857, America's population surpassed Britain's (which then included the whole of Ireland). From 1870 to 1910, America's share of global manufacturing increased from 23.3 percent to 35.3 percent, while Britain's share declined from 31.8 percent to 14.7 percent. One careful calculation suggests that, by 1910, America's income per capita was 26 percent higher than Britain's.[3]

The direction of the flow of technology and ideas was reversed. In the first half of the nineteenth century, Americans stole most of their productivity-boosting ideas from the mother country. Ambitious bankers such as Junius Morgan went to London to learn their craft. In the second half of the nineteenth century, the relationship was reversed. Charles Tyson Yerkes, a shady tycoon from Chicago, took over much of the London Underground, building three new lines, introducing electric trains, and consolidating the lines into something like a single system. J. P. Morgan turned Morgan Grenfell &

Co. into a province of his global empire. H. J. Heinz built a factory in Peckham. Frank Woolworth opened the first overseas Woolworth's in Liverpool.

Having once mocked the Americans as technological laggards, the British began to fear them as rivals. The late Victorian and Edwardian periods saw a spate of books on America's growing industrial might. And having once suffered from a colonial cringe, the Americans became more and more dismissive of their former masters. One of the first "moving pictures" shown in the United States, in 1896, featured "Uncle Sam knocking a diminutive bully, John Bull, to his knees."[4]

PROMETHEUS UNBOUND

During these years, territorial expansion, rapid immigration, and railroad construction continued unhindered. The United States completed its expansion with the addition of Alaska in 1867 and Hawaii in 1898: by 1900, the country was three times larger than it had been when the British were kicked out, with 3,002,387 square miles under the flag. The population increased from 40 million in 1870 to 99 million in 1914, growing at an average rate of 2.1 percent a year, compared with 1.2 percent in Germany, 1.9 percent in Britain, and 0.2 percent in France. Two-thirds of the growth came from natural increase, reflecting the population's optimism about the future, and the other third from immigration, reflecting the rest of the world's conviction that America was the land of opportunity.

The giant sucking sound of the era was the sound of immigrants being pulled into the United States from Europe. In the 1880s alone, 5.3 million people moved to the United States, or 10.5 percent of the 50 million people who lived there at the start of the decade. These immigrants were an undoubted plus for the economy.[5] They were disproportionately young adults with few dependents and a drive to make it. They were all by definition adventurers who were willing to risk an ocean voyage to a new world for a chance of a better life. They provided the hands and muscles that built the machines, roads, and bridges of a rapidly industrializing nation: by 1920, immigrants and their children constituted more than half of manufacturing workers. Many immigrants also possessed valuable skills: the Scandinavians who flooded to the upper Midwest were farmers, while the eastern European Jews who gravitated to New York were merchants and traders. Skilled British immigrants continued to do what they had done throughout American history: bring Britain's industrial secrets in metallurgy, weaving, and chemicals across the Atlantic.

It is fitting that many of the greatest buildings erected in this era were railway terminals: Grand Central Station in New York (1871), Union Station in Chicago (1881), and Union Station in Washington, D.C. (1907), were all marble temples to the steam engine. Railways were the greatest prosperity-producing machines of the age. "The town that is distant a hundred miles by rail is so near that its inhabitants are neighbours," Anthony Trollope wrote on a trip to the United States in the 1860s, "but a settlement twenty miles distant across the uncleared country is unknown, unvisited, and probably unheard of by women and children. Under such circumstances the railway is everything. It is the first necessity of life, and gives the only hope of wealth."

The second half of the nineteenth century saw a massive expansion in America's "only hope of wealth": railroad companies added more than thirteen miles of track every day for forty years from 1870 onward, increasing total mileage by a factor of five, and ensuring that, by 1917, America possessed 35 percent of the world's railway mileage (see chart opposite). The number of people per mile of completed railroad fell from 6,194 in 1840 to 571 in 1880 to 375 in 1890. A disproportionate amount of this building was in the hitherto sparsely inhabited West.

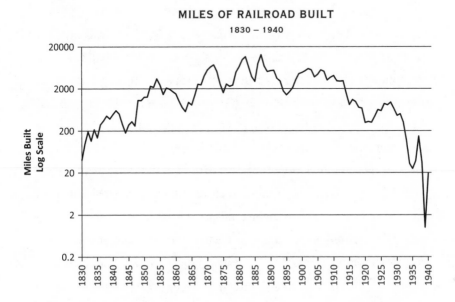

MILES OF RAILROAD BUILT

1830 – 1940

Railroads reduced the cost of moving stuff around: according to one estimate, by 1890 the cost of rail freight was $0.875 a ton-mile compared with $24.50 per ton-mile for wagon freight, a reduction of 96 percent. They speeded up connections: the transcontinental railroad reduced the time it took to get across the continent from six months to six days. They also boosted reliability: you could more or less guarantee that you would get to where you were going on time. Trains could pull dozens of wagons' worth of stuff: David Wells calculated that, in 1887, the country's railway freight was equivalent to every person carrying a thousand tons one mile or every ton a thousand miles.[6]

Railways also acted as industrial stimulants in their own right. In the 1880s, 200,000 people were employed building railroads and another 250,000 people were running them.[7] About half the steel produced in the three decades after the Civil War went into making rails.

Railways did more than just connect the disconnected and speed the flow of goods: they changed the direction of traffic. Before the railway age most goods flowed north to south (or vice versa) along the coast or America's generous river system. With the railway they increasingly flowed east to west. People poured into what had been vast open spaces and started cultivating crops and raising cattle. And the products of all their labor then poured back to the East Coast and thence to the rest of the world. It was as if a giant had applied a lever to an entire country and turned it on its axis.[8]

America changed more in these years than it did in any other period. This chapter will look at two sets of changes—the technological transformation that saw the arrival of new materials (steel and oil) and new technologies (cars and electricity); and the geographical transformation that saw the West integrated into the American (and global) economy. The next chapter will stay with the same period and look at the business titans who refashioned the economy.

THE AGE OF INNOVATION

The years between 1865 and 1914 saw the arrival of an astonishing range of fundamental innovations: a new basic material (steel), a new basic fuel (oil), a new power source (electricity), a new personal mobility machine (the motorcar), a new communication device (the telephone), and countless smaller innovations that sometimes harnessed the bigger ones and sometimes went off in their own directions. From 1860 to 1890, the U.S. Patent Office issued half a million patents for inventions—more than ten times as many as were issued in the previous seventy years and far more than in any other country.

Yesterday's fast follower, America, now occupied a place that it has occupied ever since: bravely carving out the technological frontier so that other countries could follow in its wake.

The age of steel arrived with a gust of wind in 1856 when an Englishman, Sir Henry Bessemer, discovered that blowing cold air through molten pig iron causes the oxygen in the air to bind with the carbon in the pig iron, expelling the impurities automatically. Steel had been used since the beginning of civilization, most commonly for weapons but also for fine cutlery. Sheffield was already famous for its steel in Chaucer's time. Yet steel played almost no role in the first Industrial Revolution because it was so difficult to make in bulk. Henry Bessemer changed all this. Bessemer had developed a new type of artillery shell but the cast-iron cannons of the day were too brittle to handle it. He was experimenting with ways of making a stronger metal when a gust of wind happened to blow over some molten iron, superheating the metal and generating steel. Bessemer quickly designed an industrial process that could duplicate this happy accident. A Bessemer mill could manufacture a ton of high-quality "crucible" steel at the expenditure of just 2.5 tons of fuel (coke), while old-fashioned mills took seven tons of coal to make one ton of lower quality "blister" steel. Bessemer's was only the first of a cavalcade of innovations that continues to this day. A decade later the Siemens-Martin process (open-hearth furnaces) increased productivity still further. After that, steelmakers learned how to use scrap metal to reduce waste. By the end of the century, the cost of producing a ton of steel had fallen by 90 percent compared with the midcentury (see chart on page 100).

America proved better than any of its rivals in harnessing these improvements: a country that produced only 380,000 tons of steel in 1870 produced 28.4 million tons in 1913. America had a huge comparative advantage in steel. It had the factors of production lying in the ground: once the transportation infrastructure was constructed

WHOLESALE PRICE OF BESSEMER STEEL
1867 – 1902

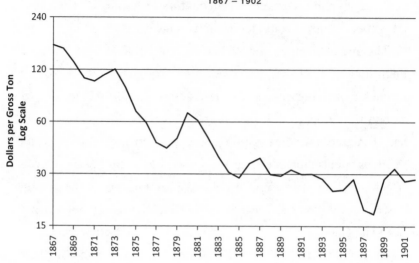

they could be brought together relatively cheaply. It also had a blank slate: whereas Britain, the world's leading steel power at the beginning of the period, had invested heavily in old steelmaking techniques, America introduced new plants and new methods.

The steel revolution changed the face of industrial America. John Fitch described the sheer might of the new steel furnaces:

> The very size of things—the immensity of the tools, the scale of production—grips the mind with an overwhelming sense of power. Blast furnaces, eighty, ninety, one hundred feet tall, gaunt and insatiable, are continually gaping to admit ton after ton of ore, fuel, lime, and stone. Bessemer converters dazzle the eye with their leaping flames. Steel ingots at white heat, weighing thousands of pounds, are carried from place to place and tossed about like toys. . . . Cranes pick up steel rails or fifty-foot girders as

jauntily as if their tons were ounces. These are the things that cast a spell over the visitor in these workshops of Vulcan.[9]

It also changed the geography of production. Cleveland, Bethlehem, Chicago, Birmingham, and Youngstown became, to a greater or lesser extent, steel towns; Pittsburgh became a steel city. These new steelmakers could not produce the silver metal fast enough to satisfy demand. During the course of a single decade—the 1880s—the proportion of America's railways that were made out of steel increased from 30 percent to 80 percent.[10] America became a steel country in much the same way that it is currently a silicon country. Steel rails knitted the continent together far more efficiently than iron rails. Steel rails lasted roughly ten times longer than iron rails and could support greater weight: heavier locomotives pulled longer trains loaded with more stuff. Steel pipelines, combined with steel pumps and compressors, carried the oil and gas that powered the industrial machine. Steel bridges spanned rivers and steel frames supported skyscrapers. Steel put cheap tools in everybody's hands and cheap utensils on everybody's tables. This is why steel gave America its richest man, in the shape of Andrew Carnegie, and its biggest company, in the form of U.S. Steel.

If America's new economy was built out of steel, it was lubricated by oil. In 1855, Benjamin Silliman, a chemist at Yale University, published his "Report on the Rock Oil, or Petroleum from Venango Co., Pennsylvania, with special reference to Its Use for Illumination and Other Purposes." Three years later Edwin Drake began drilling for oil at Titusville, Pennsylvania, applying techniques used in salt wells. Though the Civil War briefly put a halt to the drilling, as soon as the war was over America witnessed an "oil rush" reminiscent of the California gold rush, and northwestern Pennsylvania was soon littered with makeshift oil wells and crude refineries where men refined oil much as they distilled whiskey, boiling the liquid and smelling it to see if it could be used for kerosene. Though the mountainous terrain of the Pennsylvania oil fields made transportation difficult, the construction of an oil pipeline in 1865 removed the bottleneck: oil flowed from Pennsylvania to railroad tanker cars and tanker ships and thence to giant refineries. Demand and supply soon surged. From 1880 to 1920, the amount of oil refined every year jumped from 26 million barrels to 442 million. And as Pennsylvania's oil fields ran down, new sources of oil were discovered, most notably in Texas and California. The chart below shows the astonishing decline in the price of kerosene paid by consumers from 1860 to 1900, a decline that was repeated between 1920 and 1930.

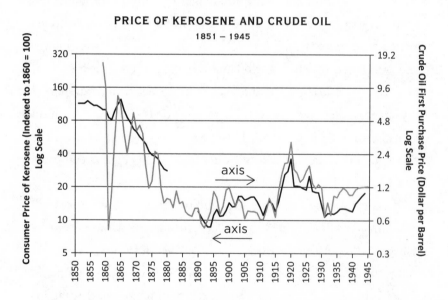

PRICE OF KEROSENE AND CRUDE OIL
1851 – 1945

Thanks to the combination of new oil finds and the expertise of its oil companies, America dominated the age of petroleum for roughly a century from Drake's first oil strike until the rise of the Gulf States in the 1960s. America's access to cheap oil quickly reshaped the country's consumption habits. In the nineteenth century, the main use for oil was as a source of light. (John D. Rockefeller got his start in the oil industry by buying a factory that made oil for kerosene lamps, when kerosene lamps were still a novelty.) People also used it to lubricate the machines that were at the heart of the machine age. In the twentieth century, oil became the nation's primary source of energy: as gasoline and diesel for cars, fuel oil for industry, heating oil for homes.

More than any other country, America was built on cheap oil. Americans could live in far-flung suburbs because filling their cars was cheap. They could build sprawling houses or locate them in climate-challenged places because fuel was abundant. California was America's prime example of what happens when you build a civilization on the basis of cheap fuel: people choose space over proximity and retailers quickly adjust to a less dense civilization by offering giant shopping malls and drive-throughs. Occasional oil shocks such as the one in the 1970s represented a fundamental threat to America's way of life and promoted lots of talk about kicking the oil habit. As soon as the oil price declined, Americans returned to their earlier habits.

The 1880s saw the introduction of two revolutionary new technologies, electric power and the internal combustion engine. Economists call these "general purpose technologies" because they are great inventions in their own right that lead inexorably to lots of smaller inventions that, taken together, completely change the tenor of life. Electricity was such a powerful new technology that contemporaries regarded it as a variety of magic. It can be generated easily and transmitted long distances with minimal leakage, and without smoke or fumes. Yet if it's not handled correctly it can kill you in a flash. The internal combustion engine combines the power of a steam engine with the flexibility of a horse. Electricity gave birth to electric tools for factories and homes; elevators; electric railways and underground trains; washing machines, stoves, irons, refrigerators; and, of huge significance for the sweltering South, air-conditioning. The internal combustion engine gave birth not only to direct offspring—cars, trucks, and buses—but also to more indirect ones, such as suburbs, supermarkets, motels, McDonald's, and, indeed, Motown.

The United States cannot claim a patent on these great inventions. The groundwork for the electricity revolution was laid by a United Nations of innovators. Alessandro Volta, an Italian, invented the first battery. James Prescott Joule, an Englishman, showed how a magneto could convert mechanical energy into electricity. Michael Faraday, also an Englishman, produced the first electric generator, a copper disk that rotated between the poles of a horseshoe magnet, in 1831. A German, Karl Benz, developed the first internal combustion engine on New Year's Eve, 1879, a mere ten weeks after Edison unveiled his electric light, and produced the first motorcar six years later, in 1885. But America can certainly claim to have democratized these general-purpose technologies more successfully than any other country. America's genius lay in three things that are rather more subtle than invention: making innovations more user friendly; producing companies that can commercialize these innovations; and developing techniques for running these companies successfully.

Thomas Edison is remembered as one of America's greatest inventors, a natural genius who grew up in the Midwest without much formal education, picked up the skills he needed in small workshops, and ended up with more patents to his name than any other American, including the first iterations of some of the world's most popular consumer goods, such as the first phonograph (in 1877) and the first long-playing record (in 1926). Yet there was more to Edison than this: his greatest claim to fame is arguably not as an inventor but as a systematizer of invention. He realized that America needed more than just folksy tinkerers with bright ideas. It needed professional innovators: people who could produce brilliant ideas on a regular basis, just as factories were producing products, and who could fit those innovations into a broader system of supply and demand. To that end he created America's first industrial laboratory at Menlo Park, New Jersey, in 1876 and staffed it with German PhDs, skilled craftsmen, and "absolutely insane men." He wanted to produce "a minor invention every ten days and a big thing every six months or so," and he wanted his laboratory's products to have commercial value. "We can't be like the old German professor who as long as he can get his black bread and beer is content to spend his whole life studying the fuzz on a bee!"[11]

He did not invent the first electric light, for example. Moses Farmer lit his home in Salem, Massachusetts, with glowing platinum wires in 1859. Pavel Yablochkov, a Russian, devised an arc lamp, or "Yablochkov candle," in 1876. Joseph Swan, an Englishman, patented the first incandescent lightbulb in 1878 and publicized his invention by lighting first his home, then a lecture theater in Newcastle, and finally the Savoy Theatre in London. What Edison did do was to pave the way for the mass adoption of electric lights. He invented an efficient lightbulb that could be manufactured in bulk. He established electric-generating stations that could provide power for those lights. His first great breakthrough took place on October 22, 1879, when he applied electricity to a cotton-thread filament suspended in a vacuum glass bulb. Thousands of people traveled to Menlo Park to see his "light of the future" that could light the world without a flame and be turned on and off with the flick of a switch. In 1882, standing in the office of his banker, J. P. Morgan, he flicked a switch and lit up Lower Manhattan with power generated from his electric power station in Pearl Street. It is a measure of how startlingly new the technology was that General Electric had to post notices in public places advising people not to try to light the new electric lights with matches.

The spread of the new technology was patchy. Electric lights caught on like wildfire: in 1885, there were 250,000 lightbulbs in use, and by 1902, 18 million. The electrification of urban transport was rapid. By the early twentieth century, nearly five billion passengers rode electrified streetcars every year, and Chicago and New York had both introduced electrified mass-transit systems, with Chicago electrifying its elevated lines in 1896 and New York opening its first electrified underground line in 1904. The electrification of buildings was much slower. Electricity was expensive because power plants were small and many producers, particularly Edison, favored direct current (DC), which lost power over long distances. For once the great systematizer of innovation was on the wrong side of history. On the thirtieth anniversary of the lighting up of Lower Manhattan, in 1912, only 16 percent of homes had electricity.

The pace of adoption sped up after the turn of the century: producers shifted from DC to the more efficient alternating current (AC)—in 1902, 61 percent of generating capacity was AC, and in 1917, 95 percent—and houses were connected to the grid as a matter of course. The average output of electric power per capita doubled every seven years from 1902 to 1915 and then doubled every six years from 1915 to 1929. The nominal price of electricity fell from 16.2 cents per kilowatt-hour in 1902 to 6.3 cents per kilowatt-hour in 1929—an inflation-adjusted decline of 6 percent a year.[12] But again the electrification of manufacturing was slower still: it was not until the 1920s that industrial America made substantial strides into the electricity age.

At first America followed Europe's lead in treating cars as toys for the wealthy, yachts that happened to go on land rather than water, in Richard Tedlow's phrase. In 1906, George Perkins, one of J. P. Morgan's lieutenants, bought the world's largest custom-made car, an eleven-foot-long French creation equipped with a writing desk and a washstand-table.[13] The number of registered cars crept up from just eight thousand in 1900 to seventy-eight thousand in 1905, and chauffeurs joined valets among the staff of grand houses. But then Henry Ford came up with an idea as revolutionary as any engineering innovation: making cars for "the great multitude." The first Model T, produced in 1908, was a category killer: powerful for its weight (22 horsepower and 1,200 pounds), easy to drive by the (admittedly challenging) standards of the day, light and strong thanks to the use of vanadium steel, which had several times the tensile strength of regular steel, and capable of negotiating dirt roads (all America's hard-surfaced roads in 1900, laid end to end, would not have stretched from New York to Boston, or 215 miles).[14] Ford reduced the price of the Model T from $950 in 1910 to $269 in 1923, even as he improved the quality. The number of cars on America's roads increased to 468,000 in 1910 and 9 million in 1920, and an astonishing proportion of these were Tin Lizzies: 46 percent in 1914 and 55 percent in 1923.[15]

Motorcars quickly added to the amount of power at the disposal of ordinary people: the horsepower embodied in motorcars surpassed the horsepower embodied in work animals (mostly horses) in 1910 and in railroads by 1915. Motorcars also changed the face of America: towns and cities began to sprawl, as people gained the ability to drive right to their front door, and horses, which had become more numerous in the age of rail, finally began to decline in number.[16]

The development of the motorcar was soon followed by the development of an even more exciting form of transportation—the flying machine. In 1900, the Wright brothers successfully flew a glider at Kitty Hawk, North Carolina. Then, in 1903, they added power in the form of a carburetor engine powered by gasoline.

Orville and Wilbur Wright were quintessentially American figures. In Germany and Britain, those magnificent men in their flying machines tended to be scions of the aristocracy. In America, they were products of the heartland—compulsive tinkerers who relied on local resources rather than government patronage and who were quick to commercialize their (sometimes wacky) ideas. The Wright brothers were born and bred in the Midwest. They made their living in that nursery of entrepreneurs, the bicycle business, experimenting with flying machines in their spare time, often using bicycle parts. Their first engine was built by their bicycle shop mechanic, Charlie Taylor, and used chains, resembling bicycle chains, to drive the propellers.

They owed their success to two things. They were the first aeronautical pioneers to realize that the key to producing flying machines was not producing ever more powerful engines, but developing a control system that allowed the pilot to steer the plane and maintain its equilibrium. In their first patent they didn't claim that they had invented a flying machine, but rather a system of aerodynamic control. They were also much more business-minded than their rivals: relying on their own resources rather than on the patronage of governments or plutocrats, they had to turn flying into a business as quickly as possible. In 1909, the brothers formed a company that, as well as manufacturing airplanes, ran a flight school, put on exhibitions of aeronautical daredevilry, and pioneered air freight.

Turning a hobby into a business proved difficult. You couldn't sell aircraft to regular consumers in the way that you could sell cars: they were too expensive and dangerous. Governments and business consortia were what mattered. You had to address all sorts of problems of supply and demand—hence the emphasis on flight schools and aerial displays. Patent wars proved to be expensive and distracting. At first the U.S. government didn't want to have anything to do with a couple of unknowns from Ohio, while European business consortia were suspicious of American nobodies. But a succession of successful flights with passengers, including one in which Wilbur flew around the Statue of Liberty and down the Hudson River, with a million New Yorkers looking on, turned the brothers into celebrities and provided them with a long line of customers.

The telephone was the least revolutionary of these three technologies. The telegraph had already crossed the technological Rubicon by separating the transmission of information from the transmission of physical objects. But it was certainly more revolutionary than the first words spoken on a telephone might suggest: "Mr. Watson come here—I want to see you" is hardly "What hath God wrought." Alexander Graham Bell had no doubt about the significance of what he had sired: on the evening he delivered his banal instruction to Mr. Watson, March 10, 1876, he wrote to his father, "I feel that I have at last struck the solution of a great problem—and the day is coming when telegraph wires will be laid on to houses just like water or gas— and friends converse with each other without leaving home."[17] He also grasped its commercial possibilities: though he was a professor of "vocal physiology" rather than a technologist by profession, he filed a patent for his invention in early 1876, only hours before a rival inventor, Elisha Gray, filed a competing patent.

For all its convenience the telephone spread slowly compared with, say, the radio or the internet. The number of households with phones climbed from 250,000 in 1893 to 6 million in 1907. The price of phone calls remained high and the pace of technological progress was slow. The gap between the invention of the phone and the first long-distance phone service between New York and San Francisco was twice as long (thirty-nine years) as the gap between the invention of the telegraph and the first long-distance telegraph service between the two cities (seventeen years). The reason for this was that Bell Telephone was a virtual monopoly. The only thing that kept it on the cutting edge was that the government monopolies that controlled the technology in the rest of the world were even more inefficient than a private monopoly. In 1900, the number of telephones per person was four times more than in England, six times more than in Germany, and twenty times more than in France. There were as many telephones in New York State as in all of Europe.[18]

Technologies such as cars and telephones are so eye-catching that it is easy to ignore more humble advances. Elisha Graves Otis, the founder of Otis Elevator, devised a cable-drawn "safety elevator" in 1852 that not only whisked you from floor to floor but also prevented accidents with a fail-safe break. James Bogardus, an architect, developed cage construction, using a wrought-iron cage to provide the skeleton of the seven-story Harper & Brothers building in 1854, making it easier to build high. George Westinghouse developed an automatic railroad air brake in 1869 that, using compressed air, allowed a single engineer to stop an entire train with one lever. Harvey Firestone, a mechanic working for Columbus Buggy Company in Columbus, Ohio, discovered that putting rubber tires on horse-drawn carriages could make them go faster. Henry Ford was one of the first visitors to the new tire factory, in 1895: he understood that there was no point putting the world on wheels if those wheels didn't go around smoothly.

THE RISE OF THE WEST

America's westward expansion produced some of the most iconic images of the young country: cowboys riding through the open range; boomtowns turned ghost towns; bloody battles between George Custer and the Sioux. Theodore Roosevelt decamped to the Badlands where he made his living as a rancher (and sheriff) and wrote a four-volume history of the frontier. William F. Cody

("Buffalo Bill") packaged images of the frontier, including buffalo hunts, bucking ponies, and war dances, into a blockbuster: in the winter of 1886–87, more than a million people saw it in Madison Square Garden in New York, and the next year the enormous British audience included Queen Victoria.

The West loomed even larger as the era faded into the past. Some of the greatest works of postwar American popular culture are about the West: Laura Ingalls Wilder's Little House on the Prairie series, about her settler childhood; Rodgers and Hammerstein's *Oklahoma!* (1943), about the Oklahoma land rush; George Stevens's *Shane* (1953), about a man who stands up against a cattle baron. "The West" continued to make money for Hollywood long after the railway barons had taken their final train trips. Given all this romanticism, it is important to remember that America's westward expansion was driven by hard-edged economic forces.

The meaning of "the West" changed as the country's population expanded. In 1800, the West meant Ohio. By 1850, it also meant the West Coast. The discovery of gold in California in 1848 drove thousands of people mad. Prospectors abandoned their families and walked across the vast continent, scaling the Rockies and the Sierra Nevadas, for the chance of panning gold. Stories of prospectors who made a fortune in gold were relayed back to the East Coast and magnified with the telling. The more common fate of people who wasted money, time, and effort, only to find nothing, was ignored. The gold rush was followed by the silver rush of the 1860s and 1870s, when silver was discovered in the Nevada hills.

The other great migration of the 1840s was inspired by God rather than gold. In 1847, Brigham Young led about seventy thousand Mormons on their Great Trek to escape persecution. They eventually stopped on the edge of the Great Salt Lake in Utah. Many more waves followed. Replanted in the West, this vigorously anticapitalist religion, founded on the principle of keeping wives and property in common, was quickly transmogrified and embourgeoisified. In order to win admission to the Union, Mormons had to renounce plural marriage. And in order to thrive they had to become first-class businesspeople: many of today's great Mormon business fortunes were founded in this era.

As we've seen, the 1862 Homestead Act sped up the westward movement of the population, offering settlers 160 acres for a nominal fee so long as they worked on the land they received for five years. Over the next few decades, the government gave away more than 270 million acres—about 10 percent of the land area of the United States—to 2.5 million settlers. Most of the land was west of the Mississippi River. Though some of the act's most prominent supporters doffed their hats to Jefferson's vision of a republic of "yeomen farmers," the act was thoroughly forward-looking. The government used property rights for settlers to encourage one of the greatest population movements in history. In neofeudal Brazil, the government handed out giant chunks of land to great landlords. In capitalist America, it handed land out to ordinary people on condition that they mix their labor with the soil. The 160 acres also established a minimum rather than a maximum size of farm: over the coming decades land holdings grew as failed smallholders sold their land and successful smallholders expanded.

The government also provided incentives for railroads to build track on spec in order to connect the homesteaders to the wider economy. In the decade after 1862, Congress repeatedly gave away parcels of land the size of northeastern states: the Union Pacific Railroad received the equivalent of New Hampshire and New Jersey combined. Richard White of Stanford University calculates that if you collected all the land doled out to railways in this decade together into a single state, "Railroadiana," it would rank third in the country in size after Alaska and Texas.[19] Before the arrival of the railroad, the vast western landmass was, for all intents and purposes, worthless. Moving agricultural products to the East Coast was so arduous that it wasn't worth bothering with. With the arrival of the railroad the Midwest and West became part of the national and, indeed, the global economy. The products of the prairie could be taken to New York by locomotive and shipped from there to Europe. Jefferson had imagined that self-sufficient farms might be antidotes to the market; the great story of agriculture in the second half of the nineteenth century is the integration of even the most isolated homesteads, out in the West, into the global bazaar.

The West that these settlers discovered was very different from the East Coast: a world of vast open spaces and huge distances. Families lived in the middle of nowhere. Going to the town to buy supplies or meet other human beings could be the work of a day. There was no broadcasting to break the silence of the long nights. Rail stations were hundreds of miles apart. Some fields covered sixty acres. We tend to think of civilization as getting denser as it progresses: more and more people are crowded into vibrant city centers. For many Americans the opposite happened: as the country expanded westward, settlers found themselves sitting on isolated farms surrounded by miles of nothingness.

Eventually this vast space was transformed by the laws of economics. Economies of scale and scope, efficiency-producing machines, logistics networks: all operated in the world of cattle and wheat as well as in the world of iron and oil. The railroads were part of a logistics network that eventually stretched around the world. Those "lonesome cowboys" were part of a supply chain that increased the value of Texas longhorns from three dollars in Texas to thirty dollars in Dodge. Big business did as much to change the world of the little house on the prairie as it did to change the world of small steel and oil producers.

The giant railroads loomed over the West from the very start: you couldn't lay down thousands of miles of track across several states without possessing capital and political connections. In the East, railroads had to compete against several different sorts of transport, from canals to roads. In the West, they were often the only providers of transportation—and like all monopolists they exploited their power to extract the maximum rent from their clients.

The pioneering railroad in the region was the Union Pacific, which was chartered by Abraham Lincoln in 1862. The Union Pacific formed America's first transcontinental railroad when it met up with the Central Pacific Railroad on May 10, 1869. It quickly built or acquired additional lines, which provided it with links to most of the region's great (or soon to be great) cities: Salt Lake City, Denver, and Portland. The extension of America's rail network to the West turned the country into an agricultural superpower, opening up new markets ever farther west, and turning the Midwest into the breadbasket of not only America but the world.

The railroads gave birth to some of rural America's most interesting businesses, the bonanza farms of the Red River Valley of Minnesota and the Dakotas. These farms were first created in 1873–74 when the Northern Pacific Railway went bankrupt, precipitating the Great Crash and taking another hundred or so overborrowed railroads with it. The Northern Pacific was lucky enough to have assets in the form of some 39 million acres of federal land granted to it by the government, and creditors frequently took land in settlement of their loans. George Cass, the Northern Pacific's chairman, had the bright idea of organizing the absentee owners' lands into giant farms, thereby producing more business for his railroad as an added bonus, and he brought in an agricultural visionary, Oliver Dalrymple, to set his idea in motion.[20]

The resulting bonanza farms were, in essence, agricultural factories that were governed by the same logic as the industrial factories of the East. They covered an average of seven thousand acres. They used giant steam engines and mechanized combine harvesters decades before such machines were used on family farms. They employed armies of workers, many of them migrants, marching in line with the latest equipment.[21] They operated according to the same managerial principles as other big businesses—absentee owners hired a cadre of professional managers (bookkeepers, accountants, purchasing specialists), and those managers broke the job of farming into discrete operations such as maintaining threshing machines or loading corn onto wagons. William Allen White captured the spirit of the new agriculture in an article in *Scribner's Magazine* in 1897. "The successful farmer of this generation must be a business man first and a tiller of the soil afterward. . . . He must be a capitalist, cautious and crafty; he must be an operator of industrial affairs, daring and resourceful."[22]

The cattle industry also thrived on size: America's cattle farmers were forever pushing into America's open range—first in Texas, then in the Dakotas, and then into Montana—in order to increase the size of their herds. At one point the biggest of the cattle barons, Conrad Kohrs, owned fifty thousand head of cattle grazing on 10 million acres of land spread across four states and two Canadian provinces. He shipped ten thousand head of cattle a year to the Chicago stockyards to be slaughtered and transported east.

The cattle industry required two things to thrive: barbed wire and cowboys. Barbed wire boosted productivity by providing a convenient way of distinguishing between private property and no-man's-land. Farmers first tried to make up for the shortage of wood in the West by building fences with plain wire but it did not stop animals from roaming. Then, in the 1870s, several entrepreneurs came up with the idea of twisting wire to make it more like a thorn. Joseph Glidden, a farmer, filed one of the first patents in 1874. "The greatest discovery of all time," as the advertisers had it, barbed wire quickly spread across the West, with competing entrepreneurs squabbling over patents and producing endless variations on the theme: the bible of barbed wire, Robert Clifton's *Barbs, Prongs, Points, Prickers, and Stickers* (1970), lists 749 varieties. The American Barbed Wire Company, which eventually consolidated patents, owned its own iron ore site. The XIT Ranch in Texas, created in the 1880s, covered 3 million acres and had six thousand miles of barbed wire. John Warne Gates described the wire poetically as "lighter than air, stronger than whiskey, cheaper than dust." Native Americans described it, equally poetically, as "the devil's rope."

America's giant cattle farms needed cowboys to drive the cattle from Texas via the open range to the railheads in Kansas in Dodge City or Wichita. On an average drive, ten cowboys (each with three horses) were responsible for moving three thousand cattle. A thousand-mile drive could take up to two months (you could go faster, but the cattle lost so much weight that you couldn't sell them when you reached your destination). By 1877, the cattle trail was so well established that five hundred thousand cattle a year were passing through Dodge.

It was the farmers' willingness to turn themselves into capitalists, "cautious and crafty," that lay behind America's emergence as an agricultural superpower. American farmers engineered an ecological transformation by turning the native grasslands of the Midwest and California into a vast sea of grain. They engineered a biological transformation by turning the scrawny animals that we encountered in the first chapter into fat four-footed food factories. Sadly, they also engineered an ecological catastrophe. Bison were placid creatures that had grazed in massive herds on the American plains for millennia and coexisted with Native Americans, who never killed enough to deplete the herds. Between 1872 and 1874, white hunters killed more than 4.3 million bison, slaughtering them with such brutal efficiency that tens of thousands, stripped of their skin, were left to rot, almost killing off the species entirely.[23]

The proportion of total U.S. land devoted to farming increased from 16 percent in 1850 to 39 percent in 1910, where it remains, more or less, to this day.[24] The real (inflation adjusted) value of U.S. farmland per acre more than doubled over the same period.[25] This vast expansion was driven by the conversion of unproductive land in already settled regions into farmland, as well as by westward expansion. Such conversion was laborious and expensive: tree stumps had to be uprooted, waterlogged land drained, stones cleared, brush removed. Wheat production rose from 85 million bushels in 1839 to 500 million in 1880 to 600 million in 1900 to 1 billion in 1915.

American farmers were in the forefront of technological innovation because there was never enough labor around. Between 1840 and 1880 the number of man-hours required to produce 100 bushels of wheat fell from 233 to 152, and the number of hours required to produce 100 bushels of corn from 276 to 180.[26] The combine harvester, which was introduced in the 1880s, merged a reaper and a thresher into a single machine. The early combines were so big and cumbersome that they were only used on the biggest farms. Over the years they were shrunk, streamlined, and adapted to a wider range of crops such as corn, beans, and peas. Seed machines meant that you could plant seeds more easily and efficiently.

American farmers were also in the forefront of biological innovation. The quality of wheat improved as immigrants brought in hardy strains such as "Turkey Red" from the Russian steppes, and scientists invented new varieties of wheat that were adapted to local circumstance. More than 90 percent of the wheat planted in 1919 consisted of varieties that had not been planted before the Civil War.[27] The quality of the animals also improved thanks to a combination of animal eugenics, better nutrition, and improved veterinary care. The average milk yield per cow increased by 40 percent between 1850 and 1900, from 2,371 pounds per year in 1850 to 3,352 pounds in 1900.[28]

Luther Burbank, a botanist who earned the sobriquets of "the wizard of horticulture" and the "plant wizard," deserves a place next to other great agricultural innovators such as Cyrus McCormick and John Deere. Born in Massachusetts in 1849, he started his career as a biological innovator by developing the blight-resistant russet potato (the strain used in most McDonald's French fries). He used the proceeds from selling the rights to his potato to move out west, to Santa Rosa, California. There he developed or inspired more than eight hundred varieties of plants, fruits, and flowers, including the "July Elberta" peach, the "Santa Rosa" plum, the "Flaming Gold" nectarine," and the "spineless cactus," which can be fed to cattle.

At the same time, Americans got better at turning animals into food and then delivering that food to the dinner table. In the 1830s, several abattoirs in Cincinnati developed ways of improving the ancient art of slaughtering hogs by introducing a "disassembly line": workers attached carcasses to a wheeled chain that then whisked them from the slaughtering floor to the cooling rooms. They later improved the "line" by building upward, turning abattoirs into skyscrapers of death: the hogs were driven up a ramp and slaughtered on the top floor and cut and dressed on the next, with the various cuts of the hog dropped into curing and salting tanks in the cellar.[29]

Cincinnati's innovation had a massive impact. Other local businesses applied the same continuous production process to the waste products of hog slaughtering: Procter & Gamble got its start in business turning pig lard into soap.[30] The great abattoirs of Chicago to the north copied the idea and applied it with even greater ruthlessness to cows: the dead steer were suspended on hooks on a moving line. They sped past gutters, slicers, splitters, skinners, sawyers, and trimmers at such a speed that Sarah Bernhardt described the spectacle as "horrible and magnificent."[31] It was during a visit to one of these abattoirs that Henry Ford got the idea of the mass assembly line.

Gustavus Franklin Swift made another breakthrough with the introduction of refrigerated railroad cars in 1877. Before Swift, cattle had been driven long distances to railroad shipping points and then transported live in railroad cars. Swift realized that he could save a lot of money if he slaughtered the cattle in the Midwest and transported them in refrigerated railway cars to the East. Transporting the steaks rather than the steers, as it were, not only did away with the need for long cattle drives (and the ensuing weight loss), but also reduced the weight of what you were transporting by half. Even by the standards of the time Swift was an enthusiastic practitioner of vertical integration: he even owned the rights to harvest ice in the Great Lakes and the icehouses along the railway tracks that replenished the ice. He quickly built a huge empire—by 1881, he owned nearly two hundred refrigerated cars and shipped something on the order of three thousand carcasses a week—and a highly fragmented industry consolidated into a handful of companies (Swift as well as Armour, Morris, and Hammond).

Americans also got much better at food preservation, with the onward march of preserving, canning, pickling, and packaging. The first American canning center opened in Baltimore in the 1840s. Some of the most enthusiastic customers were explorers who wanted to carry their provisions to the West. Gail Borden started producing condensed milk in 1856 and, as his new product took off, tried to apply the same technique to tea, coffee, potatoes, and pumpkins.[32] John Landis Mason invented the Mason jar, which made it easier to preserve food at home, in 1859. The Union army ate canned food during the Civil War. Joseph Campbell started canning tomatoes, vegetables, jellies, condiments, and mincemeats in 1869, the same year that H. J. Heinz began selling packaged foods. By 1910, the country produced more than 3 billion cans of food, thirty-three cans per person, and food processing accounted for 20 percent of manufactured output.[33] Domestic iceboxes took the food preservation revolution into people's homes, reducing spoilage, particularly of milk and meat, and decreasing airborne disease. One academic study estimates that ice was responsible for 50 percent of the improvement in nutrition in the 1890s.[34]

Farmers excelled at codifying all these new ideas, technological and biological, into a systematic body of knowledge. The U.S. Department of Agriculture, founded in 1862, created a network of A&M colleges devoted to the "agricultural and mechanical arts."

They also got much better at managing uncertainty through the development of futures markets. Farming is risky: numerous acts of God, from severe weather to biological blight, can ruin a crop and leave a farmer with no income. A bumper crop on the other side of the world can mean that prices drop like a stone. Selling an option on crops while they are still in the ground can provide a hedge against the future. The second half of the nineteenth century saw the development of specialized options markets in a range of agricultural products. The Chicago Board of Trade, which was founded in 1848, started selling futures in wheat, corn, and rye in 1868. The Kansas City Board of Trade, founded in 1856, traded futures in hard red winter wheat; and the Minneapolis Grain Exchange, founded in 1881, did the same for hard red spring wheat.

The final ingredient in the recipe was cheap transportation: for all

the rural anger against the railroad monopolies, the railroad companies actually cut their costs. From 1852 to 1856, it cost 20.8 cents to
transport a bushel of wheat from Chicago to New York. By the early
1880s, the cost had fallen to 8.6 cents, and by 1911–13, it had fallen to
5.4 cents. The cost of shipping a bushel of wheat across the Atlantic
fell from 14.3 cents a bushel to 4.9 cents a bushel. In the early 1850s
the price of wheat in Chicago had been 46 percent of that in Liverpool. By the outbreak of the First World War, the Chicago and Liverpool prices were virtually identical: previously isolated markets had
been turned into a single world market.[35]

All these developments linked the once-isolated West into the
global economy. The process of plugging the West into the world enriched the West by making its land and resources much more valuable. It also enriched the world by providing it with a new source of
wheat and meat. The railroads attracted people from the wild blue
yonder through blockbuster advertising campaigns, subsidized their
travel across the Atlantic, and then lent them money to buy tracts of
land. They also kept agents in the eastern seaports to make sure that
"their" immigrants weren't poached by rival companies. The Union
Pacific was particularly keen on Irish laborers, who were regarded as
talented diggers, and Chinese "indentured" laborers who, apart from
being cheap, were thought to be good with explosives. James J. Hill
was keen on Scandinavians on the grounds that he thought they had
high characters. The Dakotas even baptized a nonexistent city with
the name Bismarck in the hope of attracting German immigrants.

The combination of westward expansion and technological innovation brought a leap in agricultural productivity. Real output per
worker in the agricultural sector grew at about 0.5 percent a year in
the nineteenth century, with growth particularly rapid in the two
decades after 1860 at 0.91 percent a year.[36] In 1900, the average agricultural worker produced about two-thirds more stuff than in 1800.

The productivity revolution changed the face of rural America. Women and children were increasingly liberated from backbreaking toil: women focused on domestic economy, empowered by new machines such as the sewing machine and inspired by new fads such as "scientific housework"; and children spent more time on education. The productivity revolution also changed America as a whole. America's cattlemen and cowboys turned beef from the luxury of the rich, as it still was in Europe, into a regular treat for the masses. America's wheat farmers showered the country with cheap bread and flour, with the price of wheat falling by half in just four years, from 1868 to 1872.[37] Diets became richer and less monotonous: Americans could eat peaches from Georgia, oranges from Florida, asparagus from California, as well as staples such as beef from the Midwest and cod from New England. The term "dietician" (from "diet" and "physician") entered the language for the first time in 1905 as people began to worry not about having too little to eat but about having too much.[38]

Four

THE AGE OF GIANTS

———————

T HE SECOND HALF of the nineteenth century saw a revolution in the scale of economic life. When John Jacob Astor died in 1848, he left a fortune of $20 million, making him America's richest man. His company, the American Fur Company, employed only a handful of full-time staff, who worked out of a single room. When Andrew Carnegie sold the Carnegie Steel Company to J. P. Morgan in 1901, he pocketed $226 million, making him the world's richest man. Morgan combined Carnegie Steel with a few other steel companies to forge a leviathan that employed 250,000 people, more than the country's armed forces, and had a market value of $1.4 billion.[1]

The revolution in organizational scale was also a revolution in human scale: the men at the heart of this revolution were veritable giants of energy and ambition. They exercised more power than anybody other than kings or generals had exercised before. And they thought in the biggest possible terms—no dream was too grand or ambition too extreme. They are some of the few businesspeople who deserve comparison with Alexander the Great, Caesar, and Napoleon.

Rockefeller controlled 90 percent of the world's refinery capacity. Carnegie produced more steel than the United Kingdom. Morgan twice saved America from default, acting as a one-man Federal Reserve. Having reinvented the private sector, they reinvented the voluntary sector as well. A striking number of America's most important social institutions—from the universities of Chicago and Stanford to the Rockefeller and Carnegie foundations—were created by men who were born within a few years of each other in the 1830s.

These outsize figures have attracted outsize opprobrium. Ida Tarbell accused them of being "robber barons." Teddy Roosevelt dubbed them "malefactors of great wealth." Henry Adams described Jay Gould as "a spider" who "spun huge webs, in the corner and in the dark." A popular Broadway show called Morgan "the great financial Gorgon."

There is some justification for this hostility: people seldom achieve great things without being willing to ride roughshod over the opposition. All that riding can go to the head: Henry Ford tried to prevent the First World War by taking a peace ship to Europe, in just one example of several deranged political missions. Some of Tarbell's robber barons were undoubtedly guilty of terrible things. Daniel Drew was a former cowboy who fed his cattle salt so that they would bulk up on water before they were weighed—the origin of the phrase "watered stock." James Fisk, who coined the phrase "never give a sucker an even break," watered and sold so much Erie stock that the once-prosperous railroad went bankrupt. Jay Gould bribed legislators to get deals done, bribed stockholders, and even kidnapped an investor. He once said, "I can hire one half of the working class to kill the other." A striking number of them paid three hundred dollars a year for a "substitute" in order to escape serving in the Union army.

For the most part, however, these businesspeople were neither "robbers" nor "barons." They made their own money rather than inheriting it. Andrew Carnegie arrived from Scotland at the age of thirteen without a penny in his pocket. John D. Rockefeller's father was a snake-oil salesman, bigamist, perhaps even a rapist, who abandoned his family seasonally and eventually deserted them entirely for his other, younger wife. Collis Huntington grew up in the aptly named Poverty Hollow in Harwinton Township, Connecticut.

These men got rich by rolling up their sleeves and seizing their chances. "When it's raining porridge," Rockefeller's sister once said, "you'll find John's dish right side up." Carnegie started life as a bobbin boy, endeared himself to the leading businesspeople in Pittsburgh, and by his early thirties had become a millionaire even before investing a dollar in steel. Rockefeller borrowed a thousand dollars from his father at the start of the Civil War, invested it in a food distribution business, emerged from the war with seventy thousand dollars, and purchased a light-fuel factory. Cornelius Vanderbilt started his business career ferrying people in a flat-bottomed boat from New Jersey to New York, traded up to a steamer, and then traded up again to locomotives. "Law, rank, the traditional social bonds—these things meant nothing to him," T. J. Stiles noted. "Only power earned his respect, and he felt his own strength gathering with every modest investment, every scrap of legal knowledge, every business lesson."[2] Collis Huntington came to California as part of the gold rush but quickly decided that there was more money to be made selling axes and shovels to the miners. J. P. Morgan was the only one who was born to the purple, and he massively increased the power of his bank. One of the striking things about creative destruction is that it can affect members of the same family in very different ways: the very force that made Andrew Carnegie the world's richest man impoverished his father, a handloom weaver who saw his skills devalued by the arrival of steam-powered weaving mills in the 1830s and who never found a niche in life, despite leaving Scotland for America.

The robber barons all made a point of "giving something back," building philanthropies on the same scale as their companies. Carnegie tried to make a reality of equality of opportunity by founding almost three thousand public libraries. Rockefeller founded two universities, Rockefeller University and the University of Chicago, and gave a fortune to other institutions of higher education. Leland Stanford left so much of his wealth to Stanford University that his widow had to liquidate assets in order to stay afloat.

The main defense of these men from public opprobrium, however, is not that they rose from nothing or founded charities. It is that they helped to produce a massive improvement in living standards for all. These men were entrepreneurial geniuses who succeeded in turning the United States into one of the purest laboratories of creative destruction the world has seen: men who grasped that something big but formless was in the air and gave that something form and direction, men who squeezed oil out of the rocks and created industrial machines out of chaos. In a famous passage, Winston Churchill wrote, "At last I had authority to give directions over the whole scene. I felt as if I were walking with destiny." The men who presided over the industrial scene in this golden age of capitalism were also walking with destiny.

The titans all grasped that the material basis of civilization was changing. Carnegie realized that America was entering the steel age. The man who could provide the best steel at the lowest price would be a modern-day King Midas. Rockefeller realized that it was entering the oil age. Henry Ford realized that it was entering the age of mass mobility. Lesser figures realized that it was entering a mass consumer age and set about providing the consumer goods for the masses. "Put all your good eggs in one basket and then watch that basket," Andrew Carnegie once advised. This advice worked if you chose the eggs that were destined to transform the economy.

They also recognized that, with the arrival of the railway and the telegraph, the nature of both time and space had changed. They did everything they could to acquire timely information and to speed up production and delivery. "The old nations creep on at a snail's pace," Carnegie wrote. "The Republic thunders past with the rush of an express." They grasped that the same forces that were shrinking America were also shrinking the world: having built an American leviathan, Rockefeller quickly expanded abroad.

These great entrepreneurs earned their place in history not by inventing new things but by organizing them. This involved three elements: spotting innovations that had the potential to revolutionize industries; bringing distant factors of production together, often moving matériel huge distances; and integrating previously discrete economic activities, from the production of raw materials to the sale of finished products.

Carnegie became a steel king by discovering the latest techniques and taking them to scale. In 1875, he sank his fortune into building a vast state-of-the-art steelworks in Pittsburgh and its environs. Calculating that Pittsburgh already gave him important advantages because it sat at the intersection of major rivers and railroads and close to coalfields and iron fields, he capitalized on these advantages by integrating his business both vertically and horizontally. He acquired coke-oven works to guarantee his carbon supply, iron mines to secure his ore, and railroads and shipping lines to ensure the steady flow of raw materials to his mills and finished products to his customers.

Carnegie established an enduring advantage by moving first and building solid defenses. Yet he was always on the lookout for disruptive innovations that might threaten his mastery of the industry. In 1883, he bought his biggest rival, the Homestead Steel Works, which included a huge plant served by tributary coalfields and iron fields, a

425-mile-long railway, and a line of lake steamships. The bigger he got, the more he could reduce costs. "Cheapness is in proportion to the scale of production," he claimed. "To make ten tons of steel a day would cost many times as much per ton as to make one hundred tons." In 1888, when he saw that a new plant using the open-hearth method was producing better results than the Bessemer process, he immediately ordered six more furnaces to be built. "Every day's delay in building . . . is just so much profit lost."

Carnegie made sure that he invested some of his prodigious profits in research and development. A passage about a German chemist he discovered in the 1870s summed up his attitude:

> We found . . . a learned German, Dr. Fricke, and great secrets did the doctor open up to us. [Ore] from mines that had a high reputation was now found to contain ten, fifteen, and even twenty per cent less iron than it had been credited with. Mines that hitherto had a poor reputation we found to be now yielding superior ore. The good was bad and the bad was good, and everything was topsy-turvy. Nine-tenths of all the uncertainties of pig-iron making were dispelled under the burning sun of chemical knowledge.[3]

Rockefeller adopted a similar strategy. He found the oil industry in a state of chaos—wildcatters dug holes wherever they felt like it, including in the main streets of towns; overproduction cut profit margins to nothing; oil was left to go to waste—and set about producing order. He spotted the importance of the refining business before anyone else. (His business partner Henry Flagler's favorite quotation, which he kept displayed on his desk, was "Do unto others what they would do unto you—and do it first.") This allowed him to produce more oil at a lower cost than any of his competitors. He systematically eliminated those competitors by either inviting them to join his Standard Oil Company, which he founded in 1870, or, if like Ida Tarbell's father they refused to sell, driving them out of business. "The Standard was an angel of mercy," he said, "reaching down from the sky and saying 'Get into the ark. Put in your old junk. We'll take all the risks.'"[4] By the late 1870s, firms in his alliance controlled more than 90 percent of the country's oil business.

These alliances were part of a bigger plan to bring everything possible under a single roof. Rockefeller built pipelines to connect his oil fields in Pennsylvania with refineries in New Jersey, Cleveland, Philadelphia, and Baltimore. He built his own barrel-making factory, which, in 1888, saved him $1.25 a barrel at a time when he was using 3.5 million barrels a year. He used his superior scale to negotiate special deals with railroads: guaranteed volume in return for reduced costs. He increased revenues by converting oil into a growing range of useful products such as lubricating oil, paraffin, naphtha for road surfacing, and gasoline. The bigger he grew, the more ambitious he got. In the mid-1880s, he built three giant refineries that could handle 6,500 barrels a day compared with the previous maximum of 1,500. By 1890, he was also using a fleet of tank wagons to deliver Standard Oil to the consumer's door, completing his control of the whole process.

Rockefeller had no use for such old-fashioned notions as competition and free markets. "The day of individual competition in large affairs is past and gone," he declared. "You might just as well argue that we should go back to hand labor and throw away our efficient machines." For him, business combinations were the organizational equivalents of steam engines. The fact that some combinations might abuse their influence was "no more of an argument against combinations than the fact that steam may explode is an argument against steam. Steam is necessary and can be made comparatively safe. Combination is necessary and its abuses can be minimized."[5] The fact that the price of oil fell so precipitously under his sway proves that there was something in this: Rockefeller used his organizational genius to lower unit costs rather than to bilk the public. The result of declining unit costs was rising output per hour.

J. P. Morgan applied the same organizational genius to the world of money. For the most part, economic life at the time took place behind a veil of ignorance.[6] The government did not produce any sound figures on, say, employment, imports or exports, or the money supply. Corporations kept their balance sheets from prying eyes, including, for the most part, the prying eyes of shareholders. Most companies didn't bother to issue reports. Those that did mixed fact with fiction: Horace Greeley commented in the *New York Tribune* in 1870 that if the Erie Railroad's annual report was true, then "Alaska has a tropical climate and strawberries in their season."[7] Stock was issued on a whim. This played into the hands of professional investors such as Jay Gould and James Fisk, who could exploit (and often create) rumors or who could launch great schemes, such as the 1870 scheme to corner the gold supply.

Morgan brought three things to this fog-filled world. He brought a trained intelligence. He had studied mathematics (among other subjects) at Göttingen in the days when Germany was the center of the academic world, and proved to be such a good student that his professor asked him to stay on as a graduate student. He brought global contacts. Morgan's father had made his career in the City of London, then the capital of global finance, selling America to Britain and Britain to America, and Morgan spent several years in London before moving back to New York. And he brought more information about Anglo-American business than anyone possessed before. He had started his business career reorganizing railroads, then America's most complicated industry as well as its biggest, and went on to reorganize everything from steel to agricultural products to transatlantic steamships. He and his lieutenants sat upon dozens of boards. Nobody knew more about American business from the inside out than J. P. Morgan.

Morgan used his unique position to shape American capitalism in its glory days. This sometimes meant creating companies from scratch. Morgan had a sharp eye for world-changing innovations: he lent Thomas Edison the money to establish the Edison Electric Illuminating Company in 1878, and was the first person to install electric lights in his house (much to the annoyance of his neighbors, because the generator made an infernal racket).[8] More often it meant reducing costs by improving organization and getting rid of overcapacity.

Morgan's great love was for orderly progress—"He liked his capitalism neat, tidy, and under banker's control," as Ron Chernow put it in his splendid book on the House of Morgan.[9] Morgan promoted order in the private sector by forming trusts. He promoted order in the general economy by stepping in and helping the system operate. He twice saved the U.S. government from default. In 1895, he organized a consortium of bankers to prevent a run on America's gold holdings by supplying the Treasury with gold in return for federal bonds. For a brief moment, Morgan controlled the flow of gold in and out of the United States. In 1907, as the stock market collapsed and banks imploded, he locked his fellow capitalists in a room in his house at 219 Madison Avenue and told them to come up with a plan to prevent a market meltdown. Banker-imposed order could do more to promote higher productivity than unrestrained competition.

The serious question about these titans is not whether they were greedy or selfish. Greed and selfishness are common human emotions that afflict paupers as well as plutocrats. It is not even whether they cut commercial corners. America had not yet encountered many of the great challenges of a sophisticated capitalist economy, let alone formulated rules to deal with them. The serious question is whether they made themselves rich at the expense of the rest of the population. The Supreme Court certainly found them guilty of trying to create monopolies. Even conservative economists tend to qualify their praise for their entrepreneurial vigor with worry about their competition-crushing ambitions. But the charge of monopoly needs to be qualified: not all monopolies are bad. Monopolies tend to be less problematic in developing countries than in developed ones. Developing economies typically suffer from what economists call "institutional voids": they lack the institutions that make markets work properly, so companies have to expand into all sorts of areas, from securing supplies to improving distribution.[10] Monopolies are also less problematic during periods of rapid technological change when innovators are making big bets on new technologies. The Aluminum Company of America (Alcoa) was a monopoly owing to its ownership of a new system for extracting aluminum from alumina and bauxite. No one could compete. Yet Alcoa not only kept its costs and prices down but also continued to innovate, developing a whole new industry of lightweight pots and pans, a revolution in domestic life.

The titans prospered by exploiting economies of scale rather than by price gouging. They also prospered by creating markets where none existed before—and by providing those markets with ever-cheaper products. Steel production rose from 20,000 tons in 1867 to more than a million tons a decade later, as prices fell from $166 to $46 a ton. Oil production rose from 8,500 barrels of refined crude in 1859 to more than 26 million barrels in 1879, as prices declined from $16 a barrel in 1859 to less than one dollar in 1879, and remained at one dollar for the rest of the century.

"THE GREATEST SINGLE DISCOVERY OF MODERN TIMES"

The rise of the business titans went hand in glove with the rise of a new business organization. This was the publicly owned joint-stock corporation. Nicholas Murray Butler, the president of Columbia University from 1902 to 1945, provided the most succinct summary available of the historical importance of the business corporation:

> I weigh my words, when I say that in my judgment the limited liability corporation is the greatest single discovery of modern times, whether you judge it by its social, by its ethical, by its industrial or, in the long run—after we understand it and know how to use it—by its political, effects. Even steam and electricity are far less important than the limited liability corporation and would have been reduced to comparative impotence without it.

New technologies such as steam and electricity clearly had the capacity to change the world. Strong-willed businesspeople such as Carnegie and Rockefeller clearly had the capacity to change the world as well. But the thing that brought all of this together and transformed capacity into action was this unique organizational technology.[11] Companies could improve on the workings of the market in two ways: they could coordinate the flow of products from raw materials to finished products by creating managerial hierarchies; and they could shape the future by allowing entrepreneurs to make big bets on particular products or processes.

Before the mid-nineteenth century, companies came in two distinct forms: partnerships and chartered companies. Partnerships were flexible and easy to create. But they had two big drawbacks: impermanence and unlimited liability. They were typically dissolved when a partner died or lost interest in the business. Such dissolutions were often acrimonious. Each partner was personally liable for the company's debts if the firm got into trouble, at a time when bankruptcy could lead to imprisonment. This meant that people tended to form partnerships with relatives and coreligionists rather than strangers. Chartered corporations could offer permanence and limited liability by separating the business as a corporate entity from the people who operated it or invested in it. But you couldn't create corporations without getting a charter from the government. This could be time-consuming and tedious. Palms had to be greased and hoops jumped through. Governments also tried to use companies to achieve public purposes: in order to win the privilege of corporate permanence and limited liability you had to agree to build a bridge or further the government's imperial ambitions.

Chartered companies played an outsize role in the history of America. The country was first settled by chartered companies such as the Massachusetts Bay Company and the Virginia Company. The voyages that brought the settlers to the United States were paid for by "adventurers" who bought shares in the companies. The initial settlers usually had a stake in the companies themselves. The companies also owned much of the land collectively. American representative government was arguably formed in 1630 when the Massachusetts Bay Company transformed itself from a company into a commonwealth and converted its stockholders from members of a limited business venture into representatives in a public government.[12]

The American Revolution gave chartered companies a new lease on life. In Britain, chartered companies went into decline after the Bubble Act was passed in 1720 to deal with the problems created by the South Sea Company. (The reaction to the South Sea Bubble was an early example of the government's response to a financial panic being worse than the panic itself.) In postrevolutionary America, the states enthusiastically created chartered companies. More than 350 businesses were incorporated between 1783 and 1801. Two-thirds of these were in the business of providing inland navigations via turnpikes or toll bridges. The rest provided an assortment of services—banking, insurance, manufacturing, and, in the case of John Jacob Astor's company, animal skins.[13]

Still, even though America was far more generous with its chartered companies than Britain, the form suffered from inherent limitations: chartered companies were narrowly conceived and politicians had too much power. The first half of the nineteenth century saw one of the great revolutions in capitalism. A succession of legal decisions liberated the corporate form from its shackles: by the end of the Civil War, anybody could create a company, provided they paid a small fee and met various requirements (such as minimal capitalization) for the vague purpose of pursuing business. Henceforth, businesspeople found it much easier to raise large amounts of money from "the public," and the public found it much more convenient to invest in companies. It also changed the balance of power between the state and the private sector: instead of businesspeople lobbying governments for the privilege of incorporation, state governments lobbied businesses for the privilege of their presence. These new companies had the rights of "natural persons": they could own property collectively and enter into legal contracts (including suing and being sued). But they did not have the disadvantage of natural persons: they were potentially immortal and they could operate across borders.

The greatest of the robber barons liked to keep controlling shares in what they regarded as "their" companies. Carnegie disliked public ownership, reasoning that "where stock is held by a great number, what is everybody's business is nobody's business," and structured his corporation into a series of partnerships, each controlled by Carnegie himself, and subject to an overall "Iron Clad Agreement" that forced any partner who wanted to get out to sell his stake back to the company at book value. He only adopted the corporate form in 1900 when a lawsuit by Henry Clay Frick left him with no choice. John D. Rockefeller also structured his company as a succession of interlocking partnerships under his personal control. Henry Ford increased his control of his company in the mid-1920s by turning it into a sole proprietorship.

Nevertheless the logic of scale and scope meant that the corporate form advanced, unevenly but relentlessly, at the expense of other sorts of ownership. Before the 1880s, companies had seldom been capitalized at more than $1 million. In 1900, John D. Rockefeller's Standard Oil Company was capitalized at $122 million. Before the 1880s, companies had seldom employed more than a few hundred people. In 1900, several companies employed more people than the American government. "If the carboniferous age were to return and the earth were to repeople itself with dinosaurs," John Bates Clark wrote in 1901, "the change that would be made in animal life would scarcely seem greater than that which had been made in business life by these monster-like corporations."[14]

The corporate revolution began with the railroads. The railroads needed two things that private companies had not needed before. They needed large quantities of capital to finance rails and rolling stock. The total amount of capital spent on canals from 1815 to 1860 was $188 million. The total amount of money spent on railroads by 1860 was more than $1.1 billion.[15] It was impossible to raise this amount of capital by tapping the traditional resources of friends and family. They also needed armies of managers. The railroads quickly dwarfed other organizations in terms of employees: in the mid-1850s, the Erie Railroad employed four thousand people, while the Pepperell Manufacturing Company of Biddeford, Maine, one of the country's largest manufacturing companies, employed a few hundred. And they kept growing: in 1900, the Pennsylvania Railroad employed more than one hundred thousand.[16] Railroads not only operated on a bigger scale than business organizations had operated on before, they ran bigger risks: if they got their schedules wrong giant lumps of steel, traveling at sixty miles an hour, ran into each other. The scale of the railway revolution would have been impossible without a corporate form that guaranteed their longevity and limited liability that protected investors.

Alfred Chandler argued that, along with their other achievements, the railroads created a new species of economic man: the professional manager who is selected on the basis of his competence and knowledge rather than family ties to the owner. Railroad managers didn't own the organizations they worked for, but nevertheless devoted their entire careers to advancing their interests. ("The individual withers, and the whole is more and more," Charles Francis Adams told Harvard undergraduates when trying to define the essence of the modern corporation.) They operated within the context of a complicated hierarchical structure that defined what they were supposed to do, but they nevertheless had a high sense of their individual calling. They read periodicals such as the *Railroad Gazette* and learned books such as Marshall Kirkman's *Railroad Revenue: A Treatise on the Organization of Railroads and the Collection of Railroad Receipts* and Arthur Wellington's *The Economic Theory of the Location of Railways*. They pioneered many of the management methods that have since become commonplace: the likes of Daniel

McCallum of the New York and Erie, Benjamin Latrobe of the Baltimore and Ohio, and J. Edgar Thomson of the Pennsylvania Railroad devised new accounting techniques that made it possible to measure the performance of individual operating units and devised organizational charts that carefully defined the role of each cog in a huge machine.

The railways linked the world of rational management to the world of finance capital. The railways' voracious demand for capital did more than anything else to create the modern New York Stock Exchange. Though the exchange had been founded in 1817, it did not come into its own until the railway boom of the midcentury. The precursor to the Dow Index included no fewer than ten railroads as well as a steamship operator, Pacific Mail, and a telegraph company, Western Union. Before the railroad age, a busy week on the stock exchange might involve a thousand shares. In the 1850s, million-share weeks were not unknown. Railroads still accounted for 60 percent of publicly issued stock in 1898 and 40 percent in 1914. Wall Street also became the center for the market for railroad debt. In 1913, there was $11.2 billion worth of railroad bonds, versus $7.2 billion of common stock.

The railroads spawned a new investor culture. Business newspapers such as the *Commercial & Financial Chronicle* (founded in 1865) and the *Wall Street Journal* (founded in 1889) devoted more coverage to the railroads than to anything else. Henry Varnum Poor edited the *American Railroad Journal* before giving his name to the ratings agency Standard & Poor's. Sophisticated investors (including many foreigners) learned to hedge against risk by buying a "market basket" of railroad securities, just as today's investors buy a basket of leading industrial stocks.

Investors were keen on acquiring information and hedging against risk because the new business was so unstable. Joseph

Schumpeter noted that the American railroad boom, far more than any of the European railroad booms, meant "building well ahead of demand" and therefore operating deficits for unspecifiable periods. The railroad barons had no choice but to engage in speculation on a massive scale: they needed to assemble unheard-of quantities of matériel in order to build businesses that initially had no customers. Speculation could easily lead to sharp practices or even outright fraud. The railroads produced a breed of speculators, brilliantly satirized in Anthony Trollope's *The Way We Live Now* (1875), who were more interested in gaming railroad stocks to make a quick buck than in actually building railroads. In the so-called Erie War of 1868, Daniel Drew and his allies James Fisk and Jay Gould secretly printed millions of dollars of bonds in the Erie Railway Company in order to stop Cornelius Vanderbilt from taking it over. Speculation was particularly common in the transcontinental railroads, which, as Richard White has demonstrated, were rife with overbuilding, insider dealing, and other sharp corporate practices.

This combination of "building well ahead of demand" and endemic speculation meant that the industry was far from the model of rational planning that Alfred Chandler praised. The railroads didn't fit together into a national system: there was no single national gauge for different lines and you sometimes had to travel for miles by horse and cart to get from one line to another.[17] At the same time, the West had more track than it knew what to do with: in 1890, America west of the Mississippi had 24 percent of the country's population but 43 percent of its railroad mileage.[18] The industry was plagued by instability: in the last quarter of the nineteenth century, more than seven hundred railroad companies, which together controlled over half the country's rail track, went bankrupt. "The generation between 1865 and 1895 was already mortgaged to the railways," Henry Adams noted laconically, "and no one knew it better than the generation itself."

Despite these irrationalities, the corporation went on to conquer America's industrial heartland. Having been more or less confined to the railways in the 1860s, vertically integrated companies dominated most of the country's big industries by 1900: not only steel and oil but also technology and consumer goods. AT&T was founded in 1885, Eastman Kodak in 1888, and General Electric in 1892. The men who created these corporations typically followed the same sequence of moves that we have seen with Carnegie and Rockefeller. They made bet-the-farm investments in new plants. They grew as big as possible as fast as possible, turning their lower costs into barriers to entry. (Reid Hoffman, the founder of LinkedIn, calls the modern equivalent of this technique "blitzscaling.")[19] They integrated "forward" and "backward." And they tried to drive sales as high as possible by cutting costs and mass advertising.

The final area to fall to the corporation was retailing. In 1850, retailing was completely dominated by mom-and-pop stores. Within a generation, a handful of giants had joined the crowd of midgets. These giants exploited the new national rail network to increase the range of goods available in their stores while slashing prices. In 1858, Rowland Hussey Macy founded a fancy goods shop in New York that grew into a department store chain. In 1859, George Francis Gilman opened a small shop selling hides and feathers that grew into the Great Atlantic & Pacific Tea Company (A&P). By 1900, the chain had almost 200 stores in twenty-eight states selling a rather more ambitious collection of goods than just hides and feathers. Frank Woolworth expanded even faster: opening his first successful "five-cent store" in Lancaster, Pennsylvania, in 1879, he expanded to 12 stores by 1889, and 238 by 1909, and was looking abroad for new business.

The most striking innovation was the rise of the mail-order business. Aaron Montgomery Ward (in 1872) and Richard Warren Sears and Alvah Roebuck (in 1886) created mail-order companies that allowed Americans to order products from a catalogue. These companies revolutionized rural life: people who had hitherto only had access to a handful of goods now had access to everything that their country could offer, from the most mundane (such as farm supplies) to the most exotic (such as the Heidelberg Electric Belt, which, worn around the waist for brief periods, supposedly provided a "wonderful cure for seminal or vital weakness").[20]

The most interesting figure in this retail revolution was Richard Sears. Like many entrepreneurs in this era, Sears started his career in the railway business (which was also at that time the telegraph business). He used his position as stationmaster-cum-telegraph master to collect information on the prices of many of the commercial items that, through catalogues and deliveries, passed through him. He focused on watches, because they offered such high margins, and made his first fortune by selling a job lot of watches that had fallen into his hands. He invested the money he had made from selling the job lot into establishing a mail-order business so that he could sell yet more watches. He quickly realized that he was in the mail-order business rather than the watch business, and started advertising an ever-expanding collection of goods in his catalogues. In 1902, Sears was fulfilling 100,000 orders a day, selected from a catalogue that ran to 1,162 pages. This demanded a huge machinery of storage, delivery, and coordination, which in turn demanded an ever-larger investment of capital.

In 1906, Sears and his business partner, Alvah Roebuck, took the company public and opened a $5 million mail-order plant in Chicago, the largest business building in the world, featuring an assembly line for customer orders. "Miles of railroad tracks run lengthwise through and around this building for the receiving, moving and forwarding of merchandise," boasted the Sears catalogue. "Elevators, mechanical conveyors, endless chains, moving sidewalks, gravity chutes, apparatus and conveyors, pneumatic tubes and every known mechanical appliance for reducing labor, for the working out of economy and dispatch are to be utilized here in our great works." One of the first people to visit this industrial marvel was the ever-curious Henry Ford.

THE URGE TO MERGE

The corporations that spread across the American business world, from transport to production to retailing, all had one thing in common, the quest for size. As the market became more mature, the quest for size inevitably led to mergers. The years between 1895 and 1904 saw a merger mania. Before the mania, consolidation had tended to take the form of vertical integration, as companies purchased their suppliers and distributors. The merger boom added horizontal integration to the mixture. Horizontal and vertical integration reinforced each other: as soon as it was born, U.S. Steel acquired massive iron ore deposits in the Lake Superior region, and by 1950, it owned 50 percent of all the country's iron ore deposits.[21]

Two people were at the heart of the age of consolidation: Rockefeller and Morgan. In 1882, Rockefeller masterminded the first giant merger by transforming the Standard Oil alliance, a loose federation of forty companies, each with its own legal and administrative identity (to satisfy individual state laws), into the Standard Oil Trust. The alliance had already succeeded in eliminating competition among its members through exchanges in stock. Shareholders in the member companies gave their voting shares to a central trust company in return for tradable trust certificates that conferred the right to income but not votes. The trust form carried this to a new level. In legal terms, a trust is a device that vests custodianship of assets in the hands of a trustee or group of trustees who have a legal duty to act in the interests of the owners of the assets. In business terms it is a device that allows businesspeople to centralize control. Rockefeller used the trust device to create an integrated company with a single headquarters, at 26 Broadway in New York City, a single ownership structure, and a single managerial strategy. Rockefeller shut down thirty-two of his fifty-three refineries and expanded the twenty-one remaining plants, reducing the cost of refining from 1.5 cents per gallon to 0.5 cents.[22] Companies in a wide variety of industries, notably sugar, lead, and whiskey, followed Rockefeller's example.

Congress retaliated by passing the Sherman Antitrust Act, prohibiting contracts or combinations in restraint of trade, in 1890. The New Jersey legislature then retaliated to the retaliation by making it easy to create holding companies, which could hold shares in subsidiary companies. In 1899, Standard Oil of New Jersey became the oil giant's formal holding company, controlling stock in nineteen large and twenty-one smaller companies. By 1901, two-thirds of all American firms with $10 million or more of capital were incorporated in the state, allowing New Jersey to run a budget surplus of almost $3 million by 1905 and paying for a rash of new public works. Other states fought back by embracing trusts. The New York legislature enacted a special charter for the General Electric Company to keep it from absconding to New Jersey. No state was more assiduous in wooing corporations than Delaware. By 1930, the state had become home to more than a third of the industrial corporations on the New York Stock Exchange: twelve thousand companies claimed legal residence in a single office in downtown Wilmington.

The most powerful of the trusts was "the money trust," as Charles Lindbergh, father of the famed aviator and a congressman from Minnesota, dubbed Wall Street, and the most powerful money-truster by far was J. P. Morgan. Having demonstrated his prowess in consolidating railroads during the great shakeout produced by the depression of the 1890s, Morgan extended his skills to a wider range of industries as the economy recovered, but overcapacity remained.

The result was the great merger wave of 1895 to 1905, which saw more than 1,800 manufacturing firms absorbed into consolidations. Morgan and his allies bought out the existing owners by offering them the value of their firm in preferred stock with an equivalent of common stock as a sweetener. They then merged various competing companies together in order to reduce excess capacity. The theory was that the preferred stock would rise as investors competed for a share of the gains from consolidation and the common stock would do well in the long run because the newly consolidated companies would produce a steady profit. Morgan typically placed his allies (often Morgan partners) on the boards of these new companies in order to keep a watchful eye on them.[23] In 1900, he and his partners had a place on the boards of companies accounting for over a quarter of the wealth of the United States.

There can be no doubt that Morgan succeeded in transforming the face of corporate America. He created new companies such as General Electric, American Telegraph and Telephone (AT&T), the Pullman Company, National Biscuit (Nabisco), International Harvester, and, of course, U.S. Steel. He increased the total amount of capital in publicly traded manufacturing companies from $33 million in 1890 to more than $7 billion in 1903. He created the world of the "big three" or the "big four." Naomi Lamoreaux calculates that, of the 93 consolidations she studied in detail, 72 created companies that controlled at least 40 percent of their industries and 42 controlled at least 70 percent. These 42 included General Electric, which had been formed from eight firms and controlled 90 percent of its market;

International Harvester, which had been formed from four companies and controlled 65 to 75 percent of its market; and American Tobacco, which had been formed from 162 firms and controlled 90 percent of its market.

Whether he succeeded in creating a more efficient economy is more debatable: Morgan was a much more problematic figure than, say, Carnegie or Rockefeller. The success rate of these behemoths was mixed. The most favorable assessment of the success rate of these mergers was published by Shaw Livermore in 1935. He collected information on 136 mergers that were big enough to shape their industries, studied their earnings from 1901 to 1932, and concluded that 37 percent were failures and 44 percent successes.[24] The creation of U.S. Steel ended a long period of falling prices in the steel industry (see chart below).

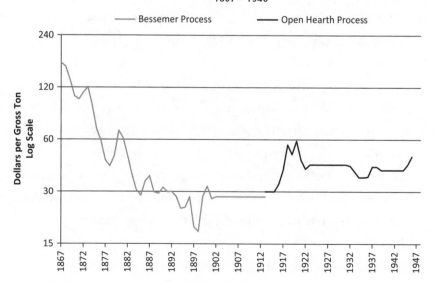

WHOLESALE PRICE OF STEEL
1867 – 1946

THE EVOLUTION OF THE CORPORATION

This period of banker dominance was relatively brief. The merger movement resulted not in the triumph of bank-centered capitalism, but in the consolidation of the widely held company at the heart of capitalism. The widely held company had already triumphed in the railroad sector. Now it triumphed in the manufacturing sector as the new behemoths financed their consolidations by issuing securities, and other companies went to the national exchanges in order to compete with them. These widely held companies typically separated ownership from control. Some founders such as Andrew Carnegie severed their connections completely. Others kept some shares but seldom enough to dictate policy. The day-to-day business of running companies devolved to salaried managers who held little or no stock. The founders made their opinions known through boards of directors, but they were typically counterbalanced by salaried managers and by representatives of the banking houses that had engineered the mergers in the first place. Big capitalism now meant widely held capitalism: companies that were owned by the public and controlled by professional managers.

By 1914, Ford Motor Company was one of the very few big privately owned companies to survive. Paradoxically, the large company that held out most firmly against public ownership was also the one that was responsible for perfecting America's greatest management breakthrough: mass production. Mass production was rooted in Eli Whitney's "uniformity system" for manufacturing first cotton gins and then muskets in the late eighteenth century. Henry Ford took this philosophy to a new level, not only breaking every task down into its smallest component parts but adding a moving assembly line.

Long lines of workers now stood at their stations repeating the same mechanical task over and over. Ford built the moving assembly line into a vast system of production and distribution in which everything was designed to boost efficiency and maximize control. Vertical integration meant that his employees made almost everything in-house. A national network of seven thousand dealers meant that Tin Lizzies were available in the smallest towns. "In the past," Frederick Taylor wrote in *The Principles of Scientific Management* (1911), "the man has been first; in the future the system must be first."

Just as significantly for the rise of managerial capitalism, America embraced the standardization of innovation as well as production. This happened slowly. Most companies preferred to rely on improvisation—either scouring the public records for new ideas or getting them informally from chats with local inventors. The Patent Office did a good job of disseminating information by displaying models and blueprints in its offices in Washington, D.C., and by publishing information in relevant magazines. *Scientific American* featured lengthy descriptions of the most important new technologies, printed lists of patents granted, and even offered to send its readers copies of the complete specifications for patents in return for a modest fee. America did an equally good job of producing "innovation hubs"—that is, places where tinkerers got together to discuss the art of tinkering. Hardware stores and telegraph offices acted as magnets for tinkerers. Telegraph offices stocked books and journals about electrical technology. Companies practiced what is now called "crowd sourcing" and "open innovation" on the grounds that there were more smart people outside the organization than inside. Western Union executives kept an eye on their frontline employees for bright ideas and frequently lent them money to commercialize them. J. P. Morgan decided to invest in Edison's incandescent lighting project because two of his partners were friendly with Western Union's patent lawyer. Big companies also invested heavily in developing their ability to scan the market. T. D. Lockwood, the head of AT&T's patent department, explained, "I am fully convinced that it has never, is not now, and never will pay commercially, to keep an establishment of professional inventors or of men whose chief business it is to invent."[25]

Lockwood was the owl of Minerva: as the century turned, invention was in fact becoming a corporate function, like accounting or advertising, and inventors were becoming company men (see chart below). Thomas Edison was the harbinger of a new age with his "invention factory" in Menlo Park and a plan to produce a big invention every six months. By the turn of the century, everyone was trying to follow in his footsteps. The proportion of patents granted to individuals rather than to firms fell, from 95 percent in 1880 to 73 percent in 1920 to 42 percent in 1940.[26] In 1900, General Electric,

U.S. PATENTS ISSUED FOR INVENTIONS
1901 – 2000

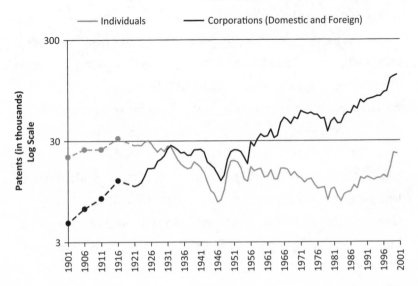

desperate to develop a new incandescent lightbulb as its patent on the old lightbulb ran out, created an R&D lab under the control of Willis Whitney. AT&T created a lab that soon earned its keep by solving technical problems that stood in the way of providing a coast-to-coast telephone service. The lab's accumulation of "a thousand and one little patents," in the words of the company's president, kept competitors at bay.[27] DuPont established a laboratory in 1911, Kodak in 1913, Standard Oil of New Jersey in 1919. Wherever you found the frontier of knowledge, there you would find a corporate R&D lab.

Giant companies, owned by the public, dominated by professional managers, bent on producing ever-larger quantities of standardized products, and determined to produce as much as possible in-house, including ideas, now sat at the heart of the American economy.

Not everybody was happy about this.

Five

THE REVOLT AGAINST
LAISSEZ-FAIRE

———◆———

MERICAN HISTORY HAS BEEN punctuated by great speeches:
Lincoln's Gettysburg Address, John Kennedy's inaugural,
Martin Luther King Jr.'s "I Have a Dream" speech. William
Jennings Bryan's "Cross of Gold" speech was another one. It not only
gave voice to the deepest feelings of a significant section of the popu-
lation. It marked a turning point in American economic policy.

When he addressed the Democratic Convention in Chicago in
July 1896, Bryan was only thirty-six, a former Nebraska congressman
turned journalist, a mere boy among the grizzled old bosses of the
party. But the plains were on fire with fury. Bryan's supporters had
prepared the ground for his appearance by seizing control of the
party apparatus. Bryan was the greatest orator of his age, with a powerful voice, "clear as a cathedral bell," and a gift for language. He
used every rhetorical trick in the book to work his audience into a
frenzy of righteous indignation.[1]

He proclaimed that the habitual arguments of the advocates of
the gold standard, that silver would disturb the business interest of

the country, was based on a false conception.[2] "The man who is employed for wages is as much a business man as his employer; the attorney in a country town is as much a business man as the corporation counsel in a great metropolis; the merchant at the cross-roads store is as much a business man as the merchant of New York." The farmers who grew the nation's grain were businessmen as fully as the brokers who sold it. The establishment branded these rural radicals as belligerent. But who wouldn't be belligerent in defense of their homes and their families? "We have petitioned and our petitions have been scorned. We have entreated and our entreaties have been disregarded." The establishment lambasted them for special pleading on behalf of the countryside. But aren't the advocates of the gold standard advocates of the urban interest—and don't the great cities rest on "our broad and fertile prairies"? "Burn down your cities and leave our farms, and your cities will spring up again as if by magic. But destroy our farms and the grass will grow in the streets of every city in the country." The advocates of the gold standard had thrown down the gauntlet. The people had a duty to respond. He ended with a great rhetorical flourish:

> If they dare to come out in the open field and defend the gold standard as a good thing, we will fight them to the uttermost. Having behind us the producing masses of this nation and the world, supported by the commercial interests, the laboring interests, and the toilers everywhere, we will answer their demand for a gold standard by saying to them: You shall not press down upon the brow of labor this crown of thorns! You shall not crucify mankind upon a cross of gold!

As he uttered this phrase Bryan bowed his head and stretched his arms out wide, the very image of a crucified Christ. The delegates looked on in silence. Then, as they realized that he had reached the end of his speech, they erupted in applause, wave upon wave, getting louder and louder, and joined by shrieks and hollers. The convention adopted the silver plank immediately and adopted Bryan as its presidential candidate the very next day.

For the previous few decades, the Democratic Party had been dominated by supporters of big business in general and the gold standard in particular. They had chosen the thoroughly conservative Grover Cleveland as their champion. But opposition to the gold standard had been growing for years as farmers complained of deflation, and "silverites" (including many owners of silver mines) argued that silver was a more humane, as well as a more convenient, alternative. At the Democratic conference, the Cleveland Democrats were roundly denounced as agents of capitalism and apostles of the barbarous religion of gold. David Bennett Hill, a U.S. senator for New York, had the difficult job of championing the Cleveland cause. "Why don't you ever smile and look pleasant?" a reporter inquired. "I never smile and look pleasant at a funeral," Hill replied.

For all its brilliance, Bryan's speech proved to be a disaster for his cause. By splitting the Democratic Party asunder over gold, he inaugurated a long period of Republican dominance of politics. By raising the issue of the gold standard, he turned an informal policy into a formal one. One of the first things William McKinley did when he moved into the White House in 1897 was to sign the Gold Standard Act, which made gold the standard for all currency.

Silver was only one of a long list of lost causes that Bryan championed. He led the Democratic Party to defeat three times (in 1896, 1900, and 1908). He tried to convert the diplomatic corps to temperance by banning alcohol at diplomatic functions when he was secretary of state under Woodrow Wilson, thereby perhaps contributing to the fractious mood of international affairs. He opposed America's entrance into the First World War. He acted for the state of Tennessee when it prosecuted John Scopes for teaching evolution. Teddy Roosevelt called him a "blithering ass," and H. L. Mencken "a poor clod . . . deluded by a childish theology, full of an almost pathological hatred of all learning, all human dignity, all beauty, all fine and noble things."[3]

Yet Bryan had a habit of coming out on top in the end. His widow, editing his memoirs in 1925 after his death, claimed that, for all his failures during his life, his policies had triumphed in one area after another: federal income tax, popular election of U.S. senators, female suffrage, a Department of Labor, more stringent railroad regulation, monetary reform, and at the state level, initiatives and referenda. They have continued to triumph after his death—America eventually abandoned the gold standard in 1971 under a Republican administration.

Bryan's greatest success was that he extended the realm of politics. Hitherto respectable Americans had regarded the gold standard as an immutable fact about the world rather than a political construct. Bryan argued instead that the gold standard was a cross that one group of people (the speculators) had invented to torture another group (the farmers). Bryan applied the same skepticism to laissez-faire in general. Hitherto respectable Americans had regarded the laws of the market as much the same as the laws of nature. Bryan and his allies claimed that politicians could tame the market for the common good.

THE WORLD ACCORDING TO GROVER

To understand how shocking Bryan's Cross of Gold speech was, it is worth looking at the man Bryan replaced as the head of the Democratic Party. Grover Cleveland was the only president to serve two nonconsecutive terms: he was both the twenty-second and twenty-fourth president. He was also the only president to get married in the White House. He believed in sound money, small government, and sturdy self-reliance. ("The expectation of paternal care on the part of the Government . . . weakens the sturdiness of our national character," he once said.) And he clung to his principles with a bull-like determination despite the pressure of special interests, the tug of public opinion, and the vicissitudes of the economy (Cleveland had the physique as well as the temperament of a bull, weighing three hundred pounds at one point). In 1887, he vetoed a bill to provide a tiny sum for seed grain for Texas farmers devastated by a drought on the grounds that he could "find no warrant for such an appropriation in the Constitution. . . . I do not believe that the power and duty of the General Government ought to be extended to the relief of individual suffering which is in no manner properly related to the public service or benefit." He stuck to his laissez-faire principles during the panic of 1893 as banks collapsed, industrial production fell by 17 percent, and unemployment rose to 12 percent. In the 1894 midterm elections, voters stampeded to the Republicans. But Cleveland stuck to his guns: he intervened in the Pullman strike to keep the railroad and the postal service working, using the Sherman Antitrust Act to obtain an injunction against the strike and to prosecute Eugene V. Debs, the American Railway Union's leader.

Cleveland had grown up in a world that was defined by small government as both a fact and an ideal. As late as 1871, the federal government employed only 51,071 people, of whom 36,696 worked for the post office. This produced a ratio of one nonpostal employee per 2,853 people.[4] With the exception of the Civil War years, consolidated (combined federal, state, and local) government spending was significantly less than 10 percent of GDP between 1800 and 1917 (see charts opposite).

U.S. GOVERNMENT EXPENDITURES
1800 – 1917

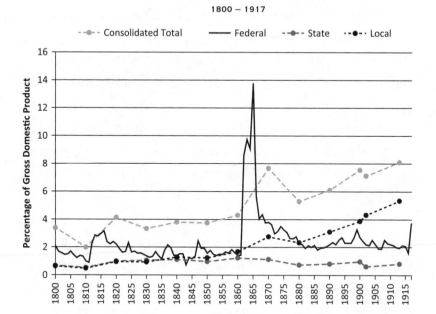

U.S. FEDERAL GOVERNMENT EXPENDITURES
1800 – 1917

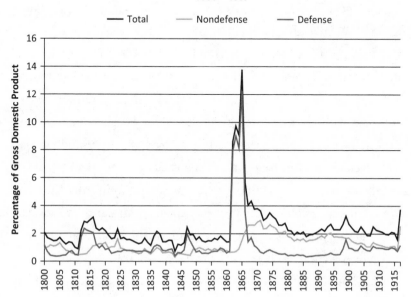

Citizens could get through their lives without any contact with the federal government other than the post office. April 15 was just another spring day: there was no income tax to pay. Washington, D.C., was one of the world's sleepiest capital cities: there was no Federal Reserve to look after the country's money, no Department of Education, Commerce, and the rest of it. The inhabitant of the White House had precious little to do and, if for some strange reason he got it in his mind to do something, nobody to help him do it: Cleveland had to answer the telephone himself, just as he had to open his own front door.

To the extent that there was any government at all, it was done at the lowest possible level. The government as a whole collected only eight cents for every dollar of income generated by the economy, and six of those eight cents were spent by local government. American government was in many ways still the government described in Tocqueville's *Democracy in America* (1835)—a government of town hall meetings.

The government was overshadowed by giant corporations. Charles W. Eliot, the president of Harvard, gave a sense of what this disparity meant at the local level in his 1888 essay "The Working of the American Democracy": the Boston & Maine Railroad employed eighteen thousand people, had revenues of some $40 million a year, and paid its highest salaried officer $35,000. At the same time, the Commonwealth of Massachusetts employed six thousand people, had revenues of $7 million, and paid no salary higher than $6,500.[5]

The astonishing growth of the American economy after the Civil War—an expansion that is unprecedented in human history—had taken place with little interference from Washington. America survived for seventy-seven years, from 1836, when the Second Bank's charter ran out, to 1913, when Woodrow Wilson created the Federal

Reserve, without a central bank or much of a monetary policy other than to stick to the gold standard. The cost of living rose by a scant 0.2 percent a year. Employers had a free hand to hire and fire their workers. America pursued an open-door policy toward European immigrants (though not toward Chinese immigrants, who were singled out by the Chinese Exclusion Act of 1882). And most Americans liked it that way: the prevailing wisdom was that all you needed to create a good society was a sound currency and a Bill of Rights and the free market could do the rest.

The Founding Fathers had been careful to put limits on both the scope of the state and the power of the people. They had defined people's rights into a Bill of Rights. They had divided government into separate branches in order to create checks and balances. "In framing a government which is to be administered by men over men," James Madison opined in *The Federalist Papers*, "the great difficulty lies in this: you must first enable the government to control the governed; and in the next place oblige it to control itself." They had also built in an element of meritocracy. Senators were given six-year terms to make sure that they kept an eye on the long term—George Washington famously likened the Senate to a saucer into which you pour your tea to cool it. They were also appointed by state legislatures rather than directly elected, in order to ensure that they were overwhelmingly chosen from the "better men" of society. Supreme Court justices had jobs for life.

The Founding Fathers' system of checks and balances was tested by a huge growth in the voting population under Andrew Jackson (see chart on page 158). By the second half of the nineteenth century, almost all white males enjoyed the right to vote and an astonishing proportion of them exercised that right: 83 percent in 1876, 81 percent in 1888, and 74 percent in 1900. Yet for decades the barriers to

U.S. VOTER PARTICIPATION RATE
1824 – 2012

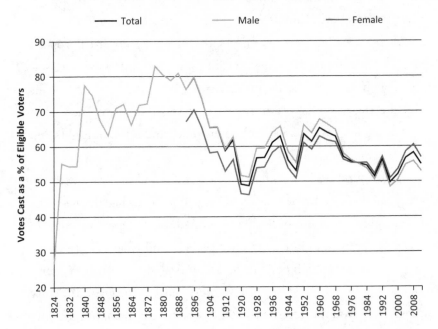

—— Total   —— Male   —— Female

democratic excess that the Founders had constructed continued to work in part because Washington was so divided and in part because the newly enfranchised masses didn't expect that much from the federal government.

Between Abraham Lincoln and Teddy Roosevelt, America had a succession of passive presidents. Writers have competed with each other to lament this development. James Bryce devoted an entire chapter of his 1888 classic *The American Commonwealth* to the subject of "why great men are not chosen president." Morton Keller wrote that "the nineteenth-century American presidency consisted of a mountain of greatness (Lincoln) bounded on either side by lowlands of mediocrity." Andrew Johnson never went to school and did not learn to write until his wife took him in hand. Grover Cleveland never visited Europe, never visited America west of the Mississippi, and first saw Washington, D.C., when he moved into the White House. But it's not clear that this was a bad thing: Bryce also noted that this succession of mediocrities served America's needs at the time: "The proportion of first-rate ability drawn into politics is smaller in America than in most European countries," he argued, because public affairs are not as exciting as "the business of developing the material resources of the country."[6]

Presidential passivity was compounded by divided government. For the twenty years from 1874 to 1894, there were only two brief periods when a single party controlled both the presidency and Congress—the Republicans in 1889–91 and the Democrats in 1893–95. The party that finally broke this stalemate, in the mid-1890s, was the more business friendly of the two. The Republicans controlled the federal government for the next sixteen years, to a degree rarely known in the United States. The party chairman, Mark Hanna, the man who did more than anyone to make William McKinley president, was a Cleveland iron ore magnate. The Speaker of the House, "Uncle Joe" Cannon, confounded every social reformer with the resounding retort, "This country is a hell of a success."[7]

The Supreme Court acted as a vigilant guardian of the rights of property and freedom of contract. The Court used the first section of the Fourteenth Amendment of 1868, which ruled that states could not "deprive any person of life, liberty, or property without due process of law," and which had originally been passed to guarantee the legal rights of free slaves, to strike down attempts to regulate business. In the *Santa Clara* case (1886), the Court made it clear that it regarded a corporation as a legal person and therefore subject to the protection of the law. In *Pollock v. Farmer's Loan & Trust Company* (1895), the Court struck down the federal income tax, five to four. In *United States v. E. C. Knight Company*, the Court defanged the

Sherman Antitrust Act. The federal government had felt certain that it would win its antitrust case against the American Sugar Refining Company on the grounds that the company controlled 98 percent of the country's sugar supply. Instead, the Court ruled that a monopoly of manufacturing did not constitute a monopoly of commerce, since it was perfectly possible to make things without trading them.

The Supreme Court was particularly strict about freedom of contract in labor cases. In *Toledo, Ann Arbor and North Michigan Railway Company v. Pennsylvania Company* (1893), it ruled that a legal act performed by an individual worker—quitting work—became illegal if it was part of a combination, a decision that it confirmed in ex parte Lennon in 1897. This effectively made strikes illegal. In *Lochner v. New York* (1905), it struck down a New York statute prohibiting bakery employees from working more than ten hours a day or sixty hours a week on the ground that it infringed freedom of contract. In 1918, it struck down the Keating-Owen Child Labor Law of 1916, which prohibited the shipment of goods manufactured by child labor from one state to another, on the grounds that it attempted to regulate production and therefore to exercise power reserved to the states.

The monetary equivalent of the U.S. Constitution was the gold standard. Advocates of the gold standard occupied the most powerful economic offices in the country: the presidency, the secretaryship of the treasury, and the leading offices in the country's biggest banks—and for understandable reasons. Gold has always been acceptable as a means of exchange, and hence a store of value, as far back as history reaches. The fact that the supply of gold was limited meant that gold was one of the most solid defenses of liberal society against the temptation to debauch the currency, the monetary equivalent of property rights. The universal acceptance of gold as a means of exchange made it easier to trade goods across borders.

America has been engaged in a vigorous debate about the relative merits of "hard" and "soft" money from the foundation of the republic. The Founding Fathers—and particularly Alexander Hamilton—understood that commercial societies need to have a solid store of value that everybody can trust if they are to operate efficiently. But America vacillated until 1834 over whether silver or gold was the best store of value (it initially chose to define its dollar in terms of troy ounces of silver but nevertheless, at the same time, issued gold coins with the price of gold locked in at a fixed rate to silver). It also repeatedly suspended its commitment to "hard" money to finance its innumerable wars, starting with the War of Independence. Printing money proved to be the only feasible way of paying for troops and weapons, because it was impossible to raise money from taxes or overseas borrowing fast enough. But even if printing money worked in the short term, it invariably produced inflation and retrenchment in the longer term: George Washington's continentals allowed him to keep his troops paid and provisioned for several years after being issued in 1775, but eventually became worthless.

The Civil War was an extreme example of this pattern. It took years of painstaking work to restore the value of America's currency after both the North and the South introduced fiat currency during the war. The South's experience proved particularly disastrous: printing half a billion dollars' worth of "graybacks," which were not convertible into gold, produced such a severe bout of inflation that money was quickly rendered worthless. Southerners couldn't trade with people in the rest of the country, let alone across the world. Even the North's more measured experiment with "greenbacks" took some time to overcome. In 1875, the Specie Payment Resumption Act forced the federal government to retire enough greenbacks from circulation by January 1879 that the dollar was returned to its prewar gold value of $20.67 per troy ounce of gold.

The monetary debate was further complicated by the discovery of a vast new supply of silver, Nevada's Comstock Lode, in 1859. When the big increase in the supply of silver (from 2,000 pounds in 1858 to 719,000 pounds in 1864 to 2.5 million pounds in 1876) led to a sharp fall in its price (from $2.73 per ounce in 1864 to $0.53 per ounce in 1902), the West's silver barons hit on a brilliant idea for pushing the price back up: force the federal government to buy their product and use it as currency. The Sherman Silver Purchase Act of 1890 was one of the most remarkable pieces of special-interest legislation in American history. It not only forced the federal government to purchase almost all the silver that the mines were producing, which amounted to millions of pounds every month, and turn it into silver coins, it also threatened to destabilize the currency. The law required the Treasury to buy the silver with a special issue of Treasury notes that could be redeemed for either silver or gold. But in the metals markets, silver was worth less than the government's legal exchange rate for silver and gold. So investors were presented with a magic money tree: they bought silver in the metals markets, exchanged that silver in the Treasury for gold dollars, sold those gold dollars in the metals markets for more than they had paid for the silver, and then took their expanded supply of silver back to the Treasury. Carried to its logical conclusion this would have reduced America's gold supply to zero.

America's East Coast establishment rallied to save gold from the mounting threats from western silver barons and midwestern farmers. Grover Cleveland halted the run on the Treasury's gold supplies by pressing Congress to repeal the Sherman Act in 1893. Conservatives championed gold as a bulwark not just against economic chaos but against civilizational collapse. The *Chicago Tribune*, a leading Republican newspaper, compared the advocates of fiat currency to the revolutionaries of the Paris Commune. The *Illinois State Register*, a leading Democratic paper, described them not just as "inflation-ists" but as "lunatics."[8] The more that old certainties dissolved, the more desperately liberals clung to the gold standard. The gold standard thus became self-vindicating: pleas that the gold standard was harming the economy were treated as proof that it was "working."[9]

Critics of the gold standard have likened this worship of the yellow metal to a primitive fetish. But it is much more than this. The exchange value of gold as a percentage of a fixed basket of goods and services had remained stable since Sir Isaac Newton, master of the British mint, in 1717, set the pound sterling at 4.25 per ounce of gold. The price remained at that level until 1931, when Britain abandoned the gold standard. The United States followed in 1933. One of the most remarkable things about the economic expansion of the second half of the nineteenth century was that it took place without the distraction of inflation.

The "official liberalism" of Supreme Court justices and bankers reflected general educated opinion. There was a broad and deep consensus that the market was a stern but ultimately benign ruler: obey the market and society would get richer; disobey the market and not only would society get poorer but you would reap all sorts of perverse consequences. Minimum wages would lead inexorably to higher unemployment, for example. Laissez-faire economics ruled not just in the economics departments but across the broad range of intellectual life. William Lawrence, an Episcopal bishop, said that there was "an elementary equation" between men's wealth and God's grace."[10] Lawyers believed that freedom of contract was at the heart of Anglo-Saxon law. From the 1860s onward, a new school of social Darwinists argued that laissez-faire was supported by evolution as well as God.

Social Darwinism was invented in Britain. Francis Galton, Charles Darwin's cousin, applied Darwin's ideas to the human species, formulating what he regarded as the science of eugenics. Herbert Spencer, a journalist at the *Economist*, elaborated his ideas but, just as importantly, coined the immortal phrases: "survival of the fittest" and "nature red in tooth and claw." American intellectuals enthusiastically imported these ideas. Spencer was one of the most revered public intellectuals in post–Civil War America—"a great man, a grand intellect, a giant figure in the history of thought," in Richard Hofstadter's phrase.[11] William Graham Sumner preached social Darwinism from a chair at Yale University.

The country's great businessmen were particularly keen on social Darwinism. James J. Hill argued that "the fortunes of railroad companies were determined by the law of the survival of the fittest." John D. Rockefeller, comparing the production of a great business to the production of the American Beauty rose, said that the "survival of the fittest" is "the working out of a law of nature and a law of God." Andrew Carnegie invited Spencer to visit his steelworks in Pittsburgh. Social Darwinism provided a perfect explanation as to why the "higher types" of men should be left as free as possible. Leave them free and they would discover more effective ways to combine land, labor, and capital. This would draw society ever upward as the masses followed in their wake. Leave them free and they would also devote their surplus fortunes and energies to philanthropic activities, applying the same genius to reorganizing education, welfare, and health care that they had already applied to iron, steel, and oil. Tie their hands and the whole of society would suffer.[12]

American culture was also saturated with belief in self-help and upward mobility. Calvin Cotton argued, "This is a country of self-made men, than which there can be no better in any state of society." Mark Twain and Charles Dudley Warner insisted, in the preface to the British edition of *The Gilded Age: A Tale of Today* (1873), that "in

America, nearly every man has his dream, his pet scheme, whereby he is to advance himself socially or pecuniarily." Horatio Alger's stories of men who had risen by dint of hard work sold in the millions. Orison Swett Marden's *Pushing to the Front* (1894), which argued that anybody could succeed providing that they had enough determination and energy, went through 250 editions. Immigrants, who had often fled authoritarian European regimes, brought an intense commitment to the ideals of opportunity and achievement.

Grover Cleveland's America was thus a remarkable outlier: it was easily the world's most democratic country, but it was also the world's most laissez-faire. Some 80 percent of American white males could vote. But they didn't use their votes to restrict business's freedom, partly because the political system put barriers in their way, but more importantly because they didn't think that the government owed them a living.

The decades after 1880 saw these constraints on the power of the government tested by two developments: the rise of political protest against the status quo in both rural and urban America, and the rise of a Progressive intellectual movement that redefined attitudes to the "state" and the "market." But in many ways the ground for these developments was prepared by a revolution within capitalism itself, as giant corporations began to undermine the logic of laissez-faire. Two presidents—Teddy Roosevelt and Woodrow Wilson—played a leading role in translating America's changed mood into policy.

CAPITALISM VERSUS LAISSEZ-FAIRE

The changing structure of industry put a question mark next to many of the central tenets of laissez-faire: a doctrine that seemed perfectly suited to Tocqueville's world of small-scale independent tradesmen and wide-open spaces was far more difficult to sustain when companies employed thousands of people across state lines and millions of people crowded into great cities.

The first to break the spell of laissez-faire were the railroad companies. By far the most efficient way of moving people and goods long distances, railroads quickly became entangled with politics because they operated on such a grand scale. They raised questions of interstate commerce because they crisscrossed state lines. They raised questions of the common good because they held the fate of so many other businesses, not least farmers, in their hands. And, most important of all, they raised questions of eminent domain because, by their very nature, they drove through land that other people owned. Accordingly, their whole business model necessitated contact with the government, which provided them with cheap land in order to persuade them to build rail lines in the middle of nowhere.

Even the most conservative Americans recognized that railroads were a special case. The first Supreme Court judgment sanctioning extensive interference in the market related to railroads. In *Munn v. Illinois* (1876), the Supreme Court ruled that railroads were a specific class of property "clothed with a public interest" because the public had no realistic alternative but to use their services. This meant that the states had a right to regulate railroad rates in the public interest.[13] The first piece of national business legislation was also introduced to deal with the railroads. The 1887 Interstate Commerce Act, which was signed into law by Cleveland, created the Interstate Commerce Commission in order to ensure fair rates and stamp out rate discrimination. The railroads were also the first American businesses to be nationalized (albeit briefly), during the First World War. America even "nationalized" time in order to satisfy the railroads. In laissez-faire America, time was local: town worthies would set the church clock to noon when the sun passed directly overhead. This played havoc with railroads, which needed to schedule activities across the entire continent: dangerous havoc when trains collided with each other. On Sunday, November 18, 1883, America divided itself into two standard time zones to make railroad coordination easier.[14]

The railroads were the first great crony capitalists. They bought politicians, bribed judges, and, in Henry Adams's phrase, turned themselves into "local despotisms" in one state after another. In 1867, Crédit Mobilier, a construction company founded by the principals of the Union Pacific Railroad, skimmed off millions from railroad construction, bribing politicians to turn a blind eye in the process. The politicians embroiled in the scandal would eventually include a vice president, Schuyler Colfax, and a vice-presidential nominee, Henry Wilson; the Speaker of the House, James Blaine; and a future president, James Garfield. The 1869 "war" between Cornelius Vanderbilt and Jay Gould for control of New York's Erie Railroad involved hired judges, corrupted legislatures, and under-the-counter payments.

The railroads changed the nature of lobbying as well as its scale. They used their lobbies to fight their competitors and to beg favors from the government, blurring the line between economic and political competition. They played out their disputes on a national and not merely regional scale. The creation of the Interstate Commerce Commission ensured that the railroads had to lobby federal regulators as well as local and national politicians.

The robber barons continued the railroads' assault on the old-fashioned world of laissez-faire, prompting Rutherford B. Hayes to complain in his diary that "this is a government of the people, by the people, and for the people no longer. It is government by the corporations, of the corporations, and for the corporations." The barons tried to buy as much political influence as possible: one wit said that John D. Rockefeller did everything to the Pennsylvania legislature except refine it. They also crowded into the legislatures themselves. The Senate was widely ridiculed as "a millionaires' club." William Clark, a Democrat from Montana, was worth $100 million; John Dryden, a Republican from New Jersey, was worth $50 million; and the power behind William McKinley's throne, Mark Hanna, a Republican from Ohio, was worth between $7 million and $10 million.

The growing density of civilization tested the limits of laissez-faire. The number of people per square mile increased from 10.6 in 1860 to 35.6 in 1920. The proportion of the population who lived in places with eight thousand inhabitants or more increased over the same period from 16.1 percent to 43.8 percent. Great cities such as New York and Chicago were honeycombed with tenements.

This produced obvious problems with human and animal waste. In the old rural America, nature had been able to take care of itself. In the new urban America, sanitation and pollution became pressing problems. The streets were crowded not just with people but also with animals: pigs scavenging in refuse piles, cows tethered in yards to provide milk, and, above all, horses carting loads, pulling carriages, and providing entertainment. Water supplies were contaminated by human and animal waste. Dead bodies generated disease: in one year alone, 1880, the New York City authorities removed the carcasses of almost ten thousand dead horses.[15]

It also produced industrial pollution on a terrifying scale. In the old rural America, the little pollution produced by the textile mills and smithies simply disappeared into the atmosphere. In the new industrial America, it was dangerously concentrated. Smoke turned the sky black at midday; soot covered everything in a film of filth. Herbert Spencer was so appalled at the state of Carnegie's Pittsburgh, with its noise, smoke, and filth, that he pronounced that "six months here would justify suicide." Rudyard Kipling felt the same way about

Chicago: "Having seen it I desire urgently never to see it again. The air is dirt."[16]

The combination of overcrowding and pollution helps to explain one of the most puzzling facts of the era: that, despite an improvement in overall living standards and a reduction in the real price of food, the average height of native-born American males declined by more than 2.5 percent from 68.3 inches for the 1830 birth cohort to 66.6 inches for the 1890 birth cohort.[17]

Industrial life was dangerous as well as dirty. The great machines that drove industrialization—the locomotives that rushed from city to city; the molten furnaces that produced the steel that made the locomotives; the skyscrapers that blocked out the sky—all brought terrible dangers along with them. Steelworkers were spattered by molten metal or killed by exploding furnaces. Oil workers might be crushed by a collapsing derrick. Mine workers were crushed by collapsing mine shafts (in 1869, an explosion at the Steuben shaft in Pennsylvania killed 110 miners) or slowly poisoned by asthma and black lung disease.[18] Steamboats exploded and sank. Trains killed hundreds of people (and thousands of cows) every year. Between 1898 and 1900, there were as many Americans killed by trains as there were British soldiers killed by the Boers.[19] Growing speed was purchased at the expense of thousands of lives.[20]

Finally, great corporations also produced great concentrations of wealth that tested America's belief in equality of opportunity. America's new plutocrats were increasingly keen on flaunting their wealth as Schumpeter's spirit of creative destruction gave rise to Thorstein Veblen's disease of conspicuous consumption. They were also increasingly keen on adopting European airs and graces. They competed to get themselves admitted into the *Social Register* (first issued in 1888). They joined gentlemen's clubs and country clubs (and, in once-egalitarian Philadelphia, even joined cricket clubs). They sent their children to exclusive schools and universities that were modeled on British public schools and Oxbridge. Matthew Josephson captured the mood:

> "Nature's noblemen" all joined in the frenzied contest of display and consumption. Mansions and châteaux of French, Gothic, Italian, barocco and Oriental style lined both sides of the upper Fifth Avenue, while shingle and jigsaw villas of huge dimensions rose above the harbor of Newport. Railroad barons and mine-owners and oil magnates vie with each other in making town houses and country villas which were imitations of everything under the sun, and were filled with what-nots, old drapery, old armour, old Tudor chests and chairs, statuettes, bronzes, shells and porcelain. One would have a bedstead of carved oak and ebony, inlaid with gold, costing $200,000. Another would decorate his walls with enamel and gold at a cost of $65,000. And nearly all ransacked the art treasures of Europe, stripped medieval castles of their carving and tapestries, ripped whole staircases and ceilings from their place of repose through the centuries and lay them anew amid settings of a synthesis age and a simulated feudal grandeur.[21]

These giant fortunes produced a growing sense of injustice. The old idea that every man could become a boss was harder to maintain in a world where companies employed 250,000 people. And the old idea that people got what they deserved was more difficult to justify when the sons of robber barons behaved like feudal lords—when, for example, one of William Vanderbilt's sons, Cornelius, built a mansion in Newport, Rhode Island, the Breakers, that boasted 65,000 square feet and 70 rooms, and another son, George, retaliated by building a house in North Carolina, the Biltmore, that boasted 175,000 square feet and 250 rooms, as well as farms, a village, a church, and agricultural laborers.

RISING DISCONTENT

The storm of creative destruction that swept across the country in the aftermath of the Civil War whipped up great concentrations of anger as well as wealth. The anger began far from the center of capitalist civilization, in the countryside rather than in the towns, and particularly in the wide-open plains of the Midwest, with the Granger movement. The Grange, or Order of the Patrons of Husbandry, was a secret order founded in 1867 to advance the interests of America's farmers, still the largest occupational group in the country, though no longer an absolute majority of all workers, and still in most people's minds, not least their own, the repositories of America's core values. The Grange was a two-headed beast: a self-help movement that encouraged its members to look after themselves by getting an education and clubbing together to purchase their supplies and market their products; and a political movement that agitated for better conditions. At its height it claimed 1.5 million members, with local branches all over rural America.

The Grangers had a lot to complain about. They were wrong to complain that the railroad barons were being given a free lunch: as we have seen, the only way to encourage the railroads to build tracks in the middle of nowhere was to give them a chance to make a decent return. Hundreds of railroads went bankrupt in the second half of the nineteenth century. They were wrong to complain that Rockefeller and his ilk were being given special treatment: it is common commercial practice to give people discounts for bulk purchases, and a reasonable one, too, given their lower unit costs. But they were right to complain that they were sometimes the victims of monopolies: whereas people on the East Coast usually had a choice of which mode of transport they could use (perhaps a rival railroad or a canal or a road), farmers in the Midwest were reliant on one monopoly provider. Farmers coined the term "railroaded" to mean cheated. They were also right that farming was in long-term decline as a source of employment, though wrong about the reasons for this decline: the basic reason Americans were moving from the countryside to the towns was not manipulation of the system by sinister forces but the productivity improvements that they themselves were introducing.

Rural discontent produced new political parties such as the People's Party or the Populist Party, as it was more commonly known. It also produced fierce activists such as Mary Elizabeth Lease, who urged Kansans to "raise less corn and more hell," and, of course, William Jennings Bryan. The Populist Party platform, adopted at the party's first convention in Omaha on July 4, 1892, perfectly expressed the growing critique of capitalism:

> We meet in the midst of a nation brought to the verge of moral, political and material ruin. . . . The fruits of the toil of millions are boldly stolen to build up colossal fortunes for the few, unprecedented in the history of mankind; and the possessors of these in turn despise the republic and endanger liberty. From the same prolific womb of government injustice are bred two great classes—tramps and millionaires.[22]

From the 1880s onward, angry workers joined angry farmers. Organized labor had not really existed in the first half of the nineteenth century because most workers were craftsmen who sold their work directly to their customers. After the Civil War, however, industrial unrest became a feature of American life, just as it became a feature of life across the industrial world: there were 37,000 strikes between 1881 and 1905, for example, with the largest number in the building trades and mining industry, but the most divisive in the industries at the heart of the second Industrial Revolution, such as railways and steelmaking.

In 1886, more than 600,000 workers walked out of their workplaces in a tsunami of 14,000 strikes, against 11,562 businesses, that became known as the Great Upheaval. The strikes peaked in a national strike for the eight-hour day on May 1. In 1894, the Pullman strike brought the U.S. transportation network to a standstill until Grover Cleveland intervened. In the same year, the "great coal strike" shut down coal production in Pennsylvania and the Midwest and almost paralyzed large swaths of American industry.[23]

The bloodiest battle was the Homestead strike in 1892, which pitted Andrew Carnegie and Henry Clay Frick against the workers. Or rather it pitted Frick against the workers because Carnegie, determined to keep his reputation as a friend of the workingman, decided to go on one of his many holidays and let Frick bear the brunt. By 1892, Homestead employed 4,000 workers in a vast plant seven miles east of Pittsburgh, on the banks of the Monongahela River. Frick tried to rationalize labor costs by linking wages to the price of steel (which was declining) rather than to the company's profits. The Amalgamated Association of Iron and Steel Workers resisted; Frick built a three-mile-long stockade around the factory, complete with barbed wire, 2,000-candlepower searchlights, and rifle slits, and employed 300 men from the Pinkerton detective agency to protect his strikebreakers. Pitched battles followed, leaving 16 dead and the public shocked. When the strikers won the first round of the battle, forcing the Pinkertons to surrender, the governor of Pennsylvania ordered 8,500 troops to break the strike and seize the mill.

The most important cause of these protests was deflation, which gripped the economy from the end of the Civil War to 1900 and which was particularly severe from 1865 to 1879. Overall prices declined by 1.9 percent a year from 1865 to 1900. The prices of some commodities fell much more, with agricultural prices falling by 29 percent between 1870 and 1880 and nonfarm prices by 13 percent (see chart opposite). Deflation discombobulated four overlapping groups of people: producers, borrowers, employers, and employees. Producers were forced to reduce the price of their goods. The nominal price of corn plummeted from 50 cents a bushel in 1890 to 21 cents six years later. Farmers found themselves in a race to produce more and more in order to maintain their nominal incomes. Borrowers had to pay back the cheap dollars that they had borrowed with more expensive dollars plus more expensive interest on those dollars. This was a recipe for class and regional conflict: deflation transferred wealth from borrowers in the South and the West to lenders in the East. The burden of deflation didn't just fall on the little men: industries with high fixed costs such as railroads had to pay a premium for their plant and machinery. Employers had to reduce their workers' nominal wages in order to keep themselves competitive and support the interest on their debts. And employees received declining nominal wages. Again this was a recipe for conflict: workers focused on the fact that their wages were being cut rather than on the fact that their money would go further (John Maynard Keynes later called this "the stickiness of nominal wages"), and employers had yet more incentive to replace uppity workers with obedient machines.

The protests were also driven by something more nebulous than deflation: anxiety about the sheer scale of change. In *Drift and Mastery* (1914), Walter Lippmann argued that William Jennings Bryan's

PRICES AND WAGES
1860 – 1905

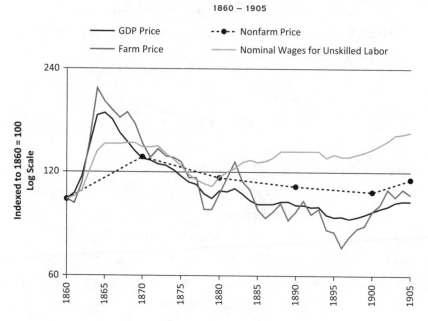

presidential campaign was animated by the desire to defend the traditional American way of life against "the great organizations that had come into the world." "He thought he was fighting the plutocracy; as a matter of fact he was fighting something much deeper than that; he was fighting the larger scale of human life."[24] Lippmann's "larger scale of human life" was a sign of something deeper still: the relentless reorganization of the economy. America reorganized on a massive scale. The proportion of American workers who worked on farms shrunk from half in 1880 to a quarter in 1920 (the word "urbanization" was coined to describe the phenomenon in Chicago in 1888). Fifteen million immigrants arrived from Europe between 1890 and 1914—many of them Catholics from southern Europe, who did not naturally meld with the country's traditional Protestant stock. And workers reorganized on an equally massive scale to try to master the changes: by 1914, about 16 percent of the labor force was unionized, a lower proportion than in Denmark (34 percent) or Great Britain (23 percent), but a higher proportion than in France or Germany (14 percent).[25]

THE CULT OF GOVERNMENT

The Progressive intellectuals inhabited a different world from the rural radicals or trade union activists: they were middle-class professionals who made comfortable livings as professors, journalists, lawyers, and government officials and who instinctively looked down on the worker, particularly those born abroad, wondering whether they should be allowed to vote, or even to have children.[26] But they were nevertheless central to the anti-laissez-faire coalition. They provided reformers with the two things that they needed to go ahead: outrage and organization. They took problems that people had long taken for granted and told them that they couldn't tolerate them any longer. And they produced reforming organizations with the same enthusiasm that businesspeople produced companies.

The Progressives' greatest achievement was to encourage a change in American attitudes to government. Before they got to work, Americans were optimistic about business and cynical about government. A couple of decades later, Progressives had persuaded a significant number of people that the opposite was the case. Muckraking journalists exposed the dark side of America's leading tycoons: Ida Tarbell published a nineteen-part magazine series in *McClure's Magazine* arguing that Standard Oil's rise had been produced by "fraud, deceit, special privilege, gross illegality, bribery, coercion, corruption, intimidation, espionage or outright terror." Louis Brandeis, the "people's attorney" and future Supreme Court justice, polemicized against "the curse of bigness" and banks that gambled with "other people's money." Henry George wondered why the "enormous increase in the power of producing wealth" had not "made real poverty a thing of the past." "Capital is piled on capital," he argued, "to the exclusion of men of lesser means and the utter prostration of personal independence and enterprise on the part of the less successful masses."[27] Henry Demarest Lloyd proclaimed that "wealth" was lined up against "commonwealth."

The era's most talented novelists added their voices to the muckraking cause. Upton Sinclair exposed the horrific conditions in the meatpacking industry in Chicago. Frank Norris denounced the Southern Pacific Railroad as "an excrescence, a gigantic parasite fattening upon the life-blood of an entire commonwealth" in *The Octopus*.[28] Theodore Dreiser portrayed the compulsion of tycoons in his trilogy based on Charles Yerkes.

Many leading Progressives broadened their attacks on the ills of big business into an attack on the economic foundations of capitalism. In 1869, Charles Francis Adams, a descendant of two presidents, worried that society had "created a class of artificial beings who bid fair soon to be masters of their creator. It is but a few years since the existence of a corporation controlling a few millions of dollars was regarded as a subject of grave apprehension, and now this country already contains single organizations which wield a power represented by thousands of millions . . . they are already establishing despotisms which no spasmodic popular effort will be able to shake off." The Progressives enthusiastically endorsed this argument, presenting giant corporations as a challenge to America's great tradition of decentralized power and popular democracy. Why should companies enjoy such generous legal privileges, they asked, without accepting broader responsibilities to society?

The Social Gospel movement did a lot to change attitudes. In the glory days of laissez-faire, leading churchmen had argued that the laws of the free market were sanctified by God. In the Progressive Era, some leading churchmen argued the opposite—that capitalist individualism was not only incompatible with the Christian ethic but positively repugnant to it. Walter Rauschenbusch, a Baptist minister and theologian, complained that "for a century the doctrine of salvation by competition was the fundamental article of the working creed of the capitalistic nations." But this was a mistake. Christians should try to end competition because it was "immoral"—a denial of the notion of "fraternity" that is at the heart of Christianity. To give free rein to competition is to "dechristianize the social order."

The flip side of demonizing business was sanctifying the state. Woodrow Wilson, the philosopher king of Progressivism, argued that Americans had devoted too much effort to limiting government and not enough to making it "facile, well-ordered and effective." Herbert Croly translated the pro-state arguments of British Fabians such as Beatrice and Sidney Webb into American idiom in his *The Promise of American Life* (1909) and then kept it before the public by founding the magazine *The New Republic* in 1914.

These pro-statist attitudes profoundly shaped the new academic science of economics. Richard Ely (and others) launched the American Economic Association in 1885 with a manifesto calling laissez-faire "unsafe in politics and unsound in morals." Washington Gladden, a charter member of the AEA, condemned individual liberty as an unsound basis for democratic government. Progressive economists loudly applauded eugenic and nativist themes. Three years after its foundation, the AEA offered a prize for the best essay on the evils of unrestricted immigration.

The Progressives completed their assault on Grover Cleveland's world by reengineering the political system. They mounted an all-out assault on the Founding Fathers' regime of checks and balances on the grounds that restrictions created cabals and that democracy required openness. Thirty-one states, starting in Oregon and spreading across the West, adopted direct primaries to reduce the power of the party bosses. In 1913, America ratified the Seventeenth Amendment to allow voters to elect senators directly rather than allowing state legislatures to appoint them. Seven years later, the Nineteenth Amendment gave women the right to vote. They would have liked to have gone much further. Teddy Roosevelt regarded the Constitution as a "stubborn obstacle to overcome in the fight for his Progressive political agenda," in the words of William Bader.[29] Woodrow Wilson believed that America could no longer afford to have a presidency fettered by eighteenth-century checks and balances if it was to cope with the world of giant corporations. It needed instead a complete constitutional revolution—a powerful prime minister on the British model supported by vigorous party discipline.

THE CLOSING OF THE FRONTIER

The development of a European-style elite on the East Coast coincided with the closing of the American frontier in the West. The open frontier had given America its energy and optimism. The world's first new nation had thrown much of its energy into settling the frontier—and as one frontier was settled another was opened up still further to the west. The quintessentially American image was of the pioneer family in their covered wagon trekking into new territories. European countries were so crowded together that they had little choice but to go to war for territory or to expand abroad. The quintessentially American advice was "Go west, young man." America had so much space on the frontier that it recruited millions of Europeans with the promise not just of life and liberty but also of free land. In 1893, Frederick Jackson Turner, a young historian at the University of Wisconsin, announced a radical new thesis at the annual meeting of the American Historical Association in Chicago: the frontier had finally closed.

The end of the frontier struck most Americans, not least Turner, as a change for the worst. The frontier had given America its egalitarian stamp: people who chafed under the yoke of Boston Brahmins or New York nabobs could simply move west. Now even the West was settled—and San Francisco had its very own Nob Hill. The frontier had acted as a guarantee of America's rugged individualism. Now America was going the way of decadent Europe and becoming a settled civilization. The frontier had given America its endless sense of possibility. Now even the vast spaces of the West were parceled out and divvied up.

What the Mediterranean Sea was to the Greeks, breaking the bond of custom, offering new experiences, calling out new institutions and activities, that, and more, the ever-retreating frontier has been to the United States directly, and to the nations of Europe more remotely. And now, four centuries from the discovery of America, at the end of a hundred years of life under the Constitution, the frontier had gone, and with its going had closed the first period of American history.[30]

Turner overstated his case. Productivity growth accelerated after the closing of the frontier: indeed the completion of America's internal market, with the integration of the West Coast, made it easier to conquer new economic frontiers. America remained a country of cheap land and vast open spaces. People continued to move around in huge numbers: southern blacks started to move to northern cities from 1900 onward and "Okies" fled the dust bowl for California. Turner nevertheless put his finger on something: America had begun its long transformation from a land of infinite possibility to a land of limits and trade-offs.

Bryan was the obvious man to give expression to this new America, limited by the closing of the frontier, topped by a new ruling class, and roiling with discontent. Nobody was better at proclaiming, "I'm mad as hell and I'm not going to take this anymore." But he was too eccentric a figure and too tricky a customer to reach the very pinnacle of national life. The politician who did much more to turn the new spirit of activism into legislation was not a Democrat but a Republican—Teddy Roosevelt.

ENERGY IN THE EXECUTIVE

On December 3, 1901, Theodore Roosevelt, who had succeeded to the presidency when William McKinley was assassinated by an anarchist, delivered his first annual message to Congress. Roosevelt started off celebrating the country's achievements. Business confidence was high, he said; prosperity was abounding; progress was accelerating. He praised the industrialists who had helped to build this prosperity: "The captains of industry who have driven the railway systems across the continent, who have built up our commerce, who have developed our manufactures, have, on the whole, done great good to our people." He insisted that they deserved their outsize rewards—individual ability determines the difference between "striking success" and "hopeless failure," and businesspeople will only be tempted to exercise that ability if they have a chance to win "great prizes." He also warned against unnecessary meddling. "The mechanism of modern business is so delicate that extreme care must be taken not to interfere with it in a spirit of rashness or ignorance."

He ended his speech on a very different note, however: "It should be as much the aim of those who seek for social betterment to rid the business world of crimes of cunning as to rid the entire body politic of crimes of violence." And as he warmed to his job, Teddy the Reformer got the upper hand from Teddy the Conciliator. All the talk of the "rashness" of reform and the "delicacy" of business was forgotten as TR embraced the Progressive cause.

For TR was an activist by temperament. Alice Roosevelt Longworth, his daughter, said that he had to be "the bride at every wedding, the corpse at every funeral and the baby at every christening." Henry James called him the "the very embodiment of noise." Louis Hartz said that he was "America's only Nietzschean president." He was also a unique combination of a patrician and an intellectual: as an intellectual he endorsed Hegel's conception of the primacy of the state and as a patrician he looked down on nouveaux riches businesspeople.

In 1902, he ordered his attorney general to bring an antitrust case against the proposed merger of the Burlington, Great Northern, and Northern Pacific railroads, the largest amalgamation in the world after U.S. Steel. The Supreme Court sided with the government in 1904, ordering the combination dissolved. TR followed up with forty-four additional prosecutions, including actions against the Beef Trust, the Sugar Trust, DuPont, and, of course, Standard Oil. In 1903, he established a Department of Commerce and Labor and equipped it with a Bureau of Corporations charged with investigating and exposing business malfeasance. In 1905, having been elected to the presidency in his own right with 56.5 percent of the vote, he unveiled an activist program that was "calculated to curl the hair of industrialists." In 1906, he signed the Hepburn Act, increasing the government's ability to regulate railroad rates, the Pure Food and Drug Act,

Whales were one of the main sources of oil for lighting, turning whaling into one of America's most lucrative—and dangerous—enterprises.

As this painting of a farm in the Mahantango Valley in Pennsylvania shows, Americans lived cheek by jowl with animals of all descriptions for a long stretch of U.S. history.

The 1794
silver dollar.

The Louisiana Purchase, in 1803, nearly tripled the size of the United States at a cost of $15 million, draining the treasury and forcing the country to borrow from Baring Brothers.

1800–1850: THE NORTH WAS A HIVE OF ENTREPRENEURIAL ACTIVITY

A blacksmith
at the forge.

Samuel Slater's mill in Pawtucket, Rhode Island, the first mechanical cotton mill in America.
Slater was a practitioner of industrial espionage, having memorized the secrets
of a British mill where he had worked.

Cyrus McCormick, founder of the McCormick Harvesting Machine Company, was granted a patent for his machine in 1834. Thanks to McCormick, farmers who once broke their backs using scythes could now work while seated, like princes of the prairie.

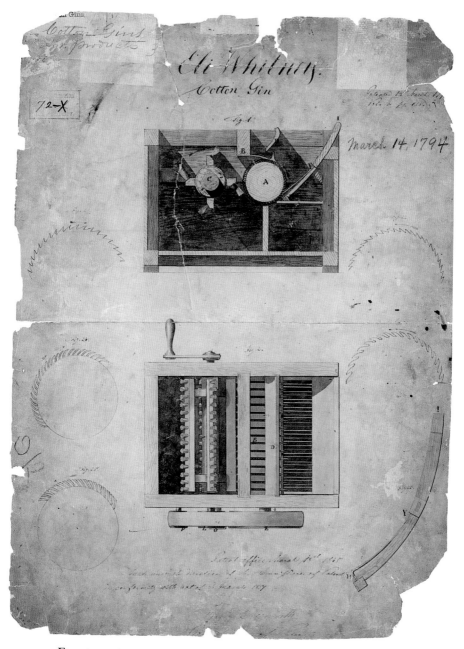

Eli Whitney's patent application for the cotton gin, which revolutionized the productivity of the cotton economy.

SHERIFF'S SALE.

John Warburton and others, vs. Robert Taylor.
Attachment in the St. Louis Circuit Court.

Whereas, on the 14th day of April, 1845, an order was made in the above entitled cause, by the Hon. John M. Krum, Judge of the 8th Judicial Circuit of the State of Missouri, ordering and directing the undersigned, Sheriff of the County of St. Louis, to sell the property attached by virtue of the writ of attachment in this case, in the manner prescribed by law, which said property is described as follows, to wit:

1 Negro woman, named AMERICA, aged about 25 years; and her child, aged about 18 months.

Also, twin negro boys, aged about 5 years, named FRANK and WILLEY.

Now, therefore, I, the said Sheriff, will, on *Monday*, the 25th day of August, inst., between the hours of nine and five o'clock, of that day, at the east front door of the Court house, in the City and County of St. Louis, State of Missouri, sell the said attached property above described, to the highest bidder, for cash, in pursuance of said order.

WILLIAM MILBURN, Sheriff.

St. Louis, Aug. 13, 1845.

REPORTER PRESS, ST. LOUIS

The Southern economy was based on the most inhuman of foundations:
the ownership of human beings.

The Erie Canal, which opened in October 1825, helped to create a water route from New York to the Great Lakes. The canal spurred western expansion and helped to turn Detroit, Cleveland, and Chicago into urban hubs.

The Room in the McLean House, at Appomattox C. H., in which GEN. LEE surrendered to GEN. GRANT.

General Robert E. Lee (seated, first from the left) meets General Ulysses S. Grant
on April 9, 1865, to fix surrender terms for the Confederacy.

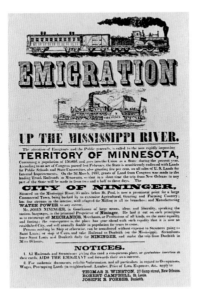

Two posters advertising immigration to the new territories: Minnesota in 1857 and Oklahoma in 1879. Settlers flooded west, tempted by the offer of large plots of land for a nominal fee as long as they agreed to work the land for a certain period of time.

A gold prospector circa 1850. Prospectors abandoned their families and sometimes walked across the vast continent, scaling the Rockies and the Sierra Nevadas for a chance to strike it rich.

The Pony Express linked the east and west coasts by combining a new technology, telegrams, with an old one, ponies.

The Westport Landing at Kansas City, circa 1865.

In an 1872 painting by John Gast, pioneers follow an allegorical figure of America westward by foot, horse, stagecoach, wagon, and railroad.

A group of men pose on a steam locomotive at City Point, Virginia, in the 1860s.

A painting by Thomas Hill depicts the ceremony held at Promontory Point, Utah, on May 10, 1869, marking the completion of the transcontinental railroad.

The great East River suspension bridge connecting the cities of
New York and Brooklyn, circa 1883.

Bessemer steel manufacture: heating and casting steel ingots in 1876. "Bessemer converters dazzle the eye with their leaping flames," John Fitch wrote after a visit to one of America's "workshops of Vulcan."

A Standard Oil advertising poster, 1900. In that year Standard Oil was capitalized at $122 million and John D. Rockefeller controlled 90 percent of the world's refinery capacity.

Trains transporting goods to and from a factory in Philadelphia, circa 1900. Industrialists aimed to bring as much production as possible under a single roof.

A steelworks in Pittsburgh, Pennsylvania, in the early 1900s. Steel gave the United States its richest man, in Andrew Carnegie, and its biggest company, in U.S. Steel.

European immigrants on Ellis Island. Nearly 12 million immigrants arrived in the United States between 1870 and 1900.

increasing its ability to tackle adulterated and poorly labeled food, and introduced income and inheritance taxes and prohibition of corporate political funds.

TR wanted to use government as a mediating force between what he thought were the two most dangerous forces in industrial society: businesspeople who pursued wealth regardless of the common good, and the mob who could be whipped up into a frenzy by jealousy and rage. He proclaimed, with withering patrician disdain, "Of all forms of tyranny the least attractive and the most vulgar is the tyranny of mere wealth, the tyranny of plutocracy." Yet at the same time he warned against muckraking, populism, and mob rule. "If Bryan wins," he argued, "we have before us some years of social misery, not markedly different from that of any South American republic."[31] He declared that "every man holds his property subject to the general right of the community to regulate its use to whatever degree the public welfare may require it." "I believe in corporations," TR confessed, "but I believe that they should be so supervised and so regulated that they shall act for the interest of the community as a whole." His aim was to prove that the government of the United States was more powerful than any aggregation of capital—yet it never crossed his mind that government might itself turn into an interest group in its own right, determined to interfere in the delicate balance of corporate life, not to pursue the common good but to advance its own interests.

TR was succeeded by a more conventional Republican. William Howard Taft pointedly argued that it was not the mission of the federal government "to be spectacular in the enactment of great statutes laying down new codes of morals or asserting a new standard of business integrity."[32] It was the business of government to establish predictable rules and let business generate wealth. But the ever-restless TR reemerged as a candidate for the Bull Moose Party in 1912 with an even more sweeping set of proposals: a vigorous battle against "the trusts," further vilification of the malefactors of great wealth, direct elections to nullify unpopular judicial precedents and remove stubborn judges. Though he lost the election, the overall results provided testimony to how far the revolt against laissez-faire had progressed. Woodrow Wilson and Teddy Roosevelt won 69 percent of the vote between them. Taft, the candidate of business Republicanism, came in third with just 23 percent of the vote. The Socialist Party, which had been founded in 1901, stormed onto the national stage: Eugene Debs, its presidential candidate, won almost a million votes and the party got more than a thousand candidates elected to various local government jobs.

If TR represented the patrician face of disdain for business, Woodrow Wilson represented the academic-bureaucratic face. The "Princeton schoolmaster" reinforced and extended many of TR's progressive measures. In 1913–14, as Europe rushed into war, Wilson signed a succession of pieces of far-reaching legislation. The Sixteenth Amendment, passed by the states in 1909 and authorized by Congress in 1913, introduced income tax. The Clayton Antitrust Act strengthened the 1890 Sherman Act and restricted interlocking directorships. The Federal Trade Commission Act created a body designed to root out and crush restrictive trade practices. One of Wilson's most important reforms was the Federal Reserve Act, which he signed into law on December 23, 1913. The act produced an institutional revolution: twelve Federal Reserve banks that came into being in November 1914 and soon began to expand America's credit supply to a degree that had not been possible under the old, restrictive gold regime. It also created an intellectual revolution: by substituting the sovereign credit of the United States for gold, it empowered central bankers to play the role that had once been played by an inflexible monetary mechanism, on the one hand, and the capricious, though necessary, intervention of private bankers like J. P. Morgan, on the other.

To be sure, America continued to peg its exchange rate to the gold standard and the Federal Reserve Act put gold limits on credit expansion to the tune of 40 percent gold backing for newly issued Federal Reserve notes and 35 percent backing behind member bank deposits at the Federal Reserve Bank. But over the next half century, whenever the limits were within reach of gripping, they were gradually lowered until, in 1968, they were wholly eliminated. As will be discussed in chapter 9, President Richard Nixon removed the final ties to gold on August 15, 1971. Since then, monetary policy has been largely at the discretion of the Federal Reserve's Open Market Committee.

The change in the tenor of life was perhaps best represented by J. P. Morgan's appearance before Arsène Pujo's congressional committee. In 1905, Morgan had contained the crisis by forcing his fellow bankers to support the banking system. In 1912, Pujo, a congressman for Louisiana's seventh district, forced him to appear before his committee and railed against his machinations. The Pujo Committee concluded that the money trust held 341 directorships in 112 companies with assets of $22 billion, and in 1913, after Morgan's death, his directors quietly resigned from forty of the companies. Many angry defenders of the status quo ascribed J. P. Morgan's death in Rome a few months after appearing before the committee to the strain of his public vilification. This is an exaggeration—it would be more reasonable to blame his death on his habit of smoking twenty huge cigars a day and refusing to exercise—but the Pujo Committee nevertheless represented the end of an era in which bankers could combine the function of titans of finance and central bankers.

Wilson's greatest contribution to ending the age of laissez-faire was acquiescing to something that, for many years, he tried to prevent: America's entry into the First World War. America's declaration of war on Germany in April 1917 fundamentally changed the relationship between state and society. The federal government was forced to raise taxes to hitherto undreamed-of levels to pay for a conflict that, according to Hugh Rockoff of Rutgers University, cost the country about $32 billion, or 52 percent of GNP at the time.[33] In 1917, taxes were raised across the board. Income taxes were made more progressive, with a top rate of 67 percent. Large estates were taxed at up to 25 percent. Stringent taxes were imposed on corporate profits with the goal of restraining war profiteering. After the war, ordinary citizens had to pay taxes. The government also had to borrow money through a succession of devices such as Liberty Bonds.

The federal government also tried to steer the economy, creating a phalanx of new federal agencies such as the War Industries Board, the Food Administration, and the Fuel Administration, staffing them with economists and other experts and giving them the power to fix prices and establish targets. The War Industries Board tried to regulate the sale of alcohol as well as coordinating government purchasing and fixing prices in more than sixty "strategic" industries. It also nationalized the railroads to ensure the smooth traffic of goods around the country.[34] The government even resorted to policing people's speech: the Sedition Act of 1918 criminalized any expression of opinion that used "disloyal, profane, scurrilous or abusive language" about the U.S. government, flag, or armed forces. And the act was vigorously enforced: Eugene Debs was thrown in jail. For pure liberals, it was never to be a "bright, confident morning" again.

America unwound much of this federal activity after the war. Wilson's Washington leviathan was beached. Freedom of speech was restored. The railways were put back into private hands. But the war nevertheless left a permanent mark. America remained in the thrall of the government experts who had staffed the new federal agencies. The wartime agencies provided the foundations for the far more ambitious New Deal agencies that were created over a decade later: the War Industries Board gave birth to the National Industrial Recovery Act and the Food Administration gave birth to the Agricultural Adjustment Administration.[35] "Almost every government program undertaken in the 1930s reflected a World War I precedent," Hugh Rockoff concludes, and "many of the people brought in to manage the New Deal agencies had learned their craft in World War I."

The war cast a long shadow in international as well as national affairs. Even though the American people reverted to their traditional isolationism once the war was won, America continued to be far more involved in European and Asian affairs than it had been before 1917. In 1920 through 1940, the United States spent 1.7 percent of its GDP on its army and navy, roughly double the proportion it had spent between 1899 and 1916.[36] In 1915, the national debt was $1.191 billion. John D. Rockefeller could have paid it off many times over from his own pocket. By 1919, it had risen to more than $25 billion.

THE NEW WORLD VERSUS THE OLD

America did not move as far away from laissez-faire as Europe did at the time. The American Constitution provided far more solid defenses against socialism than most European constitutions. American culture was more committed to free-market capitalism than European culture. America suffered far less during the war than the other great powers. The United States lost 126,000 men compared with France's 1,570,000; Britain's 908,000; Germany's 1,773,000; Austria's 1,200,000; and Russia's 1,700,000. Austria, shorn of its eastern European empire, ceased to be a great power. Germany, burdened with reparations imposed by the Treaty of Versailles and humiliated by defeat, went into a sort of national psychosis. Russia fell victim to the Bolsheviks. France was a wreck. Britain struggled to retain its former glory with a weakened economy and a failing empire.

America's Progressives looked like teddy bears compared with Europe's antiestablishment parties. The British Labour Party was pledged to ensure the common ownership of the means of production, distribution, and exchange. Germany boasted two fiercely anticapitalist parties: the left-wing Social Democratic Party and the right-wing Nazi Party. The Russian Bolsheviks made good on their promise to establish a dictatorship of the proletariat. By contrast, America's Progressives merely wanted to make capitalism work more smoothly and its trade unions wanted a bigger share of the capitalist pie. America also enjoyed another burst of probusiness government in the 1920s. Warren Harding and Calvin Coolidge succeeded in reversing many of the measures implemented during the Progressive Era and reasserting the traditional freedoms of business.

That said, America nevertheless moved significantly to the left: the America of 1918 was a very different country from the America of the late nineteenth century. It had most of the accoutrements of a modern state-dominated society: an income tax, a central bank, and a swelling bureaucracy. And it had a significant group of people who thought that the major problem was that this hadn't gone far enough.

Six

THE BUSINESS OF
AMERICA IS BUSINESS

———◆———

THE TWO PRESIDENTS who followed Teddy Roosevelt and Woodrow Wilson—Warren Harding and Calvin Coolidge—brought a complete change to public life, replacing activism with restraint and noise with silence. They abandoned dreams of reinventing American capitalism and cutting a dashing figure on the world stage, and embraced, instead, the ideals of living a quiet life and conserving presidential power.

For Progressive historians, the two men were disgraceful do-nothings—detours on the glorious road toward state activism. Harding played poker once a week with his chums, not all of them model citizens, and golf twice a week, honing his game by hitting balls on the White House lawn for his Airedale, Laddie Boy, to retrieve.[1] Coolidge prided himself on never working more than four hours a day and never sleeping less than eleven hours a night. "His ideal day," H. L. Mencken quipped, "is one on which nothing whatever happens."

Harold Laski complained about "conscious abdication from power." John Morton caviled about "the temporary eclipse of the presidency." The reality of the era is much more interesting: Harding's and particularly Coolidge's commitment to doing nothing was philosophical as well as temperamental, an ideological weapon rather than a personal vice. Theirs was an active inactivism.

Harding and Coolidge both devoted themselves to keeping government small. They worked with tax cutters in Congress, which was controlled by Republicans throughout the 1920s, to lower the top rate of tax. They populated their administrations with small-government conservatives, most notably Andrew Mellon, secretary of the treasury from 1921 to 1932—and, incidentally, the third-richest man in the country after John D. Rockefeller and Henry Ford—who rolled back taxes on excess profits, slashed estate taxes by half, and reduced the national debt. Coolidge twice vetoed a measure to boost farm prices by dumping crop surpluses abroad and vetoed a bill for the federal government to operate a hydroelectric site at Muscle Shoals. He also pushed the newly founded Bureau of the Budget to instill the principle of austerity in government departments. "The kind of government he offered the country," remarked Mencken, "was government stripped to the buff."[2]

Harding and Coolidge both believed that business rather than government was the engine of social progress. "The man who builds a factory builds a temple," Coolidge declared, in one of his few expansive statements. "The man who works there worships there." Harding's plea for a "return to normalcy" has been widely dismissed as the dullest of battle cries. It was certainly a cry for a return to the regular rhythms of life before the disruption of the Great War. But it was also more than this—a cry for a return to the heroic days of American business when entrepreneurs spun giant companies out of brilliant ideas and when heroic individuals, unencumbered by government interference, built iron horses and flying machines. The job of the president was not to be engaged in a frenzy of activity. It was to provide a stable foundation upon which businesspeople could create wealth.

The 1920s was arguably the last decade when the size of government could be restrained, and the United States the last rich country where that arduous feat could be performed. European countries had already built mighty government machines to provide their people with welfare and to protect themselves from their fractious neighbors. The neighbors got more fractious by the day. By contrast, the United States could still practice the art of frugal government. It was protected from invasion by strong cultural ties with Canada to the north, the vast deserts of northern Mexico to the south, and wide oceans on either side. Coolidge hardly exaggerated when he remarked that "if the federal government should go out of existence, the common run of people would not detect the difference in the affairs of their daily life for a considerable length of time."[3] Government played such a marginal role in American life that, for the first time since the birth of mass political parties in the age of Andrew Jackson, male electoral participation rates fell from 63 percent in 1916 to 52 percent in 1920, and sank further still in 1924.

This hands-off principle was marred by countertrends. These Republican presidents were increasingly hostile to the free movement of goods and people: for example, in his address to Congress in 1924, Coolidge praised tariffs for securing "the American market for the products of the American workmen" and enabling "our people to live according to a better standard and receive a better rate of compensation than any people, anytime, anywhere on earth, ever enjoyed." The decade was framed by two tariffs: the Emergency Tariff of 1921 and the Smoot-Hawley Tariff of 1930. The 1924 Immigration Act, which remained in effect until 1965, severely limited the number of immigrants and restricted the flow to favored countries with which America already had strong blood ties, mostly in northern Europe.

America also embraced something that no other liberal democracy has dared: for fourteen long years, from 1920 through 1933, it was illegal to produce, transport, or sell alcohol. Though this oppressive regime did nothing to reduce the proportion of American GDP that was spent on alcohol, it did create an innovative new business in the form of bootlegging.

The bootleggers of the 1920s provided a mirror image of the entrepreneurs of respectable society. America's gangsters, many of them immigrants who found more conventional careers closed to them, built business empires from nothing by dint of the clever use of management innovations and new technology. Al Capone franchised out the management of his gambling dens and brothels to local clients in return for the provision of centralized services, notably protection. Those franchises were early adopters of ticker tape to keep them up to date with the news, and cars to keep them ahead of the police.

The era also got off to a difficult start. The immediate aftermath of the war had an almost surreal quality to it: anarchist outrages, hyperpatriotic demonstrations, angry strikes, Communist plots, all piled upon one another. The United States experienced perhaps the most intense deflation in its history with wholesale prices falling by 44 percent between June 1920 and June 1921. In 1920, bellwether companies such as Anaconda Copper, Bethlehem Steel, and U.S. Steel saw their annual revenues fall by 49 percent, 46 percent, and 44 percent, respectively. Farm production dropped by 14 percent in 1921. The unemployment rate jumped from 2 percent in 1919 to 11 percent in 1921. The depression lasted some eighteen months, during which policy makers practiced the same passive response that was practiced during the crisis of 1893, and later in the crises of 1996 and

2007. Then the unexpected collapse was followed by an equally unexpected and sharp recovery. As James Grant has observed, it was "the crash that cured itself."[4]

Adding to the country's problems was the worst surge in strikes in American history (see chart below). During the war, Samuel Gompers's American Federation of Labor (AFL) had enthusiastically supported the war effort but surreptitiously negotiated more recognition and higher wages. With the outbreak of peace, it tried to make its gains permanent with coordinated strikes in key industries such as steel and meat.

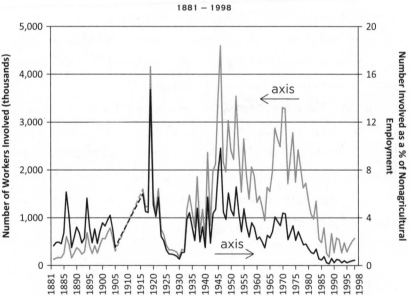

WORKERS INVOLVED IN STRIKES
1881 – 1998

Yet the storm blew over almost as quickly as it blew in. American employers successfully counterattacked the strikers by raising (sometimes justified) fears of communism. By 1920, trade unions were back in the same position they had been in in 1910. The Supreme Court shifted the balance of power back toward the bosses: in 1921, the Court made secondary boycotts illegal (*Duplex Printing Press Co. v. Deering*), and in 1923 (*Adkins v. Children's Hospital*), it ruled against minimum wages. Trade union membership plummeted—the AFL lost about a million members between 1920 and 1925 alone—and trade union activism withered. In 1929, 286,000 workers (1.2 percent of the workforce) staged 900 strikes, compared with 4 million workers (21 percent of the workforce) staging 3,600 strikes in 1919.

From 1921 through 1929, U.S. GDP grew by 5 percent a year in real terms—one of the best performances for an advanced country on record. America also witnessed one economic miracle after another. On May 20, 1927, Charles Lindbergh made the first solo flight across the Atlantic, signaling the arrival of a new age of globalization. (Calvin Coolidge dispatched a warship to collect both Lindbergh and his plane.) On October 6 of the same year, Al Jolson spoke the first words in the motion picture premiere of *The Jazz Singer*, signaling the arrival of modern mass entertainment. By the end of the decade, America's share of the world's manufacturing had risen to 42 percent from 36 percent in 1914. Even America's growing protectionism was qualified by the size of the internal market and the legacy of decades of free immigration: in 1930, 15 percent of Americans had been born abroad and 36 percent had at least one parent who was born abroad.

MAKING SENSE OF THE TWENTIES

The 1920s were dominated by three great themes. The first was the rapid improvement in productivity, particularly in the first half of the decade. This improvement was at its most startling in the car industry. By 1924, a Model T was rolling off the production line every ten seconds. Just a dozen years earlier it had taken fourteen hours to put together a single car. The increase in productivity can also be found outside the manufacturing sector—in offices, with their army of young female secretaries, who could be relied on to do the maximum of work for the minimum of pay before getting married, and in chain stores, with their emphasis on low costs and frugal service. With the trade unions quiescent after the initial postwar discontent, and inflation at zero, companies were able to capture a princely proportion of these productivity improvements in corporate profits. The level of corporate earnings doubled between 1913 and 1925. The number of companies listed on the stock market quintupled. And the total value of stocks increased from $15 billion to $30 billion.[5]

The second was the modernization of the economy thanks to the expansion of the service sector and the rise of the cities. The 1910 census noted that America had crossed an important threshold, with more people working in the service sector than in agriculture. The service sector continued to expand rapidly in the 1920s with the addition of new professions, such as "human resource managers," to old ones, such as teachers.

At roughly the same time, the number of city dwellers exceeded the number of country dwellers. A nation that had defined itself in terms of prairies and cowboys began to define itself in terms of skyscrapers and city slickers. Skyscrapers reached ever higher: between 1930 and 1931, Manhattan acquired two of its greatest landmarks, the Chrysler Building and the Empire State Building, and the amount of office space in the borough roughly doubled. A succession of new magazines—*Time* (1923), the *American Mercury* (1924), and the *New Yorker* (1925)—flattered the new urban sophisticates, helping to ignite the culture wars that rage to this day. The *New Yorker* boasted that it was "not edited for the old lady in Dubuque." F. Scott Fitzgerald wrote airily about "the vast obscurity beyond the city." H. L. Mencken used the Scopes trial to create the impression that rural

America, particularly southern rural America, was populated by stump-toothed idiots (interestingly, the textbook that Scopes used was, in fact, a crude hymn to the wonders of eugenics). William Jennings Bryan, who famously clashed with the eminent attorney Clarence Darrow during the case, died after the trial, bringing to a close one of the most influential public careers in American history.

The third theme was arguably the most interesting: the democratization and dissemination of the great innovations of the laissez-faire era: electricity, automobiles, and airplanes, and at a more abstract level, the business corporation itself. The 1920s was a decade of growing prosperity for the masses as well as overheated markets. Average Joes had access to things that had once been luxuries for the rich (such as their own homes) or that hadn't existed a few years before (such as cars and radios). Suburbs sprawled. Houses were networked into the electricity grid and water supply. And by 1929, 3 million American households, or one out of every ten, owned shares, with disastrous consequences.

THE HORSELESS CARRIAGE

The motorcar sat at the center of the American economy, produced in America more efficiently than anywhere else in the world, and consumed more enthusiastically. By the mid-1920s, 80 percent of all the world's cars were located in the United States: America boasted a motorcar for every 5.3 people compared with one car for every 44 people in England and France. A car that cost the average worker the equivalent of nearly two years' wages before the First World War could be purchased for about three months' earnings by the mid-1920s. Thereafter the price stabilized, but quality continued to improve: you got more car for your buck (and more ways of financing the bucks you needed to buy your car).

The automobile industry revolutionized the distribution of wealth. In 1924, Henry and Edsel Ford ranked second and third in a federal government list of top taxpayers (Rockefeller was still number one), and Mrs. Horace Dodge ranked ninth. It also had a domino effect on the rest of the economy—it stimulated demand for oil to power it, rubber and glass to provide it with tires and windshields, roads to ease its path, garages to house it, gas stations to provide it with fuel and repairs, and numerous services to house, feed, and otherwise satisfy the newly mobile population. One calculation in 1929 suggested that the auto economy had created over 4 million jobs that had not existed in 1900, or one-tenth of the overall workforce.

There was almost no aspect of American life in the 1920s that was not transformed by the motorcar. Bootleggers used "getaway cars" to escape the police. Streetwalkers found a new place to ply their trade: in *Middletown* (1929), Robert and Helen Lynd reported that, of the thirty women charged with sex crimes in the local juvenile court in 1924, nineteen had been in cars.[6] Suburbs, which had originally been created by electric trams, spread still farther, blossoming into veritable "autopias." Billboards, gas stations, and food stands mushroomed. The White Castle hamburger chain began in 1921 in Wichita, Kansas; Howard Johnson opened his first drugstore soda fountain in Quincy, Massachusetts, in 1925; Harland Sanders developed his chicken recipe in 1930 at his "Servistation" in Corbin, Kentucky.[7]

The number of trucks also increased rapidly, from zero in 1909 to three hundred thousand in 1920 to six hundred thousand in the late 1920s. These trucks forced railroads to compete for the first time. They also offered something that the railroads could not: delivery to your door rather than to the train station. This saved an enormous amount of time and effort: instead of having to unload your produce at the station, reload it onto a horse and cart, and then transport it to its final destination, you could take it all the way from origin to destination in a single journey.

The combustion engine arguably transformed the lives of the 44 percent of people who lived in rural areas even more than the 56 percent who lived in cities. Henry Ford made sure that his Model T was capable of surviving rural America's dismal roads by providing it with independent wheel suspension, rugged parts, easy-to-repair engines, and even kits to help farmers turn their car into a tractor.[8] Farmers destroyed some 9 million working animals, particularly horses and mules, during the decade, freeing pastureland for more remunerative uses, and replaced them with motorized vehicles of various sorts.[9] The number of tractors increased from about 1,000 in 1910 to 246,000 in 1920 to 920,000 in 1930. These tractors also became more versatile thanks to the emergence of direct power drives, which allowed them to transfer power directly to implements they towed, and pneumatic tires, which allowed them to tow much heavier loads. The number of combine harvesters grew from 4,000 in 1920 to 61,000 in 1930 and then to 190,000 in 1940. The spread of Tin Lizzies in rural areas was good for the gene pool as well as social life: people who had been forced to socialize within a few miles could suddenly cover much more distance.

The combustion engine took over public as well as private transport, as the number of buses surged and their price declined. The first recognizably modern motor bus was introduced by the Fageol brothers in Oakland, California, in 1921, in the form of the Fageol Safety Bus. Buses might not be able to compete with streetcars when it came to romance—a "Bus Named Desire" doesn't have quite the right ring—but they were more practical: they didn't need expensive tracks; they could vary their routes; rubber tires reduced noise and absorbed shocks.[10] Soon intercity buses were challenging trains just as local buses had challenged streetcars: the first coast-to-coast bus service in 1928 made the journey from Los Angeles to New York in five days, fourteen hours, and made 132 stops.

The 1920s saw a big improvement in the quality of the country's roads as well as the vehicles that cruised them. In 1900, America's 2 million miles of road were largely dirt tracks connecting farms to towns. Indeed, one reason European cars made so little progress in America was that their chassis were too low to survive the rigors of America's dirt tracks. Woodrow Wilson inaugurated a new age when he signed the 1916 Federal Aid Road Act, which provided federal grants to states engaged in the development of their roads and bridges. Howard Mason Gore, the secretary of agriculture, introduced more order into the emerging national system when he approved a uniform system of numbering and marking highways in 1925: east-west roads were assigned even numbers, north-south roads odd numbers, and transcontinental highways were designed in multiples of ten. Road builders developed asphalt and concrete for road surfaces. The first road atlas to report on the condition of specific routes was introduced in 1926.[11] Robert Gordon estimates that the development of a nationwide network of paved roads increased the speed of automobile travel by a factor of at least five between 1905 and 1920.[12]

America also began to add the air to its transportation routes. The commercial aircraft industry was slow to get off the ground because flying was so dangerous. In the 1900s, airplanes were associated with daredevils. In the 1910s, they were associated with the military (the Wright brothers sold their first aircraft to the Army Signal Corps and foreign militaries). By the end of the 1920s, they were finally seen for what they were to become: part of the mass transportation system that moved people around a vast country at unprecedented speeds.

The Post Office laid the foundation of the postwar boom by

establishing a national air network to speed up the delivery of the post (thirty-one of the first forty U.S. Post Office pilots were killed in the first six years).[13] In 1925–26, the government threw open these postal routes to competitive bids from private companies. This electrified the nascent industry: more than five thousand people competed for contracts, the first of which was given to Walter Varney, the founder of Varney Airlines, the corporate ancestor of United Airlines, to fly mail from Pasco, Washington, to Elko, Nevada. Dozens of entrepreneurs realized that there was money to be made from transporting people as well as parcels. By 1928, when the first statistics for scheduled air transportation were collected, the United States already had 268 aircraft in domestic operations and 57 in international operations.[14]

THE MARCH OF THE ELECTRONIC SERVANTS

The combustion revolution was only equaled in significance by the electricity revolution. In the early twentieth century, the electricity industry witnessed the biggest boost in productivity of any sector of the economy thanks to two developments: the construction of large central stations powered by high-pressure boilers and efficient turbines, and the construction of power transmission networks over ever-larger areas. Over the next three decades, the amount of electricity that Americans used increased tenfold—from 6 billion kilowatt-hours in 1902 (or 79 kilowatt-hours per person) to 118 billion kilowatt-hours in 1929 (or 960 per person). Over the same period, the cost of that electricity declined by 80 percent—from 16.2 cents per kilowatt-hour in 1902 to 6.3 cents in 1929.

The electrification of America's factories in the 1920s was at the heart of the growth in productivity. Though electricity was a well-established technology in 1920, its impact on productivity had been limited by old-fashioned industrial design. Prior to the 1920s, most American factories were powered by big steam engines. These steam engines sat in the basement and then powered machines on the upper floors through vertical shafts that ran up the side of the building, and horizontal shafts on each floor of the building. At first factory owners were reluctant to waste all their sunk costs: they simply replaced the steam engines with electrical motors and expected the workers to put up with the inconvenience of tall buildings and lots of horizontal shafts. But during the 1920s, they realized that it sometimes pays to start from scratch: they started powering their machines with individual motors and laying out their factories horizontally rather than vertically.

Henry Ford summarized the importance of this change:

The provision of a whole new system of electric generation emancipated industry from the leather belt and line shaft, for it eventually became possible to provide each tool with its own electric motor. This may seem only a detail of minor importance. In fact, modern industry could not be carried out with the belt and line shaft for a number of reasons. The motor enabled machinery to be arranged in the order of work, and that alone has probably doubled the efficiency of industry, for it has cut out a tremendous amount of useless handling and hauling. The belt and line shaft were also tremendously wasteful—so wasteful indeed that no factory could be really large, for even the longest line shaft was small according to modern requirements. Also high-speed tools were impossible under the old conditions—neither the pulleys nor the belts could stand modern speeds. Without high-speed tools and the finer steels which they brought about, there could be nothing of what we call modern industry.

Paul David has identified electrification as an example of an innovation that only has its full effect when it is accompanied by other changes such as a reorganization of work. For electrification to boost productivity you don't just need to add electricity to the old production process. You have to shift from the "group drive" (in which electric power simply replaces steam power in a plant that retains the huge shafts and belts of an earlier era) to "unit drive" (in which each machine is equipped with its own electric motor).

These small electric motors powered an ever-increasing number of household appliances. Entrepreneurs invented dozens of devices that could use the new energy source to improve people's lives. In the same year that the Communists seized power in Russia, General Electric celebrated a different revolution—the rise of "electric servants" that are "dependable for the muscle part of the washing, ironing, cleaning and sewing. They could do all your cooking—without matches, without soot, without coal, without argument—in a cool kitchen." A survey carried out by Chicago's Electric Company in 1929 showed that more than 80 percent of residents had an electric iron and vacuum cleaner, 53 percent had a radio, 37 percent had a toaster, and 36 percent a washing machine. Refrigerators (10 percent) and electric heaters (10 percent) were much rarer.[15]

THE WIRELESS AGE

The most revolutionary device that people plugged into their sockets was the radio. Starting in the 1890s, telecom engineers figured out how to free themselves from wires by sending data and voice signals over the air. In 1901, Guglielmo Marconi, an Italian, established the British Marconi Company to transmit Morse code over the airways to ships. In 1907, Lee de Forest developed a triode or tube that could divide up the radio spectrum into different channels or frequencies. In 1915, Bell engineers succeeded in using long radio waves to transmit speech from Arlington, Virginia, to Panama, Hawaii, and Paris.

Modern commercial radio was born with the 1920s: the first radio news program was broadcast on August 31, 1920, by station 8MK in Detroit, Michigan (it survives to this day as the all-news radio station WWJ), and the first licensed broadcast was delivered in Pittsburgh, Pennsylvania, on November 2, 1920. The new technology spread like wildfire. By 1924, there were 556 radio stations and 25,000 "transmitting stations" manned by amateurs. By 1930, almost half the households in the country (46 percent) had radios. The 1920s might better be described as the radio decade than the jazz decade (though listening to jazz was one of the most popular uses of the radio).

The radio was freedom in a box: suddenly people who had never had a chance to listen to professional musicians or dramatists could turn their sitting rooms into private theaters cum concert halls. All they needed to do was to buy a radio and everything else was free. The revolution was driven by profit-seeking entrepreneurs rather than, as was the case in much of Europe, government commissions. George Westinghouse, an electrical magnate, established KDKA in order to stimulate demand for his radio sets. Growing demand for radio sets stimulated more innovation—particularly the introduction of vacuum tubes in 1925. And the advertising boom provided a reliable source of cash. Soon hundreds of radio stations were plying their trade.

General Electric's Radio Corporation of America (RCA) was one of the landmark stocks of the 1920s, referred to simply as "Radio": its price rose by a factor of one hundred between 1924 and 1929, before falling to almost nothing by 1931. Radio stars were some of the best-paid performers of the era: at its peak in 1933 the *Amos 'n' Andy* show earned its two stars an annual income of a hundred thousand dollars, higher than the earnings of the president of NBC or RCA.

This most democratic of mediums inevitably changed politics. Harding became the first president to speak on the radio when he dedicated the Francis Scott Key Memorial Bridge at Fort McHenry in Baltimore harbor in 1922. Silent Cal was a surprisingly enthusiastic broadcaster. The 1924 Democratic National Convention was broadcast in all its chaotic glory. Franklin Delano Roosevelt made the medium his own when he used it to deliver his fireside chats to the nation during the Great Depression, speaking to a frightened country like a wise old uncle who knew exactly what to do. Radio also provided a platform for less cuddly figures: Father Charles Coughlin, the "radio priest," received an average of 4,000 letters a week, rising to 1.2 million in February 1932, when he attacked Hoover as "the Holy Ghost of the rich, the protective angel of Wall Street"; Huey Long broadcast for hours on end and christened himself "the Kingfish" after a character in *Amos 'n' Andy*; Gerald L. K. Smith kept his audience enthralled with his intricate and all-enveloping conspiracy theories.

The cinema spread almost as fast as the radio. The nickelodeon (so called because it charged an admission price of five cents) exploded on the scene in 1906–7. Grand movie palaces, complete with exuberant decorations, elaborate organs to provide the sound, and warm-up acts featuring singers, dancers, and comedians, arrived in 1911. The Roxy Theatre in Midtown Manhattan had 6,200 seats and dressing rooms for 300 performers. By 1922, some 40 million people, 36 percent of the population, attended the cinema once a week. The introduction of sound in 1928 gave the medium another boost. By the late 1920s, more than 70 percent of the population was regularly going "to the movies" and America was producing 80 percent of the world's films. Popular entertainment went the same way as other forms of industrial production: people who had previously made their own entertainment became the passive consumers of entertainment that was made in Hollywood's great dream factories.

THE AFFLUENT SOCIETY

The arrival of "electronic servants" signaled something new in history: mass affluence. In the late nineteenth century, most American households lived a hand-to-mouth existence. They spent half or more of their income on basic sustenance and they were always one paycheck away from poverty. In the 1920s, ordinary people had a chance of living the American dream—buying their own houses and filling them with consumer goods that had not even existed a generation earlier.

The 1920s saw one of the two biggest housing booms in American history—more than a million houses were built in 1925 alone, and by 1929 about half the houses in the country were owner-occupied. The housing boom had ripple effects. Owner-occupiers did what owner-occupiers always do—filled their houses with furniture, pictures, and gadgets, and purchased various forms of insurance to protect their families and possessions. One of the most popular books of the era, Sinclair Lewis's *Babbitt* (1923), tells the story of a real-estate agent in the fictional Midwest suburb, Floral Heights, where only three houses are more than a decade old. The houses are temples to electronic conveniences: gramophones the size of cabinets, hot-water radiators, vacuum cleaners, electric fans, coffeemakers, toasters. Lewis sneers at the standardized nature of all these products—he describes one room as being "as neat, and as negative, as a block of artificial ice"—but Floral Heights represented the democratization of wealth and opportunity as the productivity gains of the previous decades transformed the lives of ordinary Americans.

THE COMPANY GOES PUBLIC

Democratization extended to the core institution of American business life, the business corporation: the total number of shareholders increased from about a million at the turn of the century to up to 7 million in 1928. The most enthusiastic practitioner of popular capitalism was AT&T, which increased the number of stockholders from 10,000 in 1901 to 642,180 in 1931. The principal stockholders of the country's biggest railroad (Pennsylvania Railroad), the biggest public utility (AT&T), and the biggest industrial corporation (U.S. Steel) owned less than 1 percent of the shares.

"Democratization" might seem like a strong word given that a majority of the public did not own stock. It nevertheless captures an important change. You didn't have to be a captain of industry or Wall Street banker to own stock: you could be an ordinary person saving for your retirement. In 1929, about 50 percent of all corporate dividends went to people who earned five thousand dollars a year or below.[16] America's biggest companies had adopted a form that they were to maintain until the 1970s: owned by scattered investors rather than dominant founders, as they once had been, or powerful institutions, as they were from the 1970s onward.

The advent of widespread ownership went hand in hand with two other developments. The first was the consolidation of companies. In their classic *The Modern Corporation and Private Property* (1932), Adolf Berle and Gardiner Means noted that the country's big companies kept getting bigger. From 1909 to 1928, America's two hundred largest companies grew by an average of 5.4 percent a year, compared with 2 percent for other corporations.[17] From 1921 to 1928, they grew at 6.1 percent a year, compared with 3.1 percent for smaller companies. By 1929, the magic two hundred controlled almost half of the country's corporate wealth, worth $81 billion. This rapid growth of big companies was driven in part by the public markets, which allowed them to raise money more easily and use that money to consolidate their grip on their respective markets.

The second was the rise of professional managers. The most important fact about the modern corporation was the separation of ownership and control. The millions of new owners of America's great companies could not exercise their property rights directly by running their companies themselves. They had to hire professional managers to do it for them. This redefined the nature of property: company owners no longer owned plant and machinery but instead owned bits of paper that were traded on the public markets. It also redefined "ownership" by making it easier to earn an income from shares without bothering about the tedious question of how the company was run. Berle and Means likened the new shareholders to the new factory workers: just as factory workers surrendered the direction of their labor to their industrial masters, so the new shareholders surrendered the direction of their capital to their managerial masters.[18]

The 1920s inaugurated a golden age for American managers that lasted until the mid-1970s. In the Gilded Age, managers had to answer to the owners. In the first two decades of the century, they had to answer to bankers (as was still the case on the Continent). By contrast, small shareholders had no choice but to hand the day-to-day management to professionals. The downside of this was that managers were able to feather their own nests at the expense of owners.

Corporate hierarchies elongated. The upside was that they could try to shape their business environment by adopting the long view.

Corporations embraced the soft side of management as well as the hard side. They developed intricate personnel management systems to make the best use of their workers. They adopted sophisticated public-relations techniques to burnish their image in the public mind. They also invested heavily in advertising, establishing in-house advertising divisions, forming relationships with professional advertising companies, and generally trying to turn selling into an art. Advertising spending reached the highest point as a proportion of GDP in the early 1920s (see chart below).

U.S. AD SPENDING
1919 – 2007

The most ambitious managers advocated "welfare capitalism"— that is, providing their workers with pension plans, health-care benefits, and profit-sharing plans. George Johnson, a shoe entrepreneur, introduced an eight-hour workday, a forty-hour workweek, and comprehensive medical care. Philip Wrigley proved that he could embrace social reform and make gum at the same time by introducing an income insurance plan and a pension system. Lewis Brown, an asbestos magnate, introduced collective bargaining, the eight-hour workday, a forty-hour workweek, and regular surveys of employee opinion.[19]

These new professionally managed corporations extended their reign into new areas such as distribution and retail. Chain stores that specialized in no-frills services expanded rapidly in the 1920s, using their massive scale to put pressure on their suppliers and their national footprint to reach into the expanding suburbs. The victims of the new chain stores were not just mom-and-pop stores that couldn't match them on price. They were also the mail-order stores that by the late 1920s were forced to open physical stores, often in the suburbs. Creative destruction brought an inevitable political reaction: the losers banded together and eventually persuaded the Federal Trade Commission to pass retail price maintenance.

HENRY FORD VERSUS ALFRED SLOAN

The most significant corporate battle of the 1920s pitted Ford's entrepreneur-focused conception of the corporation against General Motors' management-focused conception. Ford Motor Company started the decade with a massive advantage: in 1921, Ford had 56 percent of the American market, compared with GM's 13 percent. Henry Ford was universally hailed as America's greatest businessman. But by the end of the decade, the two companies were neck and neck—and by the end of the 1930s, GM was significantly ahead of Ford.

The architect of this change was Alfred Sloan, who moved to

General Motors after a brief career manufacturing ball bearings and became president of the company in 1923. Sloan understood that management had become a driver of productivity in its own right: whereas Ford boosted productivity by devising new ways of producing things, Sloan boosted it by developing new ways of getting people to work together. Sloan was almost the living embodiment of the managerial ethic—about six feet tall but weighing only 130 pounds, completely absorbed in his work with no time left over for hobbies; a colleague likened him to the roller bearings that he had once manufactured: "self-lubricating, smooth, eliminates friction and carries the load."[20]

Sloan embraced the idea of the multidivisional firm. Oliver Williamson has called the multidivisional firm the most important innovation in the history of capitalism in the twentieth century.[21] This may be overstating it, but there can be no doubt about its importance. Multidivisional firms were well suited to an age of giant organizations: they allowed companies to combine the virtues of size with focus. They were also well suited to an age of consumer capitalism, allowing companies to generate specialized divisions that focused on producing and servicing particular products. These divisions were sufficiently close to the market to follow changes in fashion as carefully as smaller companies but also sufficiently close to the rest of the corporation to be able to draw on vast resources.

The first company to adopt the multidivisional form was DuPont shortly after the First World War. DuPont had grown exponentially during the war in order to supply the Allies with nitroglycerin. But the outbreak of peace provided it with a problem: Should it shrink back to its former size (allowing skills to wither and workers to be laid off)? Or should it find new uses for its new capabilities? The company decided on the latter course and created several divisions to market different products, such as paints. Individual executives were given responsibility for the management of production and sales of their products (or product lines). Their divisions became profit centers and their performance was evaluated by top management with the help of such tools as ROI (return on investment).[22]

Alfred Sloan applied the idea to America's biggest manufacturing company. Sloan realized that car buyers were no longer grateful to receive whatever they were given ("You can have any color you want so long as it's black"). They wanted to exercise that most American of virtues, individual choice, and they wanted to use that choice to communicate something about themselves: what sort of people they were and how much money they had to spend. He also grasped that he could not satisfy this demand without completely reorganizing his firm.

Sloan divided his company into different divisions responsible for different types of cars: from Chevrolets designed to compete with the Model T to Cadillacs designed for the elite. He gave high-flying managers responsibility for operating these divisions, but at the same time held these managers responsible for their overall performance. "From decentralization we get initiative, responsibility, development of personnel, decisions close to the facts, flexibility," Sloan said. "From coordination we get efficiencies and economies."[23]

Sloan sat at the very heart of this leviathan of an organization, in GM's headquarters in Detroit, using his ability to allocate capital to command the entire machine. He continually adjusted his company's structure in response to internal and external pressures. *Fortune* magazine argued that GM had "escaped the fate of those many families of vertebrates whose bodies grew constantly larger while their brain cavities grew relatively smaller, until the species became extinct . . . because Mr. Sloan has contrived to provide it with a composite brain commensurate with its size."[24]

GM pioneered techniques for stretching the market by making it easier to borrow against future earnings, and stimulating it by investing in advertising. The company introduced "installment buying" in 1919 with the creation of the General Motors Acceptance Corporation. It also invested an unprecedented $20 million in advertising over the next decade.

It is notable that Ford only really rebounded after the Second World War when it copied GM's enthusiasm for management: Henry Ford II, only twenty-eight years old when he took over, copied GM's organizational structure, hired GM executives to give that structure life, and brought in a group of "Whiz Kids" who had worked for the Army Air Corps during the war—and who included Robert McNamara—to install statistical controls.

The multidivisional form swept all before it. Francis Davis, a former manager at DuPont, showed how multidivisional management could be used to galvanize a failing company. When Davis took over the United States Rubber Company in 1928, it was a loss-making mess: a disparate collection of inefficient operating units with no formal operating structure. Davis used the multidivisional form to impose order by gathering financial and strategic decision making in a central staff, measuring the performance of the various divisions, and getting rid of the underperformers. Davis restored the company to profitability and started investing in research, developing a new foam-rubber cushion in 1934 and introducing rayon cord into its tires in 1938.

AMERICA IS FLAT

The *American* Telephone and Telegraph Company, the Aluminum Company of *America*, the *American* Radiator and Standard Sanitary Corporation, the *American* Can Company, the *American* Woolen

Company, the Radio Corporation of *America* . . . the names of some of the country's biggest businesses suggest that there was another great development driving American life along with democratization. This was the development of an integrated national market.

The first thirty years of the century saw striking advances in the integration of the South into the national market. This was not the result of enlightened reform from on high or political pressure from below. Rather it was the result of a technological innovation that originally had nothing to do with the South whatsoever: the development of a mechanism for controlling the climate and thereby making it possible to work in the sweltering heat. In 1902, Sackett & Wilhelms Lithographing & Printing Company in New York was struggling with the fact that varying levels of humidity made it difficult to print in color. Printing in color required the same paper to be printed four times in different-colored inks—cyan, magenta, yellow, and black—but if the paper expanded or contracted even a millimeter between print runs, as happens when humidity changes, the whole effect is ruined. Sackett & Wilhelms asked the Buffalo Forge Company, a heating company in Buffalo, New York, if it could devise a system to control humidity. Buffalo Forge assigned the problem to Willis Carrier, a young engineer on minimum wage. And Carrier figured out an ingenious solution: if you circulated the air over coils that were chilled by compressed ammonia, you could maintain the humidity at 55 percent. The birth of the New South can be dated from that moment.

The earliest customers for Carrier's innovation were companies that made products that suffered from excessive moisture, such as textiles, flour, and razor blades, or that created lots of internal pollution, such as turning tobacco plants into cigarettes. Then, in 1906, Carrier began exploring a whole new market—"comfort." He targeted movie theaters as the ideal test ground for what he took to describing as his "weather maker." Historically movie theaters had been forced to shut down in the summer because they were even hotter than the outside world. Carrier understood that if you made them colder than the outside world, people would visit them for the cold air as well as the hot action. New York cinemas started to install air-conditioning in the 1910s. By 1938, an estimated 15,000 of the country's 16,251 cinemas had air-conditioning, and the "summer blockbuster" was becoming a feature of the entertainment calendar.

Southern companies gradually realized that air-conditioning changed the competitive landscape: once they had eliminated their biggest regional disadvantage, their energy-sapping climate, they could deploy their regional advantages, their relatively cheap and flexible workforce (an early government study found that typists became 24 percent more productive when transferred from a humid office to a cool one). In 1929, Carrier provided an entire office block, the Milam Building in San Antonio, Texas, with air-conditioning. Air-conditioning did more than make the workplace bearable. It also enabled the South to manufacture products sensitive to heat and humidity such as textiles, color printing, and pharmaceuticals, as well as to process food. One of Carrier's earliest clients was the American Tobacco Company's plant in Richmond, Virginia, which used air-conditioning to dispel the miasma of tobacco dust in the environment. Textile companies, particularly in the Carolinas, began to process cotton in the South rather than sending it north. Eventually a huge swath of northern companies, plagued by powerful trade unions, relocated production to the Sun Belt, turning a region that had once been deemed too hot for modern industry into the heart of the new economy.

The Great Migration of blacks from the South to northern industrial cities (notably New York and Chicago) also lessened the region's isolation. Hitherto the North and the South had been almost two separate countries when it came to their labor markets. Even after the abolition of slavery, most blacks moved only within the South, and then not very far. But the combination of the economic boom of the 1920s and the passage of restrictive immigration acts changed this: some 615,000 blacks, or 8 percent of the southern black labor force, moved north, many of them to fill jobs that would once have been filled by foreign immigrants. By 1925, Harlem had become "the greatest negro city in the world," in the words of James Weldon Johnson, the executive secretary of the NAACP, with 175,000 African Americans occupying twenty-five blocks of New York City.[25] Migration produced immediate economic benefits for the migrants: even though blacks earned less than whites, they still earned significantly more than they would have back home. It also released masses of cultural energy from the collision of southern black culture with northern opportunities in the form of the Harlem Renaissance and the rise of black jazz.

At the same time, the South saw the emergence of national companies. The most significant of these was Coca-Cola, which had been founded in the 1880s but emerged on the national scene in the 1920s under the overall guidance of Ernest Woodruff (who bought the company in 1919) and his son Robert Woodruff (who became CEO in 1923). Robert Woodruff regained control of the company from the bottlers who had held it hostage. He also demonstrated a genius for publicity, buying acres of advertising along America's highways and popularizing a slogan, "The pause that refreshes," that captured the mood of a harassed but energetic nation.

Clarence Saunders revolutionized the retail industry when he opened America's first self-service retail store in Memphis in 1916, the Piggly Wiggly. Hitherto, shops had kept all their goods behind the counter: shoppers told the staff what they wanted, waited while their purchases were bagged up, and then handed over their money.

Saunders came up with the idea of getting the customers to do the work. Customers entered through a turnstile, proceeded down a line of shelves laden with goods, putting what they wanted in a basket, and paid the cashier at the end of their journey. Saunders proclaimed that his labor-saving idea would "slay the demon of high prices."

By 1932, Saunders had an empire of 2,660 Piggly Wigglys across the country doing more than $180 million in business. He built a big house in Memphis—the Pink Palace—that now serves as a museum and contains a model of the first Piggly Wiggly store. But he didn't rest on his laurels: he fought off a speculative raid from Wall Street and experimented with a "shopping brain" that allowed shoppers to add up the cost of the goods as they went.

THE END OF AN ERA

The 1920s can sound a little like paradise before the fall—a world of technological wonders and material progress, of mass prosperity and broadening optimism. There were already a couple of serpents in this paradise, however.

One was consumer debt. The early years of the twentieth century saw the birth of a mass consumer credit industry as people got used to seeing their real income grow year in and year out. Department stores and mail-order companies played a leading role in sparking the revolution, extending loans to working-class people as well as the elite and evaluating people's creditworthiness on the basis of various bureaucratic formulas rather than personal knowledge. Other consumer companies adopted similar models. The car companies led the way, but dozens of other consumer businesses eventually followed, with companies establishing "easy payment" plans for pianos, radios, phonographs, vacuum cleaners, even jewelry and clothes. The size of household debt crept ever upward—from $4,200 in 1919 to $21,600 in 1929 (both in 2017 dollars).[26]

The biggest debt was on houses. In the period between 1890 and 1930, mortgages became much easier to obtain, with lower down payments and more options for second and even third mortgages. The value of outstanding mortgages soared from about $12 billion in 1919 to $43 billion in 1930—with many families availing themselves of those second and third mortgages.

But what happened if the merry-go-round of higher pay and more borrowing slowed for a while? Hubert Work, a Republican Party operative, unwittingly put his finger on the problem when he delivered a speech designed to scare voters away from the Democrats:

> Today a large amount of our people have more at stake than their profits or their jobs. They owe money on their homes, their radios, their automobiles, their electric washing machines and many other luxuries. They have laid wagers on continuing prosperity. Let there be a break in the endless chain of prosperity and this whole structure of personal credit will collapse and bury millions beneath it with hardship unprecedented in any former period of depression.[27]

Another serpent was America-first nationalism. The anti-immigration acts shut off the country from its long-standing supply of cheap labor. Annual immigration dropped from 1 percent of the native population for the period between 1909 and 1913 to 0.26 percent from 1925 to 1929. The growth rate of the population fell from 2.1 percent between 1870 and 1913 to 0.6 percent from 1926 to 1945. The reduction in immigration not only reduced the supply of labor (making it easier for trade unions to organize) but also reduced the long-term demand for houses. This made it more difficult to sell the houses that had been built in such numbers during the credit boom.

But why bother to worry about these serpents? The American growth machine was humming, America's potential rivals were tearing themselves apart, and in 1928, America elected a new president who looked eminently qualified to act as a national snake charmer.

Herbert Hoover had spent his life amassing perhaps the best résumé of any new president to date, as a mining engineer, international businessman, and star member of America's great and good. John Maynard Keynes commended his "knowledge, magnanimity, and distinterestedness." Sherwood Anderson noted that he had "never known failure." As head of food relief during and after the Great War, he had saved as many as 2 million people from starvation; as secretary of commerce under Harding and Coolidge, he had been a powerful force in both administrations—"secretary of everything," as one newspaper called him; "secretary of commerce and undersecretary of all the other departments," as a Washington wag put it.[28] He did invaluable work improving the operation of America's internal market by standardizing the sizes for the parts of all machines. Adding to that, he was also a literary prodigy: his *American Individualism* (1922) is one of the best books on America's defining trait and his *Fishing for Fun and to Wash Your Soul* (1963) is a fine meditation on that very civilized pastime.

Hoover was a subscriber to an interventionist brand of Republicanism, which emphasized the party's responsibility to keep nudging the economy in the right direction. "The time when the employer could ride roughshod over his labor is disappearing with the doctrine of 'laissez-faire' on which it is founded," he wrote in 1919.[29] He had an almost Fabian belief in the power of science, planning, and efficiency, a belief that colored his personal life as well as his approach to government. "It has been no part of mine to build castles of the future," he reflected, "but rather to measure the experiments, the actions, and the forces of men through the cold and uninspiring microscope of fact, statistics and performance." Where he broke with the Fabians was in the belief that intervention should be the work of business's friends rather than its enemies. He believed in using the power of government to make business work better—for example, by simplifying rules and by smoothing out the business cycle. One of Hoover's first acts on becoming president was to draw up an ambitious plan to recruit the best brains in the country to compile a body of knowledge and a plan of action to guide the country in "the next phase of the nation's development." "In a society of temperate, industrious, unspectacular beavers," *Time* magazine commented, "such a beaver-man would make an ideal King-beaver."

Yet even Hoover's abilities were soon to be tested beyond breaking point. The United States had enjoyed the bright side of creative destruction with three decades of barely punctuated economic growth culminating in seven years of unprecedented prosperity. It was about to experience the dark side.

Seven

THE GREAT DEPRESSION

———◆———

I N STRAIGHTFORWARD GEOGRAPHIC TERMS the New York Stock
Exchange could hardly be more peripheral to the vast American
landmass: it nestles on the far tip of Manhattan Island just south
of the wall that the first Dutch settlers built to protect themselves
from the Native American population. In economic terms, however,
it constitutes the beating heart of American capitalism: it pumps
credit through a continent-size economy (and far beyond) and regis-
ters the health of the entire American enterprise. Whether you are in
the business of making toothpaste in Cincinnati, cars in Detroit, or
computers in Silicon Valley, you probably trade your shares on the
New York Stock Exchange.

Wall Street first established itself at the heart of the U.S. economy
in the 1920s. The number of brokerage offices—people who sold
stocks to retail customers—jumped from 706 in 1925 to 1,658 in late
1929. Trading volume increased from 1.7 million shares a day in 1925
to 3.5 million in 1928 and 4.1 million in mid-October 1929. Six times
as much common stock was issued in 1929 as in 1927. The Street was
awash in credit. New investors could buy on 25 percent margin—that

is, borrowing 75 percent of the purchase price. Regular customers could buy on 10 percent margin.[1]

Some of the wisest people in the country applauded the bull market. In 1927, John Raskob, one of the country's leading financiers, wrote an article in *Ladies' Home Journal*, "Everybody Ought to Be Rich," advising people of modest means to park their savings in the stock market.[2] A year later, Irving Fisher, one of the country's most respected economists, declared that "stock prices have reached what looks like a permanent high plateau."

Others were more skeptical: as the market took off in 1927, the commerce secretary, Herbert Hoover, condemned the "orgy of mad speculation" on Wall Street and started to explore ways of closing it down.[3] The orgy proved more difficult to stop than to start. Giant corporations diverted a growing share of their profits from productive investment to stock market speculation. New investors continued to buy on margin (the story has it that Joseph Kennedy sold all his stocks in July 1928 when a shoeblack insisted on regaling him with inside tips). Money flooded in from abroad as Wall Street offered better returns than anything else going. The thirty-stock Dow Jones Industrial Average—the prevalent market measure at the time—leapt from 191 in early 1928 to 381 on September 1, 1929.

At last the music stopped. In October, the market fell by 37 percent. People who had bought on margin were wiped out. Many professional investors were ruined. Images of stockbrokers jumping out of windows were seared on the national consciousness.

For a while it looked as if the Great Crash might be one of those freakish comets that streak across the sky every now and again without leaving a trace. Stock ownership was still confined to a minority of the population.[4] Not a single major company or bank collapsed in the rout. By April 1930, the Dow Jones Industrial Average was back to where it had been at the start of 1929—that is, roughly double the level it had been in 1926. The *New York Times* breezily declared that the most important news story of 1929 had been Admiral Byrd's expedition to the South Pole.[5]

But, as our chart below makes clear, the bounce on Wall Street was short-lived and the fall resumed. The stock market continued to plunge until, at its bottom in 1932, stocks were worth a mere 11 percent of their high-water mark and Wall Street was reduced to a ghost town. Two thousand investment houses went out of business. The price of a Big Board seat fell from $550,000 before the crash to $68,000. Securities firms declared "apple days"—unpaid vacation days each month to allow destitute brokers to go out and supplement their income by selling apples on the sidewalks. The Empire State Building, which John Raskob had commissioned in 1929 as a

DOW JONES INDUSTRIAL AVERAGE

PLOTTED MONTHLY, JAN 1921 – DEC 1940

monument to "the American way of life that allowed a poor boy to make his fortune on Wall Street,"[6] was nicknamed the "Empty State Building."[7] The Union League Club had a room wallpapered with worthless stock certificates.

Historians have questioned the extent to which the Wall Street crash caused the Great Depression. One leading business historian has gone so far as to argue that "no causal relationship between the two events of late October 1929 and the Great Depression has ever been shown." This is unconvincing. Econometric analysis suggests that, by itself, change in asset prices has a significant effect on GDP, accounting for nearly 10 percent of GDP growth in the postwar years.[8] Given that stock and asset holdings relative to GDP were roughly the same in the years 1927 to 1932 as in the postwar years, the collapse of the stock market must have had a significant "wealth effect." The 2008 crisis was another reminder that financial crises impose damage on the general economy if they are accompanied by toxic assets that are highly leveraged.[9] In the 1920s stocks provided the toxic assets and call money funded by brokers' loans provided the leverage. The financial crisis produced contagious defaults that rippled through the rest of the economy. General economic activity declined from late 1929 to the first few months of 1933. By 1932, industrial production, real GDP, and prices had declined by 46 percent, 25 percent, and 24 percent, respectively, from their 1929 levels. Stockholders saw much of the value of their assets evaporate. Businesses reduced their investment from $13 billion in 1929 to less than $4 billion in 1933.

Workers saw their jobs go up in smoke. In March 1933, hundreds of thousands of unemployed workers, unable to get either jobs or public assistance, marched through New York City, Detroit, Washington, D.C., San Francisco, and other cities.

Contraction in one industry routinely produced contraction in another. The car industry reduced its production of cars by two-thirds between 1929 and 1933. That in turn produced a decline in demand for steel, which produced a decline in demand for ore and coal. Real private investment in buildings (residential and nonresidential) fell by 75 percent. That in turn produced a decline in demand for bricks, mortar, nails, logs, and everything that goes into making a building. Again and again a decline in production meant a decline in demand for labor, which spread throughout the economy: less construction not only meant less demand for the people who put buildings together, such as plumbers and roofers, but also the people who supplied the raw materials, such as loggers, and the people like Babbitt who sold the finished houses.

Unemployment was at its most severe among men in the great industrial centers. In Cleveland, Ohio, the unemployment rate reached 50 percent in 1933, and in Toledo, Ohio, 80 percent. Edmund Wilson, one of the era's best-known writers, described what he found in Chicago, that hog butcher to the world, on a visit in 1932. He came across an old Polish immigrant "dying of a tumor, with no heat in the house, on a cold day." He visited a flophouse, where "a great deal of TB" and "spinal meningitis" had gotten out of hand and broken "nine backs on the rack." Hundreds of people descended on one garbage dump when the garbage truck delivered its load and dug in "with sticks and hands." The foragers even seized spoiled meat and "cut out the worst parts" or sprinkled them with soda. One widowed housekeeper removed her glasses before picking up the meat "so she would not be able to see the maggots."[10]

The land of plenty was transformed into a land of plight, the land of opportunity into a land of broken dreams. The despair of the decade was memorialized in a succession of sometimes brilliant novels: Tom Kromer's *Waiting for Nothing* (1935), Edward Anderson's *Hun-*

gry Men (1935), John Dos Passos's *U.S.A.* (1930–36), and John Steinbeck's *The Grapes of Wrath* (1939). It was also inscribed in its demography. The country's population increased by 7 percent in the 1930s, compared with 16 percent in the 1920s. Armies of people, including the Joads in *The Grapes of Wrath*, moved from hard-hit areas such as the Great Plains and the South to California, the North, or even abroad. In 1932 to 1935, for the first time in American history, more people left the country than arrived.

The Depression was deeper than anything comparable countries had experienced: at its height, about a quarter of the workforce was unemployed. It was also longer: the Depression ground on for more than twelve long years and the economy did not really return to its full productive capacity until the buildup of the World War II years (1941–45). It is arguable that America didn't suffer from one Great Depression but from two Depressions interrupted by a weak recovery. The first Depression lasted for forty-three months from August 1929 to March 1933. The second lasted for thirteen months from May 1937 to June 1938. The intervening recovery sagged: after six years of recovery, real output remained 25 percent below the historical trend, the number of private hours being worked was only slightly higher than their 1933 trough, and the unemployment rate was 11 percent.[11]

Thereafter, the economy plunged downward once again as the country was gripped by what contemporaries called "the depression within a depression," or, more pointedly, "the Roosevelt recession." Unemployment in 1939 was higher than it had been in 1931, before Roosevelt became president. It was also significantly higher than the 11.4 percent average for the world's sixteen biggest industrial economies. Testifying before the House Ways and Means Committee on May 9, 1939, Henry Morgenthau, who was not only FDR's treasury secretary but also his close friend and near neighbor in upstate New York, came close to suggesting that the New Deal had been a failure:

We have tried spending money. We are spending more than we have ever spent before and it does not work. . . . I want to see people get a job. I want to see people get enough to eat. We have never made good on our promises. . . . I say after eight years of this Administration we have just as much unemployment as when we started. . . . And an enormous debt to boot![12]

WHAT CAUSED THE GREAT DEPRESSION?

Herbert Hoover offered one answer to this question in the opening of his *Memoirs:* "In the large sense the primary cause of the Great Depression was the war of 1914–18." Hoover focused on the way that the Versailles Treaty compounded the terrible destruction of the war by burdening the Allies with mountainous debts and Germany with unrealistic reparations payments. From 1916 to 1919, the United States saw its national debt balloon from $1.2 billion to $25 billion. Almost half that debt consisted of funding loans to the Allies, who struggled to repay them even as they extracted as much money as they could from Germany in reparations. In the years 1929 to 1932, almost all the Allies repudiated their debts (Finland was an honorable exception), and America responded by embracing protectionism.

The story is actually much bigger than this. The Depression was the consequence of the shattering of a stable world order, underpinned by fixed gold-standard-linked exchange rates, and by the war and the failure of the Great Powers to adjust to a changed distribution of economic and financial power and to put a sustainable new system in its place.

Before the war, the global economic order was centered on London and enforced by the Bank of England through the gold standard. Britain was easily the world's leading financial power: two-thirds of the trade credit that kept goods flowing around the world, or about $500 million a year, passed through London.[13] The combination of Britain's overwhelming economic preeminence and the British elite's adamantine commitment to its global role meant that the system worked reasonably smoothly. The British were exceedingly good at their job, stepping in swiftly and decisively to make sure that the system adjusted. Other European powers—and particularly gold-rich France—played their part in tackling problems: when Barings Bank almost collapsed in 1890, thanks to unwise loans to Argentina, threatening to destabilize the London financial markets, the central banks of France and Russia lent money to the Bank of England and the crisis was averted. The mere knowledge that the Bank of England could call upon such large sums of money and deploy them with an expert hand was enough to reassure the markets. In Keynes's phrase, Britain was "the conductor of the international orchestra."

The First World War hastened the shift in the center of power from Europe (and Britain) to the United States. This change was already well advanced before the war. But the fact that the European powers spent so much more of their blood and treasure on the war than the United States sent it into overdrive. Before the war, four European industrial nations combined—Britain, Germany, France, and Belgium—produced substantially more than the United States. By the late 1920s, the United States outproduced the Europeans by half. Before the war, America was a net importer of capital: $2.2 billion in 1914, for example. After the war, it was a net exporter: $6.4 billion in 1919. The Allied powers ended the war owing the U.S. Treasury $12 billion in war debt, with Britain owing $5 billion and France owing $4 billion. America consolidated its global leadership by accumulating such a large proportion of the world's gold that Liaquat Ahamed likened it, in *Lords of Finance*, to a poker player who has accumulated such a huge mound of chips that the game breaks down.[14]

U.S. OFFICIAL GOLD RESERVES
1860 – 2016

With its gold supplies virtually depleted and its economy crippled, Britain was now too weak to play the role of the conductor of the international order. The question was whether the United States could mount the dais.

Working against this were European pride and American irresponsibility. The major European powers all regarded returning to the gold standard (which they had abandoned during the war) as one of their first items of business. But they failed to adjust their exchange rate to reflect their diminished economic power. The most calamitous manifestation of this was the decision by Winston Churchill, who was then chancellor of the exchequer, to return Britain to the gold standard at $4.86 per pound sterling or £4.25 per troy ounce of gold, the level that it had been before the Great War shattered European civilization—indeed, the level that it had been when America declared independence. The result of the pound's overvaluation was a triple disaster for Britain. The real economy suffered because Britain at its old exchange rate was uncompetitive, leading to unnecessary agonies as industry was squeezed, export industries such as coal mining contracted, unemployment soared, and the trade unions organized a general strike. In 1931, with 22 percent of the workforce unemployed, the British government, with its gold reserves rapidly depleting, took sterling off the gold standard for the first time in peacetime since Sir Isaac Newton established the gold parity in 1717. The pound fell by more than a third against the dollar (from $4.86 to $3.25), forcing other countries to follow suit, first the Scandinavian and Baltic states, with their close ties to the British market, then Japan, then much of Latin America.

For all Keynes's adumbrations against the "barbarous relic," the problem was not the gold standard in the abstract but the decision by almost all the developed world to fix their postwar currencies against the dollar at the prewar noncompetitive exchange rates, despite significant costs of storage and loss of interest. The fetters that doomed the international economy were not Keynes's fetters of gold but the fetters of pride. The world's major central banks to this day value gold as a reserve currency and, where appropriate, as a medium of exchange. At the end of 2017, the United States held 262 million ounces of gold and the central banks of the world's major countries (including the International Monetary Fund and the Bank for International Settlements) held 815 million ounces. Even Russia, which as part of the USSR eschewed the capitalist totem and refused to hold gold, has, since the USSR was disbanded in 1991, accumulated 59 million ounces of gold. Officially Communist China also holds 59 million ounces of Keynes's relic.

At the same time, America failed to take over Britain's role as the conductor of the international orchestra. Britain had been confident of its hegemonic role in the world. America was unsure of its new role. Some global-minded Americans saw that America's self-interest dictated that it should take a more responsible role in leading world affairs. Woodrow Wilson maintained that Europe could not be successfully rebuilt without the active participation of the United States. Thomas Lamont, the de facto head of J. P. Morgan, argued that America was entangled in the global economy through a complex web of trade and finance.

These voices were counterbalanced by isolationists, who thought that America should have little to do with the Old World and its debts, antagonisms, and wars. Warren Harding became so nervous of isolationist opinion that he refused to send official delegates to various global banking conferences, sending J. P. Morgan bankers to observe in a private capacity instead. Taking over the role of conductor would have proved difficult enough at the best of times given the complexity of the situation. It proved impossible when so many of your own citizens were determined to drag you off the dais.

One of the worst examples of America's irresponsibility was the Tariff Act of 1930, which increased tariff rates by an average of 18 percent on 900 manufactured goods and 575 agricultural products.[15] The act has become a symbol of economic idiocy. Sixty-three years later, in a television debate on the North American Free Trade Agreement, Al Gore, then vice-president, presented Ross Perot with a framed photograph of the act's sponsors, Willis Hawley, a congressman from Oregon, and Reed Smoot, a senator from Utah. It is now fashionable among some economic historians to question the extent to which the act was a cause of the Great Depression. America's tariffs had been high since the founding of the republic. The Fordney-McCumber Tariff Act of 1922 had already raised them further. Smoot-Hawley raised the average rate on dutiable goods from 40 percent to 48 percent, implying a price increase of 8 percent over a wide range of goods. Other countries had started to raise their own tariffs before Smoot-Hawley. The volume of American imports had already dropped by 15 percent in the year before the act was passed. Yet the act was a prime example of the more general problem of America's failure to take over Britain's role as a leader of the global trading order.

Smoot-Hawley was another example of the weakness of economic reason when confronted with special interests. Irving Fisher organized a petition of 1,028 economists against the act and 238 of the country's 324 newspapers urged Congress not to pass it. Walter Lippmann, America's preeminent columnist, described the tariff as "a wretched and mischievous product of stupidity and greed." George Norris, a Republican senator from Nebraska, described the act as "protectionism run perfectly mad." Thomas Lamont "almost went down on [his] knees to beg Herbert Hoover to veto the asinine Hawley-Smoot Tariff." By September 1929, twenty-three trading partners had lodged their concerns about the prospect of higher tariffs.

The American public proved admirably enlightened, siding, for the most part, with the experts rather than the special interests: the president's correspondence secretary informed him that "there has seldom been in this country such a rising tide of protest as has been aroused by the tariff bill."[16] Yet despite warnings by experts and complaints by ordinary citizens, the act got progressively worse as it ground its way through the political sausage-making machine. The bill began life as a relatively modest plan to help American farmers who had faced hard times since the early 1920s. Farmers demanded that agriculture should be given the same sort of protection as industry, where tariffs were on average twice as high. To many of its supporters, "tariff equality" meant reducing industrial duties as well as raising agricultural ones. "But so soon as ever the tariff schedules were cast into the melting-pot of revision," the *Economist* wrote at the time, "logrollers and politicians set to work stirring with all their might." The tariff's critics dubbed the bill the "Grundy tariff," after Joseph Grundy, a Republican senator from Pennsylvania and president of the Pennsylvania Manufacturers' Association, who said that anyone who made campaign contributions was entitled to higher tariffs in return. Vested interests pushed for juicier pork. Responsible politicians backed down. And eventually Herbert Hoover found himself using six gold pens to sign a monstrosity of an act that laid out specific duties for 3,300 items.

The act quickly provoked retaliation. The League of Nations (which America had not joined, despite Woodrow Wilson's best efforts) had floated the idea of a "tariff truce" in order to ward off the growing global recession. Smoot-Hawley helped to turn a truce into a war. Foreign countries responded with a wide range of tools (tariffs, import quotas, exchange controls) that reduced global trade. Furious about tariffs on their watches, for example, the Swiss imposed tariffs on American typewriters, cars, and radios. Germany declared a policy of national self-sufficiency (with the implicit threat that a self-sufficient Germany would also be an expansionist Germany). Even Britain, which had championed free trade since the repeal of the Corn Laws in 1846, embraced protectionism in February 1932, by raising tariffs and providing special preferences for the empire and a few favored trading partners. The volume of global business shrunk from some $36 billion of traffic in 1929 to about $12 billion by 1932.[17]

The Depression's tendency to feed on itself was reinforced by what Irving Fisher called "debt deflation." The explosion of lending in the 1920s had worked very well so long as people earned a regular (and rising) income. The combination of rising unemployment and stagnating (or falling) real incomes magnified economic problems. Society's debt obligations rose while its ability to meet those obligations declined. Deflation forced debtors to reduce consumption, leading to more declines in prices. Declines in prices led to general economic contraction. By the beginning of 1934, more than a third of homeowners in the average American city were behind in their mortgage payments.

Debt deflation also amplified the malign effects of tariffs in general and Smoot-Hawley's new tariffs in particular. Tariffs were levied on the volume of imports (so many cents per pound, say) rather than value. So as deflation took hold after 1929, effective tariff rates climbed, discouraging imports. By 1932, the average American tariff on dutiable imports was 59 percent, higher than it had ever been before except for a brief moment in 1830. If the Tariff Act raised duties by 20 percent, deflation accounted for half as much again. Global trade collapsed. In 1932, U.S. imports and exports were both one-third of what they had been in 1929.

Debt deflation was pronounced in agriculture. American farmers had thrived as never before during the Great War because their European competitors were frequently unable to operate. Agricultural prices doubled during the war as foreign demand surged, and farmers borrowed heavily in order to invest in agricultural machinery or reclaim marginal land. When farm prices failed to collapse after the war, as expected, farmers engaged in another round of investment and speculation. Then the climate changed. The recovery of European agriculture reduced demand for American products. But agricultural cycles being what they are, farmers couldn't change their strategy to cope with changing conditions. A cycle of debt deflation began to set in. Falling prices set off a succession of crises: overborrowed farmers could not pay back their loans; rural banks collapsed as their customers defaulted; and overcultivated marginal land produced dust bowls. Foreclosures rose from 3 percent of farms between 1913 and 1920 to 11 percent between 1921 and 1925 to 18 percent between 1926 and 1929. By 1933, nearly half of America's farmers were behind in their mortgage payments.

America's quirky banking system added fuel to the fire. The rapid growth in the demand for banking services created a highly fragmented and dismally organized system. Canada had four national banks, each with branches across the land and each with deep pockets, widely spread shareholders, and diversified customers.[18] America had some 25,000 mostly undercapitalized banks, regulated by fifty-two different regulatory regimes, and dependent on the vagaries of local economies. Bank failure was common even in good times: in the 1920s, banks failed at a rate of well over 500 a year. Between 1929 and 1933, 40 percent of the nation's banks (9,460) went bankrupt. In 1930, the Bank of the United States (which owed its name to clever marketing rather than to any official status) collapsed in the biggest bank failure in U.S. history to that date, leaving some $200 million in depositors' funds frozen.[19] In 1932, the problem became even larger: in October, Nevada's governor shut the state's banks in order to stop the wildfire from spreading, and thereafter thirty-eight states held "bank holidays."

An oddity in America's political system added yet more fuel. The Founders had created more than a three-month gap between the presidential election in November and the new president taking office in March in order to give presidents enough time to make the arduous journey from their homes to the nation's capital. This convention still held in 1932 despite the arrival of trains, motorcars, and indeed airplanes (the date was moved to January with the passing of the Twentieth Amendment in January 1933). America was consequently left without a functioning president between Hoover's humiliating defeat in November 1932, when he lost all but two states and with it any legitimacy he had preserved after the crash, and Roosevelt's assumption of the office in March. Hoover refused to take new initiatives without Roosevelt's cooperation. Roosevelt preferred to wait until he was in power in his own right. And the two men fell into a habit of glowering hostility: Hoover didn't speak a word to Roosevelt as they proceeded in a carriage to the inauguration. With Washington paralyzed, banks collapsed, businesses folded, and fear fructified.

The Federal Reserve also performed poorly. There was only one able banker on the board, Benjamin Strong, the president of the New York Federal Reserve Bank, and he died in 1928. The other board members were, in John Kenneth Galbraith's phrase, "startlingly incompetent": Daniel Crissinger, the chairman of the Federal Reserve Board from 1923 to 1927, was a minor businessman and failed congressman who owed his position to his boyhood friendship with Warren Harding.[20] The Federal Reserve was still learning on the job. The Fed hit on its most powerful tool for setting monetary policy, Federal Reserve Open Market policy, by accident. After the First World War, some newly organized Federal Reserve district banks were transacting so little business with other banks that policy makers feared that they would not be able to produce enough revenue to meet their contemplated expenses. So in the first half of 1922, Reserve banks stepped up their purchase of interest-earning government securities to improve their earnings position. This had the unanticipated effect of boosting the reserves of commercial banks across the country, forcing short-term interest rates lower. The Fed soon realized that it had an incredibly powerful tool on its hands: by purchasing securities on the open market it could ease credit conditions and interest rates and, pari passu, by selling securities it could tighten credit conditions by raising rates. In May 1922, the Fed decided to give the Federal Reserve Bank of New York responsibility for coordinating such investment of the remaining twelve Reserve banks. A few months later, it formed what is now called the Federal Open Market Committee (FOMC).

Nonetheless, the FOMC was frequently paralyzed by internal divisions. The Fed fueled the speculative frenzy of 1926–28 by keeping interest rates too low in order to sustain the value of the pound sterling by encouraging a flow of capital into Britain. It then overcompensated by raising interest rates four times in 1928 and 1929, from 3.5 percent to 6 percent, making it harder for businesspeople to borrow to invest. The Fed also contributed to the problem of bank failures by neglecting to create firewalls—for example, when the Bank of the United States went bankrupt in December 1930. Milton Friedman and Anna Schwartz demonstrate, in their monumental *Monetary History of the United States* (1963), that banking failures reduced the stock of money in circulation by over a third. The Fed then made a desperate situation still worse in the autumn of 1931 by sharply raising interest rates in order to preserve the value of the dollar.

In reflecting on this catalogue of errors, it is important to make allowance for circumstances. Policy makers still had only a hazy picture of the national economy. It took the shock of the Great Depression itself to persuade the government to employ Simon Kuznets and the National Bureau of Economic Research to prepare a comprehensive set of national income accounts. The world had never experienced anything like the Great Depression before: policy makers were sailing into a global storm without a map to guide them. At first they didn't know how bad it was going to get. A year after the crash, many Americans thought that they were in the midst of a usual, if painful, downturn—not as bad, surely, as the sudden contraction of 1920. There was plenty of good news to weigh against the bad: the 1929 unemployment rate had been 2.9 percent, one of the lowest ever; the new economy of radio, movies, and airplanes was booming; corporate profits were strong.

When it became clear that America was heading into an unprecedented storm, they didn't have a clear understanding of how the various segments of the economy interacted. To be sure, Wesley Clair Mitchell had spelled out how business cycles functioned in 1913. But that was scarcely adequate to penetrate the confusing fog of the crash of 1929. The only depression that remotely rivaled the Great Depression in severity and length was the depression of 1893. But it was still possible in those days of small government and fatalistic politics for the government to stand pat and let creative destruction take its course. By the 1930s, people expected the government to "do something" but didn't know what that "something" should be. The federal government was tiny: total expenditures in 1929 amounted to just $3.1 billion, or 3 percent of GDP. The Federal Reserve was only fifteen years old in 1929 and was still very much feeling its way. Academic economists had little to say about dealing with depressions. And even if they had known what to do, it's not clear that they would have had the machinery to make much of a difference in the time available.

NOT RISING TO THE CHALLENGE

The Great Depression's most prominent victim as it tightened its grip on the economy was Herbert Hoover: a president who had come into office as lauded as almost any in American history saw his reputation wither and die. Roosevelt's hatchet men, some of the most ruthless in the business, dubbed the Depression the "Hoover Depression," the shantytowns of the homeless that sprang up in so many American cities "Hoovervilles," and the newspapers that the homeless used to cover themselves at night "Hoover blankets."[21] Subsequent historians have branded Hoover a do-nothing Republican.

This accusation of do-nothingism is twaddle. There were certainly Republicans who believed in doing nothing: Andrew Mellon, the treasury secretary whom Hoover inherited from Coolidge, reportedly believed that the best solution to the Depression was to engage in wholesale liquidation:

> Liquidate labor, liquidate stocks, liquidate farmers, liquidate real estate. . . . It will purge the rottenness of the system. High costs of living and high living will come down. People will work harder, live a more moral life. Values will be adjusted, and enterprising people will pick up from less competent people.

Hoover was not one of them—indeed he lambasted Mellon's presumed liquidationist ideas in his memoirs and claimed credit for ignoring them. He believed firmly that modern capitalist economies needed the guidance of an activist government. Hoover met with the Federal Reserve to discuss the stock-market bubble just two days after his inauguration and he periodically backed several different ways of dealing with it, from raising interest rates to discouraging buying on margin. The first president to have a telephone on his desk, he often started the day by ringing up Thomas Lamont at J. P. Morgan to keep track of the market.[22] He reacted swiftly to the slowing of the economy by proposing a mixture of tax cuts and investment in infrastructure. He brought business leaders to the White House and extracted pledges to maintain wages and thus avert an erosion of purchasing power: Henry Ford, one of the most prominent guests at the White House, immediately cut car prices and boosted workers' wages to seven dollars a day.

Hoover's problem was that he had little appreciation of the art of politics. Even his friends worried that he was "too much of a machine." His enemies vilified him as cold and heartless. He didn't know how to tickle people's egos. He didn't know how to charge his ideas with rhetorical power. He didn't understand, in short, that you need to govern in poetry as well as prose.

Some politicians rise to the challenge of difficult times. Hoover seemed to shrink. He captured the headlines with a few bizarre statements—for example, he proclaimed, wearing his trademark funereal expression, that the best way to cure the Depression was for everyone to have a laugh, and even approached Will Rogers about writing a Depression-destroying joke. Never a people person, he retreated into a dour shell. Never a master of inspiration, he retreated into dull technocracy. Toward the end he was a visibly broken man, his eyes bloodshot, the color drained from his face, working at his desk from dawn to dusk but never able to go out among the people or inspire the nation.

Here his successor was the opposite—one of the great politicians of the democratic era. FDR was the American equivalent of a British aristocrat: brought up on a rambling estate in the Hudson Valley and educated at Groton and Harvard, he was utterly convinced of his right to rule and his abilities to execute that right. But like Winston Churchill on the other side of the Atlantic, he was an aristocrat with a common touch.

Where Hoover was dour, Roosevelt was sunny. Where Hoover gave way to despair, Roosevelt was an irrepressible optimist: for him every cloud had a silver lining and every problem had a solution. Roosevelt was the embodiment of Hamilton's principle, in Federalist No. 70, that "energy in the executive is a leading character in the definition of good government." He instinctively understood that politically it was better to do something—even if it was the wrong thing—than to stand pat and wait for times to get better. "The country needs and, unless I mistake its temper, the country demands bold, persistent experimentation," he declared in a speech at Oglethorpe University on May 22, 1932. His ideas were frequently ad hoc, contradictory, and ill thought out—Henry Stimson, the secretary of war, said that following his train of thought was "very much like

chasing a vagrant beam of sunshine around an empty room."[23] He
made numerous mistakes. One of his leading policies—the National
Industrial Recovery Act—was a failure. Nevertheless, he realized that
a problem-solving people needed a leader who would commit himself wholeheartedly to action and experiment.

No president has made better use of the bully pulpit. FDR delivered a succession of uplifting speeches—most notably his inaugural
address, in which he declared that Americans had nothing to fear but
fear itself. He grasped the power of the radio to bring him closer to
the people. Throughout his presidency he delivered a succession of
fifteen-minute fireside chats, which simultaneously reassured a nervous public and normalized radical policies. Presidents had gotten
into the habit of addressing the public like Roman senators addressing the senate (a habit that was revived by John F. Kennedy in his
"Ask not" inaugural address). FDR talked to the people as if he were
an affable uncle dropping by for a visit. "I tried to picture a mason at
work on a new building, a girl behind a counter, a farmer in his field,"
he said.

Roosevelt surrounded himself with a group of intellectuals who
were confident that they understood what ailed America and how to
fix it. These were the Brain Trusters: a group of liberal academics and
lawyers who gathered around FDR in the late 1920s and early 1930s.
"Instead of a kitchen, or a tennis cabinet, he preferred to lean on a cap
and gown cabinet," one profile opined. The founding member of the
cap and gown cabinet was Raymond Moley, a professor of law at Columbia University. Other prominent members included Adolf Berle,
a professor at Columbia Law School and coauthor of *The Modern
Corporation and Private Property* (1932), and Rexford Tugwell, a Columbia University economist. The heirs to the Progressive intellectuals of the early twentieth century, they took all the virtues (or vices)

of the Progressives to extremes. They believed above all in the power of government. Tugwell had returned from a trip to study agriculture in Europe and the Soviet Union convinced that government planning was the secret ingredient of successful farming (his critics dubbed him "Rex the Red" or "the Lenin of the New Deal"). Berle's core argument in *The Modern Corporation* was that, if left unregulated by government, modern corporations represented a major threat to the public good.[24]

The Progressives had been split down the middle over the question of big business. Louis Brandeis thought that "bigness" was in itself a curse. His solution was to use the power of government to break up concentrations of power and increase competition. Others thought that concentration was an index of efficiency and that the trick was to direct concentration to the public good. In *Concentration and Control* (1912), Charles Van Hise, the president of the University of Wisconsin, argued that America had entered a post-laissez-faire age in which business was destined to get ever bigger. There was nothing wrong with such "concentration," he argued, so long as it was balanced by government "control." The Brain Trusters sided emphatically with the pro-bigness argument—indeed, they treated Van Hise as a prophet and *Concentration and Control* as a bible. They saw the country's industrial conglomerations as representing a threat to both prosperity and freedom. Too much wealth in the hands of a few industrialists reduced demand and threatened to deprive business of its consumers, and too much power in the hands of the same industrialists undermined democracy, they asserted; but leaven concentration with control in the form of regulations and a potential vice is transformed into a virtue. America, Van Hise argued, needed to summon the power of big government to counterbalance the power of big business.[25]

MAKING HISTORY

FDR was sworn into office at noon on March 4, 1933. That day, the banking system, the vital lubricant of a capitalist economy, was in a state of collapse. According to Hoover's comptroller of the currency, "the straw that broke the camel's back" was provided by the governor of Michigan's decision to declare a statewide bank holiday on February 14, 1933. Panic ensued. Currency withdrawals rose sharply from February 15 to March 8, and the amount of currency in circulation rose by almost $2 billion. Gold withdrawals from the Federal Reserve Bank of New York surged, reducing the Fed's gold balance far below the statutorily required 40 percent of Federal Reserve notes to just 24 percent (the Fed then suspended the gold reserve requirements). As of the close of business on March 4, 1933, the banks in thirty-five of the forty-eight states had declared bank holidays, according to an estimate by Allan Meltzer of Carnegie Mellon University. On March 5, FDR, as his first order of business, closed all banks under an obscure federal mandate.

Closing banks was easier than reopening them again without triggering a resumption of bank runs. FDR discovered that his incoming administration didn't have the capability to pull off this complicated task. Fortunately, Hoover's team, led by the treasury secretary, Ogden Mills, and including Eugene Meyer, the chairman of the Federal Reserve, had devised a clever plan during its last year in office to reopen the banks without creating disruption: divide the banks into three classes according to their financial health; screen them thoroughly; and then restore them to regular operations in stages. Class A banks would open first. Class B banks would receive loans from the Federal Reserve to ensure their liquidity and open second. Class C banks would either obtain special assistance, including capital infusions in return for stock issues if necessary, or else be liquidated. FDR had, unfortunately, refused to cosign Hoover's program for reforming the banks prior to his inauguration, but nevertheless the first thing he did on assuming office was to induce the Congress to pass the Emergency Banking Act. The act gave FDR the power to offer 100 percent guarantees for bank deposits, a point that the president hammered home in his first Fireside Chat, on March 12, a tour de force in which he explained the financial situation so well, Will Rogers quipped, that even a banker could understand it.[26] Over the next few months, savers transferred billions of dollars of cash and gold from under their "mattresses" back into banks.

FDR then created a Federal Bank Deposit Corporation (FIDC, later FDIC) that guaranteed individual bank deposits up to five thousand dollars (a figure that has subsequently been raised many times). The bank runs that had once been such a conspicuous feature of capitalism now became a rarity. He also reformed the securities industry by creating the Securities and Exchange Commission and forcing companies to publish detailed information, such as their balance sheets, profit and loss statements, and the names of their directors. Hitherto Wall Street had been dominated by a handful of insiders such as J. P. Morgan, who had privileged access to information. Henceforth information was much more widely available and smaller investors could have an even chance. He also wrestled primary control of trade policy from Congress and lodged it in the White House. That reduced the power of Congress to engage in "logrolling" over trade, whereby different blocks of congressmen voted to protect each other's pet industries: Louisiana sugar growers voting in favor of Iowa potato growers, and so on.

While trying to fix the wiring of capitalism FDR devoted his first hundred days to putting people back to work. He proposed a Civilian Conservation Corps (CCC) to employ a quarter of a million young men in forestry, flood control, and beautification projects. He also proposed a Federal Emergency Relief Administration (FERA) to allocate federal unemployment assistance to the states. He engaged in bold regional development, most notably creating the Tennessee Valley Authority (TVA), to spur economic development in one of the country's most backward regions.

FDR completed his hundred days with what he regarded as "the most important and far-reaching legislation ever enacted by the American Congress"—the National Industrial Recovery Act. NIRA proposed federal regulation of maximum hours and minimum wages in selected industries and—more radical still—provided workers with the right to unionize and strike. The bill also called for the creation of two new organizations, the National Recovery Administration (NRA) and the Public Works Administration (PWA). The NRA was responsible for implementing a vast process of government-sponsored cartelization: regulating production in entire industries and raising prices and wages according to government fiat. The NRA not only suspended America's antitrust laws, it essentially organized the country's industry into a network of government-mandated trusts: an astonishing break with American tradition. The PWA created an ambitious public construction program. When he signed the final bills that emerged from Capitol Hill on June 16, FDR remarked rightly if a little immodestly that "more history is being made today than in [any] one day of our national life."[27]

The NRA's twin for rural America was the Agricultural Adjustment Act, which was supposed to prevent "overproduction" and stabilize farm prices. Americans had been leaving the land for decades as new machinery reduced demand for human muscle and city jobs offered higher wages. The 1930s added two complications to this process. Agricultural workers were forced to stay in the countryside because there were no jobs in the cities; and European demand for America's agricultural products was reduced by Smoot-Hawley. The result was that rural poverty was often even more serious than urban poverty. FDR tried to solve the problem by limiting production (by paying farmers not to produce) and boosting prices.

Action inevitably produced reaction, from the left as well as the right. Norman Thomas, the perennial Socialist presidential candidate, dismissed the New Deal as an attempt "to cure tuberculosis with cough drops." Robert La Follette, the governor of Wisconsin, a state with a long tradition of Progressivism (some of it colored by the large number of Scandinavians who settled there, with their strong commitment to good government and social equality), argued that FDR needed to go much further in securing an equitable distribution of wealth. Upton Sinclair, the muckraking novelist, ran for governor of California on a program of confiscating private property and abolishing profit. Another Californian, Francis Townsend, hitherto an obscure physician, became a national figure with his plan to pay everyone two hundred dollars a month, the equivalent of an annual payment of forty-five thousand dollars in today's money, to retire at sixty. Opinion polls showed that 56 percent of the population favored Townsend's plan, and a petition calling on Congress to enact the plan into law gathered 10 million signatures. On the right, William Randolph Hearst took to calling FDR "Stalin Delano Roosevelt" in private, and his editors took to substituting "Raw Deal" for "New Deal" in news coverage.[28] "Moscow backs Roosevelt," declared a headline in one of Hearst's twenty-eight newspapers during the 1936 election campaign.[29]

The most powerful critiques came from populists who defied easy left-right categorization. Huey Long, the governor of Louisiana and then senator for the state, as wily a politician as the country had produced, launched his Share Our Wealth Plan in February 1934 under the slogan "Every man a king and no man wears a crown." He turned his native state into an advertisement for his policies, with a program of welfare handouts and infrastructure building paid for by the windfall profits of oil: Louisiana built more miles of roads in his term than any state except New York and Texas, despite being one of the poorest states in the country, and built an impressive new university— Louisiana State University—despite being educationally backward. Charles Coughlin preached an exotic mixture of share-the-wealth populism and the Jews-are-to-blame racism from his radio studio in Royal Oak, Michigan. He denounced "the filthy gold standard which from time immemorial has been the breeder of hate, the fashioner of swords, and the destroyer of mankind," and urged his listeners to rise up "against the Morgans, the Kuhn-Loebs, the Rothschilds, the Dillon-Reads, the Federal Reserve banksters."[30] The mixture proved wildly popular: he received so many letters a day that the postal service had to give him a dedicated post office, and an edition of his speeches sold more than a million copies. Coughlin started out as a fan of FDR, declaring that "the New Deal is Christ's deal," but, unsurprisingly given Coughlin's overtowering ego and idiosyncratic politics, the two soon fell out, and Coughlin lambasted Roosevelt as an agent of various international conspiracies.

FDR dealt with these criticisms by introducing the second New Deal—Social Security to provide a safety net, the Works Progress Administration (WPA) to provide an economic stimulus, and rights for trade unions—to provide a payback to some of his strongest supporters. The Social Security bill, unveiled on January 17, 1935, and enacted into law seven months later on August 14, was by far the most significant of these measures because it was intended to provide a permanent entitlement rather than a short-term stimulus to the economy. Indeed, it was arguably the most consequential piece of U.S. domestic legislation of the twentieth century because it permanently altered the relationship between the government and the people. The United States had been a latecomer to social security: Otto von Bismarck's decision to embrace compulsory social security in Germany in the 1880s had led other European countries to follow suit. Even laissez-faire Britain introduced compulsory social insurance in the early twentieth century. America had preferred to put its faith in the local variety and voluntary action. But FDR and his New Dealers seized on the Great Depression to introduce two radical changes: bringing the federal government into the provision of social welfare and creating a Social Security program that was not dependent on need.

FDR campaigned for reelection in 1936 as a champion of the people against the powerful: the selfish and shortsighted business elite who, in his view, had condemned the country to the recession and were bent on thwarting the New Deal. In his annual message to Congress on January 3, 1936, he railed against "entrenched greed." "They seek the restoration of their selfish power. . . . Give them their way and they will take the course of every autocracy of the past—power for themselves, enslavement for the public." In a speech in Philadelphia accepting his party's presidential nomination, he compared the struggle against the British in 1776 to his own struggle against "economic royalists." FDR's address to a rapturous crowd at New York's Madison Square Garden on October 31, 1936, reeked of class hatred: Roosevelt listed his "old enemies"—the agents of "business and financial monopoly, speculation, reckless banking, class antagonism, war profiteering"—and declared that he welcomed their hatred. He returned to the Oval Office in 1937 with a bigger mandate and bigger ambitions.

EVALUATING THE NEW DEAL

The New Deal permanently increased the power of American government. It secured FDR's position as one of America's most admired (and most hated) presidents. Samuel Lubell, a political scientist, argued that there are usually two parties in America—a sun party (a majority party that drives the agenda) and a moon party (one that reacts to that agenda). The Republicans had been the sun party for the thirty years before the New Deal. After the New Deal, the Democrats remained the sun party until the election of Ronald Reagan. Lyndon Johnson engineered a solar eclipse.

FDR's victory over Alf Landon in 1936 was one of the most lopsided in American history. He won more votes than any candidate had won before—28 million and a margin of 11 million. He won every state save Maine and Vermont and rang up the highest proportion of electoral college votes (523 to 8) since James Monroe had run with virtually no opposition in 1820. FDR's coattails were long: the Democrats took 331 congressional seats, leaving the Republicans with just 89, and 76 seats in the Senate, so many that the freshman Democrats had to sit on the Republican side of the aisle.

FDR's second term was a different story. Toward the end of his first term, in May 1935, the Supreme Court had declared the National Industrial Recovery Act unconstitutional. Seven months later, it had delivered the same verdict on the Agricultural Adjustment Act. Roosevelt's attempt to bring the Court to heel by replacing elderly justices with younger and more sympathetic ones provoked furious opposition not only from middle-of-the-road voters but also from his own party, which rightly regarded "court packing" as an assault on the principle of checks and balances at the heart of the Constitution.

The court-packing debacle sucked much of the energy out of Roosevelt's second administration. The Democrats lost 6 Senate seats and 71 House seats in the 1938 midterm elections, with losses concentrated among the most enthusiastic supporters of the New Deal. When Congress reconvened in 1939, Republicans led by Senator Robert Taft pried away enough southern Democrats from the Roosevelt coalition to block much of FDR's domestic legislation. The "Roosevelt recession" dented his reputation for economic success. By the end of the New Deal era, even his staunchest supporters, such as Henry Morgenthau, were turning against him.

Yet for all his miscalculations and disappointments during his second term, FDR succeeded in forging an alliance between the two great blocs of voters who, for the time being at least, hated the Republicans more than they hated each other: the southern whites who hated them because of the Civil War and the northern ethnics who hated them because they were Protestant businesspeople. And he added lots of other voters who looked to benefit from the government—agricultural workers who wanted protection from the vagaries of the market, intellectuals who wanted to play the role of Plato's guardians, public-sector workers who profited from every expansion of government power, and African Americans who suffered particularly badly from the Depression. His was the first administration that was not almost entirely composed of white Anglo-Saxon men: his Cabinet included a Catholic, a Jew, and a woman, and Eleanor Roosevelt acted as a Cabinet member without portfolio, traveling more than a quarter of a million miles in her husband's first two terms.[31]

One of the oddest features of the 1930s was that you saw a spurt in trade union membership at a time of high unemployment (see chart on page 250). The reason for this is that the New Deal provided trade unions with a dream list of enhanced powers. This change actually began under Hoover rather than Roosevelt: in 1932, the Norris–La Guardia Act curtailed the federal court's power to issue injunctions against striking unions. This deprived America's bosses of weapons that they had used to great effect in the 1920s, and signaled a change of mood in Washington. In 1933, section 7(a) of the National Industrial Recovery Act gave workers the right to bargain collectively and choose their own representatives (though the Supreme Court invalidated the NIRA, the National Labor Relations Act [NLRA] reinstated 7(a) and established a National Labor Relations Board [NLRB] that survives to this day). This legislation provided the foundations for a spurt of trade-union membership that ensured that about a third of America's nonagricultural workers belonged to trade unions in 1945.

FDR also installed a new class of experts at the heart of policy making. The Brain Trusters brought an army of bureaucrats in their

UNION MEMBERSHIP
1880 – 1998

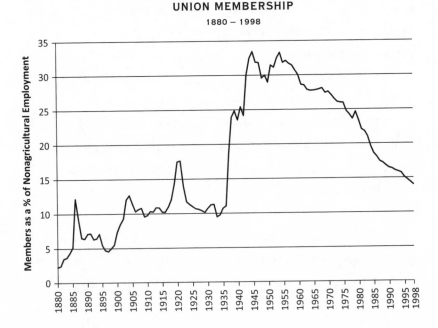

wake and charged them with implementing the New Deal's labyrinthine regulations: young lawyers, academics, and regulators, or what H. L. Mencken called "vapid young pedagogues, out of work YMCA secretaries, third-rate journalists, briefless lawyers and soaring chicken farmers."[32] When FDR arrived in Washington in 1932, it was a sleepy southern town where nothing much happened. By the end of the decade, it had replaced Wall Street as the beating heart of the country. The Justice Department's Antitrust Division expanded from a few dozen lawyers to nearly three hundred. The NRA acquired a staff of forty-five hundred. Mini–New Dealers poured into once-quiet neighborhoods such as Foggy Bottom and Georgetown and created a culture of cocktail parties, where young people enjoyed their new freedom to drink and fantasized about transforming the country. "As lively as an ants' nest that has been split open" was Mary Dewson's verdict on the city.[33]

Above all, FDR achieved the Progressives' most cherished aim of changing the relationship between the government and the people. Before the New Deal, America had been exceptional in its suspicion of big government in general and federal government in particular: the government was smaller than in most European countries and power was widely dispersed among lots of subsidiary levels of government. After the New Deal, the federal government sat at the heart of American society. In short: FDR inherited a highly decentralized political economy committed to flexible markets and transformed it into a Washington-dominated political economy committed to demand management, national welfare programs, and compulsory collective bargaining.

The most obvious change was in size: in 1930, the federal government consumed less than 4 percent of GDP and the largest government employer was the Post Office. Only a tiny minority of Americans—4 million in 1929 and 3.7 million in 1930—paid income tax.[34] By 1936, the federal government consumed 9 percent of GDP and employed 7 percent of the workforce. FDR was also busy broadening the tax base. In the late 1920s, state and local government spending had been nearly three times federal nonmilitary spending. By 1936, federal nonmilitary spending was substantially larger than state and local spending combined.

Mere figures understate the extent of the change. The New Dealers established two mechanisms that centralized power in Washington: a federal system of domestic economic programs (including infrastructure investment) that was funded by national grants and administered by state and local governments, and a national system of defense spending and old-age security. National grants to state and local governments grew from 5.4 percent of national expenditures in 1932 to 8.8 percent in 1940 (and even hit 16.4 percent in 1934). The federal government expanded its control over everything from banking to electric utilities to social insurance through regulation. It boosted its power by increasing federal income taxes in various forms (personal income tax, payroll taxes, and corporate taxes) to fund the large expansion of federal outlays.

At the same time, FDR helped to change deep-seated attitudes by keeping up a stream of praise for big government. "The old reliance upon the free action of individual wills appears quite inadequate. . . . The intervention of that organized control we call government seems necessary," he said in a Fireside Chat in September 1934. "Against economic tyranny such as this," he declared in an even more unbuttoned mood, "the American citizen could appeal only to the organized power of Government."[35] An institution that had been regarded as the very last resort of Americans now entered the mainstream.

His wiliest move, however, was to establish a government version of private, defined benefits, the most prevalent of private retirement programs. This magically transformed Social Security from a charity (which carried a stigma and could be rescinded) into an "entitlement" that people had earned by paying their payroll taxes (matched by their employers) into a fund that then earned interest on those payments. In theory, if the trust fund were to run dry, benefits would be limited to the amount that trust fund recipients had contributed. In practice, whenever the trust fund has approached zero, Congress has always chosen to replenish it (mostly from general revenues or some legislation initiative that accomplishes the same end), turning Social Security benefits into a direct government obligation. There was no precise relationship between how much you paid in and how much you got out—and certainly no paring of benefits when the fund ran low.

But that is nevertheless how people see it. FDR understood perfectly how important it was to cultivate this illusion: when he was challenged about financing Social Security with a payroll tax rather than through income tax, he replied: "We put those pay roll contributions there so as to give the contributors a legal, moral, and political right to collect their pensions and their unemployment benefits. With those taxes in there, no damn politician can ever scrap my social security program. Those taxes aren't a matter of economics, they're straight politics."[36]

America's conversion into a New Deal nation was far from smooth. FDR's superb wartime leadership rescued him from the mounting domestic failures of his second four-year term. The alliance between liberal northerners and conservative southerners proved fractious: the conservatives repeatedly broke ranks to vote with the Republicans. After the war, Social Security was far from universal. In 1946, only one in six Americans aged sixty-five and older received monthly benefits and a third of workers were exempt from payroll taxes. The "unholy alliance" of Republicans and southern Democrats repeatedly frustrated the further expansion of the New Deal state.[37]

In particular, the cost of keeping southern Democrats in his alliance was excluding agricultural and domestic workers from the Social Security program, in order to keep black workers in the South "in their place."[38] FDR nevertheless won the long war: by creating a large administrative machine at the heart of Washington and persuading everybody that Social Security is an earned entitlement rather than a charitable gift, he created a system that has turned out to be politically impossible to shrink, however large the unholy alliance's temporary advantage.

FROM POLITICS TO ECONOMICS

The real measure of the New Deal is not how successful it was in creating a political coalition, but how successful it was in getting the country out of the Great Depression. Here the record is much more negative. The most damning judgment on the New Deal is provided by the second depression. Though the economy began to recover in 1935–36 in the wake of FDR's huge stimulus package, the recovery quickly ran out of steam. FDR's much-ballyhooed job creation in the public sector was offset by job destruction in the private sector. In May 1937, the recovery crested well short of the 1929 levels of employment. By August, the economy had begun to go downhill again. This time around the collapse was bigger than the one that had destroyed Herbert Hoover. Stocks lost more than a third of their value. Corporate profits plunged by between 40 percent and 50 percent. Steel production in the last quarter of 1937 sank to 25 percent of its level in the middle of the year. The ranks of the unemployed expanded to 10 million people, or 20 percent of the workforce.

We have seen that FDR inherited the blueprint for his most successful reform—of the banking system—from his predecessor. His talent was as a salesman rather than as a policy maker. At the same time, many of the policies that he actually originated were counterproductive. Even if they boosted America in the short term, they were damaging in the longer term, plunging the country back into a second depression and ensuring that the Great Depression lasted longer in the United States than in most other countries.

The biggest disaster was his attempt to micromanage the economy through price-fixing and regulation. The NRA was a strange beast: in part a capitalist version of the Soviet Union's Gosplan, in part an all-American version of Mussolini's corporatist capitalism that tried to cartelize firms that made up four-fifths of the nonagricultural economy.[39] The NRA encouraged big businesses to collaborate to set the prices of their products and the wages and prices that went into making them. The NRA also required firms to pay higher wages and accept compulsory collective bargaining. Firms that complied with these strictures were allowed to display a blue eagle insignia: more than 2 million quickly signed up. Firms that failed to comply with the rules were often driven out of business. Blue eagle signs soon became ubiquitous in store windows and on billboards. Hugh Johnson, the former general who was put in charge of the NRA, became one of the most recognizable men in America. In September 1933, a quarter of a million Americans marched behind the blue eagle in a parade down New York's Fifth Avenue. By 1934, NRA codes covered over five hundred industries employing over 22 million workers: 77 percent of private, nonagricultural employment and 52 percent of total employment.

The NRA's aim was to prevent the problem of overproduction. But the method was absurdly bureaucratic—the NRA's 540 codes determined who could produce what and how much they could charge for it. The codes even decreed whether customers could choose their own chicken from a coop or butcher shop or whether they had to be allotted it randomly. The result was to entrench the power of established companies: insiders flourished thanks to guaranteed markets at elevated prices, part of which funded high wage rates, but outsiders could not prosper however hard they worked or cleverly they innovated. In *The Wealth of Nations,* Adam Smith had warned that "people of the same trade seldom meet together, even for merriment and diversion, but the conversation ends in a conspiracy against the public, or in some contrivance to raise prices." The major tire makers (Goodyear, Goodrich, and Firestone) got together and wrote the NRA tire code. The price of tires (and therefore cars) immediately soared. NRA bureaucrats prosecuted small producers who had the temerity to offer discounts to their customers or to work at forbidden hours.

The NRA quickly produced a flood of complaints, a flood that was made all the worse by the fact that its head, Hugh Johnson, was an alcoholic who disappeared for days on end on monumental benders. Small businesses complained that big businesses were using the NRA to crush them between the vise of high prices and tight regulations. Consumers complained that they were getting less for their money. The National Recovery Review Board, headed by Clarence Darrow, worried that many codes spurred "the exit of small enterprises" and hastened the "always growing autocracy" of the big companies. Yale's Irving Fisher told Roosevelt that "the NRA has retarded the recovery and especially retarded re-employment." FDR responded to the complaints with a series of adjustments that had the perverse effect of making the contraption ever more complicated. Creative destruction was nowhere to be seen.

The Supreme Court did FDR an unexpected (and certainly unacknowledged) favor by ruling that much of the NRA was unconstitutional (the case that broke the NRA's back involved the vexed issue of whether you could choose your own chicken at a butcher's shop). But the administration's prejudice against competition had consequences for FDR's other priorities. The number of antitrust cases brought by the Department of Justice, for example, fell from an average of 12.5 a year in the 1920s to an average of 6.5 a year in 1935 to 1938. The National Labor Relations Act strengthened the power of the big trade unions and turned a blind eye to collusion. There was little competition in a wide range of industries—cars, chemicals, aluminum, glass, and anthracite coal—and prices and wages remained at the same level they had been before the Supreme Court acted. In the middle of America's worst-ever recession, insiders in protected industries enjoyed wages about 20 percent higher than they had achieved historically.[40]

The Agricultural Adjustment Act was just as much of a mess. The act tried to use a combination of set-asides, price-fixing, and transfer payments to deal with the perceived problem of declining agricultural prices. Some farmers were paid not to produce on part of their land. Farm prices were fixed to the purchasing power at the height of favorable farm prices in 1910. And millers and processors were forced to pay for much of the cost of the program. The whole system was controlled by the secretary of agriculture.

There were some glaring design faults with this. The government had to pay farmers a lot of money not to grow things at a time when (according to the president) a third of the population was ill fed. The price of both food and clothes increased in the year after the Agricultural Adjustment Act was introduced. The Department of Agriculture had to hire thousands of bureaucrats in Washington as well as more than a hundred thousand part-timers to determine how much land farmers should be allowed to cultivate and then to make sure that they were abiding by the rules. "Our economy is not agricultural any longer," William Faulkner observed. "We no longer farm in Mississippi cotton fields. We farm now in Washington corridors and Congressional committee rooms."[41]

Poor design inevitably led to perverse consequences. Farmers exercised their entrepreneurial energy in gaming the system—claiming subsidies for setting aside parts of their farms and then growing the same crops on other pieces of land. Southern cotton farmers were particularly ruthless in taking advantage of the subsidies by throwing sharecroppers off their land while continuing to produce themselves.[42]

A second problem was policy uncertainty. Businesspeople crave certainty as much as almost anything: certainty allows them to make long-term plans and long-term investments. FDR added to the already uncertain business environment by constantly shifting policies and priorities. The New Deal was a hodgepodge of often inconsistent policies—at various times FDR tinkered with inflation and price controls, deficit spending and budget balancing, cartelization and trust-busting, bashing business and harnessing it for the common good, reclaiming land from the wilderness and consigning reclaimed land back to the wilderness.

FDR and his people also took momentous decisions in the most cavalier manner. In 1933, Roosevelt, backed by large majorities in Congress, decided to put America on something called the Gold Exchange Standard. He prohibited private individuals from owning or trading gold, forcing them to exchange their gold coins and bars for banknotes, and restricted the market in gold to exchanges between central banks. He also set an arbitrary price for gold at $35.00 an ounce, a big jump from the $20.67 per ounce that had prevailed since 1835, in order to push up prices and erode debt burdens, particularly agricultural debt burdens.[43] His policy worked for a while: the seasonally adjusted Consumer Price Index rose at an annual rate of 3.2

percent from April 1933 to October 1937. But then prices fell at a 3 percent annual rate from October 1937 to August 1939. By the end of 1939, prices were still well short of their level in the 1920s.

The bloodiest consequence of arbitrary decision making was the great pig massacre. In 1933, the agriculture secretary, Henry Wallace, ordered the slaughter of six million piglets in order to boost the price of pork.[44] Knives were sharpened and pigs sacrificed throughout the land as a result of a single bureaucratic edict. Though the New Deal was often justified as a triumph of rationalism in politics, it also empowered single individuals to make almost arbitrary decisions that resounded through the economy.

Lammot du Pont II explained what all this meant from the business perspective in 1937:

> Uncertainty rules the tax situation, the Labor situation, the monetary situation, and practically every legal condition under which industry must operate. Are taxes to go higher, lower or stay where they are? We don't know. Is labor to be union or non-union? . . . Are we to have inflation or deflation, more government spending or less? . . . Are new restrictions to be placed on capital, new limits on profits? . . . It is impossible to even guess at the answers.[45]

FDR made uncertainty worse by attacking businesspeople as a class, and worse still by attacking some leading businesspeople as individuals. During the 1930s, the IRS showed a worrying habit of carrying out audits of anti-Roosevelt business leaders such as Andrew Mellon, scion of the banking dynasty and Hoover's treasury secretary. It turned out that FDR's "first-class personality" contained a malicious and indeed vindictive streak. Such overt class warfare made businesspeople nervous as well as angry: why invest if you were going to be demonized as a speculator and perhaps singled out by the

IRS? Even Roosevelt's own side worried that his antibusiness vitu-perations were proving counterproductive. Raymond Moley reflected that he was "stunned by the violence, the bombast, the naked dema-goguery" of Roosevelt's Madison Square Garden speech. "I began to wonder whether he wasn't beginning to feel that the proof of a mea-sure's merit was the extent to which it offended the business commu-nity."[46] Roy Howard, a sympathetic reporter, warned FDR that "there can be no real recovery until the fears of business have been allayed."[47] Adolf Berle warned that "you could not have a government perpetu-ally at war with its economic machinery." He noted that business was demoralized for good reason: "Practically no business group in the country has escaped investigation or other attack in the last five years. . . . The result has been shattered morale. . . . It is therefore necessary to make that group pull itself together."[48]

If FDR's relationship with business was conflicted at best and hos-tile at worst, his relationship with labor was almost fawning—Roosevelt the patrician was a friend of the workingman and an ally of the workingman's organizations, particularly trade unions. Labor was an important part of FDR's New Deal army: trade unionists came out in large numbers in both 1932 and 1936, not just to vote for him but also to burn shoe leather for him. The National Labor Rela-tions Act, or Wagner Act, of 1935 placed tight limits on what firms could do against unions, but few limits on what unions could do against firms: unions had the right to organize while employers had an obligation to deal with "duly recognized union representatives." The act also imposed a policy of "equal pay for equal work," which made it all but impossible for companies to pay people according to their seniority, let alone their individual merit.[49]

The unions immediately capitalized on the combination of con-stitutional power and economic recovery to press home their advan-tage, mounting successful membership drives and shifting the locus of popular protest from hunger marches to trade union halls. They were particularly successful in mass-production industries such as steel and car making. In the 1920s, following the failure of the 1919 steel strike, the conventional wisdom held that the mass-production industries, with their high wages and union-busting bosses, would escape unionization. The Wagner Act changed all that. Trade union membership increased from 13 percent of the workforce in 1935 to 29 percent in 1939. The total number of days lost to strikes rose from 14 million in 1936 to 28 million in 1937.

Unionization might have been even more successful if it hadn't been for the long-running battle between craft unions and industrial unions. The AFL grew from 2.1 million members in 1933 to 3.4 million in 1936. At the same time it experienced severe internal stresses over whether to preserve its traditional craft organization. The 1934 and 1935 AFL annual meetings in (then blue-collar) San Francisco were both fiercely divided between traditionalists and modernizers who wanted to organize by industry. After their second defeat, nine modernizers, led by John L. Lewis, the head of the United Mine Workers of America, got together to organize the Committee for Industrial Organization (CIO) to "encourage and promote workers in the mass production industries." Though these activists failed to reform the AFL, which first denied the 4 million members of the CIO full membership, and then, in 1936, expelled them completely, they certainly had a big impact on America's mass-production sector. The most damaging strikes were in the steel mills and car factories, where a few determined activists could bring entire operations to a halt. In what became known as "the great GM sit-down strike," the United Auto Workers (UAW) shut down a giant GM plant in Flint, Michigan, from December 30, 1936, to February 11, 1937.

The strongest evidence against the New Deal is the unemployment rate: in 1939, 17.2 percent of Americans, or 9.48 million, were out of a job, compared with 16.3 percent, or 8.02 million, in the last year of Hoover's administration. The League of Nations composed an index of unemployment for sixteen countries during the 1930s. In 1929, the United States had the lowest unemployment rate at 1.0 percent, compared with an average of 5.4 percent. By 1932, the United States had fallen to eighth place with 24.9 percent, compared with an average of 21.1 percent. By 1938, it had fallen to thirteenth place with 19.8 percent, compared with an average of 11.4 percent.[50]

BUSINESS AND THE DEPRESSION

Even when it was running well below its potential, the U.S. economy was still a mighty beast: for example, in the depths of the "depression within a depression" in 1938, the United States' national income was nearly double the combined national incomes of Germany, Japan, and Italy.[51] The economy grew by about 20 percent between 1936 and 1940 alone. The number of retail stores increased from 1.5 million in 1929 to 1.8 million in 1939. The proportion of Americans with indoor flush toilets increased from 20 percent in 1920 to 60 percent in 1940. Steinbeck's Joad family, who were supposed to be symbols of poverty, owned the car that they drove across the country.

The great revolutionary forces that had been so evident in the 1920s continued to operate in the 1930s. Output per hour increased at a respectable 1.8 percent annual rate during the 1930s, and multifactor productivity rose at an annual rate of 1.5 percent. Technological advances from phones to airplanes continued to shrink distance. In 1935, the Sikorsky S-42 flying boat made the first nonstop flight from San Francisco to Honolulu, a distance of 2,400 miles. Donald Douglas took the aircraft revolution to new heights with a succession of innovations that reduced cost while increasing range. The DC-3, which he introduced in 1935, could hold twenty-one passengers, cruise at 195 miles an hour, and fly for a thousand miles without refueling. With three refueling stops, the DC-3 could fly from New York to Los Angeles in just fifteen hours. By the end of the decade, 90 percent of the world's airlines had DC-series planes in their fleets. Global firms continued to trade across borders despite tariffs, wars, expropriations, and exchange controls—and some, such as Ford and General Motors, became masters of running clone companies in various countries that looked and felt as if they were "local" rather than global.

The Great Depression created opportunities even as markets contracted and governments expanded. Discount companies boomed: Joe Thompson created the modern convenience store in the form of 7-Eleven. IBM mushroomed in response to demands for data from the new government bureaucracies (after the passage of the Social Security Act the federal government had to maintain a file on almost every employee in the country). The end of Prohibition proved a bonanza for people in the booze business: Erwin Uihlein seized the opportunity provided by the end of Prohibition to revive his family brewery business, Schlitz Brewing, quickly turning it into the second-largest brewery in the country.

The Depression forced companies to think harder in order to make ends meet. Procter & Gamble, America's leading consumer goods company, provided a good example of how a company could respond to hard times. P&G spent so heavily on addictive radio programs that they were nicknamed "soap operas." By the late 1930s, it was paying for five hours of programming on network radio every weekday, interweaving crude plugs for Tide or Crisco with edge-of-the-seat plots. This coincided with a corporate reorganization that put senior executives in charge of particular brands, and encouraged them not just to invent new products but also to give them personalities that could be sold to consumers.

The 1930s saw a big advance in the science of management as companies struggled at once to squeeze unnecessary costs and to seize new opportunities. In 1933, Marvin Bower, a young professional with a JD from Harvard Law School and an MBA from Harvard Business School, bumped into James McKinsey, a former professor at the University of Chicago and founder of a firm of accountants and engineers. Bower had come to the conclusion that America had plenty of professionals (bankers, lawyers, accountants, and the like) who knew how to put companies' affairs in order after they had failed, but no professionals who knew how to prevent them from failing in the first place, and he persuaded McKinsey to add a new breed of management consultants to his company's roster. Bower methodically built McKinsey into a giant, providing advice to almost all of America's greatest companies, and remained the "Firm's" guiding spirit until his death in 2003.

The United States continued to lead the world in producing a product that was now more valuable than ever, escapism. The more dismal the daily grind became, the more successful American entrepreneurs became at bottling daydreams. Hollywood enjoyed a golden decade: the studios produced some five thousand films in the 1930s and audiences boomed. Walt Disney invented a new type of film, the feature-length cartoon, with *Snow White* in 1937, adding to the already extensive stock of formats, from screwball comedies to musicals to cops-and-robber epics to westerns. Metro-Goldwyn-Mayer produced blockbusters—and indeed classics for the ages—with *The Wizard of Oz* (1939) and *Gone with the Wind* (1939).

Charles Revson and Max Factor built successful businesses selling female beauty products—the glamorous antidotes to W. H. Auden's "low, dishonest decade." Revson established Revlon in the very depths of the depression in 1932 and quickly expanded. Max Factor took over his family's company in 1938, as the depression within a depression tightened its grip, and set about transforming it from a Hollywood makeup studio into a global brand. Other forms of entertainment flourished. The Nevada legislature legalized gambling in 1931, in part because the market for divorce had collapsed, as couples decided to stay together in tough times. The game of Monopoly became a bestseller after its introduction in 1935. Pulp fiction authors such as Erle Stanley Gardner (the creator of Perry Mason) entertained millions.

All this energetic business activity produced a paradox: multifactor productivity (MFP) grew almost as fast in the "stagnant" 1930s as it did in the booming 1920s. It also grew across a much broader range of fronts. Some of this growth was a result of crisis-driven rationalization as businesses closed their less productive plants. This was particularly true in the automobile sector. Some of it was due to much more investment in the future. Railroads such as the Pennsylvania and the Chesapeake and Ohio (C&O) took advantage of cheap labor and materials to upgrade their lines. Railroads in general improved their links with road haulage. Science- and technology-dependent companies took advantage of idle brainpower to make long-term investments in scientific research. The number of people employed in R&D in the manufacturing sector increased from 6,250 in 1927 to 11,000 in 1933 to 27,800 by 1940.

The chemical industry enjoyed a particularly rich decade. DuPont discovered the first synthetic fiber, nylon, after almost ten years of research and development. Owens-Illinois developed fiberglass, also after intensive investment, and spun off a new company, Owens-Corning Fiberglass, to exploit the product. Nylon became a vital component not just of women's stockings but also of parachutes.

Other discoveries in the era included neoprene (1930), polyvinylidene chloride (1933), low-density polyethylene (1933), acrylic methacrylate (1936), polyurethanes (1937), Teflon (1938), and Styrofoam (1941).

FDR'S WARTIME RENAISSANCE

It was the Second World War rather than FDR's New Deal that finally pulled the United States out of the slough of despond.

War has played an outsize role in American history: including the Revolutionary War that gave it birth, America has spent a quarter of its history at war (see table below).

EVENT	START DATE	END DATE	NUMBER OF MONTHS
REVOLUTIONARY WAR (1775–1783)	Apr 19, 1775	Sep 3, 1783	101
PEACE	Sep 4, 1783	Jun 17, 1812	346
WAR OF 1812 (1812–1815)	Jun 18, 1812	Mar 23, 1815	33
PEACE	Mar 24, 1815	Apr 24, 1846	373
MEXICAN-AMERICAN WAR (1846–1848)	Apr 25, 1846	Feb 2, 1848	21
PEACE	Feb 3, 1848	Apr 11, 1861	158
CIVIL WAR (1861–1865)	Apr 12, 1861	May 9, 1865	48
PEACE	May 10, 1865	Apr 20, 1898	395
SPANISH-AMERICAN WAR (1898)	Apr 21, 1898	Aug 13, 1898	4

PEACE	Aug 14, 1898	Apr 5, 1917	224
WORLD WAR I (1917–1918)	Apr 6, 1917	Nov 11, 1918	19
PEACE	Nov 12, 1918	Dec 7, 1941	277
WORLD WAR II (1941–1945)	Dec 8, 1941	Sep 2, 1945	44
PEACE	Sep 3, 1945	Jun 24, 1950	58
KOREAN WAR (1950–1953)	Jun 25, 1950	Jul 27, 1953	37
PEACE	Jul 28, 1953	Oct 31, 1955	27
VIETNAM WAR (1955–1975)	Nov 1, 1955	Apr 30, 1975	234
PEACE	May 1, 1975	Aug 1, 1990	183
PERSIAN GULF WAR (1990–1991)	Aug 2, 1990	Feb 28, 1991	7
PEACE	Mar 1, 1991	Oct 6, 2001	127
IRAQ/ AFGHANISTAN/ OTHER (2001–2014)	Oct 7, 2001	Dec 28, 2014	159

WAR TOTAL	707
PEACE TOTAL	2,168
TOTAL MONTHS	2,875
PERCENTAGE AT WAR	24.6

Some of these wars were wars of conquest (in addition to America's eleven formal wars, the country also waged an ongoing campaign against Native Americans). Some were wars for survival: the British came close to snuffing out the new nation in 1812. The Civil War was an existential war that determined the nature of the country. These wars shaped both politics and economics. Five American presidents, Andrew Jackson, Zachary Taylor, Ulysses S. Grant,

Teddy Roosevelt, and Dwight Eisenhower, became national figures as military commanders. The income tax was introduced to finance wars. Wars, particularly the Civil War, led to bouts of inflation and sharply rising interest rates that partly contained inflationary surges.

The Second World War was by far the most expensive of these wars, consuming an average of 30 percent of the nation's GDP from 1942 to 1945. War spending provided the stimulus that the economy needed—America's war spending skyrocketed from $1.4 billion, about 1.5 percent of GDP, before the war to $83 billion, or over 36 percent of GDP, by 1945. Unemployment, the great scourge of the 1930s, disappeared. The war put people back to work—and indeed extended the workforce to women as the men went off to fight. It forced companies to devise new techniques to boost output as they did their best to contribute to the war effort. The result was the biggest boom in American history: real GDP almost doubled from 1939 to 1944.[52]

The war miraculously turned a negative into a positive: the government might make a bad substitute for the decisions of millions of consumers in peacetime, but it was the ideal consumer when it was also the sole consumer, buying tanks and planes, especially when it was backed by cost-plus contracts, which virtually eliminated uncertainty. The U.S. government made the wise decision to work hand in glove with America's biggest companies rather than either trying to do everything itself or distributing its largesse among small companies. America's thirty-three largest corporations accounted for half of all military contracting. General Motors alone supplied one-tenth of all American war production.[53] "If you are going to try to go to war, or to prepare for war, in a capitalist country," Henry Stimson reflected, "you have got to let business make money out of the process or business won't work." It also harnessed their competitive instincts by encouraging, say, Henry Ford to compete against Henry Kaiser to see who could do the most for the war effort. To complete this benign picture, all the major union leaders announced "no strike" pledges.

The result was a productivity miracle. The war underlined America's natural advantages as a continent-size power far away from the cauldron of conflict that was Europe: America was virtually self-sufficient in material resources, and its vast industrial heartland was perfectly safe from Japanese or German bombers. The war also demonstrated the extraordinary might of the big businesses that had been developing since the Civil War. During the war, America turned out 86,000 tanks, 12,000 warships and merchant ships, 65,000 smaller boats, 300,000 planes, 600,000 jeeps, 2 million army trucks, 193,000 artillery pieces, 17 million handguns and rifles, 41 billion rounds of ammunition, and, most demanding of all in terms of resources, two atomic bombs. By one estimate, U.S. output per worker hour was double Germany's and five times Japan's.

The two most impressive laboratories of productivity were Henry Ford's factory in Willow Run and Henry Kaiser's shipyard in Richmond, California. Henry Ford built his gargantuan Willow Run plant thirty-five miles southwest of Detroit to produce B-24 bombers in less than a year. At its height, the Run employed more than forty thousand workers. Glendon Swarthout, a novelist, commented on the factory's "insane, overpowering immensity." Charles Lindbergh called it "a sort of Grand Canyon of the mechanized world."[54] The plant became more efficient as the war ground on, turning out 75 planes a month in February 1943, 150 a month in November 1943, and, at its peak, 432 a month in August 1944.

Henry Kaiser was so obsessed with hitting the government's targets that he revolutionized the entire shipbuilding business. In 1941, it took 355 days to produce a Liberty ship. Six months later, the production time had been reduced to less than a third of that time. In November 1942, in a test case, workers put together one ship in four days, fifteen hours, and twenty-six minutes—and though that pace was impossible to sustain, the average time to produce a ship was reduced to just seventeen days, earning Henry Kaiser the admiring sobriquet "Sir Launchalot" as well as extraordinary profits. Kaiser achieved this by abandoning the traditional method of building a ship from keel upward, rivet by laborious rivet, and instead introduced a system of prefabrication and mass production: the giant Richmond shipyard was transformed into a giant assembly line with tens of thousands of workers, each responsible for a tiny part of the whole.

The U.S. economy was so productive that it could turn out consumer goods as well as war machines. In Britain and Germany, the consumer economies all but collapsed during the war. In America, consumer spending rose by 10.5 percent from 1940 to 1944 in real terms. Ordinary Americans splurged on makeup, stockings, and films. Even gambling boomed: racing fans wagered two and a half times more on horses in 1944 than they had in 1940. Americans started half a million new businesses during the war and built eleven thousand new supermarkets.[55] The arsenal of democracy was also a temple of mass consumption.

THE ARSENAL OF CAPITALISM

The wartime boom laid the foundations of the golden age of the 1950s and 1960s. The government upgraded the country's capital stock by pouring money into new factories and industrial equipment that were later taken over by the private sector. The country's stock of machine tools *doubled* from 1940 to 1945, for example. The government also upgraded the country's human capital by unconsciously running a huge on-the-job training program. Soldiers came back from the front with new skills, from organizing groups of people to repairing jeeps. Factory workers (including women) returned to civilian life with their human capital enhanced.

The United States thus entered the postwar era with immense advantages: a system of mass production that was by far the best in the world; an infrastructure that was geared to getting the best out of that system of mass production; and a workforce that had all the human capital it needed to make the best of this system.

This system had two serious flaws: mass production sacrificed quality for quantity and human engagement for predictability. This was already clear during the wartime boom. America outproduced Germany and Japan because it focused on quantity rather than quality. The Wehrmacht employed small batches of highly engineered machines—425 different kinds of aircraft, 151 types of trucks, and 150 different motorcycles. The United States produced long runs of mass-produced warhorses. This was a formula for victory during the war: in a memorandum to Hitler in 1944, Albert Speer, Germany's armaments minister, argued that the Americans "knew how to act with organizationally simple methods and therefore achieved greater results," whereas the Germans were "hampered by superannuated forms of organization."[56] But in the long run it proved to be a problem as the Germans and the Japanese learned how to combine quality with quantity—the Germans by targeting high-quality niches and the Japanese by producing the Toyota system.

America's addiction to mass production was rendered all the more troublesome by the power of the trade unions—a power that had been unleashed by the Wagner Act of 1935, temporarily tamed by the demands of the war, but then reinforced by the postwar boom. The unions not only used their hold over the mass-production system to extract relatively high wages and entitlements that could only go up; they also used it to resist the introduction of clever new ideas such as total quality management.

It took many decades for these problems to become clear. But as we tell the story of the postwar boom, it is worth remembering that there were design flaws in America's great prosperity machine.

Eight

THE GOLDEN AGE OF
GROWTH: 1945–1970

———————————◆———————————

T HE UNITED STATES EMERGED from the Second World War a
giant among midgets. A country with 7 percent of the world's
population produced 42 percent of its manufactured goods,
43 percent of its electricity, 57 percent of its steel, 62 percent of its oil,
and 80 percent of its cars. Before the war, Alvin Hansen, a Harvard
economist, had worried that America was entering an era of "secular
stagnation," a phrase that we will encounter again in later chapters.
For twenty-five years after the war, the economy boomed and Harvard economists, looking for an ax to grind, began to focus on the
evils of affluence.

Postwar America was a land of opportunity. Returning troops
without a penny in their pockets could get into college and buy a
house courtesy of the GI Bill. Blue-collar workers without more than
a high school education could afford to raise a family in the suburbs.
Opportunity bred optimism: Americans looked forward to a future
of ever-rising living standards and the government embraced ever-
loftier goals.

This was a world in which everything was shiny and new—in which brand-new families brought brand-new houses (with garages) and filled them with brand-new things. In 1946, 2.2 million Americans plighted their troth—a record that stood for thirty-three years. In the same year, 3.4 million babies were born. The babies kept coming—3.8 million in 1947, 3.9 million in 1952, and more than 4 million every year from 1954 to 1964. Some 15 million houses were built in the United States between 1945 and 1955. The number of households with televisions increased from 172,000 by 1948 to 15.3 million by 1952. Clever gadgets multiplied—automatic car transmissions, electric clothes dryers, long-playing records, Polaroid cameras, automatic garbage disposals, remote controls. . . . The number of new cars sold increased from 69,500 in 1945 to 2.1 million in 1946 to 5.1 million in 1949 to 6.7 million in 1950 to 7.9 million in 1955. And what cars! These were landbound yachts, with elaborately crafted chrome features, enough room to contain a family, and the power of a hundred horses.

This was also a world in which growth had become self-reinforcing. The U.S. economy grew by an average of 3.8 percent a year from 1946 to 1973 and real household income increased by 2.1 percent a year (or 74 percent over the period). America reaped the fruits of the massive investment in productive capacity over the previous two decades. During the Great Depression, FDR had poured money into transport (the Golden Gate Bridge) and energy (the Tennessee Valley Authority and the Hoover Dam). It sowed as well as reaped. The GI Bill provided returning veterans with a wide range of government services, such as low-cost mortgages (which helped to spark the construction boom) and education subsidies (which turned America into a world leader in the proportion of young people who went to college).

In recent decades, as Robert Gordon has pointed out, productivity growth has been concentrated in a narrow range of economic activities—entertainment, communications, and IT. In the postwar years, people experienced rapid improvement in almost every aspect of their lives—housing, education, transportation, health care, and working conditions. Even farming saw a growth surge, with productivity growing by 4 percent a year from 1945 to 1960, compared with 1 percent a year from 1835 to 1935. Farms were consolidated as successful farmers exploited economies of scale and unsuccessful ones sold out. Farmers installed new machinery in the form of giant combines, mechanical cotton pickers, and tractors. The early 1950s was the peak period for tractor sales in America as the remaining plowing horses and mules were phased out. They also exploited new forms of fertilizer. The mechanization of cotton picking boosted productivity and diminished job creation across the South and encouraged millions of black laborers to move to higher-paying jobs in northern factories.

The government embraced a Keynesian policy of demand management regardless of which party held the White House. In 1946, Congress passed the Employment Act, which set the country the Goldilocks goal of full employment, full production, and stable prices, and also established the Council of Economic Advisers. Politicians interpreted Keynesianism in increasingly expansive terms—not just as a way of heading off depression but also as a way of ensuring permanent prosperity.

How did America get into such a happy state?

WAR AND PEACE

The United States emerged from the war relatively unscathed compared with either its allies or enemies. Europe, America's traditional rival for global hegemony, was shattered. An estimated 36.5 million Europeans died of war-related causes compared with 405,000

Americans.[1] Agricultural production halved. Industrial production was set back decades: Germany produced as much in 1946 as it had in 1890.[2] Great cities such as Berlin and Warsaw lay in ruins. "Here is a burial ground. Here is Death," was how Janina Broniewska, a Polish writer, described Warsaw when she returned there after its liberation.[3] Some 25 million Russians and 20 million Germans were homeless.[4] By contrast, apart from Japan's bombing raid on Pearl Harbor, the war left the vast American homeland untouched.

Many economists, not least Alvin Hansen, worried that the economy would contract as soon as the war stimulus was removed, much as it had in 1918. Not at all. Pent-up demand for houses, cars, and consumer goods, as Americans made up for the deprivations of the depression and war, kept the economy in high gear. Manufacturers applied the productivity-boosting techniques that they had learned during the war to even the most obscure corners of the consumer economy: Swanson invented its famous TV dinners, aluminum trays of meat and vegetables that took exactly the same time to cook, as a way of keeping busy after the market for rations for U.S. troops had dried up. Americans carried the wartime spirit of solidarity into the postwar years: if they could beat the most evil empire the world had seen by fighting together abroad, surely they could build a land of prosperity by working together at home.

The country's preeminence was reinforced by two decisions that it made in the last days of the war and the early days of the peace. The first was the decision to remain wary of the European fashion for socialism. America's comrade-in-arms, Great Britain, celebrated the end of the war by voting to build a New Jerusalem. The Labour government, winning with a massive majority, nationalized the commanding heights of the economy, introduced a cradle-to-grave welfare state, and promised a rolling program of socialism. The nationalized industries suffered from overmanning and declining productivity. The rolling program ran into the sand.

Though there were plenty of New Deal intellectuals in Washington who wanted to build their own Jerusalem, they were kept on a tight leash. Even during the war, America had refrained from nationalizing its big industries, preferring instead to provide private companies with bulk orders and let them come up with the goods. After the war, it was even keener to get back to normal. The government helped people to buy houses and get educations but dismantled the wartime regime of central planning.

The country had Harry Truman and Dwight Eisenhower to thank for such wisdom. Truman had a regular guy's hostility to big ideas and big spending. "I don't want any experiments," he told his adviser Clark Clifford. "The American people have been through a lot of experiments, and they want a rest from experiments."[5] Eisenhower prided himself on being apolitical: he embraced moderate social reforms (Barry Goldwater accused him of running a "dime-store New Deal") but also believed in balancing the budget and controlling government spending. The conservative movement also played its role. European countries were all dragged to the left by vibrant socialist movements: Communists got 26 percent of the vote in France, 23.5 percent in Finland, 19.5 percent in Iceland, and 19 percent in Italy.[6] America alone was dragged to the right by a conservative movement that loathed government. Millions of Americans read Friedrich Hayek's *The Road to Serfdom* (1944), or at least the *Reader's Digest* condensed version. Businessmen clubbed together to support the American Enterprise Institute, which moved from New York City to Washington, D.C., in 1943. Ayn Rand won a mass audience for her celebration of unfettered individualism in *The Fountainhead* (1943) and *Atlas Shrugged* (1957). Even in the immediate aftermath of a war in which American and Russian troops had fought on the same side, anticommunism was rampant: a 1946 poll revealed that 67 percent of Americans opposed letting Communists hold government jobs, and a 1947 poll that 61 percent of respondents favored outlawing the Communist Party.[7]

The second decision was to embrace the rest of the world. America resisted the temptation to return to splendid isolation as it had done after the First World War. It rejected the temptation to punish its opponents as the Europeans had done at Versailles, recognizing the wisdom of Herbert Hoover's advice to Harry Truman in 1946 that "you can have vengeance, or peace, but you can't have both." On the contrary: it decided that its long-term interest lay in rebuilding capitalism on a global scale, embracing free trade, and offering help not only to its exhausted friends but also to its defeated enemies. The United States could "never again be an island to itself," Henry Stimson, one of the grandees of the American foreign policy establishment, observed. "No private program and no public policy, in any sector of our national life, now escape from the compelling fact that if it is not framed with reference to the world, it is framed with perfect futility."

America laid the foundations of a liberal trading regime by slashing tariffs on dutiable imports from an average of 33 percent in 1944 to 13 percent just six years later. It also laid the foundations of global economic management with the creation of the International Monetary Fund and the World Bank at a conference at a hotel in Bretton Woods, New Hampshire, in July 1944. The General Agreement on Tariffs and Trade (later the World Trade Organization) followed in 1947. It laid the foundations of global political management with the creation of the United Nations in 1944–46. The Marshall Plan provided Europe with some $13 billion for rebuilding in the years 1948 through 1952, more than all previous foreign aid combined. Ernest Bevin, Britain's foreign secretary, described Marshall's speech at

Harvard on April 28, 1947, as "one of the greatest speeches in world history."

The architects of the new world order were hardheaded men, not starry-eyed idealists. They realized that a new struggle was on the horizon, between capitalism and communism; they understood that U.S. companies needed global markets to sell their goods. "The Plan presupposes that we desire to restore a Europe which can and will compete with us in the world markets," Allen Dulles, the CIA director, wrote, referring to the Marshall Plan, "and for that very reason will be able to buy substantial amounts of our products."[8] The U.S. share of world trade in manufactured goods increased from 10 percent in 1933 to 29 percent in 1953, providing millions of jobs for American workers. There was no doubt as to who was in charge of the new world. John Maynard Keynes was the moving spirit behind the Bretton Woods meeting, and by far the most intellectually distinguished figure there, but America's treasury secretary, Henry Morgenthau, and his deputy, Harry Dexter White, made the key decisions: the conference attendees bowed to Keynes but listened to Morgenthau and White. Keynes was so appalled by America's ruthless determination to replace, rather than supplement, Britain as the world's superpower that he complained that it wanted to "pick out the eyes of the British Empire."[9]

America quickly moved from the hot war against the Axis powers to the cold war against the Warsaw Pact. This war added a dark hue to the country's optimism: a people who embraced the future also worried about global annihilation. In March 1955, Dwight Eisenhower stated matter-of-factly that the United States might employ nuclear weapons "as you use a bullet or anything else."[10] In 1962, during the standoff over Russia's deployment of nuclear weapons in Cuba, the world came as close to Armageddon as it ever has, with John Kennedy personally calculating the chances of nuclear war at about 25 percent. Still, the cold war also added some discipline to a society that could have been lost in affluence. If the best and brightest went into social activism in the 1960s, and financial engineering in the 1990s, they went into the Pentagon and the CIA in the 1950s.

FROM BRAWN TO BRAIN

The America that emerged from the Second World War was still overwhelmingly a manufacturing economy—a place where people made *things* that you could touch rather than simply dealt in bits and bytes, and where blue-collar workers were honored rather than regarded as leftovers from a bygone era. The Dow Jones was dominated by industrial companies such as General Electric and Westinghouse. The proportion of workers employed in the manufacturing sector reached its highest point in American history in 1943 at 30 percent of the workforce (back in 1870 it had only been about 18 percent).

U.S. WORKERS EMPLOYED IN MANUFACTURING
1870 – 2000

The rate of return on higher education actually declined in the immediate aftermath of the war because demand for blue-collar workers was so high. This was one of only two times in American history when this had happened: the other was the mid-1970s, when a sharp economic downturn coincided with a flood of baby-boom graduates onto the market.

And yet this was the manufacturing sector's swan song: the 1956 census revealed that there were more Americans doing white-collar jobs than blue-collar ones, and the most far-sighted commentators asked whether manual workers would go the way of agricultural workers. Peter Drucker coined the phrase "knowledge worker" to describe the rising class. Daniel Bell spotted a "post-industrial society" emerging in the womb of industrial society. Americans began to regard their prowess in winning Nobel Prizes as a measure of the country's economic virility—between 1943 and 1969, America won twenty-one Nobel Prizes in Physics, far more than any other country, though eleven of the winners were European refugees. Over the postwar period as a whole, it established a striking and sustained lead over every other country.

Postwar America led the world in creating a knowledge economy. American higher education provided a unique mixture of access and quality. The proportion of eighteen- to twenty-four-year-olds enrolled in institutions of higher education increased from 9.1 percent in 1939 to 15.2 percent in 1949 to 23.8 percent in 1959 to 35 percent in 1969. This was at a time when only the children of the elite plus a handful of scholarship winners went to university in Europe. At the same time, American universities prided themselves on their commitment to promoting research: increasingly professors were awarded tenure on the basis of their publications and universities ranked on the basis of their research records.

The GI program gets much of the credit for this great leap

forward: by 1956, when the original program ended, approximately 7.8 million veterans, or about half of all those who had served in the armed forces, had taken part in the program, providing the country with 450,000 engineers, 360,000 teachers, 243,000 accountants, 180,000 doctors, dentists, and nurses, 150,000 scientists, 107,000 lawyers, and thousands upon thousands more trained professionals.[11] In fact, it was part of a succession of meritocratic initiatives. The President's Commission on Higher Education published a landmark study, "Higher Education for American Democracy" (1947), that described quotas directed against Jews and Negroes as "un-American." The Educational Policies Commission published "Education and National Security" (1951), a rousing report that called on Americans to "invest a larger proportion of their economic resources in the education of individuals of superior talent."[12] The Early Admissions and Advanced Placement (AP) programs tried to liberate bright children from the lockstep uniformity of the average American high schools. The National Merit Scholarship Corporation, which was established in 1955, tried to boost public respect for intellectual excellence.

At the same time, America avoided the mistake of turning higher education into a nationalized industry, allowing public and private universities to flourish side by side and encouraging the creation of new sorts of institutions. Universities were the suns in a constellation of knowledge-related organizations that included think tanks such as the Brookings Institution in Washington, D.C., and the RAND Corporation in Los Angeles, and national institutes such as the National Institutes of Health. America also awarded research grants on the basis of competitive bids rather than bureaucratic influence.

The United States led the rest of the world in its investment in "big science." The man who did more than anybody else to convert the political establishment to the idea that science was a vital economic input rather than an expensive luxury was Vannevar Bush. Bush united the three worlds at the heart of what Eisenhower called the military-industrial complex: he was a sometime dean of engineering at MIT; the director of the Office of Scientific Research and Development, in charge of six thousand scientists, during the war; and the founder of a science company, Raytheon. He was also a confidant of Harry Truman and then of Dwight Eisenhower. A talented propagandist, his 1945 report "Science, the Endless Frontier," which urged the government to fund basic research in partnership with academia and industry, captured the public imagination with its judicious mixture of references to America's frontier past and its technological future. Bush noted that national security now depended on basic science: you couldn't produce atomic bombs without understanding the laws of physics. He then added that economic security depended on basic science too: basic science provides the scientific capital that can be turned into prosperity-producing products. "New products and new processes do not appear full-grown. They are founded on new principles and new conceptions, which in turn are painstakingly developed by research in the purest realms of science."[13]

Bush's vision of basic science was quickly made flesh. The Defense Department and the National Science Foundation became the prime funders of much of America's basic research—allocating money not just to great universities such as Bush's MIT but also to big companies and to hybrid research organizations that straddled the division between academia and business such as RAND, the Stanford Research Institute, and Xerox PARC.

The United States intensified its investment in the knowledge economy after the Soviets launched Sputnik on October 4, 1957, followed by the much larger Sputnik 2, with its dog, Laika, and its panel of scientific instruments just a month later. The Sputniks shook Americans out of their complacency: what will Americans find if they ever make it to the moon, a journalist once asked the physicist

Edward Teller; "Russians" came the grim reply.[14] Congress immediately declared "an educational emergency": among the hair-raising revelations at the time was that 75 percent of schoolchildren didn't study any physics whatsoever. The White House created a new post: Special Assistant to the President on Science and Technology. A year later, Congress passed the National Defense Education Act, and Eisenhower established the National Aeronautics and Space Administration (NASA). Funding for the National Science Foundation more than tripled in a single year from $40 million to $134 million.[15] The military bankrolled some of the most important science infrastructure, such as Lawrence Berkeley National Laboratory in Berkeley, California (for nuclear weapons), and the Lincoln Laboratory at MIT (for air defense).

Though the cold war hogged the limelight, the medical profession also made astonishing advances in these years. Having never exceeded $30 million a year before the war, public spending on health hit a succession of landmarks: $149.7 million in 1947, $1 billion in 1957, and $5 billion in 1966.[16] Penicillin was made widely available in the late 1940s and drastically reduced the number of deaths from pneumonia and syphilis. Other antibiotics such as streptomycin followed. Two polio vaccines were invented, in 1952 and 1957, wiping out the disease in the United States. All in all, 50 percent more new drugs were approved by the Federal Drug Administration between 1940 and 1960 than in the fifty years after 1960.[17] Against this should be set the fact that the number of cigarettes consumed per person increased from two thousand in 1940 to four thousand in 1970, with the majority of adults smoking regularly.

Atomic power was a particularly striking version of the knowledge economy. The United States created the Atomic Energy Commission in 1946 to find peaceful uses for nuclear power, in part to offset the worryingly high cost of developing the atomic bomb in the first place. Nuclear swords would not be so controversial if they could also be used as nuclear plows. Eight years later, in 1954, it passed the Atomic Energy Act to encourage private companies to build nuclear reactors. Scientists at Brookhaven National Laboratory on Long Island talked of creating wonderful new hybrids of carnations in a radioactive "Gamma Garden." Researchers at Argonne National Laboratory near Chicago experimented with potatoes, bread, and hot dogs to show that irradiation kept foods fresh and germ-free.[18]

Atomic power was one of many spin-offs from war. During the Eisenhower years, the Pentagon ate up six out of every ten federal dollars and the armed forces reached a total of 3.5 million men. Some optimists talked of "military Keynesianism" boosting the economy and spinning off innovations. Pessimists worried that the military-industrial complex would smother the civilian economy. There was a bit of both. The military-industrial complex provided a dependable source of income for some of the country's best-known companies, which were paid on a cost-plus basis. It also produced important innovations for the civilian economy: the budding computer industry in Silicon Valley owed as much to military spending as to Stanford University.

The United States even turned its immigration policy into an arm of the military-industrial complex: a country that put a strict limit on immigration in general nevertheless made an exception for world-class scientists and engineers. The policy started with German scientists fleeing Nazi Germany in the 1930s and continued with refugees from Communist dictatorships after the war, allowing the land of the free to add to its stock of brainpower while it burnished its reputation for civilized behavior.

Even as it focused on building a knowledge economy, postwar America invested heavily in transportation. Eisenhower's biggest domestic achievement was arguably the Federal-Aid Highway Act of

1956, which called for 41,000 miles of highways to be built by 1969 at an estimated cost of $25 billion. Predictably enough, the targets were missed: the first transcontinental interstate, I-80, was not finished until 1986 and the southern interstate, I-10, was not completed until 1990. Between 1958 and 1991, federal and state governments spent almost $429 billion on the system. Nevertheless, the interstate system was an astonishing achievement. As Earl Swift, the interstate's premier historian, has written, these highways "are intrinsic to our everyday life, to the modern American experience, to what defines the physical United States. They form the nation's commercial and cultural grid, binding its regions, bridging its dialects, snaking into every state and major city in the Lower Forty-eight. They've insinuated themselves into our slang, our perception of time and space, our mental maps."[19] More prosaically, they also boosted the economy, reducing the cost and inconvenience of long-distance travel, making it easier to produce national supply chains, and increasing the productivity of many established industries, such as truck driving. A study of thirty-five industries found that all but three experienced significant cost reductions due to cheaper and more versatile transport.[20]

The airways also became more crowded. The cost of flying relative to other goods declined by 8 percent from 1940 to 1950, by 4.5 percent from 1950 to 1960, by 2.8 percent from 1960 to 1980, and then stabilized while deteriorating in quality from 1980 to 2014. The number of passenger miles flown increased by 24.4 percent a year from 1940 to 1950, 14.3 percent a year from 1950 to 1960, and 9.9 percent a year from 1960 to 1980. An activity that had once been expensive and exotic, as well as a bit dangerous, became relatively cheap, commonplace, and safe. Though the mainstreaming of flying was largely driven by big companies such as Pan Am, there was also room for buccaneers such as Kirk Kerkorian, who capitalized on his wartime experience as a fighter pilot to establish his own airline,

Trans International, to fly gamblers from Los Angeles to Las Vegas. Kerkorian not only flew some of the planes himself, acting as ticket collector, engineer, and cleaner, he also joined the passengers at the gambling table.

Employed in the high-paying manufacturing sector or booming service sector, empowered by its growing network of roads, and focused on forming a family and accumulating material possessions, Americans spread out across the country's huge landscape. The population of the Pacific states increased by 110 percent from 1940 to 1960. California took over from New York as the country's most populous state in 1963. More than 80 percent of the population growth in the 1950s and 1960s took place in the suburbs. Some of these suburbs were of the old-fashioned type: bedroom communities on the edge of old towns such as Boston and New York. Others, particularly in the South and West, were completely new: "subs" with no "urbs," "theres" with no there there, such as Phoenix and Los Angeles. These new suburbs not only allowed America to exploit one of its great comparative advantages—the fact that it had so much free space—they also helped it to solve the great debate between Jefferson and Hamilton in a way that satisfied both parties: America was a land of independent yeomen who lived on large plots of land but nevertheless worked in the world's most advanced commercial civilization.

MANAGERIAL CAPITALISM

The capitalism that emerged after the Second World War was managerial capitalism. The economy was dominated by a handful of giant companies—the big three in car making (Ford, Chrysler, and General Motors), the big two in electricity (General Electric and

Westinghouse), and so on. General Motors was the world's largest car maker, IBM the world's largest computer maker, Procter & Gamble its largest consumer goods company. These companies were all remarkably solid by the standards of today's big companies, with their habit of contracting out whatever they can. They employed large armies of workers (GM employed a million people in 1960), owned solid assets in the form of factories and office blocks, and offered not just their managers but also their employees jobs for life. Many companies worked hard to turn themselves into the center of their employees' lives. Kodak had a 300,000-square-foot recreation center complete with an 18-hole golf course. The company sponsored movies, picnics, bridge, dancing, baseball, and, most popular of all, bowling (when the American Bowling Congress came to Rochester in the midfifties, 324 company teams entered the tournament).[21] "The big enterprise is the true symbol of our social order," Peter Drucker, a young émigré from Austria, wrote in *Harper's Magazine* in 1949. "In the industrial enterprise the structure which actually underlies all our society can be seen."[22]

American managers enjoyed a relatively free hand compared with their equivalents in Europe and Japan. They did not have to answer to universal banks like German managers or to the Ministry of Finance like Japanese managers. They did not have to answer to owners because the stock was in the hands of small investors (who were by their nature scattered and passive) rather than powerful families or big institutions. This allowed managers to make long-term bets: IBM and AT&T both supported research laboratories that patiently laid the foundations for the electronic revolution. It also allowed managers to present themselves as the guardians of the whole of society, not just the servants of the stockholders. "The job of management," proclaimed Frank Adams, the chairman of Standard Oil of New Jersey in 1951, "is to maintain an equitable and working balance among the claims of the various directly affected interest groups . . . stockholders, employees, customers, and the public at large."[23] Managers were industrial statesmen as well as businessmen.

Yet even the most powerful managers had to come to terms with big government and big labor. Big government was largely friendly. Eisenhower filled his cabinet with businesspeople: as well as appointing Charles Wilson, the CEO of General Motors, as secretary of defense, he appointed a couple of former General Motors distributors to Cabinet posts, leading Adlai Stevenson to quip that "the New Dealers have all left Washington to make way for the car dealers."

Big labor was more of a problem. In the eighteen months after the war, unions organized 550 strikes, involving 1.4 million workers, in order to demonstrate their newfound power, conferred by the pro-labor legal changes of the 1930s and the tight labor markets of the postwar years. The UAW launched a particularly determined strike against General Motors that was only settled when the management offered not just higher wages but company-sponsored pensions and health care. The "Treaty of Detroit" provided a template for all labor negotiations in the future: benefits that had hitherto been confined to managers were now spread to all workers.

Though the 1947 Taft-Hartley Act, which banned "closed shops" (which forced employers to hire only union workers) and compelled union leaders to swear that they were not Communists, did something to shift the balance of power back to managers, unions were still powerful. Throughout the 1950s, about a third of nonagricultural workers belonged to unions, and somewhere between two-thirds and three-quarters of Americans said that they approved of organized labor. Even Eisenhower made room in his Cabinet for the head of the plumbers union, Martin Durkin, as secretary of labor, provoking the *New Republic* to quip that the Cabinet consisted of "eight millionaires and a plumber." In 1955, the unions got stronger still when the AFL and the CIO agreed to merge into the AFL-CIO, reducing administrative overheads, eliminating duplication, and providing the combined AFL-CIO with a collective membership of 15.4 million. By the mid-1950s, almost half of large- and medium-size employers were giving their workers pensions, and more than two-thirds were providing some kind of insurance.[24] In Europe, policy makers decided to deliver welfare through the state. In the United States, thanks to the Treaty of Detroit, they delivered it through the corporation.

IN SEARCH OF PRODUCTIVITY

Americans were enthusiasts for the idea that management could be turned into a science. Immediately after the Second World War, only 5 percent of companies had management training programs in place. By 1958, more than three-quarters had. GE opened America's first corporate university in 1956 in Croton-on-Hudson, New York, with a fifteen-acre campus and a seven-thousand-volume management library. Soon ambitious GE-ers were fighting for a place: more than fifteen hundred passed through its doors in its first five years.[25] Other companies established training programs of their own (and poached as many GE veterans as they could get their hands on).

One of the most successful subdisciplines of management science was consumer research. Companies learned how to understand consumer markets by collecting reams of data, and how to shape them through mass advertising. They could give "brands" a personality: for example, Philip Morris turned Marlboro into the world's bestselling cigarette brand by advertising it as the cigarette of choice for rugged individuals. They could even take products that were designed for one group of people and sell them to new groups: Walter Haas and his company, Levi Strauss, repositioned jeans from work clothes for blue-collar laborers into leisure wear for rebellious youths and ultimately for the world.

One of the easiest ways to improve productivity was standardization. Standardization brings two quick benefits: it allows you to boost the productivity of relatively unskilled workers by simplifying once-complicated tasks, and it allows you to reap economies of scale and scope by expanding rapidly. Having established its lead as a manufacturing power in the nineteenth century by taking the principle of interchangeable parts further than European countries, and having then turned itself into the arsenal of democracy by taking the principle of standardization further than anyone else in the production of tanks and ships, America consolidated its position as the world's most affluent society by taking standardization to new levels in old industries, but also applying it to new areas, such as building houses and serving food.

William and Alfred Levitt applied standardized construction techniques to the production of new houses. They identified twenty-seven distinct steps in the production of a new home and then did everything they could to standardize or automate each of them. The construction of Levittown on Long Island was a model of efficiency: trucks dropped identical piles of lumber, pipes, bricks, copper tubing, and shingles at sixty-foot intervals; teams of (nonunion) workers moved from house to house, with each worker performing a specific function; and new houses were completed at a rate of thirty a day.[26] Within a year, four thousand houses had been built. The Levitts offered a choice of two designs: the four-room Cape Cod and the larger ranch house. Dozens of other developers produced similar houses across the country as people rushed to take advantage of generous mortgage terms—5 percent down (nothing for veterans) and thirty years to pay off the loan at fixed interest—and to stake their claim to a share in a booming country.

Other entrepreneurs used standardization to provide the inhabitants of these new suburbs with products and services that they could trust: toys for their children courtesy of Toys"R"Us, vans to move their stuff from one house to another courtesy of U-Haul, TV dinners courtesy of Swanson, and temporary jobs so that they could get into the new labor market courtesy of William Kelly. Edward J. DeBartolo became a shopping mall king by building cookie-cutter L-shaped or U-shaped shopping malls across the country. Jack Eckerd became a drugstore giant, his business doubling in size every two years from 1969 to 1975, by building identical self-service stores across the South.[27]

Starting in the mid-1950s, a young trucker called Malcolm McLean used standardization to revolutionize logistics.[28] McLean's great innovation was beautiful in its simplicity: transport goods in identical containers that can be loaded onto ships or trucks. This wasn't easy to implement. Trucks and cargo ships had to be redesigned. Docks had to be reorganized. Vested interests, particularly sometimes violent trade unions, had to be fought. But it increased efficiency so massively, reducing the amount of loading and unloading and of crating and uncrating, eliminating pilfering, reducing damage, that the idea spread. Ports that adopted containerization grew. Companies that embraced it saw their insurance premiums go down. By 1969, McLean's company, SeaLand Service, had grown into a giant with 27,000 trailer-type containers, 36 trailer ships, and access to 30 ports. One study found that, starting in the early 1970s, containerization increased trade among developed countries by about 17 percent and, with a 10- to 15-year lag, increased trade among all countries, developed as well as developing, by 14 percent.[29] Today, more than 90 percent of the world's trade cargo is transported in container ships.

Sam Walton revolutionized retailing by focusing on a group of customers who were normally ignored by retailers—the inhabitants of rural small towns. He took the established principles of economies of scale and standardization to new levels, building giant superstores on the edge of towns and putting his products on permanent sale ("everyday low prices"). And like McLean, he focused on logistics—building up a smooth supply chain and working with his suppliers to reduce prices. Once he had established his control over small-town America, Walton then advanced into more populous territory, using his cash piles to build giant new stores and his slick supply chain and low prices to crush competitors.

America discovered a new way of spreading a standardized solution at high speed in the form of franchising. Franchising is business by template: a franchiser produces a standardized business model and then asks small entrepreneurs to compete for licenses to operate that model. The franchiser cuts costs by providing central services such as administration, training, and advertising. The local operators do the heavy lifting of running their franchises on a day-to-day basis and thinking up new ways to improve the product. Ray Kroc, a milkshake salesman, opened the first McDonald's restaurant in partnership with the McDonald brothers, two small-scale Californian entrepreneurs, in 1954. One of his earliest franchisees, Jim Delligatti, came up with the idea for a Big Mac in 1967. Kemmons Wilson opened his first Holiday Inn in 1952 with all the modern conveniences (a TV and swimming pool) and no extra charge for children. Richard and Henry Bloch started franchising their tax-preparation business in 1955. By 1978, H&R Block was completing one in nine tax returns annually.[30]

CORPORATE IMPERIALISM

Confident, professional, and innovative, American companies expanded abroad at an unprecedented rate: their collective investment in Europe and Japan increased from $2 billion in 1950 to $41 billion in 1973. Many leading companies had already experimented with globalization during the age of laissez-faire. The Singer Marketing Company, as the Singer Corporation was then known, opened a plant in Britain in 1867. Ford had built its first plant in Britain, in Trafford Park in Manchester, in 1911. J. P. Morgan had become preoccupied with extending his enthusiasm for "combinations" to the global sphere toward the end of his life. But after the war, America's big companies towered over their foreign rivals: in 1954, for example, American affiliates in Britain were a third more productive, in terms of total labor productivity, than British firms in general.

U.S. companies conquered global markets in an astonishing range of areas (though luxury goods remained a European stronghold). By the mid-1960s, Ford and GM were the second- and third-biggest "European" car manufacturers after Fiat. U.S. companies made over 80 percent of Europe's computers. In Britain, Keynes's darkest fears of an American takeover had been realized: U.S. firms accounted for over half of the British market for cars, vacuum cleaners, electric shavers, razor blades, breakfast cereals, potato chips, sewing machines, custard powder, and typewriters. Kodak produced 90 percent of the film sold in Britain; Heinz accounted for 87 percent of baby food and 62 percent of baked beans; Kraft and Swift accounted for 75 percent of the processed cheese.[31]

Many Europeans looked on in despair. In *The American Challenge* (1967), Jean-Jacques Servan-Schreiber argued that America's superior ability to manage big companies across huge geographical areas was making it impossible for European companies to compete. The Americans had mastered the tools of organization that held the key to prosperity. The Europeans, on the other hand, were held back by their commitment to family ownership and gentlemanly values. The "art of organization" remained "a mystery to us," as he put it. Servan-Schreiber's book became not just a bestseller but a catalyst to action: it helped to inspire European dreams of creating a common market as big as the American market and a cadre of business schools as professional as American business schools.

Ordinary Americans enjoyed material abundance on a scale that had never been equaled before. This was the age of "the great compression," a phrase coined by Claudia Goldin and Robert Margo, in which inequality was low, opportunities abounded, and everybody seemed to have a chance of getting ahead. Low-paid farmworkers moved into better-paid jobs in the cities. Well-paid city dwellers moved from the urban core into the rapidly expanding suburbs. People with no more than a high school education bought generous plots of land and enjoyed jobs for life. Ambitious workers could climb the career ladder from the shop floor to a senior managerial position. Not everybody prospered equally: African Americans still suffered from discrimination and poverty and women were often sidelined. But for white men at least the American dream was as close to being a reality as it has ever been.

The economy was so successful that publishers produced a succession of bestsellers agonizing over the problems of affluence. David Riesman's *The Lonely Crowd* (1950) accused Americans of conformism. David Potter's *People of Plenty* (1954) accused them of consumerism. William H. Whyte's *The Organization Man* (1956) accused them of being cogs in the corporate machine. John Kenneth Galbraith's *The Affluent Society* (1956) accused them of satisfying their wants "with reckless abandon." (This was the golden age of popular sociology as well as economic growth.) The rise of the suburbs was a particular source of angst. David Riesman likened "the suburb" to "a fraternity house at a small college in which like-mindedness reverberates upon itself."[32] The idea that suburban life was too dull to endure was so widely held that Herbert Gans found it necessary to pronounce, after spending a few years living in Levittown, New Jersey, that "most new suburbanites are pleased with the community that develops; they enjoy the house and outdoor living and take pleasure from the large supply of compatible people, without experiencing the boredom or malaise ascribed to suburban homogeneity."

Writings about alienation are seldom worth the paper they are written on. Galbraith and company were nevertheless right that America was a homogeneous society. The suburbs looked as if they had been created with a cookie cutter. Supermarkets stocked their shelves with mass-produced products. The big three television companies (CBS, ABC, and NBC) measured their audiences in tens of millions: when CBS broadcast the episode of *I Love Lucy* in which Lucy had a baby to coincide with the actress who played Lucy, Lucille Ball, also having a baby, on January 19, 1953, 68.8 percent of the country's television sets were tuned in, a far higher proportion than were tuned in to Dwight Eisenhower's inauguration the following day. The highways and byways were lined with motel chains that prided themselves on providing the same facilities whether you were in the forests of New England or the deserts of Arizona. Holiday Inn advertised itself with the slogan "the best surprise is no surprise."

The country's core institutions vigorously promoted the "American way of life": competitive sports (jocks and cheerleaders were the heroes of school life), anodyne religiosity (Eisenhower said that everybody should have a religion—and he didn't mind what it was), and reverence for the flag. The proportion of Americans who were born

U.S. FOREIGN-BORN POPULATION
PLOTTED BY DECADE, 1850 – 2000

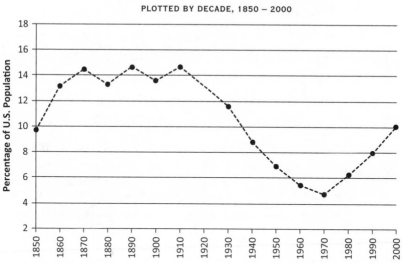

abroad declined from 6.9 percent in 1950 to 4.7 percent in 1970, the lowest figure in American history (see chart above).

The Immigration and Naturalization Service actively promoted a more homogeneous society, deporting illegals, particularly Chinese, and pressing aliens to become fully fledged Americans. The new suburbs proved to be more successful melting pots than the old cities with their ethnically based political machines. Old-fashioned ethnic loyalties dissolved into an ecumenical faith in Americanism, a point well documented in Will Herberg's *Protestant, Catholic, Jew* (1955). The fact that the golden age of American growth was also an age of declining ethnic diversity (at least when it came to immigration) and vigilant Americanism helps to explain the current rise of nativism and populism.

INTIMATIONS OF MORTALITY

The record of success in these years was astonishing. By 1960, the average American family was 30 percent richer than the average family in 1950. More than 60 percent of people owned their own homes. A quarter of American homes had been built in the previous ten years. The 1960s looked as if they would cap even this. Real GDP rose 28 percent between 1960 and 1965.

Yet beneath this glittering surface there were plenty of things to be worried about. American companies were complacent but flawed: lumbered with huge welfare costs, unwilling to think beyond standardization, and completely blind to competition from Asia. The Treaty of Detroit was eating away at the foundations of American affluence: why provide workers with a lifetime of high wages and retirement benefits for doing standardized jobs when those jobs could be done much more cheaply by foreigners or machines? And the federal government's growing habit of spending money it didn't have was, like most bad habits, proving addictive.

An age of optimism was about to give way to an age of pessimism.

Nine

STAGFLATION

————◆————

I N 1976 THE UNITED STATES celebrated its two hundredth birthday with due aplomb. The Treasury minted commemorative coins and the Post Office printed special stamps. Tall ships massed in New York and Boston. Cities mounted firework displays, with the president, Gerald Ford, presiding over one of the grandest in Washington, D.C. Elizabeth II, the queen of America's former imperial master, arrived for a state visit. Americans took particular pleasure in celebrating the country's spirit of self-reliance and self-invention, as embodied in hardworking colonial housewives, entrepreneurial rural artisans, and flinty yeomen farmers.

Yet the country's mood was hardly jolly. The 1970s was a dismal decade for the United States: the age of gold had turned into an age of lead, and many people were asking whether the American era was over. Three presidencies in a row ended in disgrace or disappointment. Richard Nixon was threatened with impeachment. Gerald Ford and Jimmy Carter were both ejected after a single term. "We have not an imperial presidency but an imperiled presidency," Gerald Ford put it in the final year of Carter's ill-starred reign.[1]

The decade was enveloped in an atmosphere of crisis. America's humiliating defeat at the hands of a small Communist power in Vietnam destroyed its self-confidence. The poisons that had been released by that war continued to eat away at its soul. The Soviets advanced menacingly, invading Afghanistan in 1979 when their puppet regime in Kabul weakened. The New Left turned to nihilism and violence. America's inner-city ghettoes were convulsed by violence and arson. The murder rate climbed to an all-time high of ten per ten thousand in the late 1970s. Richard Nixon worried in private that the United States had "become subject to the decadence which eventually destroys a civilization."[2]

Public intellectuals debated whether the 1970s should be called the "time of conflict," the "era of decline," or the "age of limits." Mancur Olson argued that democracies inevitably become the prisoners of powerful interest groups. "On balance," he concluded, "special interest organizations and collusions reduce efficiency and aggregate income in the societies in which they operate and make political life more divisive."[3] A group of MIT academics, who mysteriously called themselves the Club of Rome, outdid Thomas Malthus by arguing that the world was about to run out not only of food but also of all the basic materials of life, from oil to water; *The Limits to Growth* (1972) sold more than 12 million copies. In 1975, *Time* magazine published a cover story asking, "Can Capitalism Survive?" A nation that had emerged from the Second World War believing firmly that it was successful and good came to believe that, at the very least, it was unsuccessful and bad, and that, quite possibly, it was doomed.

Economic records of the worst kind were broken. In 1971, the United States had an unfavorable balance of trade for the first time since 1893. In 1974, the inflation rate hit 11 percent. The stock market ended the decade at the same level as it had begun.

Underlying the country's domestic problems was a sharp decline in the growth of productivity. Over the thirteen years from 1960 to 1973, output per hour increased 51 percent across the U.S. business sector. In the thirteen years from 1973 to 1986, it increased at less than half that pace (see chart below).

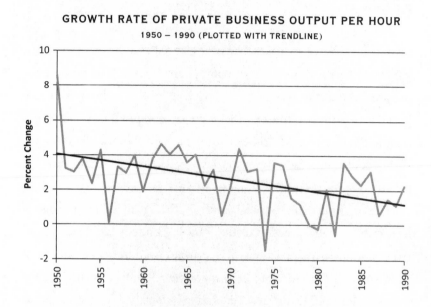

GROWTH RATE OF PRIVATE BUSINESS OUTPUT PER HOUR
1950 – 1990 (PLOTTED WITH TRENDLINE)

America was a particularly extreme example of a general trend. Europe and Japan also saw marked slowdowns in productivity growth as the low-hanging fruits (such as moving farmers off the land and into industry) had been picked and new ones proved hard to find.

Slower growth in productivity meant stagnation in living standards. From 1900 to 1973, real wages in the United States had grown at an annual rate of about 2 percent. Compounded over the years, that meant that average pay (and by implication average living standard) doubled every thirty-five years. In 1973, this trend came to an end and the average real wages of what the U.S. Bureau of Labor Statistics calls production and nonsupervisory workers began to decline. By the middle of the 1990s, the average hourly real wage of a production worker was less than 85 percent of what it had been in 1973.

FROM HUBRIS TO NEMESIS

One reason for the miserabilism of the 1970s was the excessive optimism of the previous decade: triumphant liberals had pushed the postwar economic model to a breaking point. Politicians made promises ("guns and butter") that were too good to last. Workers demanded higher wages without delivering higher productivity. Managers focused on fighting yesterday's battles rather than winning tomorrow's wars.

The key figure in the transition from the age of gold to the age of lead was Lyndon Baines Johnson. John F. Kennedy had been a relatively conservative president. His inaugural address was all about what you could do for your country rather than what your country could do for you. (The "new generation" identified in his inaugural was "tempered by war" and "disciplined by a hard and bitter peace.") He appointed so many Republicans to his Cabinet, including Clarence Douglas Dillon as secretary of the treasury, that Walter Lippmann quipped that it was the Eisenhower administration only thirty years younger.[4] Kennedy was much more interested in winning the cold war than in social reform, and was notably cautious about civil rights. "It really is true that foreign affairs are the only important issue for a president to handle, isn't it," he told Richard Nixon. "I mean who gives a shit if the minimum wage is $1.15 or $1.25 in comparison to something like this."

Kennedy nevertheless prepared the way for a spending boom by filling his Council of Economic Advisers with academic Keynesians. The council warned that the biggest problem facing the country was that the Treasury was raising too much money. The large federal surpluses would act as a deflationary brake on economic growth—a phenomenon known as "fiscal drag"—and the government needed to find ways of spending money. Predictably, there was no shortage of ideas for doing the spending: the 1964 tax cut, a program to put a man on the moon, and, of course, lots of social spending.

JFK was succeeded by a man who had none of JFK's caution. LBJ believed, with some justification, that Kennedy's assassination required a grand gesture in response. He also believed, with less justification, that his own genius deserved to be memorialized in great legislation. Standing before Congress six weeks after the assassination, he declared "unconditional war on poverty." "The richest nation on earth can afford to win it," he said. "We cannot afford to lose it." In the space of a single Congress, in 1965–66, LBJ passed a raft of laws committing America to create nothing less than a new society—"We have the opportunity to move not only toward the rich society, and the powerful society, but upward to the Great Society." He rightly outlawed discrimination in the 1964 Civil Rights Act and expanded the federal machinery designed to watch over hiring practices. He threw in the Public Broadcasting Act, the Fair Packaging and Labeling Act, and the Highway Safety Act. "He adopts programs the way a child eats chocolate chip cookies," a weary aide commented. "I'm sick of all the people who talk about the things we can't do," LBJ once said. "Hell, we're the richest country in the world, the most powerful. We can do it all."

The Great Society involved a massive expansion of the entitlement state: two new health-care entitlements, Medicare and Medicaid; the extension of Social Security disability insurance to cover temporarily disabled workers; two large increases in Social Security retirement and disability benefits; and the largest expansion in the Aid to Families with Dependent Children (AFDC) program in its thirty-year history. The federal government also funded poverty activists who encouraged people to demand their "rights."

Johnson pushed "New Frontier" economic policies to extremes, as if producing economic growth was a sheer matter of will and determination. In 1964, he bullied the Federal Reserve into keeping interest rates as low as possible at the same time as delivering a powerful fiscal stimulus by signing tax cuts into law. When William McChesney Martin, the chairman of the Fed, demurred, Johnson invited him to his Texas ranch and gave him the once-over, shoving him around the room, yelling in his face, "Boys are dying in Vietnam and Bill Martin doesn't care." When the combination of tax cuts and low interest rates began to produce inflationary pressure, LBJ doubled down on bullying and manipulation: he punished aluminum companies that raised prices by releasing some of the government's stockpile, punished copper producers by restricting exports, and even punished egg producers by getting the surgeon general to issue a warning on the hazards of cholesterol in eggs.[5]

Johnson was very much the embodiment of the spirit of the age: "Landslide Lyndon" not only massacred Goldwater in the 1964 election but brought along with him huge Democratic majorities, with his party holding more than two-thirds of the seats in both chambers. "In the early 1960s in Washington we thought we could do anything," Daniel Patrick Moynihan reflected; "the central psychological proposition of liberalism . . . is that for every problem there is a solution." In 1966, Walter Heller, one of Kennedy's top economic advisers, pronounced that the "'new economics' would assure full employment, low inflation, and steady economic growth."[6] "Steady" understates it: national income, adjusted for inflation, grew at 4 percent a year from 1962 to 1974. By 1973, the nation's real income was 70 percent higher than it had been in 1961. In the middle of the glorious 1960s, a top census official said that America's most pressing problem would be how to consume all the wealth that it was producing: "a continuation of recent trends will carry us to unbelievable levels of economic activity in our own lifetimes."[7]

Johnson's closest economic advisers underestimated the cost of all these new entitlements, not just in the long term but even in the short term. In early 1966, federal budget officials projected that Medicaid would cost under $400 million during the federal government's 1967 fiscal year. In fact, it cost nearer a billion. The cost of a day in the hospital, which had been rising by 6.4 percent a year from 1961 to 1965, rose by 16.6 percent in 1967, 15.4 percent in 1968, and 14.5 percent in 1969.[8] Federal spending on AFDC ballooned to $392 million in 1967 from a negligible amount in 1962.

Johnson's supersized liberalism also proved singularly ill-timed. LBJ increased spending on "butter" at exactly the same time that he was forced, thanks to the war in Vietnam, to increase spending on "guns." In 1968, the federal deficit hit $25.1 billion, more than the total of all deficits between 1963 and 1967. Government began to fail at everything it touched, from fighting poverty to fighting the North Vietnamese, and the proportion of Americans who said that they "trust the federal government" fell from 75 percent in the mid-1960s to 25 percent in the late 1970s. The mighty economy that LBJ believed had been capable of solving every problem began to falter. He had overloaded the system at just the time when the system was beginning to fail.

LBJ was replaced by a man who had made his career whipping up hatred of the liberal establishment. But it soon turned out that when it came to running the country rather than winning votes, the archconservative was in fact a closet liberal: a Keynesian in economics, as he told a surprised news anchor in January 1971 (who compared it to "a Christian crusader saying 'All things considered, I think Mohammed was right'"), and a progressive in social policy.[9]

Nixon presided over an even bigger expansion of the entitlement state than LBJ, oblivious to the fact that the cracks in the system were already beginning to appear. Congress created a raft of new entitlements—to free school meals, bigger unemployment checks, and enhanced disability benefits. It increased Social Security benefits by 10 percent and created an automatic mechanism to link benefits to the rate of inflation. Nixon happily supported all these measures and often initiated them (John Cogan, of Stanford University, nicely calls the chapter on Nixon in his history of federal entitlement programs "the second Great Society").[10] Total annual inflation-adjusted entitlement expenditure actually grew 20 percent faster under Nixon than it did under Johnson. In 1971, entitlement spending finally surpassed defense spending.[11] Excess was everywhere. Reality was closing in.

On August 15, 1971, Richard Nixon announced a New Economic Plan, unfortunately employing a phrase that Lenin had used to describe his economic volte-face in the 1920s. He imposed a temporary ninety-day freeze on prices, wages, salaries, and rents, to be followed by a system of prices and income controls. Henceforward, prices and wages would no longer be determined by the market, on the basis of supply and demand, scarcity and abundance, but by a wage-price review board that included several rising Republican stars, such as Donald Rumsfeld and Richard Cheney, who administered Nixon's policies through gritted teeth. He also slapped a 10 percent surcharge on foreign imports. The *New York Times*, reflecting conventional wisdom at the time, applauded its archenemy for his "bold" move. Inflation slowed for a while only to resume with renewed fury.

Nixon coupled his decision to fix prices and wages with a momentous decision to take America off the gold standard and allow the dollar to float (downward) on the global market. Since the Bretton Woods Agreement of 1944, all major nations that tied their currency to the U.S. dollar and central banks had been able to convert the dollar to gold at $35 an ounce. This system provided the basis for stable growth by imprisoning politicians in a straitjacket: if a particular national leader wanted to give his economy a temporary boost ahead of an election, the head of the central bank could restrain him by saying that this would destabilize the global system and anger other countries. Unfortunately, the system could only work if two conditions were fulfilled: if the United States maintained a large stockpile of gold and, second, if other countries refrained from hoarding dollars and then exchanging them for gold when the time seemed right. At the end of 1957, the U.S. Treasury had by far the world's largest stock of gold, with 653 million ounces. FDR's decision to elevate the price of gold to $35 per ounce in 1934, 70 percent above the market rate, had given foreign central banks an incentive to sell their gold holdings to the United States and allowed the U.S. Treasury to increase its gold holdings from 246 million ounces in 1934 to 700 million in 1949. But from 1958 onward, as American inflation accelerated and the shadow price of gold finally rose above $35 per ounce, foreign central banks began to use their excess U.S. dollars to buy gold at the fixed $35 an ounce, and America's gold hoard declined almost every year afterward. By the late 1960s, foreign holdings of dollars (nearly $50 billion) far outstripped U.S. gold reserves (about $10 billion). Between 1957 and 1972, U.S. official reserves fell by 377 million ounces. Nixon had no choice but to close the so-called gold window, stabilizing America's gold holdings at about 275 million ounces, where they remained until 1979, but his decision nevertheless jolted the global economy. In the more than forty years since then the country's gold holdings have barely budged and currently number 265.5 million ounces (see chart).

On top of the gold shock came an oil shock. America had

U.S. OFFICIAL GOLD RESERVES
1957 – 1980

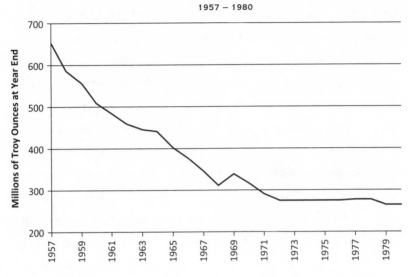

dominated the world oil industry from the birth of the oil era in the 1870s. Every time it looked as if the country was running out of oil, new fields came on line: just as the Pennsylvania fields ran dry in the early 1900s, Americans discovered vast new supplies of oil in Texas and California. This persuaded consumers to act as if cheap oil were just another of God's gifts to them: more than 80 percent of adults drove to work, and the average American car consumed 18 percent more fuel in 1973 than in 1963. But the world was changing even if Americans were becoming more self-indulgent. The oil-exporting countries had banded together into OAPEC (Organization of Arab Petroleum Exporting Countries) in 1960 to combat the downward pressure on prices. Domestic oil fields had started to run out, forcing America to turn to new fields that were much more difficult to exploit. In 1973, 36 percent of the oil that Americans consumed was imported from abroad, compared with 22 percent in 1970.

OAPEC's decision in October 1973 to impose an oil embargo on

America as punishment for its support of Israel during the Yom Kippur War thus squeezed the U.S. economy. Motorists waited in line for hours for a chance to fill their tanks and supplies frequently ran out. Tempers flared. Fists flew. In one extreme case, a station attendant was shot dead. The government tried everything it could to deal with its energy problem. Washington urged Americans to turn down their thermostats, reduced the speed limit to fifty-five miles per hour, invested in new forms of energy, and established a Department of Energy. Henry Kissinger shuttled around the Middle East trying to bring peace. Nothing changed much. The price of U.S. crude oil rose over ninefold between 1972 and 1981, sending shock waves through corporate America, starting with big energy consumers such as domestic transportation, oil refining, chemicals, steel, aluminum, and international shipping, but including the whole of the corporate world.

Above all, the oil shock entrenched America's biggest economic problem. Stagflation was a toxic combination of rising inflation and unemployment that Keynesian economists, citing the Phillips curve, which postulated a fixed trade-off between inflation and unemployment, said could never happen. In the fourteen-year stretch between 1969 and 1982, the annual rate of inflation only fell below 5 percent twice, and for four of those years it was in double digits, hitting 14.8 percent in March 1980. At the same time unemployment remained stubbornly high.

Nixon's plans to micromanage inflation to a tolerable level were doomed from the start: if anything, by creating artificial shortages in basic goods, they pushed prices upward. Gerald Ford, Nixon's successor, tried substituting volunteerism for bureaucratic management. In October 1974, wearing a WIN (Whip Inflation Now) badge on his lapel, he declared inflation "domestic enemy number one," and tried to persuade Americans to beat the scourge by driving less, heating less, wasting less, and growing their own vegetables. Some discount retailers demonstrated their commercial spirit by proclaiming that their cheap products made them champion inflation beaters. For the most part, however, the call for voluntary restraint fell on deaf ears. Jimmy Carter beat the same drum, telling Americans that they needed to substitute sacrifice for self-indulgence and stop being so wasteful. Stagflation continued regardless. By the end of the 1970s, it looked as if the world's most powerful economy had forgotten how to achieve the most basic form of economic management—stable prices.

Stagflation created political convulsions. Workers agitated for higher pay raises to keep up with the rising cost of living. Savers were upset as they saw their life savings destroyed. Taxpayers revolted as rising nominal incomes brought them into higher tax brackets. In 1978, furious that they were paying ever-higher property taxes while the services they got for their taxes were either stagnant or deteriorating, the sprawling suburbs of Southern California had had enough. Led by Howard Jarvis, an energetic antitax protester, Californians passed Proposition 13, halving their property taxes at a stroke and making it all but impossible to raise property taxes in the future.

DECLINE AND FALL

The America of the 1970s bore a striking resemblance to the Britain of the early 1900s: a great power that was suddenly struck by the possibility of its own demise. The British army had struggled to defeat a ragtag army of Boers in South Africa just as the Americans had struggled to defeat the Communists in Vietnam. The British establishment had found itself mocked by the Bloomsbury group just as the American establishment found itself mocked by the *New York Review of Books*. George Bernard Shaw quipped, in *Misalliance*, that "Rome fell, Babylon fell, Hindhead's turn will come." Americans worried that the same thing was true of Scarsdale, the Upper East Side, and Georgetown.

The most striking similarity was economic rather than military or cultural. In 1901, the year of Queen Victoria's death, Frederick Arthur McKenzie, a British journalist, enjoyed runaway success with his book *The American Invaders: Their Plans, Tactics and Progress*:

> The most serious aspect of the American industrial invasion lies in the fact that these newcomers have acquired control of almost every new industry created during the past fifteen years.... What are the chief new features in London life? They are, I take it, the telephone, the portable camera, the phonograph, the electric street car, the automobile, the typewriter, passenger lifts in houses, and the multiplication of machine tools. In every one of these, save the petroleum automobile, the American maker is supreme; in several he is the monopolist.

The sting in the tail of this passage is "save the petroleum automobile": by 1908, the United States had surpassed France as the world's leading producer of automobiles, and by the First World War, it was supreme in this area too.

Seventy-nine years later, two professors at Harvard Business School, Robert Hayes and William Abernathy, made the same case about the United States in an article in the *Harvard Business Review*, "Managing Our Way to Economic Decline." The professors noted that foreigners were devastating America's old industries such as cars and steel, and taking over high-tech businesses as well: in particular the Japanese and the Germans were doing to America what America had done to Britain.

The 1970s was the decade when America finally had to grapple with the fact that it was losing its leadership in an ever-widening range of industries. Though the best American companies such as General Electric and Pfizer powered ahead, a striking number treaded water: they had succeeded during the long postwar boom not because they had any particular merits, but because Europe and Japan were still recovering from the devastation of the Second World War, and they collapsed at the first sniff of competition. This was most obvious in two industries that had long been synonymous with America's industrial might: motor vehicles and steel.

For the first sixty years of the century, America had dominated car production: in 1950, three-quarters of the world's cars were made in the United States and a large proportion of the rest were made by American-owned companies abroad. By the early 1970s, Detroit had become fat and lazy. The big three companies kept adding layers of management because they had money to burn. They kept adding new features to their cars because they thought that their customers had money to burn. All the while they failed to pay attention to the thing that had turned them into great car companies in the first place—providing their customers with value for money. As early as 1958, a journalist described American cars as "overblown, overpriced monstrosities built by oafs for thieves to sell to mental defectives." The result was a steady rise of imports (see chart opposite).

America's champions were stuck in the mud. They devoted almost no attention to innovation: the last great innovation was the automatic transmission in 1948. They first ignored the growing market for smaller cars and, when they belatedly realized that it wouldn't go away, failed to put resources behind it. America's leading entrants to the market, such as the Chevrolet Corvair, Ford Pinto, and American Motors Gremlin, all suffered from basic problems with quality and, indeed, safety. The Ford Pinto had an unfortunate habit of bursting into flames when it was rear-ended.

U.S. MOTOR VEHICLE SALES BY ORIGIN
1931 – 2011

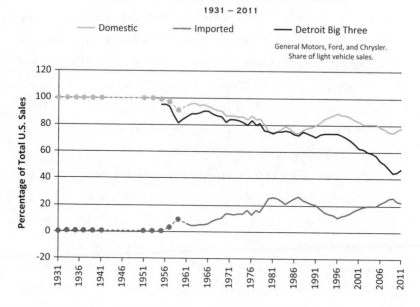

Domestic ——— Imported ——— Detroit Big Three

General Motors, Ford, and Chrysler.
Share of light vehicle sales.

They weren't even very good at doing what they regarded as their core business, devoting far too little attention to the bread and butter of the industry, reliability and safety. A striking number of these "ocean liners of the road" ran into technological icebergs as they cruised down Eisenhower's highways and left their passengers stranded by the side of the road. Ralph Nader's *Unsafe at Any Speed* (1965) became a bestseller because it diagnosed a national catastrophe. In the 1950s and 1960s, more than 2.5 million Americans were killed in car accidents, and several millions injured. Detroit also devoted far too little attention to fuel efficiency: even after the first oil shock of 1973–74, it continued to produce giant gas-guzzlers, on the assumption that high fuel prices were simply a passing peculiarity, and the world would soon return to the Elysian days of the 1950s.

U.S. car companies also fell behind their foreign rivals in terms of productivity. In 1950, American car workers were three times more productive than their German equivalents. By 1980, Japanese car workers were 17 percent more productive than the Americans.[12] The Japanese had caught the Americans napping and stolen their clothes. They borrowed American management ideas from American management gurus such as W. Edwards Deming and weaved them into a new production system based on just-in-time inventories and total quality management. The Americans by contrast stuck blindly to Henry Ford's system of mass production even as workers, under the twin influences of the counterculture and a tight labor market, refused to perform routine jobs.[13] In 1979, with the Japanese controlling 20 percent of the U.S. car market, Chrysler lost $1.1 billion, the largest business loss in U.S. history, requiring a government loan guarantee to remain in business. In 1980, Ford lost nearly $600 million, GM lost $763 million, and pressure for protectionism proved irresistible. The Japanese only preserved their access to the U.S. market by building "transplant" factories in the United States, all of which outperformed their home-grown rivals.

The steel industry suffered from the same problem of blinkered complacency. America had been by far the world's biggest steel producer for the first five decades of the century, with output fluctuating between 38 percent of the world total in 1913 and 72 percent in 1945, and U.S. Steel had been by far the world's biggest steel company. In 1937, U.S. steelworkers were anywhere between two and four and a half times more productive than their British counterparts, depending on which branch of the sector you were looking at.[14]

Then America's share of world output plunged, from 43 percent in 1953 to 11 percent in 1982. The 1959 steel strike, when United Steelworkers shut down domestic production for 116 days, was pivotal here. It broke the spell of American steel: U.S. companies that had hitherto refused to buy foreign steel on the grounds that it was of poor quality realized that they had been operating under an illusion.

Import penetration rose from less than 3 percent in 1958 to about 15 percent a decade later (see chart below).

U.S. STEEL STATISTICS
1914 – 2015

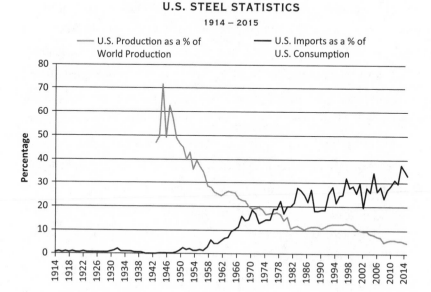

At the same time, the strike led to a boom in wages as employers tried to avert any future strike action: by the early 1980s, average wages in the steel industry were more than 95 percent higher than average manufacturing wages in general.

Foreign steelmakers, particularly the Japanese and later the Koreans, proved to be much more fleet-footed than the Americans. Japanese managers were quicker to adopt innovative techniques such as continuous casting mills. America's United Steelworkers (USW) played into their rivals' hands by negotiating higher wage rates and more restrictive work rules even as the Japanese pulled ahead in terms of productivity. In 1956, Japanese steelmakers had been 19 percent less productive than U.S. steelmakers. By 1976, they were 13 to 17 percent more productive.[15] Even as foreign supply increased, domestic demand contracted. Cities built fewer skyscrapers. There was a growing fashion for using aluminum rather than steel. U.S. Steel fell from the world's number one steelmaker to number two. Smaller steel companies merged.

The United States established its lead in consumer electronics in much the same way as it had established its lead in steel and cars: by taking the latest ideas and turning them into cheap and reliable products for the mass market. In 1955, U.S. companies controlled 96 percent of the U.S. radio-set market. By 1965, their share had fallen to 30 percent, and by 1975, it had fallen to almost zero. The same pattern held across the board, with some delays for different categories. In 1955, America had dozens of successful companies that made televisions. By the 1990s, they had all been taken over by foreign companies—Motorola's television brand by Matsushita (Japan); Magnavox, Philco, and Sylvania by Philips (Holland); RCA and GE by Thompson (France); and Zenith by LG Electronics (South Korea).

RCA provides a vivid example of the industry's habit of shooting itself in the foot. The company was late to make the shift from vacuum tubes to transistors. Blind to the transistor revolution, it nevertheless tried to diversify into computers, only to be humiliated by IBM. It devoted so much energy to computers—at one point 40 percent of its researchers' time was taken up with computers—that it failed to invest enough money in the development of color television.[16] The company sealed its fate in the 1970s when it bet the farm on its VideoDisc when the industry was moving toward videotape. Even as it lost its way in its core businesses, it engaged in a burst of diversification.

At the same time, Japan's electronic giants such as Sony, Matsushita (Panasonic), Hitachi, and Mitsubishi turned themselves into world-class export machines. There is no doubt that they cheated a bit: they protected their home markets from American imports even as they invested their profits in production facilities; they charged their domestic consumers a premium even as they charged foreigners rock-bottom prices (and sometimes even bought market share); they took advantage of America's user-friendly distribution system while keeping their own distribution system as opaque as possible. For all that, their success was built on the simple fact that they offered better goods for less money.

The same pattern was repeated in a wide swath of other industries. The footwear, clothing, and textile industries were crushed under an ever-growing pile of imports. The tire industry suffered from a double squeeze: the invention of radial tires extended the average life of tires threefold, even as foreign companies invaded American markets. With a global problem of oversupply, the Americans suffered most because they were the most expensive and least innovative. Between 1977 and 1987, thirty-seven U.S. tire firms were shut down and the industry's workforce fell by 40 percent.[17] The semiconductor industry also turned tail, though its great retreat came in the 1980s rather than the 1970s. At its peak in 1977, the U.S. semiconductor industry supplied 95 percent of the U.S. market, half the European market, and 57 percent of the world market. By 1989, the U.S. share of the world market had fallen to 40 percent and America was a net importer of chips. The problems in America's big industries had a ripple effect on the rest of the consumer economy: the number of new housing starts dropped by nearly 2 million—from 12.2 million in the 1960s to 10.4 million in the 1970s.[18]

One big theme comes through in all these case studies: the precipitous decline in the quality of American management. In the first half of the century, the United States led the world in the development of management as both a practice and a profession. Frederick Taylor thrilled the world with the discovery of "scientific" management. Harvard University shocked Oxford and Cambridge by establishing a business school. Marvin Bower turned McKinsey into the world's leading management consultancy. In the 1950s, America had been a net exporter of "management": Japanese firms hired American management gurus and European countries established business schools based on the American model. By the 1970s, everything had changed.

The obvious problem was complacency: having sat on top of the world for so long, American managers didn't notice that the world beneath them had adapted. They continued to measure themselves against the competitors next door rather than against Tokyo and Dusseldorf. The captains of the car industry airily dismissed German and Japanese cars while paying themselves ten times more than German and Japanese managers. The Beetle was a fad, they said. The Japanese could only make cheap cars for cheapskates. When Ron Hartwig, a public relations manager for GM on the West Coast, wrote to his boss in Detroit that he was seeing more and more Japanese cars on the road, his boss wrote back haughtily, "I just looked out my window in the GM Building, and I don't see any Japanese cars."[19] When it finally dawned on them that they were falling behind, they resorted to the cheapest trick in the book, accusing their rivals of cheating and demanding protection from the government.

A second problem was management's loss of focus on the quality of its products. In the 1950s, plenty of managers had climbed to the top from the company engine room or the production and engineering departments. In the 1960s and 1970s, they were replaced by accountants, lawyers, and people with MBAs. In 1980, Jackson Grayson, the president of the American Productivity and Quality Center, complained that, for twenty years, American management had "coasted off the great R&D gains made during World War II and constantly rewarded executives from the marketing, financial, and legal sides of the business while it ignored the production men." Many products were not just second-rate but even dangerous. In 1973, Nixon established a national commission on public safety that revealed a staggering toll of injuries from unsafe products in its first report: 20 million injuries, 110,000 permanent disabilities, and 30,000 deaths every year.

Too few companies were willing to go beyond hitting the numbers to shaping the markets of the future. Joseph Schumpeter noted that one of the paradoxes of innovation is that it can destroy capital in the short term even though it creates it in the long term: it makes existing skills and plants obsolete but opens up the possibility of megaprofits in the future. Managing by numbers discourages innovation because it compels managers to focus on short-term certainty at the expense of long-term possibilities.

Even America's great R&D departments lost their pizzazz. We have seen that America's ability to integrate management and R&D was one of its great strengths: General Electric and AT&T were both founded by people who were scientists before they were businessmen, and both companies invested heavily in research from the start. In the 1960s and 1970s, the executive suites and the R&D departments went their separate ways. Xerox's research department, Xerox PARC, produced a succession of blockbuster products, such as the computer mouse, that the company's managers back east knew nothing about. RCA's laboratories were widely regarded as a "country club" where scientists entertained themselves pursuing harebrained projects.

The most vivid example of the problems with American management was the fashion for conglomerates. The cynical case for conglomerates was that they allowed companies to skirt antitrust laws by expanding into unrelated businesses. Managers also advanced a more sophisticated justification: bringing a portfolio of different products under a single roof allowed them to manage risk because when one product was in a down cycle another was likely to be in an up cycle. In *The Rise and Fall of the Conglomerate Kings* (1984), Robert

Sobel noted that "conglomerates were the most exciting corporate form to appear in more than a generation, and they shook up the business scene as no other phenomenon had since the era of trust creation at the turn of the century." Some of America's leading businesspeople such as Harold Geneen, the boss of International Telegraph and Telephone, devoted their lives to building conglomerates. Some of America's leading brands also embraced diversification: Quaker Oats bought a toy company, Johnson Wax entered the personal-care business, Chesebrough-Pond's acquired a line of children's clothing. Between 1950 and 1959, 4,789 firms in the manufacturing and mining sector representing some $15.4 billion in assets were folded up into conglomerates.[20]

In fact, conglomerates had one big disadvantage that became bigger as time went on: they diverted attention away from producing first-rate products toward the secondary question of the mechanics of management. RCA was a case in point: even as it lost the competition to dominate the emerging color television market, it engaged in a burst of diversification. Its decision to buy Random House might at least be justified that it was another venture in the "communications" business. This could hardly be said of other acquisitions such as Hertz Rent-a-Car, Coronet Carpets, the Banquet Foods frozen-dinner company, and a golf clothing company.

The problem was deeper than poor management. The American system of production—producing long runs of standardized products—had allowed relatively unskilled workers to create highly standardized products for easily satisfied consumers quickly and cheaply. But it was no longer suited to a world characterized by rapid change, global competition, consumer power, and high levels of volatility. U.S. firms were faced by new competitors who didn't think that you needed to make trade-offs between quantity and quality or standardization and flexibility. Japanese producers in particular argued that they had produced a new production system that provided variety and cheapness.

URBIS ET ORBIS

As America's industrial giants weakened and its house-building machine slowed, a new phrase entered the language, "the Rust Belt." The buckles of the Rust Belt were the great industrial cities that had flourished during the era of Rockefeller and Carnegie but eventually fell into disrepair. Six of the sixteen largest cities in 1950 had lost half their population by 1980: Buffalo, Cleveland, Detroit, New Orleans, Pittsburgh, and St. Louis. Though the worst affected cities were industrial towns that had been built on a single industry, even polyglot cities such as New York and Chicago suffered badly.

America's urban nightmare, which was reflected in films such as *Taxi Driver* (1976), had deep roots. Middle-class citizens fled to the suburbs, taking their spending power and tax dollars with them. The remaining citizens were more prone to crime and dysfunction, which pushed up the demands on public services. And the combination of rising crime and growing social problems drove even more middle-class citizens out into the suburbs. But it was taken to a wholly new level by the crisis.

The most famous example was Detroit, a city that was so much the epitome of the one-industry town that its music was called Motown. The virtues that created it soon turned into vices. Mass production meant that workers had little incentive to improve their skills. Giant factories handed power to organized workers who were willing to bring the whole production process to a halt. Economic success meant that humdrum managers persuaded themselves that they were masters of the universe. And finally the car itself turned against the city that had produced it: managers and workers both used the mobility that the car provided to move out of the city and into the suburbs. In 1954, the nation's first big suburban shopping center, with parking for ten thousand cars, began drawing retail trade from downtown. In 1967, the 12th Street riot, which saw forty-three people killed and more than two thousand buildings destroyed, and was only quelled with the help of the Michigan National Guard and the U.S. Army, hastened white flight, and from 1970 to 1980, the white share of the population fell from 55 percent to 34 percent. Though the city was repeatedly dubbed the crime or murder capital of America, its police had the highest wages in the country. In 1982, Detroit's unemployment rate hit 25 percent, the same rate as in 1933. A third of the city's inhabitants were on welfare. Some 6,800 local firms had gone bankrupt in the previous two years alone.[21]

The decline of the steel industry arguably had a wider impact on urban America than the decline of the car industry, because there were more steel towns than car towns. Youngstown was the capital of "steel valley" in eastern Ohio, with the banks of the Mahoning River lined with Bessemer converters, open-hearth furnaces, strip and rolling mills, pipe plants, and other steel-related buildings, all flanked by churches, union halls, bars, and workers' homes. On September 19, 1977, remembered locally as "Black Monday," Youngstown Sheet and Tube Company closed most of its plants in the city, throwing four thousand people out of work and ripping the economic heart out of the community. Over the next decade, ten thousand more jobs disappeared.

Though New York was hardly a one-industry town like Detroit, the collapse of the city's garment industry hit it hard: the city lost four hundred thousand manufacturing jobs between 1968 and 1975, as jobs moved south to the Sun Belt (particularly North Carolina) or abroad to India and China. The general escalation of disorder hit harder still: the city lost a million people as (mainly white) New Yorkers fled to the suburbs. In the spring of 1975, the city faced fiscal meltdown: lacking the money to pay its day-to-day running expenses, unable to borrow more money, confronted by the prospect of defaulting on its obligations, the mayor, Abraham Beame, went cap in hand to the White House to ask Gerald Ford to bail the city out. Ford initially refused, inspiring the *Daily News* headline "Ford to City: Drop Dead," but then backed down on condition that the city eventually introduce a balanced budget.

Economic and social problems reinforced each other. Cities that had always suffered from severe racial problems, with real-estate agents enforcing housing segregation and the police forces largely in the hands of whites, exploded during the civil rights movement. Black citizens rioted. Black mayors were elected in many cities, addressing past injustices, but in the process driving more whites to the suburbs. In 1968, Lewis Mumford had worried about the "progressive dissolution" of America's cities. A decade later that dissolution had become rampant.

The mirror image of the decline of the cities was the continued rise of the suburbs. Manufacturing companies moved into suburban areas. By 1981, about two-thirds of all U.S. manufacturing was suburban.[22] America became a land of edge cities as back-office functions moved to office parks and retailing moved to shopping malls.

IT'S ALWAYS DARKEST BEFORE THE DAWN

By the late 1970s, there were stirrings of a better future. The high-tech boom was on the horizon: the young Bill Gates started Microsoft in Albuquerque, New Mexico, in 1975 and Steve Jobs and Steve Wozniak founded Apple in 1976. And America had not lost its talent for creative destruction, even during the decade of malaise. America's pharmaceutical industry escaped the general decline in management quality: Pfizer continued to invest heavily in R&D and developed a pipeline of blockbuster drugs. American businesspeople continued to revolutionize the consumer economy: Dee Ward Hock built Visa International, a credit card company, into a giant with 64 million customers in 1980.[23] Michael Harper turned ConAgra (short for Consolidated Agriculture) from a disorganized mess into the second-largest food company in the world.[24]

The political system also began to generate antibodies to the virus of malaise. The Brookings Institution and the American Enterprise Institute joined forces to produce more than a hundred books, journal articles, and dissertations explaining why deregulation mattered and how it could be implemented. Legislation under Jimmy Carter, one of America's most ideologically polymorphous presidents, prefigured many policies that are more commonly associated with Ronald Reagan. "Government cannot solve our problems," Carter declared in his second State of the Union address. "It cannot eliminate poverty or provide a bountiful economy, or reduce inflation, or save our cities, or cure illiteracy, or provide energy." He squeezed the size of government. He passed three "national austerity" budgets that trimmed social programs and deregulated a succession of key industries. "We have slashed government regulation and put free enterprise back into the airline, trucking and financial system of our country," he said in his speech accepting his party's nomination in 1980. "This is the greatest change in the relationship between business and government since the New Deal." He also appointed Paul Volcker, the president of the New York Federal Reserve Bank and one of the most committed inflation-fighters in the business, to the chairmanship of the Federal Reserve in August 1979. "We are face-to-face with economic difficulties really unique in our experience," Volcker said at his swearing-in ceremony. The only solution was "to slay the inflationary dragon."

Arthur Schlesinger Jr. complained that Jimmy Carter was "not a Democrat—at least in anything more recent than the Grover Cleveland sense of the word." Yet Carter was not really the right man to lead a campaign for economic renewal. He was an imperfect president—highly intelligent but also a micromanager. The American people had already given up on him by the time he discovered his inner crusader. They looked to a new man to deliver America from the furies that had consumed them. Ronald Reagan was not only determined to do battle with the devils that were destroying America, he also had something positive to bring to the equation—a burning faith in the power of entrepreneurs to revive American capitalism.

Ten

THE AGE OF OPTIMISM

———◆———

RONALD REAGAN WAS ONE of America's most unusual presidents. He was trained in Hollywood rather than in an Ivy League university or an established political machine. He didn't bother himself with the details of government: whereas Jimmy Carter worried about who should be allowed to use the White House tennis courts, Reagan talked metaphorically about building a city on a hill. "I am concerned about what is happening in government," he once quipped, "and it's caused me many a sleepless afternoon."

Yet he was also one of America's more consequential presidents. He helped to tear up the postwar social contract. He presided over wrenching change that left business strengthened and labor weakened. Despite that, he was reelected by a huge margin, with 54.5 million votes (58.8 percent of the total) to Walter Mondale's 37.6 million (40.6 percent). He left office with high approval ratings despite the mess of the Iran-Contra affair. The Republicans have spent the post-Reagan era looking for the next Reagan.

There are lots of reasons conservatives remain fixated on Reagan. Economic reasons: real gross domestic product rose by nearly a third during his presidency; inflation fell from above 12 percent when Carter left office to below 5 percent; unemployment fell from 7 percent to 5 percent. Philosophical reasons: at a time when governing seemed enormously complicated, Reagan clung to a few simple propositions. "There are simple answers," he liked to say, "just not easy ones." And psychological reasons: Reagan restored the great American tradition of optimism after Nixon's paranoia and Carter's dreariness. He combined a sunny disposition with a fine sense of theatricality, a combination that he shared with his onetime hero, Franklin Roosevelt. He did his best to embody the mythical America of rugged cowboys and wide-open spaces, spending more than a year of his presidency on his "ranch" in Santa Barbara, perpetually decked out, if the photographs are to be believed, in cowboy boots and a Stetson.

Perhaps the biggest reason for the continuing conservative infatuation, however, is his belief in freeing entrepreneurs from the shackles of government. In the 1930s, Americans turned to government to save them from the instability of the market. In the 1980s, they turned to entrepreneurs to save them from the suffocation of government.

BUSINESS UNBOUND

Reagan has three undeniable economic achievements to his name. First, he broke the power of the unions. He began his presidency by delivering a knockout blow to the Professional Air Traffic Controllers Organization (PATCO). In 1981, the air traffic controllers defied federal law (and put the country's airways in danger) by going on strike in favor of a higher base salary, a shorter working week, and a better retirement package. They miscalculated badly, underestimating the president's determination to change the social contract and management's ability to fight back, and overestimating the amount of public support they would get. Reagan gave the strikers an ultimatum: return to work within forty-eight hours or lose your job. The majority of workers refused to return to work because they didn't take his threats seriously. This proved to be a serious mistake. The public sided with Reagan. The strike quickly descended into chaos and recrimination. Managers were so successful at filling the empty slots that the airports were running at three-quarters of capacity within three days of the firings. By the end of the year, PATCO had filed for bankruptcy—and Reagan was on his way into the conservative pantheon.

Reagan's timing was impeccable: both union membership and strike activity were already on a downward trend when he came to office and continued to fall rapidly under both Republican and Democratic presidents (see charts on page 193 and page 250). Manufacturing unions were losing ground thanks to a combination of rising imports and the contracting out of jobs to foreign workers. The great industrial belt that had once been the stronghold of workers' power turned into the Rust Belt, as we've seen. A surge in immigration shifted power from workers to employers. The proportion of the nonagricultural workforce represented by unions declined from 23.4 percent in 1980 to 16.8 percent in 1989—and the workers who did remain in unions were much less likely to strike.

Reagan built on Gerald Ford's initiatives during his two and a half years as president to move the economy in a more pro-market direction (indeed, at the 1980 Republican Convention, Reagan tried to get Ford to serve as his vice-president, with a guarantee of enhanced powers, but the negotiations broke down). Reagan also continued with Jimmy Carter's policy of deregulating the economy while also fighting inflation. He appointed George H. W. Bush, his vice-president, to chair a task force on regulatory rollback, slashing the

budgets of regulatory agencies and appointing aggressive deregula-
tors to key positions in the bureaucracy. Reagan was lucky to have
inherited a man of adamantine determination in Paul Volcker: Volcker was unflinching in his commitment to slaying the dragon of
inflation despite threats of impeachment and worse. But Volcker was
also lucky in having the unflinching support of the president, despite
a federal funds rate that peaked at 22.4 percent on July 22, 1981, and
an unemployment rate that peaked at 10.8 percent in November
1982. ("If not us, who?" Reagan frequently said to his secretary of
state, George Shultz, as the political opposition mounted. "If not
now, when?")[1] Thanks to Volcker's gold-standard-like restraint on
credit expansion, inflation finally dropped to 3.2 percent in 1983 and
remained below 5 percent for the rest of the decade.

Reagan's third achievement was to introduce the biggest change
to America's tax regime since the First World War. His 1981 tax reform reduced the top personal tax rate from 70 percent to 50 percent,
and the capital gains tax from 28 percent to 20 percent. Five years
later, in 1986, he followed this up with another mammoth tax reform,
cutting the top rate of personal tax to 28 percent, cutting the corporate tax rate from 46 percent to 34 percent, and at the same time
eliminating business-friendly loopholes.

These three changes all had one big thing in common: they created the conditions for a business revival, removing the shackles that
had bound business ever tighter in the postwar years and eliminating
the inflation-related uncertainty that made it difficult to plan for the
long term. Reagan had an instinctive faith in business—business created wealth, he believed, and government consumed the fruits of that
creation. He regarded businesspeople in general and entrepreneurs
in particular as the praetorian guard of his revolution.

Reagan started his presidency with a couple of gestures that were
intended to drive home his belief that "the business of America is

business." He headed to the White House straight after his inauguration ceremony to put his name to a document imposing a hiring
freeze on the entire federal workforce. He removed the portrait of
Harry Truman from the Cabinet Room and replaced it with one of
Calvin Coolidge.[2] "Silent Cal" was his favorite president, he said,
"because he had been so silent, keeping the hand of the federal
government out of the conduct of society and allowing business to
prosper throughout the twenties."[3]

Reaganomics, as it was dubbed, produced some significant successes. The restructuring of corporate America generated a hard core
of companies that could compete effectively on the international
playing field. GE and Intel were as good as any companies in the
world. Deregulation created big opportunities for businesses of all
kinds. The deregulation of the airport sector created space for innovators such as Southwest Airlines. Deregulation in general speeded
the diffusion of new technologies. The breakup of AT&T's monopoly
of the telecom industry in 1982 spurred both a reduction in prices
and a surge of innovation. The deregulation of transportation helped
to produce a logistics revolution that reduced the cost of inputs into
the economy. There is good reason the Dow Jones Industrial Average
jumped from 951 points at the time of Reagan's first inaugural to
2,239 eight years later.

It also produced one big failure: Reagan was responsible for creating more national debt than all the presidents who preceded him
combined. Having come to office with the mission of cutting both
taxes and spending, he discovered that it was much easier to achieve
the first than the second. Reagan succeeded in slowing down the
growth of entitlement spending, no mean achievement: real per capita entitlement spending increased at its slowest rate since the early
1950s, at 1.4 percent a year from 1981 to 1989. It increased nonethe-

less, ensuring that Reagan's program of cutting taxes and increasing defense spending had to be paid for by borrowing. Some of Reagan's apologists tried to put lipstick on this pig by arguing that tax cuts would pay for themselves by generating increased revenue, an argument that flew in the face of reality. Between the fiscal years 1980 and 1990, the federal debt held by the public more than tripled from $712 billion to $2.4 trillion. The Federal Reserve was forced to impose unusually restrictive monetary policy to contain the inflation pressure and to keep interest rates sufficiently high to attract foreign capital to finance the deficits. Massive federal borrowing "crowded out" private borrowers, including those who would have put the nation's savings to more productive use, and contributed to a slowdown in productivity growth.

AFTER REAGAN

Reagan's two immediate successors tried to address the fiscal flaw in Reaganomics without returning to the micromanagement of the pre-Reagan years. George H. W. Bush, who coined the phrase "voodoo economics" when he ran for president against Reagan in 1980, raised taxes in order to plug the deficit. Bill Clinton made shrinking the deficit one of his top priorities. Bush was a one-term president: his decision to break his memorably phrased pledge not to raise taxes ("Read my lips. No new taxes") eviscerated his support on the right, while a prolonged recession soured the public against him. Clinton was much more successful. Having run for the presidency as a populist champion of the blue-collar voters who had been left behind by the economic boom and crushed by the decline of the manufacturing industry, Democratic Clinton governed as an Eisenhower Republican who believed in embracing capitalism but using the fruits of capitalist prosperity to compensate the losers.

Clinton put two policies at the heart of his presidency—balancing the budget and embracing globalization. He recognized from the start of his presidency that the federal debt held by the public, which had risen to $3 trillion in 1992, threatened to act as a long-term brake on growth, pushing up inflation and interest rates and undermining confidence. He took a page from JFK's playbook by appointing a succession of fiscal conservatives to key economic positions—Lloyd Bentsen to the Treasury and Robert Rubin to a new position as chairman of the new National Economic Council (Rubin later succeeded Bentsen at Treasury). Clinton also recognized that the combination of the end of the cold war and the information revolution was supercharging globalization. Embracing debt reduction and globalization made for complicated politics: Clinton was repeatedly forced to do battle with his friends in the liberal wing of his party while forging alliances with his enemies in the Republican caucus. The result of this political turbulence was a remarkable economic boom.

The United States became the center of the high-tech economy, with the PC revolution (dominated by Microsoft and Apple) followed by the internet revolution. The Dow Jones hit record highs in every year of Clinton's presidency as the economy boomed and regular Americans shifted their retirement savings into stocks. Between November 1995 and March 1999, the Dow rose from 5,000 points to an unprecedented 10,000.

The economic boom that Clinton finally enjoyed was driven by four profound changes that had been developing from the 1970s onward: the revival of entrepreneurialism; the deregulation of financial capitalism; the advance of globalization; and the high-tech revolution.

REVIVING THE ENTREPRENEURIAL SPIRIT

In his 1942 classic *Capitalism, Socialism and Democracy,* Joseph Schumpeter argued brilliantly that bureaucratization (including the bureaucratization of the corporation) was killing the spirit of entrepreneurialism, and with it the spirit of capitalism. Policy makers spent thirty years ignoring Schumpeter. In the 1960s, John Kenneth Galbraith even argued that the modern corporation had replaced "the entrepreneur as the directing force of the enterprise with management." But as the economy succumbed to stagnation in the 1970s, people finally began to listen. The 1980s and 1990s saw entrepreneurs regaining their position at the center of American life and established companies slimming their corporate bureaucracies in the name of flexibility and innovation.

Bill Gates created a start-up that outmaneuvered IBM and conquered the world. Howard Schultz provided America with an alternative to bad coffee with a start-up, Starbucks, that began in the far northwest of the country and then spread to every corner of the land. Fred Smith created a transportation business, FedEx, with a business plan that was so counterintuitive (send all packages to a central hub before sending them to their final destination) that his professor at Yale gave him a C when he first outlined the idea.

Americans celebrated entrepreneurship with renewed enthusiasm: *Entrepreneur* magazine, founded in 1977, boomed. George Gilder and Michael Novak praised entrepreneurs as the great agents of economic change. Peter Drucker, who had made his name dissecting big companies, most notably General Motors in *Concept of the Corporation,* published a spirited book on entrepreneurship, *Innovation and Entrepreneurship* (1985).

The new generation of entrepreneurs could draw on three resources that existed more abundantly in America than elsewhere, and that, when combined with an entrepreneur-friendly president in Washington, produced a business revolution. Financial innovators provided new sources of cash such as junk bonds from Michael Milken and venture capital from Silicon Valley's well-established venture-capital industry. Great universities provided science parks, technology offices, business incubators, and venture funds. A liberal immigration policy provided a ready supply of willing hands and brains.

Amar Bhidé of Tufts University suggests that "venturesome consumption" also promoted American entrepreneurialism. Americans were unusually willing to try new products of all sorts, even if it meant teaching themselves new skills and eating into their savings; they were also unusually willing to pester manufacturers to improve their products. Apple had a large cohort of hardcore fans who kept it going through difficult times.

A final advantage might be added to the list: legal innovation. In 1977, Wyoming passed legislation to create a new business form— limited liability companies that enjoyed the tax advantages of partnerships but also the privilege of limited liability. The reaction to this innovation was slow until the IRS signed off on the new form in 1988. Then the dam burst. Legislators across the country competed to create two new forms of companies: LLCs and limited liability partnerships. The result was a dual corporate economy. For the most part, large firms still employed the traditional corporate form that developed in the late nineteenth century. Smaller firms had a range of corporate templates to choose from that gave them an unprecedented degree of control over the extent of their liability, the rules that governed them, and the ease with which they could dissolve their firm.[4]

Embracing entrepreneurial capitalism meant more than just giving more freedom to new entrepreneurs who invented the future in their garages. It also meant redesigning established companies. The 1980s saw the big bureaucratic companies of the postwar era hitting the wall. The rate at which large American companies left the Forbes 500 increased fourfold between 1970 and 1990. Names that once bespoke corporate permanence, like Pan Am, disappeared. Corporate insurgents, like Netscape and Enron (named the most innovative company in America by *Fortune* six years in a row), emerged from nowhere and changed their industries. The established firms that survived this maelstrom only did so by doing internally what the market did externally: releasing capital and labor from dying businesses and allocating it to rising businesses, where it could be recombined with talent in imaginative new ways.

Jack Welch became the most celebrated chief executive of the era because of his willingness to apply creative destruction to one of America's most storied companies. He began his two-decade reign (1981–2001) with unflinching corporate brutality in pursuit of his belief that GE should be number one or number two in each of its chosen businesses or get out. Between 1981 and 1990, he eliminated 200 businesses, accounting for about a quarter of the company's total sales, and acquired 370 businesses, including Employers Reinsurance, Westinghouse's lighting business, and Kidder, Peabody. He also pared back the corporate headquarters and moved decision making to the business units. The restructuring resulted in a net loss of 120,000 employees, but left the conglomerate far more valuable.[5]

"Neutron" Jack was unusual in his commitment to reviving the conglomerate form. Most successful CEOs dumped the conglomerate part of the formula and focused on focus. The conglomerates that had been so popular in the 1960s and 1970s had been humiliated by foreign competitors, who took their market in one area after another, and rejected by investors, who subjected them to a "conglomerate discount" on the grounds that they would rather deal with risk by buying shares in a portfolio of companies than by allowing corporate managers to practice diversification. This inspired a generation of corporate engineers to engage in the biggest wave of corporate restructuring since the merger boom of the early twentieth century: spinning off activities that were unrelated to their core business and acquiring other companies that were. Nearly one-third of the largest U.S. manufacturing firms were acquired or merged in this era.[6]

The reengineering movement that gripped business in the 1990s went beyond the cult of focus in order to redesign companies for the era of pervasive information technology. Reengineers argued that, just as companies had not been able to capitalize on the arrival of electricity until they got rid of their multistory factories and replaced them with single-story ones, so modern companies would not be able to capitalize on the potential of the computer revolution until they reorganized their internal processes. By 1994, 78 percent of Fortune 500 companies and 68 percent of FTSE 100 firms, as the *Financial Times* list of top companies on the London Stock Exchange is known, were engaged in some form of reengineering.[7]

Whether they regarded themselves as "reengineering" or not, a growing number of companies realized that they needed radical internal reorganization in order to get the most out of new technology. By the end of the 1990s, computers could be seen everywhere, not only on the desks of white-collar workers but also, in the form of miniaturized devices, in the hands of factory-floor workers. Companies eliminated a swath of clerical workers. Henceforward, managers could do their own typing and prepare their own spreadsheets and keep their own diaries. They also encouraged frontline workers to engage in their own reordering and supply-chain management.

The other great change in this era was in the relationship between companies and the wider society. The great bureaucratic companies of the Keynesian age had accepted a litany of social responsibilities, from providing their workers with lifetime employment to funding the local opera. In the 1980s and 1990s, companies hardened their hearts. They forced their CEOs to be more ruthless with a combination of carrots and sticks: the average salary of the boss of a Fortune 500 company increased from 40 times as much as a factory worker in 1980, to 84 times as much in 1990, to 475 times as much in 2000, but at the same time the average CEO tenure declined. CEOs responded by getting rid of surplus staff, cutting unnecessary expenses, and focusing on performance.

Milton Friedman provided the intellectual justification for this more dog-eat-dog approach with his 1970 article "The Social Responsibility of Business Is to Increase Its Profits." Six years later, two finance professors at Rochester University, Michael Jensen and William Meckling, elaborated on his insights in "Theory of the Firm: Managerial Behavior, Agency Costs and Ownership Structure," which went on to be the most widely cited academic article about business ever written.[8] Jensen and Meckling argued that companies are always distorted by a tension between the owners (who want to get the best return for their money) and their agents (who will always try to feather their own nests). The managerial firm that had dominated American capitalism since at least the 1950s was run for the convenience of managers who lined their pockets with pay and perks. Jensen and Meckling argued that the best way to deal with the problem was to force managers to think like owners by paying them in stock and options, and to put their jobs on the line through the takeover market. Performance-related pay and a vigorous market in corporate control would soon restore corporate America to rude health.

The government largely stood back while all this restructuring took place on the grounds that corporate turmoil promoted wealth creation. Antitrust legislators stood pat for WorldCom's $37 billion merger with MCI, and Citicorp's $70 billion merger with Travelers.

There were a few exceptions. Rudy Giuliani stepped in to discipline two of the greatest corporate raiders, Michael Milken and Ivan Boesky, and the antitrust authorities fought an intense battle with Bill Gates. Much discussed though they were at the time, however, these exceptions did little to change the character of the era.

THE FINANCIAL REVOLUTION

Ronald Reagan inaugurated the most exuberant era on Wall Street since the 1920s. Financiers became national celebrities. Investment banks sucked in the country's jeunesse dorée with a promise of instant riches and a glamorous life. Books such as *The Bonfire of the Vanities* (1987) by Tom Wolfe and *Liar's Poker* (1989) by Michael Lewis, as well as films such as Oliver Stone's *Wall Street* (1987), glamorized life on the Street even as they pretended to demonize it. A tidal wave of money poured into various financial instruments as the economy expanded and people entrusted their retirement savings to the market. Meanwhile, the range and variety of those instruments expanded as financiers applied their brainpower to squeezing better returns out of their investments.

The change in the relationship between managers and owners extended the power of finance. In the heyday of managerial capitalism, the shareholders were essentially passive and "shareholder activism" was limited to cases so extreme that they made nonsense of the term. This changed as shareholders multiplied and their intermediaries became more powerful. The proportion of household wealth invested in stocks rather than low-risk savings accounts expanded from a tenth in 1980 to a quarter in 2000. The volume of shares traded on the New York Stock Exchange increased from about 3 million shares a day in 1960 to 160 million a day in 1990 to 1.6 billion a day in 2007.

As the number of shareholders increased, an industry developed to look after their interests: mutual funds, money managers, and the like kept a careful watch on the performance of corporate America. The owners of capital were no longer content to let managers manage as they sought fit. They believed that the price of decent returns was eternal vigilance.

The Employee Retirement Income Security Act (ERISA) of 1974 was a landmark here: it obliged all companies with retirement plans to set aside money to meet payments owed to current and future re-tirees in a separate trust fund. This created huge new pools of capital that, by law, had to be invested both prudently and productively. In practice, prudent and productive investment meant the stock market because stocks have outperformed fixed-income securities and de-posit accounts by a significant margin. ERISA created a new class of guardians—pension funds—that managed mountains of money for retirees. Some of the most vigilant guardians of money were pension funds like CaLPERS (the California Public Employees Retirement System), which looked after the interests of retired public-sector workers such as academics (who frequently spent their retirements complaining about the evils of shareholder capitalism).

The mutual fund industry, which came to life in the 1960s, fur-ther broadened and deepened the country's capital markets: by 2000, there were nine thousand mutual funds in America, some six thou-sand of which had set up shop in the 1990s. Mutual funds gave people more choice about where they could invest their retirement savings. This was even true if they participated in company plans: most com-panies allowed employees who participated in their retirement plans to choose which funds they invested in. Mutual funds allowed inves-tors to increase their power by creating pools of capital even as they diversified their risks by investing in lots of different companies.

At the same time, the computer revolution provided both owners and managers with more powerful tools than they had ever had before. Managers could use tools like ratio analysis (which allows you to measure inventory, turnover, net profit on sales, and return on investment) to measure how well the company was performing. Share owners could monitor their companies and measure their performance against other corporate assets. Day traders, sitting at home surrounded by their television screens and computer monitors, had more financial information at their disposal than lords of finance, ensconced in their paneled offices, had had in the nineteenth century.

The overregulation of Main Street banks also had the paradoxical effect of encouraging further financial innovation. The banks were so imprisoned by New Deal regulations that, by the 1980s, not a single one of the world's top ten banks was based in the United States. Half of them had been based there in the 1950s. While banks stagnated, other intermediaries innovated to take up the slack: over the thirty years after 1970, the share of financial assets held by "new" intermediaries such as money-market mutual funds, mortgage pools, and securitized loans mushroomed, while the proportion held by "traditional" intermediaries such as commercial banks, mutual savings banks, and life insurance companies declined.

Three innovations set the tone. Securitization transformed non-market assets into marketable securities. Home mortgage loans, car loans, and credit card receivables, which had been almost exclusively held in commercial and savings bank portfolios, were packaged into securities and then sold on secondary markets. Derivatives enabled investors to process a far wider range of risks. The Chicago Board of Trade, which had been established in 1848 to handle futures in grains but which moved into financial futures in the 1980s, became a dominant player. The financial services industry developed lots of ways of allowing people to borrow money so that they could acquire and transform underperforming companies: leveraged buyouts, or LBOs (which used debt to fund reorganizations); management buyouts, or MBOs (which were often used to sell off a proportion of the company); and "junk bonds."

The greatest champions of leverage were Kohlberg Kravis Roberts (KKR) and Drexel Burnham Lambert. In 1976, three young bankers with Bear Stearns, Henry Kravis, Jerome Kohlberg, and George Roberts, came up with the idea of a new kind of organization, a partnership that created a succession of investment funds, took positions in companies, and then sold them off after a fixed period of time. KKR thrived because it combined two rare skills: the ability to put together deals and the ability to manage the companies that they took over by making managers think and act like owners.

Drexel Burnham pioneered the use of high-yield bonds to take over companies. In the late 1970s, Michael Milken, based in Beverly Hills rather than on Wall Street, invented a new type of bond specifically designed for this "noninvestment grade" market that allowed companies that were too small or risky to issue regular bonds to get access to the bond market. These "junk bonds," as they were dubbed, helped to finance America's entrepreneurial revolution: Milken's clients included Ted Turner, the founder of Turner Broadcasting; Rupert Murdoch, the owner of News International; Leonard Riggio, the founder of Barnes & Noble; and William McGowan, the founder of MCI Communications, the first serious challenger to AT&T's monopoly on long-distance telephone calls. They also became some of the most valuable tools in the restructuring wars: corporate raiders used them to buy shares in the companies that they wanted to take over, with a view to using the acquired companies' assets to pay off their debts; and many targets of takeover attempts bought back their own shares from raiders at a premium. Junk bonds expanded from a mere 3.5 percent of the bond market in 1977 to a quarter of the market a decade later. Michael Milken became the symbol of the era, with his $550 million salary in a single year and his annual Predators' Ball.

Some of this looked too good to be true. Junk bonds lived up to their name: around a fifth of the bonds issued from 1978 to 1983 had defaulted by 1988. Many of the thrifts that bought junk bonds went bankrupt, as did Drexel Burnham itself in February 1990. Michael Milken was indicted on almost a hundred counts of racketeering, ending up in jail, and his company, Drexel Burnham, was forced into bankruptcy. Financial innovation continued regardless. In the 1990s, venture capital funds took over from corporate raiders as the pacesetters of capitalism, focusing on start-ups rather than mature firms, and making less use of leverage. America had far more venture capital available than the rest of the world combined: in the mid-1990s, Massachusetts had more venture capital than Britain, and California had more than the whole of Europe. All this venture capital fueled the surge of the high-tech industry. Venture capitalists were willing to take bets because they relied on the law of averages: most investments failed but a successful IPO could yield vast returns. They also provided the companies that they invested in with invaluable management advice and contacts.

As America's financial wizards worked their magic, Wall Street boomed. In 1995–96, the Dow Jones sprinted past three millennial markers—4,000, 5,000, and 6,000. The total value of U.S. investors' stock holdings increased from 55 percent of GDP in 1990 to 113 percent in 1996. This produced a powerful "wealth effect": feeling flush from gains in the value of their portfolios, investors borrowed more freely to splurge on houses and consumer goods.

Policy makers concluded the decade by deregulating the mainstream banks. This was less a surrender to the spirit of irrational exuberance than a recognition that existing regulations were producing

John Pierpont Morgan,
the greatest banker
of the Gilded Age.

John D. Rockefeller was
a titan of philanthropy
as well as business.

Andrew Carnegie became the richest man in the world when he sold his steel company in 1901.

James J. Hill, the founder of the Great Northern Railway and a pioneer in bringing transportation to the West.

Thomas Edison in his laboratory in Orange, New Jersey.
Born in the Midwest and largely self-taught, Edison had
more patents to his name than any other American.

William Jennings Bryan sitting at a conference on conservation in 1908, in Washington, DC, with
Andrew Carnegie, James J. Hill, and John Mitchell, president of the United Mine Workers.

William Jennings Bryan addressing the 1908 Democratic National
Convention (and perhaps repeating the stance he took at the
end of his "Cross of Gold" speech in 1896).

Opponents of Standard Oil criticized it as a "monster monopoly," as depicted in a cartoon from 1884.

THE RISE OF MASS PRODUCTION
AND MASS CONSUMPTION

A Marshall Field's store window, Chicago, 1909.

Workers on the assembly line at the
Ford Motor Company in 1913.

Alfred Sloan, president of General Motors, in 1928. He revolutionized the management of car companies as thoroughly as Henry Ford revolutionized mass production, turning GM into a multidivisional firm that manufactured different cars for different purses and purposes.

The Empire State Building under construction in 1930, as the Roaring Twenties turned into the miserable thirties.

THE GREAT DEPRESSION
AND THE NEW DEAL

The crowds on Wall Street on October 31, 1929, after the stock market crashed.

A "soup kitchen" feeding the hungry and homeless in Chicago on
November 16, 1930, courtesy of the gangster Al Capone.

A 1933 Clifford Berryman cartoon celebrates "the spirit of the New Deal"
in the form of cooperation between employers and employees.
"NRA" stands for the National Recovery Administration,
which took as its symbol a blue eagle.

"What we need is a new pump": a circa 1935 cartoon made fun of the idea
that the government was capable of pump priming the economy, suggesting
that the water was sloshing all over the place, to little good effect.

Members of the nascent United Auto Workers Union (UAW) during a sit-down strike in the General Motors Fisher Body Plant in Flint, Michigan, January 1937.

Passengers disembark from an American Airlines Condor plane at Newark airport in 1935.

B-24s under construction at Henry Ford's plant at Willow Run, Michigan, during World War II.

Women workers assemble the tail fuselage of a Flying Fortress B-17F bomber at the Douglas Aircraft Company in Long Beach, California.

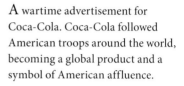

A wartime advertisement for Coca-Cola. Coca-Cola followed American troops around the world, becoming a global product and a symbol of American affluence.

Henry Ford's River Rouge factory in 1940 was one of the biggest industrial units in the world. It eventually became the heart of the mass production of 1,000 planes a day.

An aerial view of Levittown in January 1955. Levittown applied mass-production techniques to house building and brought the American dream within the reach of most white workers.

The suburban dream: mother and daughter wave goodbye to father as he drives to work in January 1949. Real GDP had increased 4.2 percent the previous year.

A re-creation of the first McDonald's restaurant, which was opened in Des Plaines, Illinois, by Ray Kroc on April 15, 1955.

The "kitchen debate" between Vice President Richard Nixon and Nikita Khrushchev during a tour of the American National Exhibition in Sokolniki Park in Moscow, 1959.

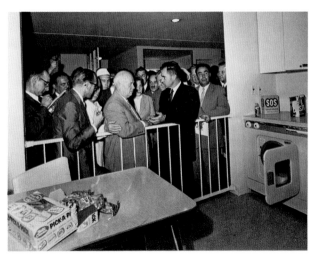

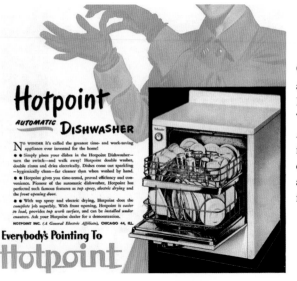

General Electric advertises an automatic dishwasher in 1948. Dishwashers and other "electronic servants" liberated Americans, particularly women, from domestic drudgery and enormously increased the amount of time available for leisure.

The IBM 360 computer was a triumph of long-term thinking. IBM spent $5 billion, or three times its annual revenue, to come up with the 360, but it paid back this investment many times over.

AMERICA'S TECH GIANTS ARE AS DOMINANT AS CARNEGIE STEEL AND STANDARD OIL WERE IN THE GILDED AGE

The Apple Campus at Cupertino, California, in 2018, as seen from the air.

Amazon's headquarters in Seattle, Washington.

the worst of all possible worlds, ensuring that America's Main Street banks were too small to compete with the big European and Japanese banks (the biggest U.S. lenders were only half as profitable as their competitors in Europe and Japan) without preventing nonbanking institutions from engaging in all sorts of (sometimes risky) innovation. Respected policy makers such as Paul Volcker had started making the case for abolishing Glass-Steagall and making it easier for banks to merge. A Supreme Court decision punched holes in the Glass-Steagall wall. In 1999, the Clinton administration finally passed a comprehensive financial reform that made it easier for Main Street banks to compete with their rivals at home and abroad. The end result was not entirely happy: worried about a world in which America's banks were too small to compete, policy makers unwittingly ushered in a world in which they were too big to fail.

GLOBALIZATION

The United States has long been a battleground for isolationists and globalizers. The isolationists point out that, as a continent-size power with a vast economy and wide oceans on either side, America can remain aloof from a messy world. The globalizers retort that, as the world's biggest economy, America's prosperity depends on the prosperity of the rest of the world. In the 1970s, the antiglobalizers began to regain their influence after being sidelined during the golden age. In the 1980s and particularly the 1990s, the proglobalizers not only regained the upper hand but expanded their creed into the Washington consensus. The protectionists did not go silent: worries about America's soaring trade deficit colored all discussions about trade. Businesspeople complained that they were being squeezed by the combination of a prolonged recession (from 1979 to 1982) and the soaring value of the dollar (from 1980 to 1985). Ronald Reagan imposed protectionist barriers against the tide of Japanese cars and forced Japanese firms to build "transplants" on American soil, as we've seen. George H. W. Bush paid a heavy price for his embrace of what he called "the new world order": Patrick Buchanan and his pitchfork army defeated him in the New Hampshire primary (forcing him to give Buchanan a slot at the Republican Convention), and Ross Perot led a protectionist third party that split the Republican vote and put Bill Clinton in the White House. The bulk of Democrats in Congress voted against the North American Free Trade Agreement (NAFTA) with Mexico and Canada. The resentment against globalization continued to mount and eventually burst forth in the form of Donald Trump's populism. But for three decades after 1980, it was the globalizers who were making the weather.

Rather than simply railing against their foreign rivals, U.S. companies began to learn from their management methods. In particular they studied Japanese companies in order to solve their biggest management problems—their overreliance on standardized production, their poor quality control, and their general addiction to producing large quantities of fairly mediocre stuff. They introduced "Japanese" management methods: total quality management (putting every worker in charge of the quality of products), continuous improvement (getting those workers to suggest improvements), just-in-time manufacturing (making sure that parts get to factories only when they are needed rather than sitting waiting for months to be used and deteriorating in the process), and self-governing teams. (We put "Japanese" in quotation marks because many of these ideas were originally thought up by American management thinkers such as W. Edwards Deming.) Philip Crosby Associates was formed to help American companies copy Japanese management techniques. By 1986, some thirty-five thousand U.S. executives had graduated from

Crosby's Quality College. In 1987, America launched its own equivalent of Japan's Deming Prize, the Malcolm Baldrige National Quality Award, to reward companies for improving quality.

America's ability to learn from the Japanese is well illustrated by the story of Soichiro Honda and the sushi cake. During a visit to Detroit in October 1989, the eighty-two-year-old founder of the car company that bears his name surprised his handlers by his emotional reaction to a cake that was delivered to his room as a welcoming gift. The cake was crafted to look like sushi. The baker had made sure that the cake was soft and sugar-free in deference to Honda's age. Honda delivered a lecture to his handlers: "You guys think that you have surpassed the Americans. You guys have become too arrogant. Look at this cake. The person who made this cake definitely put his feet in my shoes." He then summoned the pastry chef and became quite emotional when he discovered that he was only in his twenties. "Never underestimate America," he concluded.[9]

The "Japanesation" of American production solved two dogged problems: it broke down the division between "managers" and "workers" by putting self-governing teams in charge of lots of decisions, and ensured that workers were more interested in their jobs. Harley-Davidson closed the productivity gap with Japan's motorcycle companies when it introduced Japanese-style teams. Whole Foods solidified its position as the country's most profitable retailer in terms of profits per square foot by organizing itself into self-governing teams controlling everything from the company's workforce to its stock: team members vote on whether to allow a potential new hire to join the team and collectively decide what to put on the shelves.

At the same time, the U.S. population became more "global." The decades after 1970 saw the biggest surge in immigration since the late nineteenth and early twentieth centuries. In the 1990s, the number of legal immigrants topped 9 million—about a third of official population growth and by far the highest in absolute terms, and as a proportion of the population in the post-depression era.

It also saw the biggest change in the origin of immigrants in U.S. history. At the beginning of the twentieth century, 90 percent of immigrants came from Europe (though a growing proportion of these Europeans came from southern and eastern Europe rather than, as in earlier years, northern Europe). In the 1990s, only 15 percent came from Europe. Fifty percent came from the Americas and 31 percent came from Asia. By 2000, 12.5 percent of the U.S. population was Hispanic, making Hispanics a bigger chunk of the population than African Americans, and 18 percent of Americans spoke a language other than English at home. This vast increase in immigration allowed business to gorge itself on human capital—cheap labor for the fast-food restaurants and skilled labor for Silicon Valley—while deepening its connections with the rest of the world. It also provided isolationists with the matériel they required to mount a counter-offensive against globalization.

As the 1990s wore on, globalization entered its triumphalist phase. The Clinton administration reinvented America's role as an indispensable nation: now that it had succeeded in defeating communism, America took on the task of acting as the guardian of globalization. If the 1980s saw America imposing temporary trade restrictions to protect domestic producers, the 1990s saw it rolling back restrictions and striking ambitious trade deals, completing the Uruguay Round, which created the World Trade Organization (WTO), establishing Permanent Normal Trade Relations (PNTR) with China, and signing the North American Free Trade Agreement with Mexico and Canada. In the first ten years of NAFTA (1994–2004), cross-border trade surged as America set up factories across the border (*maquiladoras*) and Mexican exports to the United States increased from $51 billion to $161 billion. The United States rescued first Mexico and then the Asian currencies from financial crisis. It did everything it could to support European integration, which then reached a high point with the creation of the euro and a European Central Bank.

America's business renaissance produced a wider sense of optimism about the country's role in the world. Companies reorganized to take full advantage of globalization. New companies were born global. Established multinationals ditched the regional fiefdoms that had sprung up to deal with different national regimes and instead organized departments on a global scale. Samuel Palmisano, the chief executive of IBM, argued that IBM no longer saw itself as a federation of national firms that couple together in order to create economies of scale and scope. It saw itself instead as an array of specialized components—procurement, manufacturing, research, sales, and distribution—all of which put their activities wherever they made the most economic sense. Ford joined IBM as one of the pacesetters of this change, abolishing a score of separate national units in Europe and North America and replacing them with five product teams (some of them headquartered in Europe) that made products for the world.

Even as they tried to remove internal fiefdoms, companies contracted out as much as they could to specialized producers around the world. Many commentators dubbed this "Nikefication" because of Nike's enthusiasm for employing people in South Asia and Latin America to make its shoes. Michael Dell talked about virtual integration as companies replaced vertical integration in their own factories with long-term contracts with suppliers spread across the world. Cisco managed to become one of America's biggest manufacturers while only directly making a quarter of the products it sold. Apple contracted out almost all of its manufacturing to China.

THE ELECTRONIC FRONTIER

The last quarter of the twentieth century saw America conquer yet another frontier. This was the virtual frontier of the computer and the internet. The microprocessor revolution allowed computers to be miniaturized. The personal computer revolution put a computer on every desk. And finally the internet revolution transformed those PCs from sophisticated typewriters into nodes in the information superhighway.

The IT revolution turned the old industrial economy upside down. In the age of the robber barons, wealth was created by things that you could touch. In the information era, it is created by virtual things: software eats hardware and information eats everything. In the age of the robber barons, big was best. Giant companies had giant factories and giant workforces. In the information era, the reverse is true. From the vacuum tube to the transistor to the integrated circuit to the microprocessor, the computer industry has devoted itself to packing ever-greater computer power into ever-smaller packages. The mainframe computer has given way to the personal computer, which is giving way to the smartphone. And as computers have shrunk, companies have become more virtual: the giants of the internet age have a fraction of the workforces of the giants of the steel-and-oil age.

The United States didn't have a monopoly on the IT revolution. For a while in the 1980s it looked as if Japanese giants such as Fujitsu, NEX, Hitachi, and Toshiba might do to America's computer companies what Sony and Matsushita had done to its consumer electronics companies. The World Wide Web was developed by a Briton (Sir Timothy Berners-Lee) working in a European institution (CERN). But U.S. companies rode out the challenge from the Japanese and did far more than the British or Europeans to commercialize the web. By the end of the twentieth century, the United States dominated the information revolution just as thoroughly as it dominated the oil and steel industries in the late nineteenth century. Today most of the world's great IT companies are American, with Apple and Google dominating the smartphone market, Google the search market, and Amazon the ecommerce and server markets.

Why did the United States play such a dominant role in the IT revolution? The computer revolution had its roots in several different worlds—from the military-industrial complex to giant corporations to academia to computer hobby clubs. America excelled in three things: producing these different worlds in the first place; bringing them together in creative symbiosis; and then commercializing the ideas that they produced.

We have already seen how Vannevar Bush played a central role in forging America's unique military-industrial-academic complex. Bush was particularly keen on information technology. He founded Raytheon, a leading electronics company. He even published an essay in 1945 conjuring up the possibility of a personal computer—he called it a "memex"—that could store all your personal information, books, letters, files, records, whatever, in a single space, as a sort of enlarged "intimate supplement" to your memory.[10]

The military-industrial complex directed unprecedented re-sources into IT either directly, by doing its own research, or, more often, indirectly, by funding academic research. In 1958, the Pentagon created a new agency, the Defense Department's Advanced Research Projects Agency (DARPA), as it was quickly renamed, to fund basic research, including into producing what J. C. R. Licklider, one of its resident geniuses, termed the Intergalactic Computer Network. DARPA developed a system for linking computers together so that several individuals could share time on a single mainframe. In 1969, the group succeeded in connecting computers in UCLA and Stanford Research Institute. The number of sites in the network expanded—to 20 in 1970 and more than 2,000 in 1985—and without anyone planning it, the "net" had become a forum where academics could chat about their work. Academics remained the primary users for many years, but then the numbers exploded again: by 1993, about ninety thousand Americans regularly used the internet; by 2000, the number had increased to about 90 million Americans and 327 million people globally.

At the same time, America's big IT companies invested heavily in computer research. In the 1970s, IBM made one of the biggest business bets of the twentieth century, spending $5 billion, three times its annual revenue, to produce the System/360 computer, so called because it could serve all purposes, from scientific to defense to business. The bet paid off handsomely: IBM was so synonymous with computers that Stanley Kubrick called the power-crazed computer in *2001: A Space Odyssey* HAL, a one-letter shift from IBM. AT&T supported a giant "idea factory"—Bell Labs—that specialized in bringing together academics, material scientists, and engineers to trade ideas. In 1970, the Xerox Corporation followed AT&T's example and established a lab dedicated to pure research three thousand miles from the company's headquarters, just to make sure that it was not contaminated by groupthink.

Bell Labs produced the breakthrough that made the modern computer era possible: the transistor. Before transistors, computers had been powered by huge vacuum tubes that rendered them so large and expensive that only giant institutions like MIT could afford them. The first computer used in business, the Univac, introduced by Remington Rand in 1950, was the size of a small truck. The arrival of the first transistors in the late 1940s began the age of shrinkage: henceforth computers could become cheaper, smaller, and more personal.

Subsequent innovations took this revolution in miniature even further. In 1959, Robert Noyce invented the integrated circuit, which combined, in one small silicon chip, numerous functions that had earlier required many discrete transistors and components wired together on a circuit board. This was the equivalent in miniature of the nineteenth-century robber barons bringing various factors of production together in great industrial centers such as Pittsburgh. Thereafter scientists became so good at miniaturization that Gordon Moore, a cofounder of Intel, coined Moore's law, which dictated that the number of transistors that could be put onto a microchip would double every eighteen months.

After the war, the leadership of the electronic revolution shifted from the East Coast to the Santa Clara Valley in Northern California. The Valley had previously been called "the valley of heart's delight" on account of its orchards and fruit farms. In 1971, Don Hoefler, a journalist on a trade paper, *Electronic News,* coined the term "Silicon Valley" to describe the computer makers and silicon fabricators that were sprouting up all over the place. The Valley quickly became the most famous economic cluster in the world: the home to a disproportionate number of the tech economy's iconic companies (Hewlett-Packard, Intel, Cisco Systems, Apple, and Google) and the inspiration for a growing number of imitators across America and indeed the world: Silicon Desert (Utah and Arizona), Silicon Alley (New York), Silicon Hills (Austin), Silicon Roundabout (London).

Stanford University was particularly aggressive in building up its engineering and computer departments, and in turning its ideas into businesses. Frederick Terman, who was successively dean of Stanford's engineering department and provost of the university, has as good a claim as anybody to being the father of Silicon Valley. He built the university's engineering department into a world-class institution. He persuaded the Ford Foundation to give Stanford a generous grant in order to turn it into a West Coast equivalent of Harvard or MIT. Above all, he helped to forge the close connection between the university and local business, partly in order to fulfill Leland Stanford's plans for the university, which was to provide useful, rather than merely decorative, learning, and partly in order to prevent his most talented students from going east in pursuit of their careers. In 1939, he lent two Stanford graduates, Bill Hewlett and David Packard, $538 (the equivalent of $9,500 in 2017) to start a business in Packard's garage in Palo Alto. The company eventually employed more than a hundred thousand people and pioneered handheld calculators, electronic medical instruments, and inkjet and laser printers.

During the postwar boom, Terman used the university's growing muscle to provide start-ups with the two things they most needed: somewhere to work, turning a thousand acres of land adjacent to the campus into the Stanford Industrial Park (later Stanford Research Park), and something to live on, using university money to provide venture capital. The park's first tenant was Varian Associates, founded by Stanford alumni in the 1930s to build military radar components. Hewlett-Packard moved in in 1953. In 1954, Terman created a new university degree program that allowed full-time employees of companies to pursue graduate degrees at Stanford on a part-time basis. One of Terman's greatest coups was to persuade William Shockley, who won the Nobel Prize as the coinventor of the transistor, to move from Bell Labs to the park in 1955. Shockley was a difficult customer—an egomaniac in fact—who both attracted and repelled talent. Fairchild Semiconductor was formed in 1957 when "the traitorous eight" left Shockley Conductor because they couldn't take Shockley's abusive management style any longer.

The Valley had two other ingredients that proved essential for the commercialization of ideas: a large venture capital industry centered on Sand Hill Road and a ready supply of immigrants. Andy Grove, Intel's long-term CEO, was a refugee from Hungary. Steve Jobs was the son of a Syrian immigrant (though he was adopted shortly after birth). According to AnnaLee Saxenian, 27 percent of the four thousand companies started between 1990 and 1996 were run by Chinese or Indians (double the proportion in the previous decade). The Valley also pioneered a particularly flexible form of capitalism. Saxenian points out that in its early years Silicon Valley's great competitor on the East Coast, the Route 128 corridor in Massachusetts, was more than a match for the Valley in terms of access to research and venture capital. Yet by the late 1970s, the Valley had created more high-tech jobs than Route 128 had, and when both clusters slumped in the mid-1980s, the Valley proved far more resilient. The reason for this was that big East Coast firms such as Digital Equipment Corporation and Data General were self-contained empires that focused on one product, minicomputers, whereas Silicon Valley was much more decentralized, freewheeling, and porous: companies were constantly forming and re-forming. Silicon Valley boasted more than six thousand companies in the 1990s, many of them start-ups. Even big companies, such as Sun Microsystems, Intel, and Hewlett-Packard, were informal affairs. People hopped from job to job and from company to company. Intel was formed when two of the traitorous eight, Robert Noyce and Gordon Moore, left Fairchild and recruited Andy Grove to join them. More than anywhere else in America, Silicon Valley was a living embodiment of the principle of creative destruction as old companies died and new ones emerged, allowing capital, ideas, and people to be reallocated.

From the mid-1970s onward, the IT revolution went into high gear with two simultaneous developments, the rise of the PC and the commercialization of the internet. The arrival of the personal computer with the Altair in 1974 let loose a burst of creative activity in both software and hardware. In one of the most remarkable business deals ever negotiated, a nineteen-year-old Bill Gates persuaded IBM to use his software in all its computers. This turned Microsoft into the industry standard and Bill Gates into one of the world's richest men. IBM further speeded up the PC revolution by starting to manufacture its own PCs in 1981, thereby giving its imprimatur to the new devices. The company had sold 2.5 million by 1982 and more than 6 million by 1985. In the meantime, Apple produced computers that eschewed Bill Gates's operating system and integrated hardware and software.

The arrival of the internet with the installation of the first server at the Stanford Linear Accelerator System in December 1991 unleashed an even bigger revolution. At first the internet revolution and the PC revolution unfolded separately. The collision between the two in the 1990s brought the power of the individual computer together with the power of huge networks: people sitting at their desks (or, with the arrival of laptops and smartphones, sitting in Starbucks) could search the world's information and communicate with other internet users. Entrepreneurs designed new browsers to "read" the web. Jim Clark became the first internet billionaire when he took Netscape public in August 1995. Jimmy Wales created the world's biggest encyclopedia in the form of Wikipedia: written entirely by volunteers, it constantly evolved as people posted improvements and weeded out errors.

Google was the most successful of the new generation of internet companies, and a perfect example of what makes Silicon Valley so special. Sergey Brin and Larry Page met each other when Brin was showing new students around Stanford's computer science department. Sparks flew: though they found each other obnoxious, they had a lot in common (Brin's father was a mathematician who had fled from Moscow and Page's father was a computer scientist) and they became sparring partners and academic collaborators. They came up with an idea for quickly searching through the millions of pages that appear on the web and ranking them according to relevance. The university provided them not just with teaching from some of the world's leading academics but also with access to some of the world's most powerful computers (at one point Brin and Page used half the university's entire bandwidth) and, as their ideas took shape, commercial advice and funding. They got money from both of the Valley's top venture capitalist companies, Sequoia Capital and Kleiner Perkins. John Doerr of Kleiner Perkins advised them to hire a seasoned manager to run the company and they settled on Eric Schmidt.[11]

The internet provided entrepreneurs with opportunities to revolutionize every business under the sun just as the railways had done a century or so earlier. In 1994, Jeff Bezos, a thirty-year-old analyst with the D. E. Shaw hedge fund, established Amazon, an online bookstore in Seattle, which, thanks to Microsoft, was emerging as a tech center. Amazon is now the world's largest online "everything" store, as well as the world's largest provider of space on internet servers, and Bezos is worth more than $70 billion. In 1995, Pierre Omidyar, an Iranian-American, founded eBay, an online auction site that helps people buy and sell things. Currently the company is worth almost $30 billion and has helped to arrange millions of transactions, from the bizarre to the mundane.

The internet revolution inevitably produced lots of hoopla. The tech-rich NASDAQ 100 index went up 40 percent in 1995. In 1998, Yahoo!, a web company with 637 employees, had the same market capitalization as Boeing with 230,000 employees. The market inevitably corrected itself—the dot-com boom was followed by a dot-com bust—but the growth eventually continued on much more solid foundations with a cadre of well-managed companies leading the way.

The victors from the shake-up bear a striking resemblance to the robber barons of the late nineteenth century. They refashioned the material basis of civilization. Bill Gates put a computer on every desk. Larry Page and Sergey Brin put the world's information at everybody's fingertips. They relied on the logic of economies of scale to dominate their markets. Carnegie's great mottoes, "Cut the prices; scoop the market; run the mills full" and "Watch the costs and the profits will take care of themselves," apply just as well to makers of computers. The price of computer equipment, adjusted for quality, declined by 16 percent a year over the five decades from 1959 to 2009. But it applies even better to the social media, where your utility is determined by the size of your networks: the number of people who go on Facebook every month is much larger than the population of China. Tech companies translated vast scale into market dominance and soaring revenues.

The IT revolution changed the nature of American industry in general, not just the high-tech sector. Walmart and other giant retailers replenish their shelves on the basis of instant feedback on daily sales in all their stores across the world. Manufacturing companies keep their inventories "lean" and their costs down by using algorithms that program variables such as raw material prices and seasonal demand for their products. Bankers can calculate the value of complicated derivatives in a matter of seconds.

THE FRACKING REVOLUTION

One of the most striking changes was not in the new economy of wrestling profit from code but in the old economy of wrestling resources out of the land. Oil was old America incarnate: a world where mostly men worked with their hands and tried to extract the black substance from the land. Yet the oil industry saw one of the most surprising revolutions of the second half of the twentieth century, restoring a declining industry to rude health. This was the work of a quintessential American entrepreneur, an outsider who saw the potential in an eccentric idea and stuck with it through thick and thin.

In the 1970s, America's energy industry reconciled itself to apparently inevitable decline. Analysts produced charts to show that its oil and gas were running out. The big oil firms globalized in order to survive. George Mitchell thought that this was nonsense, because immense reserves were trapped in shale rock deep beneath the surface waiting to be freed. He spent decades perfecting techniques for unlocking them: injecting high-pressure fluids into the ground to fracture the rock and create pathways for the trapped oil and gas (fracking) and drilling down and then sideways to increase each well's yield (horizontal drilling). The result was a revolution. Shale beds now produce more than half of America's natural gas and oil at the time of this writing compared with just 1 percent in 2000. The U.S. Energy Information Administration predicts that the United States is destined to become a net energy exporter by 2022.

Mitchell was the embodiment of the American dream. His father was a poor Greek immigrant, a goatherd who later ran a shoeshine shop in Galveston, Texas. Mitchell had to work his way through college but graduated at the top of his class. He left a fortune of more than $2 billion and a Texas landscape studded with examples of his philanthropy: he was particularly generous to university research departments and to Galveston.

Mitchell was also the embodiment of the entrepreneurial spirit. He did not discover shale gas and oil: geological surveys had revealed them decades before he started. He did not even invent fracking: it had been in use since the 1940s. His greatness lay in a combination of vision and grit: convinced that technology could unlock the vast reserves of energy in the Barnett Shale beneath Dallas and Fort Worth, he kept grappling with the unforgiving rock until it eventually surrendered its riches.

After studying petroleum engineering and geology, Mitchell served in the Army Corps of Engineers during the Second World War. On leaving the army, he displayed both a rebel's mistrust of big organizations and a gambler's cunning. He made a career with Texas's scrappy independent oil producers rather than with the local giants. In his early days he struck a deal with a Chicago bookmaker to buy rights to a piece of land known as "the wildcatter's graveyard" and quickly drilled thirteen gushers. He also made a second career as an urban developer. In 1974, he built a planned community, the Woodlands, in the pine forests north of Houston, in a bid to tackle the problems of urban sprawl. It contains a mix of social housing and offices as well as million-dollar villas.

His stubbornness was his most important quality. With the major oil companies scoffing and his investors ruing their foolishness, he spent two decades poking holes in the land around Fort Worth. "I never considered giving up," he said, "even when everyone was saying, 'George, you're wasting your money.'" Then, in 1998, with Mitchell approaching his eighties, his team hit on the idea of substituting water for gunky drilling fluids. This drastically cut the cost of drilling and turned the Barnett Shale into a gold mine.

Mitchell would have been a familiar figure to the great entrepreneurs of the late nineteenth century: a man obsessed with using mechanical innovations to wrestle resources out of the unforgiving soil. But this era also saw two momentous developments that would have shocked Rockefeller and company far more than using water to extract oil out of rock: the replacement of blue-collar workers with knowledge workers at the heart of the economy and the advance of women in the workforce. Reagan, Bush, and Clinton didn't just preside over a technological revolution. They also presided over a social revolution that reached into almost every American home.

THE NEW WORKFORCE

The America of the golden age had been dominated by men and machines. It was overwhelmingly a manufacturing economy: in 1950, 36 percent of nonfarm private-sector workers were employed in manufacturing. The Dow Jones Index was ruled by industrial companies such as General Motors and Westinghouse. People who made things with their hands were widely honored, treated as the exemplars of American virtue rather than as casualties of the race for educational credentials. It was also a male-dominated economy: men went out to work and provided for their families while women stayed at home to raise the children, at most supplementing the family income with a little part-time work.

The 1980s and 1990s saw this formula of *machines + men = the American way* torn asunder. Reagan's policies certainly hastened the change: from 1979 to 1983, America lost 12 percent of its manufacturing jobs, or about 2.4 million jobs in all, thanks in part to the combination of high interest rates and a higher dollar. But they only hastened the inevitable as manufacturers learned to become more efficient and the economy progressed down the path from industry to services. Manufacturing's share of GDP declined from 23 percent in 1970 to 17 percent in 1990. Even when the manufacturing sector boomed it didn't create as many jobs as it had in the past: from 1983 to 1989, real value added by manufacturing grew by 30 percent, but employment only grew by 5.5 percent. Unforgiving competition from abroad forced manufacturing companies to reduce production costs by closing inefficient plants, adopting new technologies, or moving their operations abroad.

Meanwhile, knowledge workers advanced rapidly, particularly knowledge workers in the IT and financial-services sectors. Brain-intensive companies such as Microsoft and Apple took over from Ford and General Motors as the symbols of modern times. Even old-line companies became more brain-intensive: manufacturers focused on producing highly engineered products for precise niches rather than on standardized products for mass markets. They also devoted ever more effort to shaping perceptions of their products than on their products themselves, spending lavishly on advertising and brand management. Henry Ford had once asked why it was that "when I ask for a pair of hands a brain comes attached." By the late twentieth century it was the hands that were superfluous.

At the same time, a male-dominated economy gave way to a more gender-blind one. The proportion of men aged sixteen to sixty-four engaged in the workforce declined from 91 percent in 1950 to 84 percent in 2000, while the proportion of women rose from 37 percent to 71 percent. One of the most unpleasant side effects of the advance of the cerebral economy was the striking increase in the number of men who dropped out of the labor force entirely and became wards of the state.

The era saw what Daniel Bell dubbed the "post-industrial society" emerge from the womb of industrial America. The focus of economic life shifted from making things to irrigating ideas—from factories to office parks and from steel mills to universities. Specialists in IT and finance were in particularly heavy demand. The share of U.S. gross domestic product accruing as income to finance and insurance rose fairly steadily from 2.4 percent in 1947 to 7.6 percent in 2006. The finance industry also attracted people with ever more rarefied skills, such as PhDs in mathematics and physics. In 2007, a quarter of all graduates of the venerable California Institute of Technology went into finance.

One way to show the profound change in the economy, as brain took over from brawn, is to look at the overall weight of the economy. In the classic industrial age, America had measured its might in terms of the size of things—giant factories covering acres of land and huge mines scarring the surface of the earth. In the 1980s and 1990s, the American economy did its best to fulfill Karl Marx's prophecy that "all that is solid melts into air." The discovery of the electrical properties of silicon and advances in material science meant that everyday objects could be made smaller and lighter. Radios no longer needed to be put in hulking cabinets to house the vacuum tubes. Metal cans could be rolled into thinner tolerances. Lightweight fiber optics could replace copper. Architects could provide accommodation with less concrete or steel. At the same time, the service sector expanded: more and more workers toiled in office parks rather than in factories or, even if they did work in factories, in the business of coordinating production flows rather than actually making things.

This broke the long-established link between economic growth and more physical inputs and outputs. America's real GDP doubled between 1980 and 2000, but the raw tonnage of nonfuel raw materials consumed by the U.S. economy remained more or less fixed over these decades. This means that the only explanation of the increase in the size of GDP must lie in the world of ideas.

The declining weight of the economy relative to real GDP produced numerous benefits. It reduced waste and pollution. Companies improved their ratio of input to output and imposed a lighter burden on the world. It also sped global trade. The lighter things are, the easier and cheaper it is to move them across national borders. The logical conclusion of this is that you turn physical objects into virtual ones that can be sent from one country to another via the internet.

U.S. CONSUMPTION OF SELECTED* MINERAL COMMODITIES
*ALUMINUM, BAUXITE, CEMENT, CLAYS, COPPER, GYPSUM,
IRON ORE, LIME, NICKEL, PHOSPHATE ROCK, SULFUR, TIN.
1900 – 2015

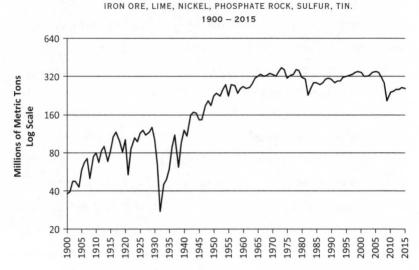

U.S. CONSUMPTION OF SELECTED* MINERAL COMMODITIES
*ALUMINUM, BAUXITE, CEMENT, CLAYS, COPPER, GYPSUM,
IRON ORE, LIME, NICKEL, PHOSPHATE ROCK, SULFUR, TIN.
1900 – 2015

Three-dimensional printing now allows people to send physical objects around the world in virtual form.

The onward march of women workers also completely changed

the tenor of American life. This was a matter of numbers: in 2000, women comprised nearly half of the total U.S. labor force and over half of these female workers were married. It was also a matter of status: women made rapid advances into the professional classes. In 2014, women ran some of America's best companies, such as PepsiCo, Archer Daniels Midland, and W. L. Gore; made up some 51 percent of professional workers; earned almost 60 percent of university degrees; and started about 40 percent of new firms.

The feminist revolution has been so successful that it is easy to forget how recent this change was. Women made early advances in some professions: by 1920, women comprised 50 percent of the clerical workforce, up from 2.5 percent in 1870, and about 90 percent of typists and stenographers. But those professions were isolated, specialized, and frequently low status. America also harnessed female labor power during the Second World War, when "Rosie the Riveter" redefined women's expectations and 5.2 million women entered the labor force. But during the baby boom, women returned to domesticity as the fertility rate rose from 2.4 in 1945 to 3.8 in 1956 and the age of first marriage for women fell from 21.5 in 1950 to 20.4 in 1970.

As recently as the 1960s, working women were confined to menial jobs and subjected to casual sexism. Kennedy's New Frontier Cabinet did not contain a single woman. The Senate contained only two, one of whom had inherited her job from her husband. In 1960, women accounted for 6 percent of American doctors, 3 percent of lawyers, and less than 1 percent of engineers.[12] Neither Princeton nor Yale had a female full professor and Harvard had only one. Harvard Business School was still all male and only 3.6 percent of students enrolled in American law schools were women.

These low figures reflected deep-seated social attitudes. A 1961 study of American college seniors showed that most female students mostly wanted to be mothers of "highly accomplished children" and wives of "prominent men." About 60 percent of women who entered college quit before graduation, often to help put their husbands through college. Wilbur Jordan, the president of Radcliffe, told incoming freshmen that a Radcliffe education would train them to be excellent wives and mothers and perhaps even to win the ultimate prize, marriage to a Harvard man.

In 1966, the Yale University publicity office described attendance at Yale as an opportunity to learn what it is to "Be a Man." In 1969, Francis Skiddy von Stade, Harvard's dean of freshmen, said that "when I see bright, well-educated, but relatively dull housewives who attended the Seven Sisters, I honestly shudder at the thought of changing the balance of male versus female at Harvard. . . . Quite simply, I do not see highly educated women making startling strides in contributing to our society in the foreseeable future. They are not, in my opinion, going to stop getting married and/or having children. They will fail in their present role as women if they do."[13]

Yet these long entrenched attitudes changed with remarkable speed. With the waning of the baby boom in the mid-1960s, women started entering the labor force in growing numbers. The labor force participation rate (LFPR) of "prime age" females (those twenty-five to fifty-four years of age) increased from 44.5 percent in 1964, to 69.6 percent in 1985, to 76.8 percent in 1999. With numbers came quality: women quickly moved up the professional scale and earned higher salaries. The percentage of annual median female wages to male wages jumped from 58 percent in 1975, to 71.6 percent in 1990, to 77.4 percent in 2010, and is continuing to go up, if not as fast as women would like.

Though this change is often associated with the women's movement and radical texts such as Betty Friedan's *The Feminine Mystique* (1963), its deeper causes were economic and technological.

When brute strength mattered more than brains, men had an inherent advantage. As brainpower became more important, the two sexes were more evenly matched. The combination of the rise of the service sector (where women can compete as well as men) and the decline of manufacturing (where they could not) leveled the playing field.

Demand was matched by supply: women were increasingly willing and able to work outside the home. The vacuum cleaner played its part. Improved technology reduced the amount of time needed for the traditional female work of cleaning and cooking. The contraceptive pill played an even bigger part. The spread of the pill not only allowed women to get married later, it also increased their incentives to invest time and effort in acquiring skills, particularly slow-burning skills that are hard to learn and take many years to pay off. The knowledge that they would not have to drop out of, say, law school to have a baby made law school more attractive.

The expansion of higher education also boosted job prospects for women, improving their value on the job market and shifting their role models from stay-at-home mothers to successful professional women. The best-educated women have always been more likely than other women to work, even after having children. In 1963, 62 percent of college-educated women in the United States were in the labor force, compared with 46 percent of those with a high school diploma. Today, 80 percent of American women with a college education are in the labor force, compared with 67 percent of those with a high school diploma and 47 percent of those without one.

The rise of female workers added significantly to the economy's output and productive potential. Women's rising employment was also made possible by rises in the productivity of other areas of the economy: it reflected the fact that it was easier to clean house or go shopping.

"WE ARE FORTUNATE TO BE ALIVE AT THIS MOMENT IN HISTORY"

There were plenty of clouds on the horizon as the twentieth century drew to a close. The financial system was much more fragile than it appeared. Globalization was much more crisis prone: the Mexican peso crisis of 1994 was followed by the Asian crisis of 1997. Some of the positives of the era were balanced by negatives. The advance of educated women coincided with a retreat for blue-collar men. In 2000, only 67 percent of males fifty-five to sixty-four years of age were in the labor force, compared with 87 percent in 1950. The rise of Silicon towns such as Palo Alto and Seattle coincided with the decline of Rust Belt towns such as Youngstown, Ohio. The "great unraveling" was already under way.

As we note in chapter 12, the crowding out of savings by the surge in entitlements required a rapid rise in consumer debt. Between 1981 and 2007, consumer debt as a proportion of disposable income grew by 8 percentage points and home-mortgage debt grew by 57 percentage points. So did America's level of anxiety. Information technology had already started to do for some white-collar jobs—particularly secretarial and clerical jobs—what machines had done for blue-collar jobs, creating a nagging fear of technological obsolescence. In 1991, at the bottom of the business cycle, a survey of workers in large corporations showed that 25 percent were afraid of being laid off. In 1995–96, with the economy booming, the figure nonetheless increased to 46 percent.[14]

At the time, though, these negatives were obscured by the positives: the stock market soared, the dollar surged, unemployment declined, trade boomed, and even pessimists such as Robert Gordon began to talk about "the Goldilocks economy." The budget turned from red to black: America's fiscal surpluses mounted from $69 billion in 1998 to $124 billion in 1999 to $237 billion in 2000, the second largest budget surplus as a percentage of GDP in the nation's history. The economy grew by over 4 percent a year. That meant that the United States was adding $500 billion of prosperity—the equivalent of the entire Russian economy—to its economy every year.

With all this talk of a "new economy" and a "productivity miracle," Clinton ended his presidency in a euphoric mood. In his final State of the Union address in 2000, he painted a picture of a new consensus of economic policy making that might prove to be just as enduring as the postwar consensus of managerial capitalism. "We are fortunate to be alive at this moment in history. Never before has our nation enjoyed, at once, so much prosperity and social progress with so little internal crisis and so few external threats." The country had more jobs and higher wages than it had ever had before. It had turned deficits into surpluses and lagging productivity growth into a productivity boom. It had replaced outmoded ideologies—Republican ideology that saw all government intervention as pointless and Democratic ideology that tried to protect all jobs from economic change—with a new pro-growth consensus. America was leading the world's most exciting technological revolution—the application of information technology to an ever-wider range of activities. "My fellow Americans," Clinton announced, "we have crossed the bridge to the twenty-first century."

Eleven

THE GREAT RECESSION

W HEN HE SWORE the oath of office on January 20, 2001, George W. Bush had the air of a man with luck on his side. He won the presidency despite losing the popular vote to Al Gore and enduring a gut-wrenching recount in Florida. He inherited a booming economy and a rising surplus as far as the eye could see. He surrounded himself with Republican veterans, many of whom had previously worked for his father. The first president with an MBA, he appointed more CEOs to his Cabinet than any previous president, including Dick Cheney, his vice-president, Donald Rumsfeld, his defense secretary, and Paul O'Neill, his treasury secretary. He immediately set about implementing an ambitious conservative agenda.

Yet Bush's luck quickly ran out. His presidency was defined by a succession of economic crises: the collapse of Enron; the severe economic contraction after the September 11, 2001, attacks that erased the budget surplus forecast and put the rising deficit in its place; the "China shock"; and, of course, the global financial crisis. The land on the far side of Bill Clinton's "bridge to the twenty-first century" proved to be much more treacherous than anybody had ever imagined.

The collapse of Enron and several other big companies raised serious questions about the soundness of the country's regulatory regime. Enron, America's biggest energy company, had invested feverishly during the 1990s in a dizzying range of businesses from wastewater treatment plants to fiber-optic cable. It had also reveled in plaudits from McKinsey and Harvard Business School for its "asset-lite" approach to management. Enron had always made aggressive use of financial wizardry to present its results in the best possible light. As the dot-com bubble burst, wizardry tipped into fraud as the company tried to cover up its losses by performing a succession of accounting tricks, such as hiding losses in off-balance-sheet vehicles named after the velociraptors in *Jurassic Park*.

Other companies suffered from similar problems—overexpansion justified by financial chicanery, compounded by cover-ups, and all intended to dupe investors. Policy makers worried that companies were becoming too adept at using spin, rumor, and accounting tricks to massage their results. In July 2002, George Bush signed the most far-reaching overhaul of corporate governance since the 1930s, the Sarbanes-Oxley Act, tightening rules for corporate audits and corporate account presentations and, most importantly, forcing corporate officers to take more responsibility for errors.

The terrorist attacks of September 11 shook America more than any single event since Pearl Harbor. The attacks provoked a huge military response that involved America invading Afghanistan, and ultimately Iraq. They also forced the country to devote massive resources to preventing future terrorist attacks. The attacks posed economic as well as strategic problems. The economy contracted sharply. The inflation rate fell to 1.1 percent—and threatened to fall even further. Even before the September 11 attacks, policy makers had been worried that America might be entering the same cycle of deflation and low growth that had plagued Japan since the 1990s. Now they had additional worries—that the global trading system would seize up under the pressure of terrorist attacks and intrusive inspections designed to prevent further such attacks.[1] Bitter conflict between America and its allies, particularly France, about the invasion of Iraq added to the sense that the global trading order was under threat.

The country's mood was darkened still further by the China shock. China's embrace of capitalism, albeit "capitalism with Chinese characteristics," which meant a leading role for the state and the Communist Party under Deng Xiaoping from the late 1970s onward, produced nothing less than an economic miracle, with the Chinese economy growing at an annualized rate of 10.1 percent a year from 1980 to 2010. China became not only the world's largest producer of labor-intensive goods such as toys, clothes, and electronics, but also the world's most popular location for multinational transplants.

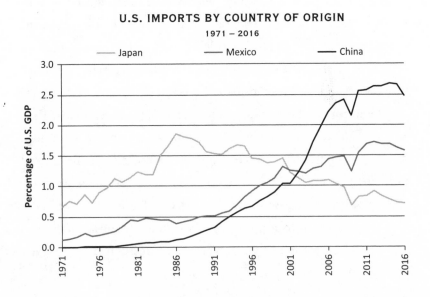

U.S. IMPORTS BY COUNTRY OF ORIGIN
1971 – 2016

China's share of world exports increased from just 1 percent in 1980 to 5 percent in 2002 to 14 percent in 2015. China surged past Mexico and Japan to be the world's leading provider of cheap imports to Americans.

China's growth was a mixed blessing: even as China provided American consumers with a cornucopia of cheap consumer goods, it deprived many American workers of their jobs. David Autor, David Dorn, and Gordon Hanson have calculated that imports from China explained 21 percent of the decline in manufacturing employment during the years 1990 to 2007—or the loss of 1.5 million jobs. In particular, America's decision to establish normal trade relations with China in 2001 was followed, in short order, by both a surge in imports from China and an unusually large fall in manufacturing employment. These job losses were concentrated among low-skilled workers who had little chance of getting equally well-paid jobs in the future: for example, the clothing industry lost about half a million jobs in the years 1995 to 2005.[2]

China's challenge was existential as well as just commercial. In the early years of the Bush administration China became the world's second-biggest economy. America had been shaken before by the rise of Japan and Germany in the 1960s and 1970s. But this was the first time that America had been confronted with a challenge from such a big country. Americans rightly worried that the twenty-first century would be China's century in the way that the twentieth had been America's century. China's surge in economic activity following Deng Xiaoping's adoption of "capitalism with Chinese characteristics" was coupled with a surprising degree of economic liberalism that accelerated through the regime of Jiang Zemin (1989–2002) and his premier, Zhu Rongji (though, regrettably, the progression toward a more liberal regime has come to a halt with the recent indefinite extension of Xi Jinping's presidential tenure).

George W. Bush added to America's troubles by allowing the federal budget deficit to grow once again after George H. W. Bush and Bill Clinton had worked so hard to contain it. Bush came to office determined to deliver on his two great election promises, however contradictory they were: cut taxes and prove that he was a "compassionate conservative" who was willing to use government power to look after the poor. He justified his first round of tax cuts on the grounds that the economy was generating a healthy surplus and government would abuse that surplus unless it was delivered back to the people ("I've learned that if you leave cookies on the plate they always get eaten"). Moreover, the White House Office of Management and Budget, the Congressional Budget Office, and the Federal Reserve projected the budget surplus indefinitely into the future, implying, eventually, the paying off of the national debt. The Federal Reserve set up a task force to find alternate securities if we eliminated the national debt, the instrument historically vital to monetary policy. The attack on the World Trade Center brought that to an end. After September 11, Bush justified a second round of tax cuts on the grounds that America needed a fiscal jolt to get the economy moving again.

He combined tax cuts with a bouquet of "compassionate" spending programs that turned him into the biggest government spender since his fellow Texan Lyndon Johnson. The administration's most unfortunate decision came in 2003, when it expanded Medicare coverage to prescription drugs, the most costly expansion in the program's history. This expansion was not only unfunded, it was made available to all retirees regardless of income. Congress happily joined in with the spending splurge: the total number of "earmarks" (spending earmarked by members of Congress for their pet projects) increased from 3,023 in 1996 to nearly 16,000 in 2005 as politicians desperately competed to buy votes with public money. Bush also added the notion of the "ownership society" to the mixture. In June

2002, he applied yet more heat to the bubbling housing market by announcing a plan ("Blueprint for the American Dream") to make it easier for people on low incomes to buy houses.

The feverish pursuit of the American dream was followed by the American nightmare.

THE FINANCIAL CRISIS

On Monday, September 15, 2008, at 1:43 A.M., Lehman Brothers, America's fourth-largest investment bank, filed for bankruptcy, precipitating the biggest financial crisis since the Great Depression and, in one way, the biggest financial crisis ever. Even at the height of the 1929 stock market crisis, the call money market functioned, albeit with annual interest rates of 20 percent. Within hours of Lehman's collapse there was a run on money-market mutual funds, hitherto regarded as almost risk-free. Within days, funding markets, which provided vital credit to financial and nonfinancial companies alike, all but seized up, setting off a severe spiral of global economic contraction. A system of financial regulation that had been carefully developed and relentlessly fine-tuned over several decades simply failed.

Lehman Brothers had its roots in the cotton economy of the pre–Civil War South: the bank's founders, Henry, Emanuel, and Mayer, immigrants from Bavaria, made their fortunes lending to cotton planters and trading in cotton. The bank branched out into other commodities, and then, after 1900, transformed itself into an investment bank, catering to the needs of America's rising industries, particularly industries that J. P. Morgan and his fellow WASPs thought too vulgar to bother with, such as motion pictures and retailing. The Lehman family also became fixtures in New York's political establishment: Herbert Lehman, Mayer's son, was governor of New York during FDR's presidency. The bank struggled during the 1980s and 1990s. In 1984, American Express purchased the company and merged it with its retail brokerage, Shearson, to create Shearson Lehman/American Express (which then in turn merged with E. F. Hutton and Co. to form Shearson Lehman Hutton Inc.). In 1990, American Express finally gave up its attempts to make sense of this dysfunctional mixture and spun off the company under its original name. This led to the most dynamic era in the company's storied history. The new CEO, Dick Fuld, revived the company's fortunes. By 2008, the company had $275 billion in assets and Fuld was the longest-serving CEO on Wall Street. Alas, Ozymandias had feet of clay: Lehman had invested massively in real estate and real-estate-related instruments, and when the housing market collapsed, so did the company.

The financial crisis had been gathering strength long before Lehman's collapse. In August 2007, BNP Paribas, a French bank, blocked withdrawals from its subprime mortgage funds. In September 2007, Britons lined up to take their money out of Northern Rock, a Newcastle-based bank, in the country's first bank run since the collapse of Overend, Gurney and Company in 1866, a collapse that had inspired Walter Bagehot to write his great book on central banking, *Lombard Street* (1873). The Bank of England was eventually forced to take the bank into public ownership. On October 24, 2007, Merrill Lynch reported its biggest quarterly loss, $2.3 billion, in its ninety-three-year history.

Lehman's collapse was a turning point, tipping markets into panic, and alerting even the most lackadaisical observers of the global scene that something was going badly wrong. By the close of business on September 15, the Dow Jones Industrial Average had fallen by 504 points (4.4 percent), stock in AIG, a trillion-dollar insurance company with operations in 130 countries, had fallen by more than half, and shares in America's two remaining investment banks, Morgan Stanley and Goldman Sachs, had lost an eighth of their value.

The crisis quickly spread to the broader economy. Millions of homeowners lost their homes or sank "underwater," with 1.7 million foreclosures in 2008 and 2.1 million in 2009, and as the list of victims spread from people with subprime mortgages with teaser rates to people with regular mortgages, consumer confidence collapsed. The University of Michigan's regular survey of households showed that American consumers had not been so pessimistic for thirty years. In the last quarter of 2008, real GDP contracted at an annualized rate of 8.2 percent. By the end of the year, global equities had lost more than $35 trillion in value and American homeowners had lost an additional $7 trillion in equity. Add in corporate entities of all sorts (nonlisted and unincorporated) and global equities had lost about $50 trillion—or close to four-fifths of global GDP for 2008.[3]

Bubbles are endemic to capitalism and human nature: think of the Dutch tulip mania in the early seventeenth century, when Dutch investors paid extravagant prices for tulip bulbs, or the South Sea Bubble in the early eighteenth century, when the British became obsessed with buying shares in a company selling government debt. People's animal spirits exceed their rational powers and they overcommit themselves, sometimes horribly so. All bubbles eventually burst, as hope and hype collide with reality, but not all bubbles burst with the same consequences. Some bubbles burst without severe economic consequences—the dot-com boom, for example, and the rapid run-up of stock prices in the spring of 1987. Others burst with severe deflationary consequences that can hold back economies for years. For bubbles to cause economic havoc you usually need to have something more than just toxic assets that can quickly lose value. You need to have a high degree of leverage by the holders of those assets. In 2008, both elements were present in abundance, just as they were in 1929.

THE ROOTS OF THE CRISIS

The origins of the crisis can be traced back to the exuberance that followed the end of the cold war. The fall of the Berlin Wall in 1989 exposed the grotesque incompetence of the Soviet system of central planning for all but the blind to see. Not only had millions died to build the Soviet regime, the Soviet paradise turned out to be a squalid hell. In the closest thing we've seen to a controlled experiment in economic regimes, Communist East Germany—the jewel in the Soviet crown—had achieved only a third of the level of productivity of capitalist West Germany. The Soviet Union was even further behind the West.

All but a handful of fanatics realized that they had been mistaken about central planning and government control. "Between the fall of the Berlin Wall in 1989 and the collapse of the Soviet Union in 1991," a senior Indian mandarin recalled, "I felt as though I were awakening from a thirty-five-year dream. Everything I have believed about economic systems and had tried to implement was wrong."[4] Governments across the world embraced competitive markets as the only alternative. The Soviets embraced perestroika and glasnost with complicated consequences. The Chinese leadership embraced state capitalism in order to prevent itself from going the way of the Soviets. India, a long-time bastion of Fabian socialism, began the slow process of dismantling the Licence Raj and introducing markets.

With globalization the height of fashion, a growing number of emerging-market countries, most notably China, followed the export-oriented economic model of the Asian Tigers (Hong Kong, Singapore, South Korea, and Taiwan): combining cheap and well-educated workforces with first-world technology and management methods, and protecting business with a stable economic policy and the rule of law. The result was an explosion of economic growth that sent shock waves through the global economy: real GDP growth in the developing world was more than double real GDP growth in the developed world from 2000 to 2007, as global multinationals opened facilities in the emerging world and emerging-market companies sprang from nowhere. The International Monetary Fund estimates that the world added about 500 million workers to the export-oriented economy between the fall of the Berlin Wall and 2005. In addition, hundreds of millions were brought under the sway of competitive forces, especially in the former Soviet Union.

Consumption in the developing world did not keep pace with the surge in income. Most emerging countries had a long tradition of saving, driven by fear of illness and destitution, and systems of consumer finance were rudimentary. The Asian economic crisis in 1997 had also reminded people of the virtues of saving. The savings rate in emerging nations accordingly soared from 23 percent of nominal GDP in 1999 to 33 percent in 2007, far outstripping the investment rate. At the same time, investment elsewhere in the world was slow to take up the slack. The result of the savings excess imbalance was a pronounced fall in global long-term interest rates, both nominal and real, from 2000 to 2005 and, at the same time, a global convergence of interest rates. By 2006, inflation and long-term interest rates in all developed economies and the major developing economies had converged to single digits. Falling interest and inflation rates in turn drove up asset prices, particularly home prices, and, importantly, de-linked monetary policy from long-term interest rates. The rapid rise in house prices took place across the rich world and not just in the United States.

The global bubble was inflated further by the malign combination of the housing boom and securitization. The average price of U.S. houses rose by 16 percent in 2004 and 15 percent in 2005.

Increasingly the firms that originated the mortgages didn't keep hold of them for the long term. Instead, they sold them on to specialists who bundled them together and then sold the newly created securities to investors. The leading securitizers were Countrywide Financial, America's largest mortgage lender, and Lehman Brothers. There are good theoretical arguments in favor of securitization. It allows mortgage lenders access to an enormous pool of global savings to fund new loans. It can also reduce risk by combining mortgages from different regions of the country. But by the early 2000s securitization was encouraging risk rather than reducing it: because the people who originated the mortgages no longer expected to keep them for very long, they didn't devote enough effort to vetting the people they were lending to. And because the chain of participants, from brokers to mortgage companies to Wall Street houses, became ever longer, accountability became ever more diffuse. Countrywide discovered that securitization allowed it to offer mind-boggling numbers of mortgages on the basis of relatively little capital and then sell off the risk to other financial intermediaries.

This was made worse still by the explosion of subprime lending, that is, lending to borrowers who, for various reasons, didn't qualify for regular (prime) mortgages. In 2000, the subprime market accounted for 7 percent of all mortgages. It serviced mainly potential homeowners who could not meet the down payment requirement of a prime loan but still had income adequate to handle the interest payments on a fixed-rate mortgage. It also dealt mainly with fixed-rate mortgages. Only a modest amount had been securitized.

Then the market began to take off thanks to the combination of financial innovation and political pressure. The number of people being offered subprime mortgages accelerated even as vetting of those people collapsed: by 2004, more than a third of subprime mortgages were being offered without a meaningful assessment of borrowers' financial status.[5] Financial firms began to accelerate the pooling and packaging of subprime mortgages into securities. The firms had no difficulty finding buyers. Demand for subprime-mortgage-backed collateralized debt obligations was particularly heavy in Europe, thanks to attractive yields and a decline in foreclosure rates that set in in the late 1990s. Indeed, in a reverse of normal business practices, many securitizers actually encouraged mortgage lenders to produce new mortgages and then sell them on.

At the same time, the Department of Housing and Urban Development pressed Fannie Mae and Freddie Mac to increase the number of poorer Americans who owned their own homes. Fannie and Freddie were peculiar beasts, government-sponsored enterprises, or GSEs. They had started life as federal agencies, Fannie in 1938 and Freddie in 1970, but had later been turned into shareholder-owned corporations, Fannie in 1968 and Freddie in 1989. Neither fish, flesh, nor fowl, they sometimes acted like regular private companies (and certainly paid their executives like private companies) but also enjoyed both the implicit backing of the government (which allowed them to borrow at rock-bottom interest rates) and close relations with politicians. Their skill at packaging mortgage loans into mortgage-backed securities and selling them on to investors, all with the implicit backing of the U.S. government, encouraged foreign savings to pour into the American housing market.

Fannie and Freddie had doubled their share of the American mortgage market from 1990 to 2000 and were responsible for about half of America's mortgage debt, despite extraordinarily thin buffers of equity capital. But in a rare display of political unity in those partisan times, both George Bush and the congressional left wanted them to expand still further and provide poorer Americans, including those with "nontraditional financial profiles," a chance to live "the American dream of home ownership." The housing department provided Fannie and Freddie with such ambitious goals that they had no choice but to invest, wholesale, in subprime securities rather than hold individual mortgages. The GSEs increased the share of subprime mortgages on their balance sheets by a factor of five between 2002 and 2004. By 2004, the GSEs accounted for somewhere between 42 percent and 49 percent of all newly purchased subprime mortgage securities (almost all at adjustable interest rates) retained on investors' balance sheets.

As the market boomed, mortgage companies began to run out of the supply of conventional borrowers. So they turned instead to "unconventional" borrowers—that is, people who didn't have enough money to make a down payment for a prime loan or earn enough money to meet the monthly payments for a fixed-rate prime mortgage. To keep the market ticking over, securitizers prodded subprime mortgage originators to offer adjustable-rate mortgages (ARMs) with initially lower monthly payments, widely known as "teaser rates." By 2005 and 2006, subprime mortgage originations had swelled to a bubbly 20 percent of all U.S. home mortgage originations, almost triple their share in 2002. A significant proportion of these were "teasers." As loan underwriting standards deteriorated rapidly, ARMs soared by the second quarter of 2007 to nearly 62 percent of first-mortgage subprime originations. Many of these new "unconventional" borrowers failed to make even the first mortgage payment. By the first quarter of 2007, the situation was dire. Almost all new subprime mortgages were being securitized, compared with less than half in 2000. Securitizers, protected by the (grossly inflated) credit ratings, found a seemingly limitless global market for their products, ranging from Icelandic banks to Asian and Middle Eastern sovereign wealth funds. The book value of subprime mortgage securities stood at more than $800 billion, almost seven times their level at the end of 2001. Fannie and Freddie made the problem even worse by cloaking the size of America's subprime problem with defective bookkeeping.

Organizational changes on Wall Street also encouraged risky behavior. Investment banks routinely took on extraordinary levels of leverage—as much as twenty to thirty times tangible capital—because the senior managers confronted what they perceived as a huge upside and limited downside. These banks had traditionally been partnerships in which the partners were jointly and severally liable for bankruptcy. As such they took on very limited debts. But a ruling in 1970 by the New York Stock Exchange that allowed broker-dealers to incorporate and gain permanent capital helped to create a fashion for leverage. Over the 1980s and 1990s, the big investment banks all transformed themselves from partnerships into public companies. To be sure, the senior officers of Bear Stearns and Lehman Brothers lost hundreds of millions of dollars from the collapse of their stocks. But these losses did not extend to their personal wealth: nobody was forced to declare personal bankruptcy and most had enough money to continue living like kings.

Wall Street was also hypnotized by ever more complex financial products that offered the promise of reducing risk by breaking it down and scattering it among a large number of buyers: inverse IOs, inverse POs, and forward-inverse IOs. Though these instruments were usually far too complex for senior bankers to understand—they had to hire a legion of "quants" with PhDs in mathematics to develop and implement them—they were nevertheless installed at the heart of the financial system: the notional value of privately negotiated derivatives increased from under $1 trillion in 1987 to more than $11 trillion in 1995.[6] It was now possible for financial institutions to take outsize risks with other people's money without the people who were supposedly running them understanding what was going on.

The early twenty-first century thus saw a classic euphoric bubble taking over the financial markets. Consumers borrowed against the value of appreciating assets such as houses. Quants developed complex financial instruments that were supposed to reduce risk but ended up shifting and concentrating it. And financial institutions ignored warning signs because they worried that, if they retrenched too soon, they would sacrifice market share to less risk-averse institutions. Their fears were given expression in a remark by Charles Prince, the chairman and CEO of Citigroup, in 2007, just before the onset of the crisis: "When the music stops, in terms of liquidity, things will be complicated. But as long as the music is playing, you've got to get up and dance. We're still dancing."

Why didn't policy makers turn off the music and stop the dancing? One reason was that the recent succession of "busts" had had a relatively mild impact on the real economy. The bursting of the dot-com bubble produced the mildest recession since the Second World War, with hardly any impact on global GDP. The 1990–91 recession was the second-most shallow. The 1987 crash, when the Dow fell 22.6 percent in a single day, and the 1998 crash, when the Dow fell 11.5 percent over three days when Russia defaulted on its foreign debts, had left no long-standing impact on GDP. Taken together, these experiences led many sophisticated investors to believe that future contractions would prove no worse than a typical postwar recession. An additional reason was that the "great moderation," which began in the 1980s, encouraged complacency about leverage. As late as April 2007, the IMF noted that "global economic risks [have] declined since . . . September 2006. . . . The overall U.S. economy is holding up well . . . [and] the signs elsewhere are very encouraging." The banking regulations adopted internationally under the Basel Accords did induce a modest increase in capital requirements leading up to the crisis. But the debates in Basel over the pending global capital accord that emerged as Basel II were largely over whether to keep bank capital requirements unchanged or even to *reduce* them. Leverage accordingly ballooned.

Moreover, there was an excess of confidence in mathematical models of risk management. One pricing paradigm, derivatives, was so successful that three of its creators—Harry Markowitz, Robert Merton, and Myron Scholes—won Nobel Prizes (and a fourth, Fischer Black, would have done so had he lived). It was also so thoroughly embraced by academia, central banks, and regulators that by 2006 it had become part of the core of the global regulatory standards embodied in Basel II. Many quantitative investment firms whose number crunching sought to expose profitable market trading principles were successful so long as risk aversion moved incrementally (which it did most of the time). The risk management paradigm nonetheless harbored a fatal flaw. In the growing state of high euphoria, risk managers and regulators failed to comprehend the size or power of the negative tail of risks that was revealed in the wake of Lehman's collapse.

Adding to all these problems was the sheer complexity of all these financial products and markets. This represented the law of unintended consequences at its most brutal: invented to evaluate and manage risks more efficiently, they ended up multiplying them massively. In despair at the complexity of these mathematical techniques, investment managers subcontracted a large part of their task to the regulatory "safe harbor" of the credit rating agencies. These rating agencies came with decades of experience and the stamp of approval from the U.S. government. Yet, in fact, their in-house analysts were no more adept at understanding the risks created by the new financial instruments than the investment community at large.

Even with the breakdown of sophisticated risk management models and the failures of the credit rating agencies, the financial system would have held together had the third bulwark against crisis—the regulatory system—functioned effectively. But under the pressure of the crisis, the regulatory system also failed. This was not just an American problem. The highly praised UK Financial Services Authority failed to anticipate the bank run that threatened Northern Rock. The global credit rating agencies bestowed ratings that implied triple-A future smooth sailing for many highly toxic derivative products. The Basel Committee on Banking Supervision, representing regulatory authorities from the world's major financial systems, promulgated a set of capital rules that failed to foresee the need that arose at the height of the crisis for much larger capital and liquidity buffers. The Federal Deposit Insurance Corporation had noted as recently as the summer of 2006 that "more than 99 percent of all insured institutions met or exceeded the requirements of the highest regulatory capital standards." U.S. commercial and savings banks are extensively regulated, and even though for years America's ten to fifteen largest banking institutions had had permanently assigned on-site examiners to oversee daily operations, most of these banks still were able to take on toxic assets that brought them to their knees.

Some critics have argued that the Federal Reserve's policy of keeping interest rates low in the aftermath of the dot-com bubble helped to create the crisis. John Taylor, one of America's most gifted economists, notes that the number of U.S. housing starts has borne a significant inverse relationship (with a lag) with the federal funds rate since 1959 and that excessively low rates in 2003 to 2005 helped to inflate the market. We note that there are plenty of reasons for the housing boom other than America's monetary policy. For one thing, America's housing boom arguably began in 1998, well before the Federal Reserve's 2001 rate cut. For another, the housing boom was a global problem: Britain saw sharp increases in house prices at about the same time as the United States, despite running a much more restrictive monetary policy.

The Federal Reserve's "easy money" critics can't establish a clear link between monetary loosening and the crisis. The policy of keeping interest rates low began as much as six years before the financial crisis, driven by worries that America might be headed for Japanese-style deflation. (This was admittedly unlikely, but if it happened, would have inflicted extensive damage to the economy.) They also fail to take into account the fact that the Federal Reserve's ability to influence interest rates through the federal funds rate (which is the only interest rate that the Fed controls) has been limited by the global savings glut. The "easy money" critics are right to argue that a low federal funds rate (at only 1 percent between mid-2003 and mid-2004) lowered interest rates for ARMs. But originations of ARMs peaked two years before the peak in home prices. Market demand obviously did not need ARM financing to elevate home prices during the last two years of the expanding bubble.

THE GREAT STAGNATION

One reason the 2008 financial crisis did not develop into a Great Depression, as happened in the 1930s, was the superior quality of the official response. Policy makers were lucky to have the example of the 1930s to draw upon as well as a great deal of thought and experience since. They were also skilled enough to make the best of their advantages: the Federal Reserve and the Treasury worked together smoothly to respond to emerging problems quickly and concoct practical but innovative solutions.

Policy makers used three policies to keep the crisis from doing even more damage: lowering short-term interest rates to boost the economy and provide liquidity to stabilize the system; rescuing major institutions, including Bear Stearns and AIG, to prevent contagions;

and applying stress tests to uncover weaknesses in the system. The Fed and the Treasury purchased shares in endangered institutions to keep them afloat. These shares were nonvoting shares to prevent the appearance of a government takeover of the banking system but also preferred shares so that the government (i.e., the public) would be first in line to receive dividends ahead of common shareholders. The Fed embarked on an experimental policy of forcing down long-term interest rates by, for example, a large-scale purchase of mortgage-backed securities. The Fed also collaborated with the Treasury and other banking institutions to restore confidence in the banks through stress tests that were intended to provide solid evidence of the banks' prospective revenues and losses.

Despite the government's successful containment of the crisis, the subsequent recovery proved frustratingly slow and weak. From 2010 to 2017, productivity as measured by business output per hour grew by a tepid 0.66 percent a year, compared with an annual average of close to 2.5 percent a year between 1948 and 2010. Serious financial crises are usually followed by long periods of slow growth.[7] This time, the overhang of household debt was particularly heavy, and the process of unwinding that debt particularly painful and drawn out. Builders started work on only about six hundred thousand private homes in 2011, compared with more than 2 million in 2005.

Worryingly, America's slowdown may have reflected something deeper: the most important indicators of economic health such as the rate of productivity growth and investment began to decline before the onset of the financial crisis. Growth rate in real GDP averaged 1.8 percent in the years 2000 to 2009, compared with 3.2 percent in 1990 to 1999. Median annual income grew by an anemic 2 percent between 1990 and 2010. America's postcrisis recovery has been slow and uneven in part because America's competitiveness problems took root long before Lehman collapsed.

The growth surge from 1998 to 2004 increasingly looks like a brief interruption of a much longer-term decline rather than the dawn of a new era of tech-driven growth. From 1913 to 1950, productivity growth averaged 3.1 percent a year. From 1950 to 1973, it averaged 3.0 percent a year. It then slowed to 1.7 percent a year from 1973 to 1998 and to 1.3 percent a year between 2004 and 2016. It was only in the period from 1998 to 2004 that it regained its pre-1970 pace with growth of 3.5 percent a year (see chart). Economists are beginning to redefine the growth potential of the U.S. economy downward. The U.S. Congressional Budget Office (CBO) suggests that the "potential growth rate" for the U.S. economy at full employment of factors of production has now dropped below 1.7 percent a year. This implies a sustainable long-term annual per capita growth rate for America of well under 1 percent.

Having looked as if it was charting a new economic course in the late 1990s, America now looks much like the rest of the advanced world. Over the past five years, output per worker for nearly two-thirds of advanced economies has risen by less than 1 percent per

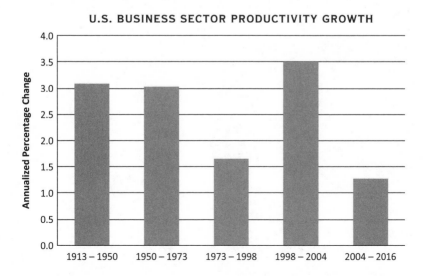

U.S. BUSINESS SECTOR PRODUCTIVITY GROWTH

year, with an unweighted average rate of about 1 percent a year. Growth in output per worker for the United States of 0.91 percent a year compares with 0.62 percent for Japan, 0.84 percent for Germany, and 0.8 percent for Britain.

Growth in the United States averaged a shade higher in 2017, owing largely to a significant reduction in the marginal corporate tax rate and the regulatory burden. But the recovery could prove short-lived: the underlying rate of productivity growth remains low, and inflationary forces are mounting. Labor markets are tightening, as America's unemployment rate slips below a 4 percent annual rate and wages and unit labor costs rise as a consequence. The incipient recovery could easily give way to stagflation: the debilitating economic environment that ultimately merges stagnant economic growth with rising inflation.

America is looking less like an exceptional nation and more like a typical mature economy: overburdened by big government, mired in slow growth, and fearful of the future. The next chapter will describe and explain America's declining dynamism.

Twelve

AMERICA'S FADING
DYNAMISM

———————

THIS BOOK HAS REPEATEDLY shown that America's greatest comparative advantage has been its talent for creative destruction. America was colonized by pioneers and forged by adventurers who were willing to take unusual risks in pursuit of a better life. Arjo Klamer once called America a "caravan" society as opposed to the "citadel" society of Europe: Americans were always on the move in pursuit of new opportunities while Europeans built citadels to protect what they already had.[1] In the second half of the nineteenth century, almost two-thirds of Americans over the age of thirty made cross-country moves compared with only a quarter of Britons who moved across their Lilliputian island.[2] "Few of us are natives of the country," Edward Bates, later Lincoln's attorney general, wrote in 1849, "we are all adventurers, coming from a distance, to seek a fortune or make a name."[3] Though Frederick Jackson Turner worried that America's pioneer spirit had ended with the closing of the frontier in 1893, the country's enthusiasm for mobility continued unabated.

The United States has rightly regarded itself as a land of entrepreneurs, where it is easier than elsewhere to found companies and then, if you are lucky and determined, to turn those companies into giants. Many of America's greatest entrepreneurs came from nowhere to build giant businesses: Andrew Carnegie was a penniless immigrant and John D. Rockefeller was the son of a snake-oil salesman. Many of America's most successful businesspeople built their fortunes by satisfying the desires of ordinary people: think of Sears and Roebuck building a giant mail-order system to deliver goods to isolated farmers or Ray Kroc building an empire on buns and burgers. In Britain, great entrepreneurs celebrated their success by winding down their businesses and buying an estate and a title. In America, there is no higher aristocracy than the aristocracy of entrepreneurs.

At the same time, America excelled in the creation of the infrastructure that is necessary for a modern capitalist economy. It laid the foundations for its industrial takeoff by building roads and canals. It led the world in the construction of a modern railway and then highways. It was the first country to link the country together with relatively cheap and comprehensive domestic flights.

America prospered in large part because it accepted that destruction is the price for creation. The world's most liberal bankruptcy laws allowed companies to go out of business. The world's biggest internal market allowed people to move to places where their skills would be more generously rewarded. The United States accepted that ghost towns and shuttered factories are the price of progress.

There is some of this classic America still in place.[4] The world's three most valuable companies at the time of this writing, Apple, Google, and Microsoft, are all American tech companies—and Amazon and Facebook come in at number six and seven. U.S. firms host 61 percent of the world's social-media users, undertake 91 percent of its searches, and invented the operating systems of 99 percent of its smartphone users. Google processes 4 billion searches a day. U.S. companies also control the infrastructure of the information economy. Amazon has almost one-third of the market for cloud computing, and its cloud-services division has grown by more than half over the past year.

Meanwhile, the United States dominates the commanding heights of global finance. The global market share of Wall Street investment banks has increased to 50 percent as European firms have shrunk and Asian aspirants have trod water. U.S. fund managers run 55 percent of the world's assets under management, up from 44 percent a decade ago. The most sophisticated new financial instruments, such as exchange-traded funds and mortgage-backed securities, were all made in America.

The United States is home to fifteen of the world's twenty leading universities and more than 60 percent of the world's stock of venture capital. America's share of the world's patents has increased from 10 percent when Ronald Reagan was elected to 20 percent today. For all the talk of China's rise, China's rulers send their children to study in American universities (and keep a gilded bolt-hole in New York in case things go wrong at home), and China's most innovative companies, such as Alibaba, list on the New York Stock Exchange, not on Shanghai's bourse.

The United States has a disproportionate number of the world's best global companies outside tech and finance too: Koch Industries, Procter & Gamble, and Johnson & Johnson are as good as any in the world. America's companies have emerged much strengthened after the corporate bloodbaths of the 1980s and 1990s. They have shed excess fat through repeated rounds of downsizing and restructuring. They have outsourced low-value-added jobs abroad. They have combined the ideas of two of the most influential business thinkers of the past thirty years into a winning formula. Jack Welch, the boss of

General Electric for two decades at the end of the twentieth century, advised companies to leave markets that they did not dominate. Warren Buffett, the twenty-first century's best-known investor, extols firms that have a "moat" around them—a barrier that offers stability and pricing power.

Yet this highly productive America exists alongside a much more stagnant country. Look at any measure of creative destruction, from geographical mobility to company creation to tolerance of disruption, and you see that it is headed downward. The United States is becoming indistinguishable from other mature slow-growth economies such as Europe and Japan in its handling of creative destruction: a "citadel society," in Klamer's phrase, in which large parts of the citadel are falling into disrepair.

The Census Bureau reports that geographical mobility has been in decline for three decades. The interstate migration rate has fallen 51 percent below its average in the years 1948 to 1971 and has been falling steadily since the 1980s. The rate of moving between counties has fallen by 31 percent over the same period, and the rate of moving within counties by 38 percent. The new immobility is particularly striking for African Americans: having migrated in large numbers from the South in the first half of the twentieth century, they are now digging in. In 2010, 76 percent of African American mothers gave birth in the same state as their own mothers, compared with 65 percent of white mothers. A study of a cohort of 4,800 African Americans born between 1952 and 1982 shows that, as they grew into adults, 69 percent of the cohort remain in the same county, 82 percent remain in the same state, and 90 percent remain in the same region. The figures for the previous generation were 50 percent, 65 percent, and 74 percent.

It is getting much harder for Americans to move to economic hotspots. A typical New Yorker now spends about 84 percent of the national median salary on rent. This makes it impossible for a regular person from, say, Kansas to move to Manhattan. House prices are always going to be higher in successful economic clusters because so many people want to live there. But today's capitals of creativity, particularly San Francisco, are also capitals of NIMBY-ism, encrusted with rules and restrictions that make it much more difficult to build new houses or start new businesses. Chang-Tai Hsieh and Enrico Moretti estimate that if it were cheaper to move to America's high productive cities, the country's gross domestic product would be 9.5 percent higher due to the gains from better jobs.[5]

Other forms of mobility are also in decline. Upward mobility is becoming more difficult: Raj Chetty of Stanford University has calculated, on the basis of an extensive study of tax records, that the odds of a thirty-year-old earning more than his parents at the same age has fallen from 86 percent forty years ago to 51 percent today.[6] A 2015 study by three Federal Reserve economists and a colleague at Notre Dame University demonstrated that the level of churning between jobs has been dropping for decades. One reason for this is that it's becoming harder to fire people—indeed, it's all but impossible to do so in the public sector—and employers are less inclined to take the risk of hiring them in the first place. Though America still has a more fluid labor market than most European countries, it is nevertheless moving in the European direction, with a cadre of protected workers who keep their jobs for longer periods and a growing group of people who are outside the formal labor market.

The United States is also losing the rugged pioneering spirit that once defined it. In 1850, Herman Melville boasted that "we are the pioneers of the world, the advance-guard, sent on through the wilderness of untried things, to break a new path in the New World."[7] Today many of the descendants of these pioneers are too terrified of tripping up to set foot on any new path. The problem starts with school. In 2013, a school district in Maryland banned, among other things, pushing children on swings, bringing homemade food into school, and distributing birthday invitations on school grounds.[8] It continues in college, where professors have provided their charges with "safe spaces" and "trigger warnings." It extends to every aspect of daily life. McDonald's prints warning signs on its cups of coffee pointing out that "this liquid may be hot." Winston Churchill once said to his fellow countrymen, "We have not journeyed across the centuries, across the oceans, across the mountains, across the prairies, because we are made of sugar candy."[9] Today, thanks to a malign combination of litigation, regulation, and pedagogical fashion, sugar-candy people are everywhere.

POTHOLES VERSUS PROGRESS

Public investment in transportation has declined from 2.3 percent of GDP in the 1960s to about 1.7 percent today, less than Europe's and far less than China's. The roads, particularly in the Northeast and California, are full of potholes. New York's John F. Kennedy International Airport is an embarrassing slum compared with, say, Shanghai's Pudong International Airport. America's trains are slow coaches compared with China's bullet trains.

The 2017 Report Card from the American Society of Civil Engineers puts some numbers to this general impression. The average age of the country's 90,000 dams is fifty-six years. Thanks to the growing density of the population, the number of "high hazard" dams has risen to at least 15,500. There are an estimated 240,000 water main breaks a year, wasting more than 2 trillion gallons of treated water. The annual cost of airport congestion and delays is almost $22 billion. Four in ten of the country's 614,000 bridges are more than fifty years old, and one in nine is structurally deficient. More than half the country's locks are over fifty years old, and almost half the vessels that use them experience delays. Electric transformers are forty years old on average. The wiring of the electricity system is so old that it is sometimes impossible to transfer surplus power from, say, the Northeast to the South.[10]

The twenty-first century has seen some mind-boggling feats of building, as advances in materials technology and engineering techniques allow us to push the boundaries of physical creation. The Burj Khalifa in Dubai, completed in 2008, is the world's tallest building, at 2,716 feet. Dubai is also building the world's biggest airport, Dubai World Central, which will be able to accommodate more than 200 million passengers. The Donghai Bridge, completed in 2005 to connect Shanghai with the deep-city port of Yangshan, is one of the world's longest bridges, at twenty miles, but the Chinese are already adding a second bridge to deal with the growth in traffic. Embarrassingly, few of these engineering marvels are being built in America.

Americans are finding it harder to start companies than they did a generation ago and harder still to grow those companies once they have started them. The share of all businesses consisting of young firms (aged five years or younger) declined from 14.6 percent in 1978 to just 8.3 percent in 2011, even as the share of firms that were going out of business remained roughly constant at 8 to 10 percent. The share of total employment accounted for by young firms declined from 18.9 percent in the late 1980s to 13.5 percent just before the great recession. The proportion of people younger than thirty who owned stakes in private companies declined from 10.6 percent in 1989 to 3.6 percent in 2014.[11]

The decline of creation has even extended to the tech sector. The number of young tech firms has declined since peaking in 2000. The number of IPOs has plunged—from an average of 547 a year in the 1990s to 192 a year more recently. In the 1990s, tech entrepreneurs used to dream of taking their companies public and becoming the next Bill Gates. Today they dream of selling their companies—or at least their bright ideas—to one of the established tech giants. They are supplicants to the established order rather than radical disrupters.

At the same time, the biggest companies are consolidating their hold over the commanding heights of the economy. Apple, Google, Amazon, and their peers dominate today's economy just as surely as U.S. Steel, Standard Oil, and Sears, Roebuck and Company dominated the economy of Roosevelt's day. The Fortune 100's share of the revenues generated by the Fortune 500 went up from 57 percent to 63 percent between 1994 and 2013.

The expansion of big companies and the decline in the rate of company creation means that the economy is becoming significantly more concentrated. The number of U.S. listed companies nearly halved between 1997 and 2013, from 6,797 to 3,485. The sales of the median listed public company were three times higher in 2013 than twenty years earlier. The *Economist* divided the economy into nine-hundred-odd sectors covered by America's economic census. Two-thirds of them became more concentrated between 1997 and 2012. The weighted average share of the top four firms in each sector rose from 26 percent to 32 percent. The consolidation was most pronounced in the most knowledge-intensive sectors of the economy.[12]

The decline in the rate of company creation since the 1980s does not necessarily indicate a decline of entrepreneurialism: lots of small companies are me-too enterprises that don't do anything to raise productivity. The United States saw an increase in the number of start-ups that went on to revolutionize their industries, such as Microsoft, Amazon, and Google. Established big companies such as John Deere also became more entrepreneurial. Nor is concentration proof of predatory monopolies. Joseph Schumpeter argued that concentration can be both a cause and a consequence of success. Successful companies race ahead of their rivals in order to enjoy the advantages of temporary monopolies. They invest the superprofits that they gain from those temporary monopolies in more R&D in order to stay ahead in the race. Great firms "largely create what they exploit," as he put it.

That said, there are reasons for deep concern. Companies are protecting themselves from competition by building all sorts of walls and moats. This is particularly true of the tech giants. They are using network effects to dominate markets: the more people you have in your network, the more valuable those networks are. They are using convenience to squeeze out potential rivals: iPhones work easily with iPads, for example. They are highly aggressive in buying up patents and suing rivals for patent infringements.[13]

There is growing evidence that consolidation is slowing the rate of the diffusion of innovations through the economy. Schumpeter argued that one of the reasons capitalism is so dynamic is that successful businesses stand on ground that is "crumbling beneath their feet." Fast followers are always "stealing" your secrets and improving upon them. This is uncomfortable for leading companies but good for society as a whole because it means that new ideas quickly spread throughout the entire economy. Worryingly, a group of researchers at the OECD, Dan Andrews, Chiara Criscuolo, and Peter Gal, argue that good ideas are taking longer to diffuse than in the past.[14] The top 5 percent of elite firms, dubbed "frontier firms," stay ahead for much longer than in the past, increasing their productivity, while the remaining 95 percent of firms remain stagnant. The information-technology industry is producing a class of superfrontier firms: the productivity of the top 2 percent of IT companies has risen relative to that of other elite firms. At the same time, technological diffusion has stalled, in part because frontier firms can hire the most talented workers and cultivate relations with the best universities and consultancies.

DEATH FROM DESPAIR

The bottom of society suffers from a tangle of pathologies that are rendering a significant number of people unemployable. Nonwork is becoming a way of life in some areas, particularly areas that were once the cradle of the Industrial Revolution. In Scranton, Pennsylvania, 41 percent of those older than eighteen have withdrawn from the workforce. In Syracuse, New York, the figure is 42.4 percent.[15] Nonwork often goes along with a life of petty crime and drug addiction: in particular an epidemic of opiates and methamphetamine is shortening lives and deepening social pathologies.

One of the most striking developments of recent years is that social pathologies that were once associated primarily with black America are now spreading to white America. For white high school graduates, the percentage of children born out of wedlock increased from 4 percent in 1982 to 34 percent in 2008. For white high school dropouts, the percentage increased from 21 percent to 42 percent. The comparative figures for blacks were 48 percent to 70 percent and 76 percent to 96 percent. Broken families create a cycle of deprivation: children who grow up in households without a father are more likely to drop out of school, produce illegitimate children, and become criminals. America's imprisonment rate is eight to ten times higher than those of the bigger European countries. Much of this has to do with the persistence of draconian drug laws that make felonies of relatively low-level drug offenses and lock those offenders up for long stretches. Imprisonment has desperate residual effects, in addition to costing the U.S. taxpayer $74 billion a year: it prevents people from completing their educations, ensures that they associate with other prisoners, and provides them with a permanent stain on their reputations. One study found that 60 percent of those released from prison were unemployed a year after release.

Angus Deaton and Anne Case of Princeton University note that the life expectancy of white working-class Americans has actually started to decline, something that has not happened since the Industrial Revolution.[16] The reduction in life expectancy is driven by an uptick in the number of "deaths from despair." The number of deaths from drugs, alcohol-related liver diseases, and suicide is going up, while progress against middle-age killers such as heart disease and cancer is slowing down. The authors argue that the most plausible explanation of all this is the gradual "collapse of the white, high-school-educated working class after its heyday in the early 1970s" due to the disappearance of high-paying jobs and the accumulation of social dysfunction. During the golden age, working-class Americans could expect stable lives and long-term advancement. Now they are increasingly living marginal lives that, as their health deteriorates, will add to the burden on entitlement programs.

EXPLAINING STAGNATION

Why is America's vaunted dynamism fading? Three explanations are popular. The first is that America is losing its long-standing sources of economic leadership. The United States led the world in three great revolutions in education—creating a mass primary school system in the nineteenth century, and creating mass high school and university systems in the twentieth century. The proportion of seventeen-year-olds who completed high school rose from 6.4 percent in 1900 to 77 percent in 1970. The proportion of high school graduates who enrolled in university rose from 45 percent in 1960 to 63 percent in 2000. Claudia Goldin and Lawrence Katz of Harvard University estimate that educational attainment increased by 0.8 years per decade over the eight decades between 1890 and 1970, and that the improvement in educational attainment contributed 0.35 percentage points per year to the growth of productivity and output per person.

Since 1980, the United States has lost its pedagogical edge. The proportion of Americans finishing high school has either stagnated or declined depending on which measure you take (James Heckman found that the percentage of eighteen-year-olds receiving "bona fide" school diplomas had fallen to 74 percent in 2000). The United States currently ranks eleventh among the developed nations in high school graduation rates. Though the proportion of twenty-five- to thirty-four-year-olds receiving a BA from a four-year college has inched up from 25 percent to 32 percent, that rise conceals lots of significant problems: for example, America has declined from number one in the world in terms of the proportion of eighteen- to twenty-four-year-olds who go to college to no better than fifteenth. American numbers are even more depressing if you look at educational attainment rather than just years spent in education. The OECD's Programme for International Student Assessment (PISA) tests for 2013 ranked American fifteen-year-olds seventeenth in reading, twentieth in science, and twenty-seventh in math.

The decline in America's relative position can be seen by comparing different age groups. Americans aged fifty-five to sixty-four are more likely to have completed high school than their peers in the OECD's thirty-four member states. Americans aged twenty-four to thirty-four are tied for ninth place in terms of finishing high school with four other countries. It is also the only country in which the graduation rate of those aged twenty-four to thirty-four is no higher than for those aged fifty-five to sixty-four.

While the positive features of America's education system have been eroded, the negative features have become more pronounced. The system is poor at training nonacademic pupils for vocational jobs. Before the Second World War, high schools in New York City required "shop" courses, including carpentry and learning how to splice electric wires, but these were phased out even as companies complained about the shortage of skilled manual workers. The system is also extremely poor at controlling costs. The cost of higher education has risen by a factor of ten since 1950 and students have gone more and more into debt to afford it: student loan debt currently stands at nearly $1.5 trillion, more than either outstanding credit card or automobile loan debt.

For most of its history, the United States has been the world's leading talent magnet. Fully 18 percent of the Fortune 500 list as of 2010 were founded by immigrants (among them AT&T, DuPont, eBay, Google, Kraft, Heinz, and Procter & Gamble). Include the children of immigrants and the figure is 40 percent. In 2012, immigrants represented about 13 percent of the U.S. population but founded 52 percent of Silicon Valley start-ups, contributed to more than 25 percent of global patents, and make up 25 percent of science and engineering workers with bachelor's degrees and 47 percent of those with PhDs. Yet the future supply of entrepreneurs and professionals is now being choked off by the country's increasingly hostile attitude to immigration and growing opportunities elsewhere. Other rich countries, such as Canada and Australia, are actively trying to woo high-quality immigrants. Indian and Chinese graduates now have many more opportunities at home.

There is much truth in all this. The United States is certainly dropping down international league tables. It also has a problem with a long tail of lower-performing schools. But it would be too much to expect the United States to maintain the sort of world domination that it enjoyed after the Second World War. America is still a world leader in higher education. Fifteen of the world's twenty top universities are based in the United States. It is better than most other countries in providing people with second chances. There is no evidence that the economy would be better served if more people went to university: about 40 percent of college graduates have been unable to find a job requiring a college education. America doesn't need more baristas with BAs.

A second argument is that the IT revolution is disappointing compared with previous technology-driven revolutions. The second Industrial Revolution at the end of the nineteenth century produced a wide range of innovations that changed people's lives in every dimension: cars replaced horses, airplanes replaced hot-air balloons, electric lights replaced kerosene and gas. The IT revolution, the argument goes, is only affecting a narrow range of activities.

This is unconvincing. The IT revolution is touching ever more aspects of daily life. iPhones can do the work of thousands: they can help you find where you want to go, act as virtual secretaries, organize your book and newspaper collections. Uber uses information to revolutionize the taxi business. Airbnb uses it to revolutionize the hotel business. Amazon allows us to order from a vast virtual catalogue and have the goods delivered within a few days or even a few hours. Morgan Stanley estimates that driverless cars could result in $507 billion a year of productivity gains in America, mainly from people being able to stare at their laptops instead of at the road.

The IT revolution provides a chance of extending to the service sector the sort of productivity gains that we are used to in the manufacturing sector. IBM and the Baylor College of Medicine have developed a system called KnIT ("Knowledge Integration Toolkit") that scans the medical literature and generates new hypotheses for research problems. Various bits of software regularly outperform legal experts in predicting the outcome of court decisions, from patent disputes to cases before the Supreme Court. New technology is enabling machines and paraprofessionals to take over many routine tasks from professionals. Programs developed by Kensho, a start-up, provide answers to financial questions such as what happens to technology stocks when there is a privacy scare. Nurses and physician assistants, equipped with computers and diagnostic tools, are doing more and more of the work once reserved for doctors. Online services and smartphone apps allow the laity to dispense with some professionals entirely, or at the very least increase their bargaining power. Every month, 190 million people visit WebMD—more than visit regular doctors in America. Educational apps are the second-most popular category in Apple's app store after games, and MOOCs (massive open online courses) are attracting millions of students. Judges and lawyers are increasingly resolving small claims through "e-adjudication." It is one of the techniques employed by eBay to settle the more than 60 million disagreements among its users each year. Contrary to the worries of economists such as William Baumol, who argued that productivity growth is inherently lower in the service sector than in the manufacturing sector, productivity growth is now limited not by the composition of the market (the manufacturing sector versus the service sector) but by the ability of innovators to develop new technologies. It is worth bearing in mind Paul David's insight that electricity didn't have much impact on productivity until companies reorganized their factories in the 1920s. The IT revolution may only be starting when it comes to productivity, particularly when it comes to the productivity of the service sector.

A third argument is that the growth rate of the workforce is decelerating. The American economy has repeatedly been boosted by the arrival of fresh waves of new workers—first farmworkers who abandoned the farm for higher paying jobs in the city and more recently women who left nonpaying jobs in the household economy to join the workforce. Now it is suffering from the reverse problem: workers are leaving the workforce and beginning to claim their pensions. The percentage of people of retirement age in the total population has increased from 6.8 percent in 1940 to 11.3 percent in 1980, and to 13.1 percent in 2010, and is set to rise relentlessly for the next twenty-five years.

This is even more unconvincing than the IT argument. The biggest problem with the argument is that the baby-boom retirement has only just begun. There is also a more subtle problem: people can continue to work much later in their life than they used to, partly because they are remaining healthy for longer and partly because work is no longer as physically demanding as it used to be. Several countries, such as Sweden and the United Kingdom, are progressively raising their retirement ages in line with the growing longevity of the population.

So why is the country stagnating? The most important reason is the growth of productivity-suppressing entitlements—the collection of social benefits (primarily Social Security, Medicare, and Medicaid) that Americans enjoy simply by right of being Americans. Aside from a jump following the Second World War, the rise of entitlements was relatively modest for the first thirty years after the introduction of Social Security in 1935. Then it took off: between 1965 and 2016, social benefits increased at an average rate of 9 percent a year. The share of GDP going to social benefits rose from 4.6 percent to 14.6 percent, a huge displacement.

The United States is now encrusted with entitlements. Fifty-five percent of all U.S. households receive cash or in-kind assistance from at least one major federal entitlement program. Almost all Americans over sixty-five receive Social Security and Medicare. Eighty percent of Americans living in households headed by single mothers receive entitlement benefits and 58 percent of American children live in families that are claiming entitlements. About 120 million Americans (two-thirds of recipients) claim benefits from two or more programs, and about 46 million (almost a third) claim from three or more programs.

This entitlement regime only bears a loose relationship to need: over 90 percent of social insurance assistance goes to a single demographic group that is defined by age rather than need—people aged sixty-five and over. The government distributes about fifty thousand dollars a year in Social Security and Medicare benefits to the typical married couple who retired at age sixty-six in 2016, just six thousand dollars less than the median income of U.S. households in general. Yet these retirees have lived through some of the most prosperous years in American history. They can also expect to live longer than any previous retirees. The burden of supporting this gilded generation will fall on current workers who have had far fewer opportunities than their seniors and have to simultaneously provide for their own children.

It is in the nature of entitlement spending that most of it is on automatic pilot: people are enrolled and payments rise according to fixed formulas. So entitlements rise at a fixed rate regardless of how the economy is performing or who is sitting in the White House. Presidents can talk about the virtue of small government as much as they like. The core entitlement programs will inevitably expand as the population ages, prices increase, and health-care costs rise. The three basic entitlement programs—Social Security, Medicare, and Medicaid—now make up almost 50 percent of the federal budget, and that number is slated to rise over the coming decades regardless of partisan political advantage.

Presidents can make a difference to the pace of growth, however. Since 1965, spending on social benefits has, counterintuitively, risen faster under Republican presidents (10.7 percent a year) than under

Democratic presidents (7.3 percent a year). Bill Clinton not only controlled spending on social benefits better than Ronald Reagan (4.6 percent a year versus 7.3 percent), he introduced radical changes to welfare (though admittedly with congressional Republican encouragement). George W. Bush added new drug benefits without providing a means for funding them, something a fiscally conservative president such as Bill Clinton would never have done. Both parties engage in competitive bidding for votes (some Republicans justify their willingness to spend public money on the grounds that if they don't spend it Democrats will). Even voters who consider themselves to be small government conservatives are wedded to entitlements—a position best expressed by the Tea Party activists who told Obama to keep his hands off "their" Medicare.

This story points to one of the oddities of entitlements that make them so difficult to reform. Americans like to think that they have "earned" their entitlements: they are simply getting back what they put into the trust funds plus interest. They make a sharp distinction in their minds between taxpayer-funded "handouts" (which can be cut) and "getting back what they put in" (which is sacred). In one AARP advertisement, a retiree proclaims, "I earned my Medicare and Social Security." This is in fact an illusion. Americans are collectively putting in less than they are getting out: making up the actuarial shortfall would require a permanent tax increase of a third or a permanent cut in benefits of a fourth.[17] Absent such changes, the Social Security trust fund will run out of money by 2034 and the Medicare fund will run out of money by 2029. But "my money returned" is an exceedingly powerful illusion that makes reform almost impossible. Victor Hugo once said that there is nothing more powerful in politics than an idea whose time has come. He was wrong: the most powerful thing in politics is a heavily subsidized benefit that the recipient believes they have fully paid for.

Most important, federal entitlements are squeezing discretionary spending. The Steuerle-Roeper Fiscal Democracy Index measures how many of America's fiscal decisions are on automatic pilot and how many are open to discretion. In 1962, about two-thirds of all federal expenditures were discretionary. In the mid-1960s, that number began falling sharply, thanks to Johnson's entitlements. In 1982, the number had fallen below 30 percent. By 2014, the number stood at about 20 percent and is slated to fall below 10 percent by 2022.

Federal entitlements are crowding out domestic savings. The following chart portrays a surprising statistical stability: the sum of social benefits to persons (entitlements) and gross domestic savings (both as a percentage of GDP) has been trendless since 1965. The steady increase in entitlements as a percentage of GDP is mirrored by a decrease, on average, in gross domestic savings as a percentage of

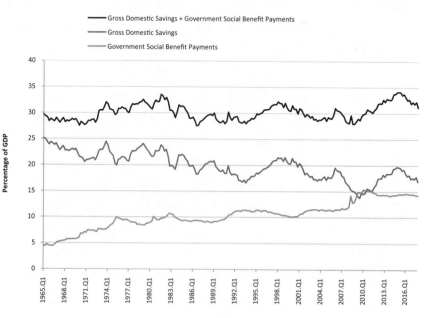

GROSS DOMESTIC SAVINGS AND GOVERNMENT SOCIAL BENEFITS
PLOTTED QUARTERLY, Q1 1965 – Q4 2017

Gross Domestic Savings + Government Social Benefit Payments
Gross Domestic Savings
Government Social Benefit Payments

GDP. This implies that entitlements are not only crowding out domestic savings, but they are also doing so on an almost dollar-for-dollar basis.

The primary driver of productivity (output per hour) is capital stock (or cumulative net investment). Gross domestic investment (net investment plus depreciation) is funded by (1) gross domestic savings and (2) since 1992, net savings borrowed from abroad (essentially America's current account deficit). Borrowing from abroad cannot be sustained indefinitely: such debt had already accumulated to $8 trillion by the second quarter of 2016. Domestic investment must eventually rely on the nation's propensity to save and invest in capital stock, which is diminishing. Worryingly, there is overwhelming statistical evidence that a significant proportion of the surge in benefit spending has been funded by the government, preempting private savings, through taxation—savings that would otherwise have funded domestic capital investment and productivity growth.

One of the most important measures of business confidence and, hence, willingness to invest is what we call the cap-ex ratio: that is, the share of liquid cash flow that companies choose to convert into illiquid equipment or buildings. Somewhat surprisingly, it turns out that just two financial statistics "explain" nearly three-fourths of the variation in the cap-ex ratio observed two quarters in the future, which happens to be the approximate time between an investment appropriation and its actual expenditures. The first is the cyclically adjusted federal budget deficit or surplus, a measure of the degree of crowding in or crowding out of private investment spending. The second is the spread between the yield on U.S. Treasury thirty-year bonds less the yield on the five-year treasury notes. This acts as a proxy for the increasing degree of uncertainty associated with physical capital investments of ever-longer-lived assets: for example, software has a three- to five-year life expectancy and nineteen years for industrial equipment.

The federal surplus or deficit statistically accounts for half of the variation in the cap-ex ratio since 1970. The remaining half is evenly split between the yield spread and other unidentified factors. In addition, given that capital stock is the primary determinant of productivity (measured as output per hour), it follows that if the savings funding capital investment continues to be diverted to funding social benefit spending, productivity growth will be further impaired.

Companies are currently more averse to making long-term investments than they have been since the 1930s (excluding the atypical circumstances of the Second World War). There are several reasons for increasing uncertainty—America's growing deficits, its angry politics, its disappointing growth rate—but they are all fueled by the entitlement crisis that is driving up the deficit, reducing

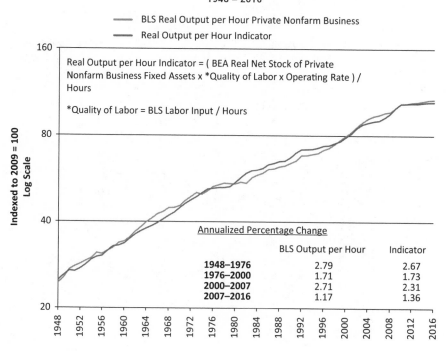

CAPITAL STOCK AND PRODUCTIVITY

1948 – 2016

—— BLS Real Output per Hour Private Nonfarm Business
—— Real Output per Hour Indicator

Real Output per Hour Indicator = (BEA Real Net Stock of Private Nonfarm Business Fixed Assets x *Quality of Labor x Operating Rate) / Hours

*Quality of Labor = BLS Labor Input / Hours

Indexed to 2009 = 100
Log Scale

Annualized Percentage Change	BLS Output per Hour	Indicator
1948–1976	2.79	2.67
1976–2000	1.71	1.73
2000–2007	2.71	2.31
2007–2016	1.17	1.36

productivity growth, and, as a result, poisoning GDP growth and politics (see chart below).

Much worse is to come: over the next twenty years the number of Americans aged sixty-five and over will increase by 30 million while the projected number of working-age Americans (eighteen to sixty-four) will increase by only 14 million. The combination of the sheer number of retirees with the legacy of decades of entitlement liberalization and expansion will create a fiscal challenge bigger than any that America has faced so far. Previous periods of high federal expenditure and debt increase have been driven largely by wars that have eventually come to an end and, as military outlays contracted, so did the debt. America is about to enter a period of high federal expenditure and debt driven by entitlements that stretch ahead, adamantine and inescapable, as far as the eye can see. Left unchecked, this means a future of growing indebtedness and repeated fiscal crises.

SHARE OF CASH FLOW BUSINESSES CHOOSE TO CONVERT INTO FIXED ASSETS
PLOTTED ANNUALLY 1929–2017, WITH RECESSION SHADING

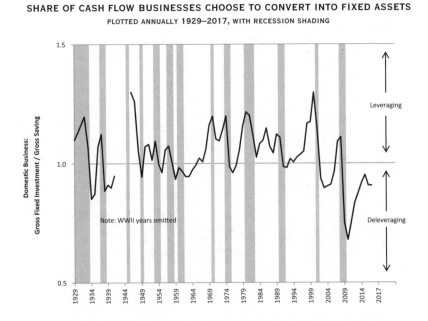

The third problem is the growth of regulation, which acts as a tax on entrepreneurs' two most valuable resources, their time and their ability to try new things. In the 1950s, the *Federal Register,* which lists all new regulations, expanded at an average of 11,000 pages a year. In the first decade of the twenty-first century, it expanded by an average of 73,000 pages a year. Federal laws and regulations now extend to more than 100 million words. State and local regulations add another 2 billion. The Dodd-Frank bill was 2,319 pages long. The 2010 Affordable Care Act is 2,700 pages long and includes a twenty-eight-word definition of a "high school." Medicare has 140,000 reimbursement categories, including twenty-one separate categories for "spacecraft accidents." Added to this is the fact that the American tax code contains 3.4 million words. This means that the land of the free has actually become one of the world's most regulated societies: in 2013, for example, it ranked twenty-seventh out of the OECD's thirty-five members when it comes to product-market regulation.

The collapse of Enron in 2001 added further to America's regulatory overload: the deregulatory language that had been so popular since the late 1970s suddenly seemed passé. The 2002 Sarbanes-Oxley legislation that followed Enron's demise reshaped general corporate governance. The 2010 Dodd-Frank Act tried to micromanage the financial services industry with thousands of pages of detailed regulations. Regulatory bodies have gotten bigger and more intrusive throughout the period of the recent slowdown. The Securities and Exchange Commission's budget reached $1.6 billion in 2018, up from $300 million in 1995. The Department of Justice has used the 1977 Foreign Corrupt Practices Act to challenge companies that have engaged in questionable behavior abroad far more recently than before 2000, and the average cost of a resolution under this act has risen, from $7.2 million in 2005 to $157 million in 2014.

America's regulatory overload makes it harder for the country to

PAGES IN THE CODE OF FEDERAL REGULATIONS
1975 – 2016

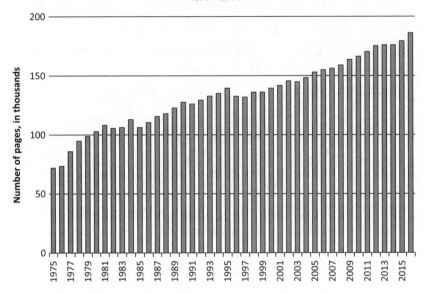

live up to its image of itself as a society of problem solvers and innovators. It adds years to most infrastructure projects because officials
have to jump through so many hoops (particularly, these days, envi-
ronmental hoops). During the Great Depression, it took four years to
build the Golden Gate Bridge. Today bigger highway projects take a
decade just to clear the various bureaucratic hurdles before workers
can actually get to work. When the New York Port Authority decided
to upgrade the Bayonne Bridge, which arches spectacularly between
Staten Island and New Jersey, so that new supertankers could glide
underneath it, it had to get forty-seven approvals from nineteen different government departments, a process that took from 2009 to
mid-2013. "The process is aimed not at trying to solve problems but
trying to find problems," Joann Papageorgis, the Port Authority official who drove through the adjustment, noted. "You can't get into
trouble by saying no."[18]

Overregulation forces business founders to endure a Kafkaesque nightmare of visiting different government departments and filling in endless convoluted forms. To open a restaurant in New York, for example, you need to deal with eleven different city agencies. It costs Americans a huge amount of time or money: half of Americans hire professionals to do their taxes compared with a minuscule number of Britons. It even turns children trying to make money for charity into criminals. In 2011, county officials closed down a children's lemonade stand near the U.S. Open golf championship in Bethesda, Maryland, because the children, who were trying to raise money for pediatric cancer, didn't have a vendor's license.[19]

Corporate regulations inevitably impose a disproportionate burden on smaller companies because compliance has a high fixed cost. Nicole and Mark Crain of Lafayette College calculate that the cost per employee of federal regulatory compliance is $10,585 for businesses with nineteen or fewer employees, compared with $7,755 for companies with five hundred or more. The complexity of the American system also penalizes small firms. Big organizations can afford to employ experts who can work their way through these mountains of legislation; indeed, Dodd-Frank was quickly dubbed the "Lawyers' and Consultants' Full Employment Act." General Electric has nine hundred people working in its tax division. In 2010, it paid hardly any tax. Smaller companies have to spend money on outside lawyers and constantly worry about falling foul of one of the Internal Revenue Service's often contradictory rules. Based on a survey of small businesses, the World Economic Forum ranks the United States twenty-ninth in terms of ease of complying with regulations, just below Saudi Arabia.

Even if overregulation provides big companies with short-term advantages, it handicaps them in the longer term, making them more bureaucratic and less innovative. Established companies expand the size of departments that deal with compliance rather than innovation. They employ senior managers who invest their time in schmoozing politicians and wooing bureaucrats rather than improving their products. The biggest cost of regulation is that it leads to the bureaucratization of capitalism—and thereby kills the spirit of entrepreneurial innovation.

One particularly depressing example of regulation is the rise of the license raj. In 1950, only 5 percent of jobs required licenses. By 2016, that number had risen to 30 percent. (The comparative figure in the United Kingdom was 13 percent.) The license raj extended its tentacles into occupations that pose no plausible threat to health or safety, such as florists, handymen, wrestlers, tour guides, frozen-dessert sellers, secondhand booksellers, and interior decorators.[20] Getting a license is time-consuming. Aspiring barbers in Texas have to study barbering for more than a year and aspiring wigmakers in Texas have to take 300 hours of classes and pass written as well as practical exams. Alabama obliges manicurists to sit through 750 hours of instruction before taking a practical exam. Florida will not let you work as an interior designer unless you complete a four-year university degree and a two-year apprenticeship and pass a two-day examination. Morris Kleiner of the University of Minnesota calculates that licensing boosts the income of licensees by about 15 percent. In other words, it has about the same impact on wages as membership in a trade union does. (Trade unionists who are also protected by licenses enjoy a 24 percent boost to their hourly wages.) Kleiner also argues that licensing slows job creation: by comparing occupations that are regulated in some states but not in others, he found that job growth between 1990 and 2000 was 20 percent higher in unregulated occupations than in regulated ones. The growth in occupational licenses also reduces geographical mobility because it requires a lot of investment of time and effort to get a new license.

The roots of this regulatory explosion reach back to the New Deal and FDR's Brain Trusters, who fervently believed that government should control a far greater share of economic decision making. But enlargement proved self-reinforcing: the coterie of new "regulators" quickly found "problems" (real or imagined) that needed to be addressed, and these government-sponsored solutions required new officials to administer and monitor them. And so on and so forth in a never-ending process.

ENTER TRUMP

Stagnation inevitably soured America's mood and roiled its politics. In almost every survey since the 2008 financial crisis, a majority of voters have told pollsters that the country is on the wrong track. Maverick political movements such as the Tea Party came from nowhere and seized the public imagination. In 2016, Donald Trump, a real estate mogul who had never stood for public office, shocked the country, the world, and probably himself by beating Hillary Clinton, one of the most experienced politicians in the country, for the presidency, with the slogan "Make America Great Again." Trump is unique among a long line of presidents. The closest historical parallel to Trump is Andrew Jackson, who was carried to the presidency on a wave of enthusiasm for the "common man" and revulsion at the patrician establishment. But Jackson's populism existed side by side with his unflinching support for the discipline of a gold standard. Indeed, Jackson was such a foe of paper money (and, famously, of the Second Bank of the United States) that he required all purchases of government land to be paid for in specie. Trump's populism knows no such discipline.

Since Trump's election, the economy has begun to recover from a near decade of stagnation. The stock market reached new heights, rising sharply straight after his election, with investors anticipating a more pro-business climate. Unemployment continued to decline. Blue-collar wage growth outstripped the rest of the economy. The wealth effect kicked in: the continued rise in house prices coupled with the sharp rise in stock prices and business asset prices added significant support to GDP. Trump addressed some of business's most pressing concerns. Federal agencies almost stopped promulgating new regulations, though how far this was a matter of deliberate policy and how far the result of the president's failure to fill administrative positions is not clear. His tax bill, which was passed by a Republican-dominated Congress and signed into law on December 22, 2017, sharply cut corporation tax. Trump's tax bill seems to have been inspired by the Republic of Ireland, which reduced its corporate tax rate from 32 percent in 1998 to 12.5 percent in 2003. On the other hand, he has pursued a dangerous policy on trade, withdrawing from the Trans-Pacific Partnership, imposing a 25 percent tariff on steel imports from various countries, notably China, and a 10 percent tariff on aluminum, and threatening another $150 billion worth of tariffs on Chinese imports.

The country's deeper problems are also growing. Incumbent companies continue to entrench themselves, not least because of their mastery of the "swamp" that Trump has singularly failed to drain. The regulatory state remains huge. The capital repatriation that is being spurred by Trump's tax reforms will increase domestic capital investment only if investors can get a reasonable rate of return; otherwise, increased cash flow will end up as higher dividends for shareholders and increased liquid assets. Trump's policy of simultaneously cutting taxes and boosting spending, particularly on infrastructure, will, if implemented, eventually increase debt and force policy makers to put their foot on the brake, particularly as the White House shows no interest whatsoever in addressing the country's ballooning entitlements (see chart below).

At this writing there are growing signs that America is in the early stages of stagflation—a dangerous combination of stagnation and inflation that can prove stimulating at first but which eventually brings wreckage in its wake, as it did in the 1970s. Record low unemployment is putting pressure on wages. But the legacy of historically low productivity growth, with nonfarm business output per hour growing at an annualized rate of less than 1 percent between 2011 and 2016, continues to dog the economy. Despite the current upturn, the deeper causes of America's fading dynamism remain unaddressed.

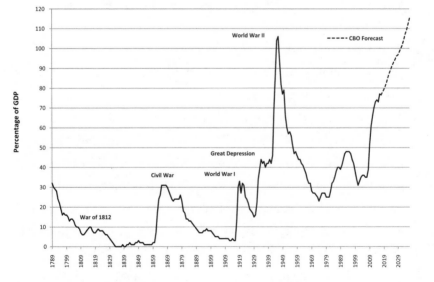

FEDERAL DEBT HELD BY THE PUBLIC
1789 – 2017, CBO FORECAST 2018 – 2037

CONCLUSION

———

I N 1933, Chicago's city fathers decided to stage a World's Fair to celebrate the city's first hundred years. The fact that the U.S. economy was in the depths of the Great Depression didn't deter the organizers from calling their fair "a century of progress" and choosing the motto "Science Finds, Industry Applies, Man Adapts." What was a few years of depression compared with Chicago's ascent from a trading post in the middle of nowhere into the capital city of the great American heartland?

This economic history is being published at a time of trouble for the United States: prolonged economic stagnation has unleashed a plague of political demons. The American people are as divided as they have been at any point since the Civil War, and American politics is as paralyzed and dysfunctional. But this book might nevertheless be subtitled "a history of progress" rather than just "a history": for all its recent troubles, America's economic history has been overwhelmingly a history of improvement. More Americans live better lives than ever before.

At the beginning of our story, American life was truly Hobbesian—"solitary, poor, nasty, brutish, and short." Americans probably enjoyed the highest standard of living in the world—higher on average than their former colonial masters back in Britain—yet by any modern measure they lived miserable lives. In 1790, the average American had a life expectancy at birth of about forty years. Three-fourths of Americans made their living from the land—plowing the fields and scattering much as people had done since the birth of agriculture. People lived one disaster away from destitution: a poor harvest could ruin an ordinary family and a shipwreck could turn a merchant prince into a pauper. Leisure was a luxury: candles and tallow lamps were so expensive that you had little choice after the sun went down but to go to bed and wait for the dawn. There were just 4.5 people per square mile, a number that increased to 6.1 in 1800 and then fell back to 4.3 in 1810. Only 5 percent of the population lived in what the census classified as urban areas.[1] Travel was slow and dangerous. The best the average American—isolated and careworn—could hope for was, in Abraham Lincoln's phrase, "a clean bed without any snakes in it."

These dismal figures were even more dismal for marginal groups such as women and blacks. Women got the rough end of the stick from both nature and nurture. The average woman gave birth to seven or eight children during her reproductive years, half of whom died in their first year. The burden of domestic drudgery fell on women. American law adopted the English practice of "coverture," whereby, as Sir William Blackstone put it, marriage creates a "unity of person between the husband and wife; it being held that they are one person in law, so that the very being and existence of the woman is suspended during the coverture, or entirely merged and incorporated in that of the husband." In other words, husbands exercised legal control over their wives' activities and owned everything their wives produced.[2]

The vast majority of American blacks were enslaved. In 1790, blacks were a much higher proportion of the population than they are today: 19 percent compared with 13 percent. They made up 43 percent of the population in Virginia, 27 percent in North Carolina, 44 percent in South Carolina, and 36 percent in Georgia. Different forms of oppression compounded each other. Black women and children worked in the fields along with the men. In 1860, the infant mortality rate for slaves is estimated to have been as high as 350 infant deaths per 1,000 births, compared with 197 for the population as a whole.[3]

Today life has improved immeasurably in every one of these dimensions. Solitary? Most Americans live in cities and even those who live in the countryside are wired into urban civilization by everything from the internet to indoor plumbing. Poor? Americans have the highest standard of living of any large nation in the world. Nasty? Most of the indignities that have dogged humankind since the birth of civilization have been either removed or tamed. There are drugs to dull the pain of childbirth or tooth extraction; indoor plumbing to civilize bodily functions; air-conditioning to protect people from the sweltering heat. You can summon light at the flick of a switch, send messages at the click of a mouse, even get a robot to vacuum your floor. In 1790, America's most famous man, George Washington, had a mouth full of false teeth, some of them made of ivory; today, only 3.8 percent of people don't have their own teeth. Short? American life expectancy is more than twice what it was at the birth of the republic.

THE PROBLEM WITH CREATIVE DESTRUCTION

The central mechanism of this progress has been creative destruction: the restless force that disequilibrates every equilibrium and discombobulates every combobulation. History would be simple (if a little boring) if progress was just a matter of light advancing at the expense of dark and prosperity at the expense of poverty. The problem is that you can't create a new world without at the same time destroying at least a bit of an old one. Destruction is more than just an unfortunate side effect of creation. It is part and parcel of the same thing: shifting resources to more productive activities inevitably involves destroying jobs and shuttering factories as well as creating new jobs and opening new enterprises. Big innovations can destroy entire industries. In 1900, there were 109,000 carriage and harness makers in America. Today there are only a handful. Even the humdrum innovation that characterizes mature industries also destroys jobs: the telephone industry reduced the number of switchboard operators it employed from 421,000 in 1970, when Americans made 9.8 billion long-distance calls, to 156,000 in 2000, when they made 106 billion calls.

The invisible force behind creative destruction is the market—that is, the myriad transactions that take place at any and every given moment. Creative destruction is also driven by two more visible forces: entrepreneurs and companies. Entrepreneurs are the heroes of creative destruction—the people with the ability to feel the future in their bones and bring it into being through sheer force of will and intellect. Entrepreneurs drive long-term growth in productivity by pursuing their dreams of building a business, launching a product, or, human nature being what it is, making a fortune. But they are seldom the easiest of heroes, or the nicest. They are almost always guilty of what might be termed imperialism of the soul: they will sacrifice anything, from their own peace of mind to the lives of those around them, to build a business empire and then protect that business empire from destruction. Great entrepreneurs are never at rest; they must keep building and innovating in order to survive. They are also prone to what the Norwegians call *Stormannsgalskap*, or the "madness of great men."[4]

One of the reasons America has been so successful is that it possesses a genius for mass-producing these flawed heroes. Charles Goodyear was so obsessed with vulcanizing rubber that he condemned his family to a life of poverty and squalor, with three of his children dying in infancy. Isaac Singer was guilty of cheating his partner out of his business and choking one of his wives into unconsciousness as well as polygamy and child neglect. John Henry Patterson, the founder of the National Cash Register Company, was a food faddist and exercise fanatic who bathed five times a day and once fasted for thirty-seven days.[5] Henry Ford launched a succession of ambitious schemes for improving the world, including eliminating cows, which he couldn't abide. In 1915, he took a ship of leading businesspeople and peace activists to Europe to try to end the First World War and "get those boys out of the trenches." "Great War to End Christmas Day," read a *New York Times* headline; "Ford to Stop It." Thomas Watson turned IBM into a personality cult, complete with company songs about "our friend and guiding hand," a man whose "courage none can stem."

The ugly side of these entrepreneurs is often just as important to their success as their admirable side, just as the destruction is as important as the creation. You cannot reshape entire industries and build companies from nothing without overdoing things. These negative qualities often end up undermining the empires that they helped to create, particularly if they get worse with age. The very stubbornness that led Henry Ford to mass-produce cars before there were many roads for people to drive them on also led him to ignore the fact that American consumers craved variety. Henry Ford's failures prepared the way for the rise of General Motors.

Great companies magnify the work of great entrepreneurs.

Great companies can succeed only by delivering big benefits to consumers—by slashing prices as Ford did, increasing choice as General Motors did, or reinventing basic products, as Tesla is doing today. At the same time, companies also succeed by riding roughshod over their competitors. They use economies of scale to drive smaller and less efficient companies out of business. They use efficiencies of production to reduce their demand for labor. They happily exploit political connections to expand more quickly than their rivals and to resist competition. "All failed companies are the same," Peter Thiel, the founder of PayPal, explains in *Zero to One* (2014), "they failed to escape competition."[6]

Creative destruction cannot operate without generating unease: the fiercer the gale, the greater the unease. Settled patterns of life are uprooted. Old industries are destroyed. Hostility to creative destruction is usually loudest on the left. You can see it in protests against Walmart opening stores, factory owners closing factories, bioengineers engineering new products. But there is plenty of hostility from the right and indeed the center too. The Southern Agrarians who protested against the industrialization of the South in the 1930s argued that the problem with capitalism is that it is always "accelerating." "It never proposes a specific goal; it initiates the infinite series." Patrick Buchanan has described globalized capitalism as "the great betrayal." "Broken homes, uprooted families, vanished dreams, delinquency, vandalism, crime, these are the hidden costs of free trade." Arthur Schlesinger Jr., a Kennedy Democrat, condemned the "onrush of capitalism" for its "disruptive consequences." Daniel Bell, another centrist, worried about the "restless discontent" of capitalism.

This unease makes creative destruction a difficult sell at the best of times. To make things worse, creative destruction is dogged by three big problems.

The first is that the costs of creative destruction are often more obvious than the benefits. The benefits tend to be diffuse and long-term while the costs are concentrated and up front. The biggest winners of creative destruction are the poor and marginal. Joseph Schumpeter got to the heart of the matter: "Queen Elizabeth [I] owned silk stockings. The capitalist achievement does not typically consist in providing more silk stockings for queens but in bringing them within the reach of factory girls in return for steadily decreasing amounts of effort. . . . The capitalist process, not by coincidence but by virtue of its mechanism, progressively raises the standard of life of the masses." Yet the poor and marginal can also be the biggest losers. And the losses are far more visible than the gains: it's easier to see the unemployed silk workers put out of business by the silk-making factories than the millions of silk stockings.

This leads to the second problem: that creative destruction can become self-negating. By producing prosperity, capitalism creates its own gravediggers in the form of a comfortable class of intellectuals and politicians. Creative destruction's enemies usually have emotions on their side: they can point to the obvious evils of "destruction." It has always been easier to make the case for ending injustice or raising minimum wages than it is for economic dynamism. And technological innovation has made it easier still by giving anybody with a camera or an internet account the ability to draw attention to any example of "destruction." They also have the "logic of collective action" on their side. It's easier for the victims of "destruction" to band together and demand reform than it is for the victors to band together.

The "perennial gale" of creative destruction thus encounters a "perennial gale" of political opposition. People link arms to protect threatened jobs and save dying industries. They denounce capitalists for their ruthless greed. The result is stagnation: in trying to tame

creative destruction, for example by preserving jobs or keeping factories open, they end up killing it. Entitlements crowd out productive
investments. Regulations make it impossible to create new companies. By trying to have your cake and eat it, you end up with less cake.

The third problem is that creative destruction can sometimes be
all destruction and no creation. This most frequently happens in the
world of money. It's impossible to have a successful capitalist economy without a vibrant financial sector: commercial banks, investment banks, hedge funds, and the like allocate society's savings to the
perceived most productive industries and the most productive firms
within those industries. At its best, finance is creative destruction in
its purest form: capital is more fleet-footed and ruthless than any
other factor of production. At its worst, finance is pure destruction.

Financial panics feed on themselves: people's desire to withdraw
their savings from risky institutions is intensified by the fact that
other people are withdrawing their savings. They panic as a herd just
as they invest as a herd. And because financial institutions tend to be
interconnected, regularly lending money to each other, the panic
spreads from one institution to another and then from Wall Street to
Main Street. To make things worse, financial panics are extremely
hard to predict. Panics often come on the heels of long periods of
stability: banks get into the habit of making risky loans precisely because they have had things so good. Some of the worst panics have
been produced by relatively small problems: the panic of 1907, a nationwide panic that triggered a serious recession, began when a group
of speculators tried to corner the stock of the United Copper Company. The corner failed; the investors suffered big losses; depositors
withdrew money from any bank with a whiff of a connection with
the speculators; and because those speculators were all well connected with the financial establishment, the panic spread.

The downswing of financial cycles is almost always more

pronounced than the upswing. This is because fear is a more power-ful emotion than greed: fearing the complete destruction of every-thing that they have worked for, people will try almost anything to save themselves from the contagion. Fear is highly contagious: what had been a mere *herding* when the market is going up becomes a *stampede* when it is going down. Panics also inflict serious damage on the wider economy. Investors will hold only the safest and most liquid assets. Cash is king and everybody bows down to it. Lenders will lend only to the best borrowers. Credit dries up. Companies col-lapse. People are laid off. Again the process is self-reinforcing: panic creates contraction; contraction creates further panic.

FROM CREATIVE DESTRUCTION TO MASS PROSPERITY

The best place to study the first problem—the fact that costs are more visible than benefits—is in the transition from the age of the robber barons to the age of mass prosperity.

This book has devoted more space to the era from the end of the Civil War to America's entry into the First World War because it was the country's greatest era of creative destruction. Railways replaced horses and carts for long-distance transport. Steel replaced iron and wood. Skyscrapers reached to the heavens. The years just before the First World War ended with a crescendo with the invention of two of humankind's most successful assaults on distance: cars and flying machines.

While all this was happening, many Americans focused on the destruction rather than the creation. Farmers complained that they were being gouged. Small businesspeople complained that they were being cheated by big businesspeople. Even Herbert Spencer, a lover of capitalism red in tooth and claw, complained about the pollution. There were good reasons for complaining: the very things that drove economic progress, industrialization and urbanization, brought over-crowding, dangerous work, and contaminated air.[7] Deaths from in-dustrial accidents in Pittsburgh per 100,000 residents almost doubled from 123 to 214 between 1870 and 1900.[8]

Politicians such as Teddy Roosevelt and Woodrow Wilson whipped up all this discontent into successful political movements. The Six-teenth Amendment to the Constitution introduced an income tax for the first time. Yet all this creative destruction nevertheless laid the foundation for the greatest improvement in living standards in his-tory. Technological innovations reduced the cost of inputs into the economy (particularly oil and steel) and, hence, the price of basic and not-so-basic commodities. The age of the robber barons laid the foun-dations of the age of the common man: an age in which almost every aspect of life for ordinary people became massively—and sometimes unrecognizably—better.

The cost of everyday items plummeted. In *Walden* (1854), Henry David Thoreau noted that "the cost of a thing is the amount of . . . life which is required to be exchanged for it, immediately or in the long-run." The Federal Reserve Bank of Dallas has built on this insight by translating the cost of basic items in 1897 into their cost in 1997 if the 1997 worker was required to work the same number of hours in order to afford them. The results are startling: a telephone would have cost $1,202 and a bicycle would have cost $2,222. That actual 1997 prices were so much lower shows how far wage-adjusted prices have fallen.

The fall in the price of food was particularly sharp: in 2000, aver-age Americans spent a tenth of their income to keep themselves fed compared with half in 1900. In 1900, scurvy, pellagra, goiter, and rickets were common because even well-fed Americans didn't get enough fruit and vegetables. Food was at such a premium that William McKinley campaigned for the presidency in 1896 on the promise of "the Full Dinner Pail." In 2000, the biggest problem was obesity: 27 percent of Americans are officially classified as obese, compared with 6 percent of French people and 2 percent of Japanese; and obesity was more prevalent among people who were eligible for food stamps than among those who were not.

The epidemic of obesity demonstrates that progress has not been as simple in diet as it has been in other areas of life: a great deal of American food is processed and saturated in fat and sugar. Still, there was plenty of poor quality food available before the rise of McDonald's and its equivalents. In 1900, 95 percent of American families used lard, 83 percent used salt pork, 90 percent used cornmeal. By 1980, those proportions had fallen to 9 percent, 4 percent, and 22 percent.[9] The fast-food revolution has coincided with a fresh food revolution as fresh food of every conceivable variety has become available all year round, thanks to cheaper transportation and advances in refrigeration.

The quality of housing improved substantially. Virginia Woolf's prerequisite for a civilized life, a room of one's own, went from being a rarity to a commonplace. In 1900, half of all family homes had more than one person per room. By 1980, only 4.5 percent of families did. In 1900, 25 percent of families shared homes with lodgers. In 1980, only 2 percent did.[10] Homes became more comfortable as well as roomier. In 1900, the majority of houses didn't have indoor lavatories or plumbing. The consequences in the most overcrowded tenements were stomach-churning—one witness described "vile privies; dirt-filled sinks, slop oozing down stairwells; children urinating on the walls, dangerously dilapidated stairs; plumbing pipes pockmarked with holes that emitted sewer gases so virulent they were flammable."[11] By 1970, 99 percent of households had running water.

Life in general got a lot cleaner. In 1900, there were animals everywhere in cities as well as the countryside: 1.4 million urban horses produced about twenty-five pounds of manure each a day and each ton of manure supported 900,000 maggots. The 6 billion flies produced every day by these maggots commuted energetically between these piles of manure and people's dinner plates.[12] Burning lights of various kinds—candles, kerosene lamps, and gas lamps—filled the air with fumes. Factories belched acrid smoke that turned everything it touched black. By 2000, the country had been thoroughly cleaned. Supermarkets sell hundreds of different varieties of cleaning items. An army of (largely immigrant) cleaners keep offices and factories spick and span. Restaurants are closed down if they fail cleanliness tests.

People's life span doubled. In 1900, the average American could expect to live for about forty-eight years. Three infectious diseases—tuberculosis, pneumonia, and cholera—accounted for almost half of all deaths. In 1918, a flu pandemic killed an estimated 500,000 to 675,000 Americans and up to 100 million people around the world—far more people than had died in the First World War itself. Medical science was so backward that Abraham Flexner, writing in his famous report on medical education in 1910, said that a random patient consulting a random physician only had a fifty-fifty chance of benefiting from the encounter. By contrast, in 2000, the average American could expect to live for seventy-seven years. The three great killer infectious diseases had been all but eliminated, and the major causes of death had shifted from infectious diseases to degenerative processes that are impacted by individual choices, primarily diet, smoking, and exercise.

Improvements were proportionately greater for minorities and women. Life expectancy for nonwhites increased from thirty-three years in 1900, fifteen years less than the white average, to just under the white average in 2000. In 1900, as many as one in a hundred women died in childbirth. A century later, the figure was one in ten thousand. The most striking advance was in the war against death in childhood. In 1900, a tenth of children died in infancy. In some parts of the country, the figure was as high as one in four. In 2000, only one of about 150 babies died in their first year.

Scientific advance played a role in this. The work of Louis Pasteur and Robert Koch led to the acceptance of the germ theory of disease and life-saving innovations such as pasteurized milk. Advancing knowledge led to better behavior: cities began to remove garbage, purify water supplies, and process sewage; citizens washed their hands and otherwise improved their personal habits. The battle against ill health proved so successful by 2000 that some inhabitants of Silicon Valley began to regard death as a problem to be solved rather than a fact to be approached with dignity. But the most important driver was rising living standards that made it possible for people to afford better food, bigger and cleaner homes, and improved health care.

As life expectancy increased, the workweek shrunk. In 1900, the average factory worker worked nearly sixty hours a week—ten hours a day, year in and year out. By 1950, the figure had declined to about forty hours, where it has more or less stayed ever since. Some people in the professional classes undoubtedly work much more than this: you can't be a first-class academic or lawyer or indeed journalist without putting in long hours. But work has also gotten nicer. In 1900, work generally meant sometimes dangerous and usually back-breaking physical labor. Farmers had to wrestle with the elements from droughts that could make the land too hard to work, floods that could drench them, and insects that constantly bit at them. Manual laborers had to wrestle with heavy machines that could kill or maim them if not properly handled. By 2000, it largely meant sitting in the office. The number of Americans who died as a result of accidents at work fell from 38 per 100,000 workers in 1900 to 4 per 100,000 in 2000.

The length of people's working life has also shrunk. In 1900, people started work young and died a couple of years after retirement. In 2000, the average American retired at sixty-two and looked forward to almost twenty years in retirement, perhaps moving from the cold Northeast to the Sun Belt. Retirement had been transformed from a brief stay in death's waiting room, probably spent living with one's children, into a new stage of life devoted almost entirely to golf, tennis, card games, and, it must be added, coping with the consequences of physical deterioration. Michael Cox, a former chief economist of the Federal Reserve Bank of Dallas, calculates that the total lifetime hours worked declined by about 25 percent over the twentieth century.

Some of the most striking advances were made against domestic toil, thanks to the arrival of "electronic servants" in the form of washing machines, stoves, microwave ovens, and dishwashers. In 1900, marriage for a working-class woman who couldn't afford servants was tantamount to a life sentence of domestic drudgery. Stanley Lebergott has estimated that the average housewife devoted forty-four hours a week to preparing meals and washing the dishes, seven hours a week to laundry, and seven hours a week to cleaning. That may be a conservative number. In the same year, employers of domestic servants in Boston, who would hardly have a reason to exaggerate the amount of work they were extracting, reported that their servants put in an average of seventy-two hours a week. What today are fairly simple tasks were then time-consuming chores: the typical housewife carried nine thousand gallons of water into the house each year, boiling most of it, and washed forty thousand diapers for her four children.[13]

Whatever the exact figures, the amount of drudgery went down relentlessly. Naomi Lamoreaux calculates that in 1925 to 1927 the number of hours devoted to basic tasks had fallen to twenty-seven hours a week for meals, six hours a week for laundry, and nine hours a week for cleaning. In 1975, they had fallen to ten hours for meals, one hour a week for laundry, and seven hours a week for cleaning.

These two sets of changes, in both the formal and domestic economies, enormously increased the amount of leisure available to ordinary Americans, particularly women. In 1900, there were only two official holidays in the United States—Independence Day and Christmas—and less than 2 percent of families took any vacation other than these two days. Expenditure on recreation represented only 3 percent of consumption.[14] Thereafter, sources of recreation kept piling one upon another—cinema, radio, television, the internet—until we reached our modern cornucopia of entertainment on demand. In 2000, the average American spent ten times as much on recreation as he did in 1900 and five times as much as in 1950.

Americans also had more hours of light to enjoy their leisure. In 1900, people's lives were shaped by the cycle of the sun: they couldn't work or play games in the evenings because the main source of lighting for most families—candles and wicks—were feeble. They were also dangerous: forget to snuff your candle and you could be incinerated in a ball of fire. One-third of New York's tenement fires in 1900 were attributed to candles, matches, or kerosene lamps. Today you can light your house for pennies a week.

AMERICA'S CHANGING SOCIAL STRUCTURE

America's occupational structure has changed beyond all recognition: a country where most people were engaged in agricultural labor has become first an industrial and now an industrial and service economy. Susan B. Carter, of the University of California, Riverside, suggests that the best way to grasp these changes is to paint a portrait of America's occupational structure at five points in time.[15]

1800

The United States was an agricultural economy: three-fourths of workers spent their lives working the land. More than 30 percent of the workforce nationally and 50 percent in the South were slaves, many of them involved in raising tobacco for export. The majority of free workers worked on family-owned farms. Everybody pulled their weight. Wives ran the households. The older children helped with planting crops and clearing the land. The younger children did sundry domestic chores. Outside of farming, the main occupations were working on ships (either in trade or whaling or fishing) or working as domestic servants.

1860

The United States was even more sharply divided into two economies than it had been in 1800. America's northern economy was the model of a progressive civilization: based on free labor, driven by market mechanisms, and characterized by relatively low levels of inequality. Most people continued to work on family farms or in small enterprises, but the logic of scale and scope was beginning to take hold. Factory workers drove skilled craftsmen out of business: textile workers, stonecutters, woodworkers, and metalworkers were all in retreat before mass production, and craft unions were beginning to form. Improved transportation (particularly the canal revolution) encouraged farmers to move west to take advantage of cheaper soil and more fertile land and to specialize in particular crops: western farmers focused on grain, while easterners focused on dairy and orchards.

A striking proportion of workers were young women and foreigners. Young women left their family farms for paid employment, particularly in the textile mills of New England. In 1860, 22.4 percent of the labor force in Rhode Island and 21.2 percent in Massachusetts consisted of females. Foreigners (and particularly Irish laborers) played a leading role in building America's canals and railroads and providing labor for its new factories.

The South might have belonged to a different historical era. The slave economy was more profitable than ever. The invention of the cotton gin had increased productivity. The Industrial Revolution in textile manufacture, particularly in Britain, had stimulated demand. And the expansion of the southern states westward, particularly into Texas and Kansas, had increased the territory that could turn into cotton fields worked by slaves. Slaves accounted for about 70 percent of the labor force in the central states of the Cotton Belt, such as South Carolina, Georgia, and Mississippi. Because slaveholders held their wealth largely in the form of enslaved agricultural laborers, they had little incentive to invest in other forms of wealth creation, such as industry or infrastructure (towns, roads, or schools).

1910

Slavery had been abolished, agriculture had shrunk to less than a third of total employment, industry had expanded to a fifth, and the United States had attained almost universal literacy, with only 7.7 percent of Americans, most of them the children of slaves, unable to read. Large-scale businesses powered by inanimate forces—water, coal, steam, and electricity—were common. The largest relative growth in employment had occurred in the white-collar sector: big businesses required managers, accountants, secretaries, and telephone operators. In 1870, white-collar workers accounted for less than 8 percent of the workforce. By 1910, they accounted for 19 percent.

The biggest beneficiaries of the boom in America's labor market were arguably Europeans who struggled to find jobs at home. Immigrants arrived in large numbers, with the invention of the oceangoing steamship making the Atlantic passage much easier, and southern Europeans joined northern Europeans.[16] Immigrants naturally located themselves where jobs were most plentiful and wages were highest: in 1910, foreign-born workers accounted for 22 percent of all workers, but less than 9 percent of farmworkers.

The biggest beneficiaries of the upgrading of America's occupational structure were women. Women accounted for 21 percent of the labor force in general, up from 15 percent in 1870, and 45 percent of the professional labor force, up from 27 percent in 1870, largely because of the feminization of the teaching profession. Women's employment was largely confined to the period of life between leaving school and getting married.

1950

America had by far the world's biggest economy and by far the world's highest standard of living. In some ways this was the old economy on steroids: manufacturing was the country's biggest economic sector, accounting for about a quarter of the labor force. In other ways, it was a very different economy in embryo. The white-collar world of professional occupations and services was growing rapidly: almost a third of female workers were employed in offices. A significant proportion of these white-collar jobs were in the government: the Pentagon was the world's biggest building and jobs in the white-collar bureaucracy multiplied like weeds. A high school diploma had become the educational norm. Universities had begun their long expansion.

The Immigration Acts of 1921 and 1924 had turned off one of the sources of growth: immigrants made up only 9 percent of the workforce in 1950, their lowest level for more than 150 years. But turning off taps can have positive consequences. Labor shortages led to higher wages and more emphasis on skills development. It also opened up opportunities for blacks, who abandoned the backward South in order to take up jobs in northern industry. The proportion of blacks living outside the South increased from 11 percent in 1910 to 32 percent in 1950. Paradoxically, America's decision to reduce its links with the European labor market helped to integrate the northern and southern labor markets.

2000

The most striking thing about the U.S. labor force was how much it depended on brain work rather than physical work: most workers manipulated symbols rather than fashioned objects. Thirty percent of workers had a college degree and fewer than 10 percent had not completed high school. Over half of the workforce worked in white-collar work—in the professions and in the service sector.

The flip side of the expansion of the postindustrial economy was the contraction of the old industrial economy. Only 13 percent of the labor force worked in manufacturing and 2 percent in agriculture. Trade unions withered: only 13 percent of the workforce belonged to unions, and union penetration was bigger in the public sector than in the private sector. At the same time, both agriculture and manufacturing became more knowledge intensive. Farmers planted high-yield crops. Factories produced shorter runs of customized products rather than long runs of standardized goods.

The relative position of women and men had changed out of all recognition. In 2000, women made up almost half of the labor force and more than half of these female workers were married: women no longer gave up their careers to have families. The share of women aged sixteen and over in the labor force grew from 34 percent in 1950 to 60 percent in 2000. The share of men of the same age groups in the labor force fell from 86 percent to 75 percent—and was expected to continue to fall in the coming decades.

The other big change in the face of the labor force was the resumption of mass immigration after the repeal of the 1920s immigration acts in 1965. The new immigrants were very different from the immigrants of the era before 1920: a far higher proportion of them came from Asia and Latin America than from Europe. A higher proportion of them were educated. Before 1920, most European immigrants came from the land. After 1965, they divided into two groups: casual agricultural laborers, mostly from Latin America, and highly educated workers from across the world. By 2000, almost 12 percent of the labor force was Hispanic.

TECHNOLOGY VERSUS ENTITLEMENTS

The twentieth century was not just the American century, but the century of the average American: never before in history have so many ordinary people enjoyed such material abundance and economic opportunity. So far the first two decades of the twenty-first century have been more troubled. Just as America's armed forces have become bogged down in prolonged wars in both Iraq and Afghanistan, so America's economy has become bogged down in a prolonged stagnation since 2009. The engines of America's great prosperity machine are no longer firing as effectively as they once did. Growth in nonfarm business output per hour from 2011 to 2016 has averaged a scant 0.7 percent annually, and real GDP growth only 2.2 percent annually.

Moreover, stagnation is producing a populist backlash that threatens to clog up those engines even more. Simon Kuznets once remarked, "We Americans are so used to sustained economic growth in per capita product that we tend to take it for granted—not realizing how exceptional growth of this magnitude is on the scale of human history." People usually respond very poorly to losing something they take for granted: first they deny they've lost it, continuing to spend the proceeds of prosperity as if nothing has changed, and then they start ranting and raving.

For all the changes from the railway age to the information age,

America still excels compared to the rest of the world in producing entrepreneurs. It sucks in talent from all over the world: Sergey Brin is the son of Russian immigrants, just as Andrew Carnegie was the son of an impoverished Scottish textile weaver. It tolerates failure: one thing that Steve Jobs has in common with Henry Ford (and indeed R. H. Macy and H. J. Heinz) is that he went bankrupt. And it encourages ambition. Mark Twain and Charles Dudley Warner's contention that "in America nearly every man has his dream, his pet scheme, whereby he is to advance himself socially or pecuniarily" remains as true now as when they wrote it in the preface to *The Gilded Age* (1873).

America's current generation of entrepreneurs is refashioning civilization just as fundamentally as the robber barons did. They are gripped by the same "madness of great men" that gripped the robber barons. Sergey Brin wants to grow meat from stem cells. Elon Musk wants to "reinvent" railways by shooting passengers down hermetically sealed tubes. Peter Thiel of PayPal proclaims that "the great unfinished task of the modern world is to turn death from a fact of life to a problem to be solved."

These great revolutions may well lay the foundations of improved prosperity just as the steel and petroleum revolutions did in the nineteenth century. Fracking is putting a downward pressure on oil and gas prices for both consumers and business. The IT revolution's impact is spreading to ever-wider areas of the economy—from information narrowly conceived to services in general and from the virtual world to the physical world.

The source of America's economic problems lies elsewhere—in the rise of entitlements and the instability of the financial system.

FIXING AMERICA'S GROWTH MACHINE

It is easy to be pessimistic about America's ability to address these problems. Social Security is not called the third rail of politics for nothing. The financial system has been prone to booms and busts since the onset of the Industrial Revolution. America's current political crisis has deep roots. In particular, the history of social benefits in the United States has exposed a deep-seated inability to square benefits with their funding. For all that, addressing these problems is far from impossible for the country that has turned a wilderness into the most powerful economy on earth.

There are several inspiring examples of countries that have successfully reformed their entitlement problems, examples that provide both general encouragement and practical blueprints. The most encouraging story is Sweden. For most of the twentieth century, the Swedish government kept on getting bigger: the government offered more and more benefits to the people and extracted higher and higher taxes to pay for them. Public spending as a share of GDP nearly doubled from 1960 to 1980 and peaked at 67 percent in 1993. The public sector added more than a million new workers between 1950 and 1990, at a time when the private sector added no new net jobs whatsoever. In 1976, Astrid Lindgren, the creator of Pippi Longstocking, received a tax bill for 102 percent of her income, and produced a fairy story about a writer, Pomperipossa, who gave up producing books for a carefree life on the dole, providing economists with a new phrase, the Pomperipossa effect.

Eventually the system hit the wall. In 1991, Sweden was plunged into what was known locally as the "black-of-night crisis": the Swedish banking system seized up, foreign investors lost confidence in the government, and mortgage rates briefly rose to 500 percent. Carl Bildt's conservative government introduced a succession of radical measures to put the country back on the right track. Sweden reduced public spending as a proportion of GDP from 67 percent in 1993 to 49 percent today. It reduced the top rate of tax and scrapped a mare's nest of taxes on property, gifts, wealth, and inheritance. The government bound itself in a fiscal straitjacket whereby it must produce a surplus over the economic cycle. Its public debt fell from 70 percent of GDP in 1993 to 37 percent in 2010, and its budget moved from an 11 percent deficit to a surplus of 0.3 percent over the same period. In 1998, the Swedes changed their system from a defined-benefit to a defined-contribution system, thereby assuring solvency. They introduced an element of privatization by allowing Swedes to put some of their pension money into a private system. Today, more than half of the population has at some point actively chosen to participate in the private market (the money for those who choose not to participate goes automatically into a state-run investment fund). Above all, they raised the retirement age to sixty-seven and introduced an automatic mechanism that raises the retirement age along with life expectancy. There is even a circuit breaker that kicks in when the economy is in recession: pensions go down if the economy can't afford them.

The Swedes introduced their radical reforms on the basis of cross-party consensus, recognizing that their "people's home," as the founders of the welfare state called it, could survive only if it managed its household finances responsibly. They also continue to worry away at the problem. The government has appointed a "commission on the future" that is trying to grapple with the implications of an aging society.

The United States is a much bigger country than Sweden—indeed, Sweden has about the same population as New York City—and far less consensus-oriented. But Sweden nevertheless holds important lessons for America, especially in its willingness to switch from a defined-benefit to a defined-contributions system that would, by definition, automatically solve the country's Social Security funding problem (no more can go out of the fund than comes in). But many other changes are applicable as well. Sweden's example shows that even the most government-addicted country can change course. Government can shrink as well as expand. Sweden also employed techniques that can be used by all democracies—depoliticizing entitlement spending by handing over reforms to a group of wise men and women and relying as much as possible on automatic formulas such as linking retirement age to expected life spans.

The United States can also draw some encouragement from the changing face of aging. The easiest way to save money is to raise the retirement age. The retirement age is currently set to rise to sixty-seven in 2022. The CBO calculates that you can add another 1 percent to GDP with a few modest tweaks to that change: bring the date forward, raise the age to seventy rather than sixty-seven, and then index it to life expectancy. Simply indexing benefits to price inflation rather than wage inflation would also save money.

The urgency of addressing this problem was underlined by the actuaries of the Social Security Trust Fund in the fund's 2017 annual report. Noting that the current system is severely underfunded, the actuaries argued that, if Social Security is to remain solvent in the long term, America has no choice but to do one of two things (or a combination of the two) forthwith: increase taxes on payrolls by 4.3 percentage points (an increase of over a third) or cut future benefits by 25 percent. The Medicare Board of Trustees also added their voices to these worries in their 2017 report, arguing that Medicare faces "a substantial financial shortfall that will need to be addressed with further legislation. Such legislation should be enacted sooner rather than later to minimize the impact on beneficiaries, providers and taxpayers."

There are no doubt people who argue that it's barbaric to oblige people to work a bit longer before receiving state benefits. But the retirement age was fixed at a time when life expectancy was much shorter. Today the average sixty-five-year-old retiree can look forward to another 19.5 years of life, compared with 12.7 years for men and 14.7 years for women in 1940 (five years after the system was set up in 1935). The retirement age was also fixed at a time when most people wore out their bodies in hard physical work. Today people are living longer and healthier lives. The Urban Institute, a think tank, calculates that 46 percent of jobs in America make almost no physical demands on their workers whatsoever.[17] Companies are learning how to adjust their workplaces to make life easier for older workers. BMW has introduced "geronto-friendly" changes to some of its production lines, such as new chairs, comfier shoes, magnifying lenses, and adjustable tables that have made older workers just as productive as their younger colleagues. Abbott Laboratories, a large U.S. health-care company, allows veteran staff to work for four days a week or take up to twenty-five extra days of vacation a year. A study of U.S. firms founded between 1996 and 2007 conducted by the Kauffman Foundation discovered the highest rate of entrepreneurial activity among people aged fifty-five to sixty-four—and the lowest rate among twenty- to thirty-four-year-olds.[18] Ray Kroc was in his fifties when he began building the McDonald's franchise system, and Colonel Harland Sanders was in his sixties when he started the Kentucky Fried Chicken chain.

The second big problem is the fragility of the financial system exposed by the 2008 financial crisis. That crisis has already led to a decade of stagnation. Another such crisis might do something even worse: undermine the legitimacy of the entire system at a time when populist anger is already fierce.

Modern capitalist economies need an innovative financial system if they are to work efficiently. Innovative financial systems improve the funding of new plants and ideas and thereby generate higher productivity and rising standards of living: think of the way that new forms of bonds helped to promote the development of mold-breaking companies in the 1980s. Sluggish capital systems starve the wider economy of investment and thereby suppress growth and retard living standards. That said, too many recent innovations have been problematic: they increase risk by promoting leverage or reducing transparency. They thus convert financiers from agents of improved productivity into rent seekers.

This creates a delicate problem: how do you guard against the destructive side of financial innovation without blunting the constructive side? One unhelpful solution has been to produce detailed rules about what financial institutions can do. This was the approach that was adopted by the Dodd-Frank legislation, on the basis of a notion of how the financial system works that significantly deviated from the reality of markets. This approach is replete with dangers: it promotes a culture of box ticking, slows down innovation, empowers lobbying groups, and, most fatally of all, leaves lots of room for financial innovators to outthink bureaucrats.

A much better solution is also a simpler one: increase the amount of capital reserves that banks are required to keep in order to operate. In the run-up to the financial crisis, banks on average kept about 10 percent of their assets as equity capital. Lehman Brothers' tangible assets fell to about 3 percent. If regulators had forced them to keep, say, 25 percent, or even better, 30 percent, to reduce the probability of contagious default—the root of the financial crisis—2008 would have been angina rather than a heart attack. Non-financial corporations rarely face insolvency because they hold back almost half their assets with equity. Both Bear Stearns and Lehman Brothers survived the

Great Depression intact in part because they were partnerships in which partners risked their own capital and so watched every investment with an eagle eye. Brown Brothers Harriman, which stayed as a partnership while other investment banks were going public, refrained from engaging in the risky practices that became so common on Wall Street and emerged virtually unscathed from the financial crisis, its credit ratings high and its balance sheet much smaller but exemplary. Sadly it would probably be impossible to force investment banks to return to the partnership form that protected them so well from disaster. They simply require too much capital to operate in a globalized world. In the absence of such discipline, the least we can do is to demand that public companies accept, in return for the privilege of going public, the obligation to hold large capital buffers to protect against the temptation to gamble with other people's money.

The objection to such a large capital requirement for all financial intermediaries is that, even if you phase it in over several years, it will suppress banks' earnings and therefore their lending. History, however, suggests otherwise. In the United States from 1870 to 2017, with rare exceptions, commercial banks' net income as a percentage of their equity capital ranged from 5 percent to 10 percent a year regardless of the size of their capital buffers. That rate edged higher in the run-up to the crisis of 2008, presumably reflecting greater risk associated with a marked expansion of commercial bank powers, but only modestly higher.

Banks compete for equity capital against all other businesses. The ratio of after-tax profits to net worth for America's non-financial corporations has, not surprisingly, displayed a similar range for nearly a century, as has the earnings price yield of U.S. common stock since 1890. In the wake of banking crises over the decades, rates of return on bank equity dipped but soon returned to this narrow range. The sharp fall of 2008, for example, was reversed by 2011. Minor dips quickly restored net income to its stable historical range. In 2016, the rate was 9 percent. The only significant exception occurred in the Great Depression. But even then, profit rates were back to 1929 levels by 1936.

What makes the stability of banks' rate of return since 1870 especially striking is the fact that the ratio of equity capital to assets was undergoing a marked contraction followed by a modest recovery. Bank equity as a percentage of assets, for example, declined from 36 percent in 1870 to 7 percent in 1950 because of the consolidation of reserves and improvements in payment systems. Since then, the ratio has drifted up to today's 11 percent. So if history is any guide, a gradual rise in regulatory capital requirements as a percentage of assets (in the context of a continued stable rate of return on equity capital)

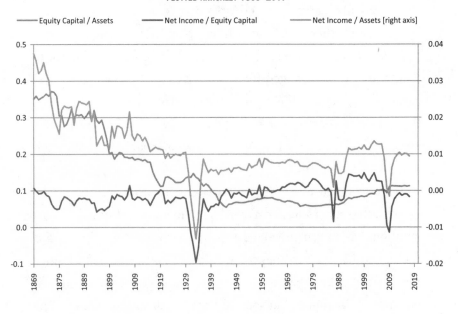

U.S. COMMERCIAL BANKS*
PLOTTED ANNUALLY 1869–2017

——— Equity Capital / Assets   ——— Net Income / Equity Capital   ——— Net Income / Assets [right axis]

*U.S. national banks prior to 1934.

will not suppress phased-in earnings since bank net income as a percentage of assets will, of arithmetic necessity, be competitively pressed higher, as it has been in the past, just enough to offset the costs of higher equity requirements. Loan-to-deposit interest rate spreads will widen and/or noninterest earnings must rise.

With lending risks sharply curtailed, a significant reduction in bank supervision and regulation will become feasible. Lawmakers and regulators will need to worry much less about the quality of the banks' loan and securities portfolios since any losses would be absorbed by shareholders, not taxpayers. This would enable the government to retire the leviathan of the 2010 Dodd-Frank Act. Government would no longer have to interfere with banks' primary economic function: to assist in the directing of the nation's scarce savings to fund our most potentially productive investments. It would also be able to focus its regulatory energies where they would be much better employed: stamping out fraud.

Thickening capital buffers and cracking down on fraud will not solve all the problems with financial intermediaries: that is an impossible task. People will always accumulate too much risk. Innovators will always dance with danger: the shadow banking system may well be the next source of crisis. Because it can never be at rest, capitalism can never be risk-free. But it will do more than our current well-intentioned but misguided arrangements to reduce the risk of contagion while preserving the dynamism of the financial system.

UNLOCKING AMERICAN GROWTH

We started the book by summoning up an imaginary meeting of the World Economic Forum in Davos in 1620 and argued that nobody would have imagined that America would eventually become the world's most powerful economy. It is fitting to end it by read-dressing the same question. Will America continue to dominate the world in the same sort of way as it has for the past hundred years? Or will we perhaps see another surprise—a fall from grace that is as un-expected as the previous rise to grace?

For the first time since it replaced Britain as the world's leading economy, the United States is now being challenged by another great power. China's economy is bigger than America's when judged in terms of purchasing power parity: $21.3 trillion compared with America's $18.6 trillion as of 2016. Its manufacturing output over-took America's more than a decade ago. Its exports are 50 percent larger. A 2017 Pew survey reveals that more people think that China is a bigger economic power than the United States in Britain (46 per-cent versus 31 percent), Germany (41 percent versus 24 percent), and Canada (42 percent versus 32 percent). China is a very different kettle of fish from imperial Britain—far larger in brute terms such as the size of its population and its landmass and, with growth rates reach-ing 10 percent in recent years, far more dynamic.

China's current success is happening at a time when the United States sometimes looks as if it has lost its way. America's politics have taken a populist turn. America sometimes seems to be unhappy with the global institutions (the IMF, the World Bank, the WTO, and even NATO) that it fathered and did so much to reinforce its power in the twentieth century.

The United States will probably enjoy less dominance in the twenty-first century than it did in the twentieth: China will account for a growing share of the world's GDP, and Europe is unlikely to tear itself apart as it did in the twentieth century. But the United States is still a long way ahead of China in terms of GDP per head: $57,608 versus $8,123 (or $15,395 at purchasing power parity). And it is doing a better job of preserving its share of global GDP than is Europe.

China also shows no signs of replacing the United States as the pacesetter of the global economy. America leads in all the industries that are inventing the future, such as artificial intelligence, robotics, driverless cars, and, indeed, finance. And for all its problems with populism, America has something precious that China lacks: a stable political regime that both constrains the power of the president and allows for the successful transition of power from one leader to the next. So far there are no tales of American billionaires buying escape-hatch homes in Shanghai or Beijing.

The United States has bounced back from previous disappointments. In the 1930s, America suffered from one of the longest and deepest depressions in history. Then it emerged from the Second World War as by far the world's most powerful economy and entered into twenty years of sustained growth. In the 1970s, America's economy was plagued by stagflation and its companies lost out to Germany's and Japan's. In the 1980s and 1990s, America seized the opportunities provided by the IT revolution and globalization to regain its position as the world's most dynamic economy. There is good reason to think that America can pull off the same trick again.

America's problems are problems of poor policy rather than senescent technology. This does not mean that they are insignificant: unless we fix them, the U.S. growth rate will be permanently reduced. But it does at least mean that they are fixable. Some suggest that America is mired in a swamp of low growth. We prefer to think that it is trapped in an iron cage of its own making: out-of-control entitlements and ill-considered regulations are forcing it to perform well below its potential, entitlements because they divert resources to consumption and away from the savings that fund capital expenditure and hence productivity improvement, and regulations because they make the distant future more uncertain, thereby discouraging businesses from investing in projects with long-term payoffs. This is an optimistic vision: Swamps by their nature are hard if not impossible to get out of. Cages can be escaped from provided you have the right keys.

We have shown that America has all the keys that it needs to open the cage. The great question is whether it has the political will to turn them.

APPENDIX:
DATA AND METHODOLOGY

One of the biggest difficulties with writing an economic history of the United States is the paucity of data for the early years. This not only makes it hard to provide a clear picture of what was going on in those years, it also makes it hard to produce time-series that go back to the founding of the republic (and beyond).

The paucity of data covering the early decades of the republic reflects the minimal demand for economic data from business. Back then, almost all economic activity was related to agriculture, which was dependent mainly on local climate, with little need for national data. From the late nineteenth century we have national railroad-car loadings and bank clearings (excluding clearings of financially dominant New York City) that were both viewed as proxies for nationwide business activity.

It wasn't until the unprecedented shock of the Great Depression that the government began to address the need for national economic statistics, employing Simon Kuznets, of the National Bureau of Economic Research (NBER), to start systematically collecting data on national income and product accounts, our most comprehensive measure of economic activity. The Department of Commerce published its first data in 1934, dating back to 1929. These data were subsequently supplemented with analyses compiled by the Bureau of the Census, the Bureau of Labor Statistics, the Department of Agriculture (Economic Research Service), and the Federal Reserve.

For the years prior to 1929, contemporary historians have had to rely primarily on a statistical framework anchored by the decennial censuses, which were constitutionally authorized beginning in 1790. The data from 1929 to date, however, can tell us a great deal about economic conditions prior to 1929. For example, if we take the growth rate of output per hour from 1929 to 2017—2.5 percent per annum— and project it backward (backcasting) to, say, 1790, we get a country with a standard of living that is measurably below the one that we are familiar with from contemporary reports. We know what type of buildings people inhabited and what sorts of transport they used not just from contemporary descriptions (and illustrations) but also from surviving examples. We also have detailed descriptions of the rations (in calories) consumed by the Continental Army and, in some cases, of the food consumed by the civilian population. This suggests a slower pace of productivity increase in the nineteenth century and the early twentieth century compared with the period 1929 to 2017.

A still-growing army of researchers have come forward to fill in this statistical void, often with novel statistical techniques.[1] Some historians have constructed what we judge to be the most credible of the various estimates of historical GDP, both nominal and real (Millennial Edition series), which sets the framework of our pre-1929 data system.[2] Their technique is described in detail in *Historical Statistics of the United States Millennial Edition*.[3] This compilation extends the Bureau of the Census's various Historical Statistics publications dating back to 1949. Using a variety of sources, we separate the Millennial Edition series' real gross domestic product (GDP) by economic sectors: households (including nonprofit institutions), government (federal, state, and local), and business (farm and nonfarm). In all cases, we take, as a given, published data from the U.S. Bureau of Economic Analysis for 1929 to the present.

The following is a description of how we estimated pre-1929 GDP for the major economic sectors:

Household GDP, composed primarily of imputed rent on owner-occupied homes, was estimated using data on owner-occupied housing units[4] (1890–present) and the number of households[5] (1850–present) from various censuses, and labor force data back to 1800 from David Weir[6] and Thomas Weiss.[7] Government GDP was estimated using data on federal, state, and local government spending. Federal government expenditure data back to 1789 are available from the U.S. Department of the Treasury.[8] State and local government expenditure data back to 1902 are available from the U.S. Department of Commerce.[9] We estimated state and local government expenditures prior to 1902 using a combination of data on revenues (1800–1900) and change in debt (1838–1902) from Sylla, Legler, and Wallis.[10] Farm GDP was estimated using data on farm income (1869–1937) from Robert Martin[11] and farm output (1800–1900) from Marvin Towne and Wayne Rasmussen.[12] Household, government, and farm GDP were then subtracted from the Millennial Edition series' GDP to arrive at nonfarm business GDP. Productivity is conventionally measured for the business sector only.

We arrived at productivity by estimating the aggregate number of business hours worked and comparing them with business output. This was done by first estimating farm and nonfarm business employment, and then multiplying employment by estimates of average weekly hours worked for the two sectors. We used data on total employment and farm employment from Weir[13] and Weiss.[14] Subtracting farm employment from total employment yields nonfarm employment, which we then scaled down to arrive at nonfarm business employment. To calculate output per hour, we need a consistent set of annual (or weekly) average hours worked. There is much anecdotal evidence of very long factory workdays in the early nineteenth century, especially for children. Our benchmark in this data series is John Kendrick's manufacturing average hours dating back to 1869. In 1869, the average weekly hours worked was 57.7, or nearly ten hours a day over a six-day week. We assumed that that was representative of all workers and that it was only modestly higher for the years prior to 1869.

The workweek started to decline and then fall rapidly in 1914, when Henry Ford doubled factory pay and lowered his workday from nine hours to eight in the belief that productivity growth after eight hours a day was modest. Observing the increase in Ford's productivity gains and profitability, most businesses soon followed suit.

The New Deal ushered in the Fair Labor Standards Act of 1938. The act applied to industries that collectively employed about a fifth of the labor force and set the maximum workweek at forty hours, with additional compensation for overtime. The average workweek has largely stabilized since.

Estimates of average weekly hours in the farming sector relied on various sources of anecdotal data. One prominent question was how to adjust for the seasons, balancing the (presumably) long hours worked during the planting and harvest season against the shorter hours worked during the winter season, to arrive at a plausible estimate for average weekly hours worked for the year as a whole. Another concern was how many hours between sunrise and sunset the proprietors of a family farm were truly working rather than tending to other household needs. While various sources informed our estimate of farm weekly hours, an examination of productivity trends by Kendrick proved particularly helpful.[15] Estimates of average weekly hours worked in the nonfarm business sector relied on data on figures on the manufacturing sector compiled by Bowden[16] and

Kendrick.[17] Multiplying farm and nonfarm business employment by their respective average weekly hours worked yields aggregate weekly hours worked, which we then annualized to arrive at aggregate hours worked.

We calculated farm and nonfarm business productivity by dividing our estimates of farm and nonfarm business GDP by their respective aggregate hours worked. We then used our productivity estimates to backcast the Bureau of Labor Statstics' (BLS) published figures, beginning in 1947, to 1800 for the farm and nonfarm business sectors.

We also used our estimates of historical farm and nonfarm GDP to backcast the BLS's data on multifactor productivity (MFP), beginning in 1948, back to 1900. We employed a simplified version of BLS's detailed estimation procedure for MFP.[18] We derived capital services from Raymond Goldsmith's data on the nation's capital stock and its depreciation rate.[19] We derived labor input from our estimates of hours worked adjusted for skills based on school enrollment data.[20] The share of income accruing to labor was derived from earnings data from Robert Margo[21] and Stanley Lebergott.[22]

NBER data on "business activity," for 1855 to 1970, linked to BEA data, has enabled us to construct a quarterly business operating rate series, which turned out to be particularly useful for analysis of the early business cycle.

The Civil War was, of course, a unique period in U.S. economic history, and we have tried to construct a subset of annual data for both the Union and the short-lived Confederacy. We also found that NBER's Business Annals for the years 1790 to 1919 (published in 1926) useful in judging the short-term qualitative direction of the economy, where quantitative data is sparse to nonexistent. A most useful general source of quantitative data was the extensive database of the Federal Reserve Bank of St. Louis.

ACKNOWLEDGMENTS

It is a pleasure to acknowledge the numerous people who have helped us write this book. At Greenspan Associates, Jeffrey Young produced tables and charts galore and checked all the numbers. Allison Theveny acted as a tireless fact checker as well as providing practical and logistical help. At the *Economist,* Celina Dunlop helped assemble the illustrations; Sheila Allen, Ingrid Esling, Mark Doyle, and Rachel Horwood acted as eagle-eyed proofreaders; and Sabrina Valaydon, Patsy Dryden, and Jennifer Brown provided valuable help. Wooldridge is particularly grateful to Zanny Minton Beddoes, the editor in chief, for granting him a three-month sabbatical that made it possible for us to spend extended periods of time working together in Washington, D.C. Outside the *Economist,* Willoughby Hood and Joseph Ashe helped with fact checking. At Penguin Press we would like to thank our copy editor for her meticulous work, and our editors, Christopher Richards and Mia Council, for rendering the sausage-making as palatable as possible. We are particularly grateful to Scott Moyers, who brought us together, suggested the project, came up with the title, and, as if that were not enough, kept us rolling forward with the judicious application of the spur and bridle. We naturally take full responsibility for any errors and infelicities that remain.

IMAGE CREDITS

Insert 1

Page 1: (top) *The Sperm Whale in a Flurry*, hand-colored lithograph by Nathaniel Currier, 1852. Springfield Museums; (bottom) *Mahantango Valley Farm*, American, late 19th century. National Gallery of Art/NGA Images.

Page 2: (top) ukartpics/Alamy Stock Photo; (bottom) map by Jacob Abbott Cummings as part of his *Atlas of Ancient and Modern Geography,* 1816. Yana & Marty Davis Map Collection, Museum of the Big Bend.

Page 3: (top) *Pat Lyon at the Forge*, painting by John Neagle, 1827. Museum of Fine Arts, Boston; (bottom) undated illustration of Samuel Slater's mill in Pawtucket, Rhode Island. The Joseph Bucklin Society.

Page 4: Advertisement for the McCormick reaper and twine binder. Front page of *The Abilene Reflector* (Abilene, Kansas), May 29, 1884. *Chronicling America: Historic American Newspapers.* Library of Congress.

Page 5: Drawing from Eli Whitney's patent for the cotton gin, March 14, 1794. Records of the Patent and Trademark Office, National Archives.

Page 6: (top) Broadside of Sheriff's Sale, notice about a sale of slaves (facsimile), August 13, 1845. Missouri Historical Society; (bottom) illustration of the Erie Canal from "Summer Excursion Routes," catalogue by Sunshine Publishing Company, Philadelphia, 1881. Digitized by the Sloan Foundation. Library of Congress.

Page 7: The room in the McLean House, at Appomattox Court House, in which General Lee surrendered to General Grant. Lithograph. Major & Knapp, Library of Congress.

Page 8: (top, left) Library of Congress via Corbis Historical/Getty; (top, right) photo 12/Alamy Stock Photo; (bottom, left) photograph of prospector by L. C. McClure, 1850. Wikimedia Commons.

Page 9: Advertisement for the Pony Express, then owned by Wells, Fargo & Company, 1861. Smithsonian National Postal Museum.

Page 10: Artist W. H. Jackson; photo MPI via Getty.

Page 11: *American Progress* by John Gast, 1872. Library of Congress, Prints and Photographs Division.

Page 12: (top) Photograph of Engine No. 133, U.S. Military R.R., City Point, Virginia, by Mathew Brady, ca. 1860–1865. U.S. National Archives; (bottom) Everett Collection Inc./Alamy Stock Photo.

Page 13: *The Great East River Suspension Bridge*, published by Currier & Ives, New York. Chromolithograph, 1883. Library of Congress, Prints and Photographs Division.

Page 14: Illustrations of operations in a steel mill by Alfred R. Waud. Wood engraving, 1876. Library of Congress.

Page 15: (top) Bettmann via Getty; (bottom) Buyenlarge via Archive Photos/Getty.

Page 16: (top) KGPA Ltd./Alamy Stock Photo; (bottom) Interim Archives via Archive Photos/Getty.

Insert 2

Page 1: (top) Photograph of John Pierpont Morgan, circa 1902. Library of Congress; (bottom) photograph of John D. Rockefeller. Studio portrait by Oscar White. 360.org.

Page 2: (top) Photograph of Andrew Carnegie, circa 1913. Library of Congress; (bottom) 1902 photograph of John J. Hill by Pach Brothers; published in *The World's Work: A History of Our Time,* Doubleday, Page & Company, 1916. University of Toronto.

Page 3: (top) Photograph of Thomas Edison in his lab. U.S. Department of Energy; (bottom) photograph of William Jennings Bryan and group by Harris & Ewing, 1908. Library of Congress.

Page 4: Photograph of William Jennings Bryan at the 1908 Democratic National Convention, 1908. Library of Congress.

Page 5: Stock montage via Getty.

Page 6: (top) Bettmann via Getty; (bottom) workers installing engines on the Ford Model T assembly line at the Highland Park plant, 1913. Ford Motor Company.

Page 7: (top) Everett Collection Inc/Alamy Stock Photo; (bottom) The New York Historical Society via Getty.

Page 8: (top) Fox Photos via Hulton Archive/Getty; (bottom) Rolls Press/Popperfoto via Getty.

Page 9: Science History Images/Alamy Stock Photo.

Page 10: Universal Images Group via Getty.

Page 11: (top) Sheldon Dick via Hulton Archive/Getty; (bottom) ClassicStock/Alamy Stock Photo.

Page 12: (top) Library of Congress via Corbis Historical/Getty; (bottom) Corbis Historical via Getty.

Page 13: (top) Courtesy of the Advertising Archives; (bottom) Bettmann via Getty.

Page 14: (top) Hulton Archive via Getty; (center) ClassicStock/Alamy Stock Photo; (bottom) Tim Boyle via Getty.

Page 15: (top) Universal History Archive via Getty; (center) Courtesy of the Advertising Archives; (bottom) INTERFOTO/Alamy Stock Photo.

Page 16: (top) Kenneth Cantrell via ZUMA; (bottom) Stefano Politi Markovina/Alamy Stock Photo.

IMAGE CREDITS

Graphs

Page 39, Discount on Continental Currency vs. Amount Outstanding: Eric P. Newman, *The Early Paper Money of America, Fifth Edition*. Iola, Wisconsin: Krause Publications, 2008, pp. 61–71, 481.

Page 41, Nonfarm Business Operating Rate: National Bureau of Economic Research, Index of American Business Activity for United States [M12003USM516NNBR], retrieved from FRED, Federal Reserve Bank of St. Louis; https://fred.stlouisfed.org/series/M12003USM516NNBR. Federal Reserve Board, Institute for Supply Management, U.S. Bureau of Economic Analysis.

Page 76, Average Price of Prime Field Hand in New Orleans: Susan B. Carter, Scott Sigmund Gartner, Michael R. Haines, Alan L. Olmstead, Richard Sutch, and Gavin Wright, editors, *Historical Statistics of the United States: Millennial Edition*. New York: Cambridge University Press, 2006. Series Bb209, vol. 2, p. 381.

Page 78, Taxable Property in the Confederacy, by State: 1861: *Historical Statistics*, series Eh50 and Eh57, vol. 5, p. 787.

Page 81, Real Gross Domestic Product per Capita: Richard Sutch, "National Income and Product," in *Historical Statistics*; Richard Easterlin, "Interregional Differences in Per Capita Income, Population, and Total Income, 1840–1950," in The Conference on Research in Income and Wealth, *Trends in the American Economy in the Nineteenth Century*, Princeton: Princeton University Press,1960; Peter H. Lindert and Jeffrey G. Williamson, "American Incomes 1774–1860," in NBER Working Paper Series, Working Paper 18396, National Bureau of Economic Research: 2012. Retrieved from http://www.nber.org/papers/w18396.pdf; Willard Long Thorp and Hildegarde E. Thorp, "The Annals of the United States of America," in Willard Long Thorp, *Business Annals*, National Bureau of Economic Research, 1926.

Page 83, Confederate Money Stock and Price Level: *Historical Statistics*, series Eh118 and Eh128, vol. 5, pp. 792–793.

Page 85, Farms and Farm Output in the Confederate States: Historical Statistics, series Eh8–Eh39, vol. 5, pp. 784–785.

Page 93, Nonfarm Business Productivity and Innovation: See discussion in Appendix: Data and Methodology.

Page 97, Miles of Railroad Built: *Historical Statistics*, series Df882, Df883, and Df884, vol. 4, p. 917; *Historical Statistics*, series Df928, vol. 4, p. 923.

Page 100, Wholesale Price of Bessemer Steel: *Historical Statistics*, series Cc244, vol. 3, p. 213.

Page 102, Price of Kerosene and Crude Oil: Ethel D. Hoover, "Retail Prices After 1850," in The Conference on Research in Income and Wealth, *Trends in the American Economy in the Nineteenth Century*, Princeton: Princeton University Press, 1960; National Bureau of Economic Research, http://www.nber.org/databases/macrohistory/contents/chapter04.html,Series 04091 and 04182, U.S. Energy Information Administration.

Page 145, Wholesale Price of Steel: *Historical Statistics*, series Cc244 and Cc245, vol. 3, p. 213.

Page 148, U.S. Patents Issued for Inventions: *Historical Statistics*, series Cg31, Cg32, and Cg33, vol. 3, p. 427.

Page 155, U.S. Government Expenditures and U.S. Federal Government Expenditures: See discussion in Appendix: Data and Methodology.

Page 158, U.S. Voter Participation Rate: *Historical Statistics*, series Eb153, vol. 5, p. 173; U.S. Census Bureau, Federal Election Commission.

Page 175, Prices and Wages: *Historical Statistics*, series Ba4218, vol. 2, p. 256; *Historical Statistics*, series Ca13, vol. 3, p. 23; *Historical Statistics*, series Cc86, vol. 3, p. 175; *Historical Statistics*, series Cc114, vol. 3, p. 181.

Page 193, Workers Involved in Strikes: *Historical Statistics*, series Ba4955 and Ba4962, vol. 2, pp. 354–355.

Page 208, U.S. Ad Spending: https://galbithink.org/ad-spending.htm.

Page 222, Dow Jones Industrial Average: *The Wall Street Journal*.

Page 228, U.S. Official Gold Reserves: Annual Report of the Secretary of the Treasury, various years, https://fraser.stlouisfed.org/title/194; International Monetary Fund.

Page 250, Union Membership: *Historical Statistics*, series Ba4783 and Ba4788, vol. 2, p. 336.

Page 280, U.S. Workers Employed in Manufacturing: *Historical Statistics*, series Dd4 and Dd5, vol. 4, p. 579; U.S. Bureau of Labor Statistics.

Page 297, U.S. Foreign-Born Population: *Historical Statistics*, series Aa22 and Aa32, vol. 1, p. 36.

Page 301, Growth Rate of Private Business Output per Hour: U.S. Bureau of Labor Statistics.

Page 308, U.S. Official Gold Reserves: Annual Report of the Secretary of the Treasury, various years, https://fraser.stlouisfed.org/title/194; International Monetary Fund.

Page 313, U.S. Motor Vehicle Sales by Origin: *Historical Statistics*, series Df347, Df348, Df350, and Df351, vol. 4, p. 832; U.S. Bureau of Economic Analysis; Thomas H. Klier, "From Tail Fins to Hybrids: How Detroit Lost Its Dominance of the U.S. Auto Market," in *Economic Perspectives*, vol. 33, no. 2, 2009, Federal Reserve Bank of Chicago; *Ward's Automotive Yearbook, 2012*, Ward's Automotive Group, Penton Media Inc., Southfield, Michigan, 2012.

Page 315, U.S. Steel Statistics: U.S. Geological Survey, 2014, iron and steel statistics, in T. D. Kelly and G. R. Matos, comps.; historical statistics for mineral and material commodities in the United States, U.S. Geological Survey Data Series 140, retrieved from http://minerals.usgs.gov/minerals/pubs/historical-statistics/.

Page 362, U.S. Consumption of Selected* Mineral Commodities: U.S. Geological Survey, 2014, various statistics, T. D. Kelly and G. R. Matos, comps.; historical statistics for mineral and material commodities in the United States, U.S. Geological Survey Data Series 140, retrieved from http://minerals.usgs.gov/minerals/pubs/historical-statistics/.

Page 370, U.S. Imports by Country of Origin: International Monetary Fund.

Page 387, U.S. Business Sector Productivity Growth: U.S. Bureau of Labor Statistics.

Page 407, Gross Domestic Savings and Government Social Benefits: U.S. Bureau of Economic Analysis.

Page 409, Capital Stock and Productivity: U.S. Bureau of Economic Analysis; U.S. Bureau of Labor Statistics.

Page 410, Share of Cash Flow Businesses Choose to Convert into Fixed Assets: U.S. Bureau of Economic Analysis; National Bureau of Economic Research.

Page 412, Pages in the Code of Federal Regulations: George Washington University Regulatory Studies Center.

Page 417, Federal Debt Held by the Public: Congressional Budget Office.

NOTES

Introduction

1. Alan Macfarlane, *The Origins of English Individualism: The Family Property and Social Transition* (Oxford: Basic Blackwell, 1979).
2. Angus Maddison, *The World Economy: A Millennial Perspective* (Paris: OECD, 2001), 28.
3. Daniel J. Boorstin, *The Americans: The National Experience* (New York: Vintage Books, 1965), 115.
4. Robert D. Kaplan, *Earning the Rockies: How Geography Shapes America's Role in the World* (New York: Random House, 2017), 133.
5. Alan Greenspan, *The Map and the Territory 2.0: Risk, Human Nature, and the Future of Forecasting* (New York: Penguin Press, 2013), 152–76.
6. Susan B. Carter, Scott Sigmund Gartner, Michael R. Haines, Alan L. Olmstead, Richard Sutch, and Gavin Wright, eds., *Historical Statistics of the United States: Millennial Edition* (New York: Cambridge University Press, 2006).
7. Charles R. Morris, *The Dawn of Innovation: The First American Industrial Revolution* (New York: Public Affairs, 2012), 242–43.
8. David M. Kennedy, *Freedom from Fear: The American People in Depression and War, 1929–1945* (New York: Oxford University Press, 1999), 615.
9. https://www.history.co.uk/history-of-america/transcontinental-railroad.
10. On March 26, 1860, the *New York Herald* carried an announcement by the Central Overland California and Pike's Peak Express Company offering mail delivery from New York "to San Francisco in eight days. The first courier of the Pony Express will leave the Missouri River on Tuesday, April 3, at 5 o'clock p.m. and will run regularly weekly thereafter, carrying a letter mail only." The first lap of this relay between New York and St. Joseph, Missouri, was by telegram. But the line ended there.
11. Ann Norton Greene, *Horses at Work: Harnessing Power in Industrial America* (Cambridge, MA: Harvard University Press, 2008), 1–2.
12. Ibid., 41.
13. Paul David, "Computer and Dynamo: The Modern Productivity Paradox in a Not-Too-Distant Mirror," Center for Economic Policy Research, No. 339, Stanford University, July 1989. See also "The Dynamo and the Computer: A Historical Perspective on the Modern Productivity Paradox," *American Economic Review* 80, no. 2 (May 1990), Papers and Proceedings of the Hundred and Second Annual Meeting of the American Economic Association, 355–61.
14. Stanley Lebergott, *Pursuing Happiness: American Consumers in the Twentieth Century* (Princeton, NJ: Princeton University Press, 1993), 37–39.
15. Housework, however, is not considered a productive input in the creation of GDP and, hence, this major advance in living standards is not captured in either OPH or MFP.
16. Deirdre Nansen McCloskey, *Bourgeois Equality: How Ideas, Not Capital or Institutions, Enriched the World* (Chicago: University of Chicago Press, 2016), 154.

17. Ernest Freeberg, *The Age of Edison: Electric Light and the Invention of Modern America* (New York: Penguin Books, 2013), 76–80.

One. A Commercial Republic: 1776–1860

1. John McCusker, ed., "Colonial Statistics," in *Governance and International Relations*, vol. 5 of *Historical Statistics of the United States: Millennial Edition,* ed. Susan B. Carter et al. (New York: Cambridge University Press, 2006), 627; Richard Sutch, ed., "National Income and Product," in *Economic Structure and Performance,* vol. 3 of *Historical Statistics of the United States: Millennial Edition,* 3.
2. Robert H. Wiebe, *Self-Rule: A Cultural History of American Democracy* (Chicago: University of Chicago Press, 1995), 17.
3. Gordon S. Wood, *The American Revolution: A History* (New York: Modern Library, 2002), 9.
4. Alan Taylor, *American Revolutions: A Continental History, 1750–1804* (New York: W. W. Norton, 2016), 375.
5. Quoted in Douglas A. Irwin, *Clashing over Commerce: A History of U.S. Trade Policy* (Chicago: University of Chicago Press, 2017), 121.
6. Taylor, *American Revolutions*, 23.
7. Ann Norton Greene, *Horses at Work: Harnessing Power in Industrial America* (Cambridge, MA: Harvard University Press, 2008), 48.
8. Alan L. Olmstead and Paul W. Rhode, ed., "Crops and Livestock," in *Economic Sectors,* vol. 4 of *Historical Statistics of the United States: Millennial Edition,* 18.
9. Oscar Handlin and Lilian Handlin, *Liberty in Expansion 1760–1850* (New York: Harper & Row, 1989), 246–47.
10. W. B. Todd, ed., *An Inquiry into the Nature and Causes of "The Wealth of Nation,"* vol. 2 of Glasgow Edition of the Works and Correspondence of Adam Smith (Oxford: Clarendon Press, 1976), 578.
11. "Fin Tech: The First Venture Capitalists," *The Economist,* December 30, 2015.
12. Walter A. McDougall, *Freedom Just Around the Corner: A New American History 1585–1828* (New York: HarperCollins, 2004), 40.
13. David Reynolds, *America, Empire of Liberty* (London: Allen Lane, 2009), 144–45.
14. McDougall, *Freedom Just Around the Corner,* 490.
15. Taylor, *American Revolutions,* 23.
16. U.S. Debt and Foreign Loans, 1775–1795, Department of State, Office of the Historian, https://history.state.gov/milestones/1784-1800/loans.
17. Baring Brothers was known as Francis Baring and Co. from 1800 to 1804, when it changed its name to Baring Brothers.
18. Robert Gallman, "Growth and Change in the Long Nineteenth Century," in *The Long Nineteenth Century,* vol. 2 of *The Cambridge Economic History of the United States,* ed. Stanley Engerman and Robert Gallman (Cambridge: Cambridge University Press, 2000), 13.
19. James McPherson, *Battle Cry of Freedom* (Oxford: Oxford University Press, 1988), 6.
20. Wiebe, *Self-Rule,* 43.
21. Ibid., 41.
22. "Median Age of the Population, by Race, Sex, and Nativity: 1790 to 1970," Bureau of the Census, *Historical Statistics of the United States: Colonial Times to 1957,* vol. 1 (Washington, D.C.: U.S. Government Printing Office, 1975), 19.
23. Walter A. McDougall, *Throes of Democracy: The American Civil War Era 1829–1877* (New York: HarperCollins, 2008), 140.
24. Daniel J. Boorstin, *The Americans: The National Experience* (New York: Vintage Books, 1965), 25.
25. Ibid.
26. Louis P. Cain, "Entrepreneurship in the Antebellum United States," in *The Invention of Enterprise,* ed. David S. Landes, Joel Mokyr, and William J. Baumol (Princeton, NJ: Princeton University Press, 2010), 348.
27. Ibid., 349.
28. H. W. Brands, *Masters of Enterprise: Giants of American Business from John Jacob Astor and J. P. Morgan to Bill Gates and Oprah Winfrey* (New York: Free Press, 1999), 33.

29. Gavin Wright, ed., "Natural Resource Industries," in *Economic Sectors,* vol. 4 of *Historical Statistics of the United States: Millennial Edition,* 275.

30. U.S. Energy Information Administration, "Annual Energy Review 2011," table E1.

31. McDougall, *Throes of Democracy,* 143.

32. Greene, *Horses at Work,* 55.

33. Ibid., 166.

34. George Rogers Taylor, *The Transportation Revolution 1815–1860* (New York: M. E. Sharpe, 1951), 15–17.

35. Ibid., 132–33.

36. Greene, *Horses at Work,* 52.

37. Louis Cain, ed., "Transportation," in *Economic Sectors,* vol. 4 of *Historical Statistics of the United States: Millennial Edition,* 762.

38. Greene, *Horses at Work,* 78.

39. Daniel Walker Howe, *What Hath God Wrought: The Transformation of America, 1815–1848* (Oxford: Oxford University Press, 2007), 214.

40. Cain, "Transportation," in *Economic Sectors,* vol. 4 of *Historical Statistics of the United States: Millennial Edition,* 770.

41. Ibid.

42. Albert Fishlow, *American Railroads and the Transformation of the Ante-bellum Economy* (Cambridge, MA: Harvard University Press, 1965), and Robert Fogel, *Railroads and American Economic Growth* (Baltimore: Johns Hopkins University Press, 1964).

43. Richard Tedlow, *The Rise of the American Business Corporation* (Chur, Switzerland: Harwood Academic Publishers, 1991), 13–14.

44. Fogel, *Railroads and American Economic Growth.*

45. McDougall, *Throes of Democracy,* 143.

46. Howe, *What Hath God Wrought,* 695.

47. Richard White, *Railroaded: The Transcontinentals and the Making of Modern America* (New York: W. W. Norton, 2011), 37.

48. Wiebe, *Self-Rule,* 56.

49. McDougall, *Freedom Just Around the Corner,* 178–79.

50. Michael Haines, ed., "Population Characteristics," in *Population,* vol. 1 of *Historical Statistics of the United States: Millennial Edition,* 21.

51. Sutch, "National Income and Product," in *Economic Structure and Performance,* vol. 3 of *Historical Statistics of the United States: Millennial Edition,* 17.

52. McPherson, *Battle Cry of Freedom,* 10.

Two. The Two Americas

1. Thomas Jefferson, "Letter to John Jay," in *Jefferson: Writings,* ed. Merrill D. Peterson (New York: Library of America, 1984), 818.

2. The framers of the United States Constitution gave the federal government authority to tax, stating that the Congress had the power to "lay and collect taxes, duties, imposts and excises."

3. Jon Meacham, *Thomas Jefferson: The Art of Power* (New York: Random House, 2013), 348.

4. Ibid., 349.

5. Ibid., 350.

6. Daniel Walker Howe, *What Hath God Wrought: The Transformation of America, 1815–1848* (Oxford: Oxford University Press, 2007), 133.

7. Ibid., 535.

8. Ibid., 534.

9. James McPherson, *Battle Cry of Freedom* (Oxford: Oxford University Press, 1988), 19.

10. Douglas A. Irwin, *Clashing over Commerce: A History of U.S. Trade Policy* (Chicago: University of Chicago Press, 2017), 133–34.

11. McPherson, *Battle Cry of Freedom,* 14.

12. Howe, *What Hath God Wrought,* 533.

13. Walter A. McDougall, *Throes of Democracy: The American Civil War Era 1829–1877* (New York: HarperCollins, 2008), 130.

14. Jeremy Atack, Fred Bateman, and William Parker, "The Farm, the Farmer, and the Market," in *The Long Nineteenth Century,* vol. 2 of *The Cambridge Economic History of the United States,*

ed. Stanley Engerman and Robert Gallman (Cambridge: Cambridge University Press, 2000), 272.

15. McDougall, *Throes of Democracy,* 131.
16. McPherson, *Battle Cry of Freedom,* 21.
17. Sven Beckert, *Empire of Cotton: A New History of Global Capitalism* (London: Allen Lane, 2014), 100.
18. Ibid., 114.
19. Ibid., 108.
20. Robert Wiebe, *The Opening of American Society: From the Adoption of the Constitution to the Eve of Disunion* (New York: Alfred A. Knopf, 1984), 359.
21. Beckert, *Empire of Cotton,* 105.
22. Ibid., 243.
23. Jacob Metzer, "Rational Management, Modern Business Practices, and Economies of Scale in Ante-Bellum Southern Plantations," *Explorations in Economic History* 12 (April 1975): 123–50.
24. Beckert, *Empire of Cotton,* 110.
25. Kevin Phillips, *Wealth and Democracy: A Political History of the American Rich* (New York: Broadway Books, 2002), 22.
26. Beckert, *Empire of Cotton,* 113.
27. Howe, *What Hath God Wrought,* 60.
28. Beckert, *Empire of Cotton,* 199–241.
29. Bhu Srinivasan, *Americana: A 400-Year History of American Capitalism* (New York: Penguin Press, 2017), 129.
30. Stephen B. Oates, ed., *The Whirlwind of War: Voices of the Storm, 1861–1865,* 46, quoting a December 1860 letter.
31. Jeremy Atack and Fred Bateman, eds., "Manufacturing," vol. 4 of *Historical Statistics of the United States: Millennial Edition,* ed. Susan B. Carter et al. (New York: Cambridge University Press, 2006), 573.
32. McPherson, *Battle Cry of Freedom,* 40.
33. Ibid.
34. Roger Ransom, ed., "Confederate States of America," in *Governance and International Relations,* vol. 5 of *Historical Statistics of the United States: Millennial Edition,* 77–78.
35. Michael Barone, *Shaping Our Nation: How Surges of Migration Transformed America and Its Politics* (New York: Crown Forum, 2013), 154.
36. Richard White, *Railroaded: The Transcontinentals and the Making of Modern America* (New York: W. W. Norton, 2011), 467.
37. Richard White, *The Republic for Which It Stands: The United States During Reconstruction and the Gilded Age, 1865–1896* (New York: Oxford University Press, 2017), 28.
38. Irwin, *Clashing over Commerce,* 211.
39. Stanley Engerman, "Slavery and Its Consequences for the South," in *The Long Nineteenth Century,* vol. 2 of *The Cambridge Economic History of the United States,* 356.
40. Ransom, ed., "Confederate States of America," in *Governance and International Relations,* vol. 5 of *Historical Statistics of the United States: Millennial Edition,* 776.
41. Roger Ransom and Richard Sutch, *One Kind of Freedom: The Economic Consequences of Emancipation* (Cambridge: Cambridge University Press, 1977); Susan Carter, ed., "Labor," in *Work and Welfare,* vol. 2 of *Historical Statistics of the United States: Millennial Edition,* 20.
42. Srinivasan, *Americana,* 127.
43. White, *The Republic for Which It Stands,* 220.
44. Ibid., 47–48.
45. Beckert, *Empire of Cotton,* 113.
46. E. Merton Coulter, *James Monroe Smith, Planter: Before Death and After* (Athens: University of Georgia Press, 1961), 67.
47. White, *The Republic for Which It Stands,* 422.
48. McDougall, *Throes of Democracy,* 553.
49. Barone, *Shaping Our Nation,* 157.
50. Friedrich Ratzel, *Sketches of Urban and Cultural Life in North America,* trans. and ed. Stewart A. Sehlin (1876; New Brunswick, NJ: Rutgers University Press, 1988), quoted in Michael Lind, *Land of Promise: An Economic History of the United States* (New York: Harper, 2012), 125.

Three. The Triumph of Capitalism: 1865–1914

1. In fact, Heinz had more than fifty-seven varieties. This was a rare example of undue modesty in advertising.
2. Joaquin Miller was a pen name. His given name was Cincinnatus Heine Miller.
3. Marianne Ward and John Devereux, "Measuring British Decline: Direct Versus Long-Span Income Measures," *Journal of Economic History* 63, no. 3 (September 2003): 826–51.
4. Robert J. Gordon, *The Rise and Fall of American Growth: The U.S. Standard of Living Since the Civil War* (Princeton, NJ: Princeton University Press, 2016), 198.
5. Charles Hirschman and Elizabeth Mogford, "Immigration and the American Industrial Revolution from 1880 to 1920," *Social Science Research* 38, no. 4 (December 1, 2009): 897–920.
6. Albert Fishlow, "Transportation in the 19th and Early 20th Centuries," in *The Long Nineteenth Century,* vol. 2 of *The Cambridge Economic History of the United States,* ed. Stanley Engerman and Robert Gallman (Cambridge: Cambridge University Press, 2000), 601.
7. Samuel P. Hayes, *The Response to Industrialism 1885–1914* (Chicago: University of Chicago Press, 1957), 8; Jack Beatty, ed., *Colossus: How the Corporation Changed America* (New York: Broadway Books, 2001), 111.
8. Richard White, *Railroaded: The Transcontinentals and the Making of Modern America* (New York: W. W. Norton, 2011), xxiv.
9. John Steele Gordon, *An Empire of Wealth: The Epic History of American Economic Power* (New York: HarperPerennial, 2004), 242.
10. Fishlow, "Transportation in the 19th and Early 20th Centuries," 595.
11. Quoted in Daniel Yergin, *The Prize: The Epic History of Oil, Money & Power* (New York: Simon & Schuster, 1991), 79.
12. Gordon, *The Rise and Fall of American Growth,* 119.
13. Ron Chernow, *The House of Morgan: An American Banking Dynasty and the Rise of Modern Finance* (New York: Touchstone, 1990), 142.
14. Gordon, *The Rise and Fall of American Growth,* 158.
15. Ibid., 154–55.
16. Ibid., 131.
17. Ibid., 181–82.
18. Ibid., 185.
19. Richard White, *The Republic for Which It Stands: The United States During Reconstruction and the Gilded Age, 1865–1896* (New York: Oxford University Press, 2017), 119.
20. Charles R. Morris, *The Dawn of Innovation: The First American Industrial Revolution* (New York: Public Affairs, 2012), 275.
21. H. W. Brands, *American Colossus: The Triumph of Capitalism, 1865–1900* (New York: Anchor Books, 2010), 251–52.
22. Ibid., 249–50 for the quote, and 249–56 for bonanza farms in general.
23. White, *The Republic for Which It Stands,* 296.
24. Alan Olmstead, ed., "Agriculture," in *Economic Sectors,* vol. 4 of *Historical Statistics of the United States: Millennial Edition,* ed. Susan B. Carter et al. (New York: Cambridge University Press, 2006), 11.
25. Ibid.
26. White, *The Republic for Which It Stands,* 219.
27. Naomi Lamoreaux, "Entrepreneurship in the United States, 1865–1920," in *The Invention of Enterprise,* ed. David S. Landes, Joel Mokyr, and William J. Baumol (Princeton, NJ: Princeton University Press, 2010), 371.
28. Jeremy Atack, Fred Bateman, and William Parker, "The Farm, the Farmer and the Market," in *The Long Nineteenth Century,* vol. 2 of *The Cambridge Economic History of the United States,* ed. Stanley Engerman and Robert Gallman (Cambridge: Cambridge University Press, 2000), 260.
29. Morris, *The Dawn of Innovation,* 205–6.
30. Ibid., 207.
31. Ibid., 205–6.
32. Daniel J. Boorstin, *The Americans: The National Experience* (New York: Vintage Books, 1965), 315.
33. Gordon, *The Rise and Fall of American Growth,* 74.

34. White, *The Republic for Which It Stands*, 515.
35. Atack et al., "The Farm, the Farmer and the Market," in *The Long Nineteenth Century*, 253.
36. Thomas Weiss, "Long Term Changes in U.S. Agricultural Output per Worker, 1800 to 1900," NBER Working Paper Series on Historical Factors in Long Run Growth, No. 23, National Bureau of Economic Research, 1991.
37. White, *The Republic for Which It Stands*, 219.
38. Boorstin, *The Americans*, 323.

Four. The Age of Giants

1. Richard S. Tedlow, *Giants of Enterprise: Seven Business Innovators and the Empires They Built* (New York: HarperBusiness, 2001), 421–22.
2. Quoted in Bhu Srinivasan, *Americana: A 400-Year History of American Capitalism* (New York: Penguin Press, 2017), 66–67.
3. Richard Tedlow, *The Rise of the American Business Corporation* (Chur, Switzerland: Harwood Academic Publishers, 1991), 41.
4. Peter Collier and David Horowitz, *The Rockefellers: An American Dynasty* (New York: Holt, Rinehart and Winston, 1976), 25.
5. H. W. Brands, *Masters of Enterprise: Giants of American Business from John Jacob Astor and J. P. Morgan to Bill Gates and Oprah Winfrey* (New York: Free Press, 1999), 81.
6. H. W. Brands, *American Colossus: The Triumph of Capitalism, 1865–1900* (New York: Anchor Books, 2010), 71–72.
7. John Steele Gordon, *An Empire of Wealth: The Epic History of American Economic Power* (New York: HarperPerennial, 2004), 231.
8. Ron Chernow, *The House of Morgan: An American Banking Dynasty and the Rise of Modern Finance* (New York: Touchstone, 1990), 46.
9. Ibid., 111.
10. See, for example, Tarun Khanna, Krishna G. Palepu, and Jayant Sinha, "Strategies That Fit Emerging Markets," *Harvard Business Review*, June 2005.
11. See John Micklethwait and Adrian Wooldridge, *The Company: A Short History of a Revolutionary Idea* (New York: Modern Library Chronicles, 2005), 55–79.
12. Jack Beatty, ed., *Colossus: How the Corporation Changed America* (New York: Broadway Books, 2001), 19.
13. Tedlow, *The Rise of the American Business Corporation*, 12.
14. John Bates Clark, *The Control of Trusts* (New York: Macmillan, 1901), 17.
15. Tedlow, *The Rise of the American Business Corporation*, 14.
16. Ibid., 16.
17. Richard White, *Railroaded: The Transcontinentals and the Making of Modern America* (New York: W. W. Norton, 2011), 2.
18. Ibid., 209.
19. Tim Sullivan, "Blitzscaling," *Harvard Business Review*, April 2016.
20. Charles Morris, *The Tycoons: How Andrew Carnegie, John D. Rockefeller, Jay Gould, and J. P. Morgan Invented the American Supereconomy* (New York: Times Books, 2005), 174; Srinivasan, *Americana*, 209.
21. Naomi Lamoreaux, "Entrepreneurship, Organization, Economic Concentration," in *The Long Nineteenth Century*, vol. 2 of *The Cambridge Economic History of the United States*, ed. Stanley Engerman and Robert Gallman (Cambridge: Cambridge University Press, 2000), 430.
22. Thomas McCraw, "American Capitalism," in *Creating Modern Capitalism: How Entrepreneurs, Companies and Countries Triumphed in Three Industrial Revolutions*, ed. Thomas K. McCraw (Cambridge, MA: Harvard University Press, 1995), 325.
23. Naomi Lamoreaux, ed., "Business Organization," in *Economic Structure and Performance*, vol. 3 of *Historical Statistics of the United States: Millennial Edition*, ed. Susan B. Carter et al. (New York: Cambridge University Press 2006), 487.
24. Lamoreaux, "Entrepreneurship, Organization, Economic Concentration," in *The Long Nineteenth Century*, 427.
25. Naomi Lamoreaux, "Entrepreneurship in the United States, 1865–1920," in *The Invention of Enterprise*, ed. David S. Landes, Joel Mokyr, and William J. Baumol (Princeton, NJ: Princeton University Press, 2010), 386.

26. Robert J. Gordon, *The Rise and Fall of American Growth: The U.S. Standard of Living Since the Civil War* (Princeton, NJ: Princeton University Press, 2016), 572.
27. Lamoreaux, "Entrepreneurship in the United States, 1865–1920," in *The Invention of Enterprise*, 387.

Five. The Revolt Against Laissez-Faire

1. Richard White, *The Republic for Which It Stands: The United States During Reconstruction and the Gilded Age, 1865–1896* (New York: Oxford University Press, 2017), 841.
2. H. W. Brands, *American Colossus: The Triumph of Capitalism, 1865–1900* (New York: Anchor Books, 2010), 547–48.
3. A. Scott Berg, *Wilson* (London: Simon & Schuster, 2013), 260.
4. Thomas McCraw, "American Capitalism," in *Creating Modern Capitalism: How Entrepreneurs, Companies and Countries Triumphed in Three Industrial Revolutions*, ed. Thomas K. McCraw (Cambridge, MA: Harvard University Press, 1995), 346.
5. Kevin Phillips, *Wealth and Democracy: A Political History of the American Rich* (New York: Broadway Books, 2002), 305.
6. William Leuchtenburg, *The American President: From Teddy Roosevelt to Bill Clinton* (Oxford: Oxford University Press, 2015), 4–6.
7. Samuel P. Hayes, *The Response to Industrialism 1885–1914* (Chicago: University of Chicago Press, 1957), 144.
8. White, *The Republic for Which It Stands,* 275.
9. Ibid., 831–35.
10. Robert Wiebe, *The Search for Order, 1877–1920* (New York: Hill and Wang, 1967), 41.
11. Richard Hofstadter, *Social Darwinism in American Thought* (Philadelphia: University of Pennsylvania Press, 1944), 32.
12. Wiebe, *The Search for Order, 1877–1920,* 135.
13. White, *The Republic for Which It Stands,* 363.
14. David Reynolds, *America, Empire of Liberty* (London: Allen Lane, 2009), 249–50.
15. White, *The Republic for Which It Stands,* 500.
16. Robert J. Gordon, *The Rise and Fall of American Growth: The U.S. Standard of Living Since the Civil War* (Princeton, NJ: Princeton University Press, 2016), 219.
17. White, *The Republic for Which It Stands,* 478–81.
18. Gordon, *The Rise and Fall of American Growth,* 310.
19. Ibid., 237.
20. Claude S. Fischer, *Made in America: A Social History of American Culture and Character* (Chicago: University of Chicago Press, 2010), 24.
21. Matthew Josephson, *The Robber Barons* (New York: Harcourt Brace and Company, 1934), 234.
22. Quoted in Michael C. Jensen, "The Modern Industrial Revolution, Exit, and the Failure of Internal Control Systems," *Journal of Finance* 48, no. 3 (July 1993): 832.
23. White, *The Republic for Which It Stands,* 799–800.
24. Walter Lippmann, *Drift and Mastery* (New York: Mitchell Kennerley, 1914), 80–81.
25. Robert Margo, "The Labor Force in the Nineteenth Century," in *The Long Nineteenth Century,* vol. 2 of *The Cambridge Economic History of the United States,* ed. Stanley Engerman and Robert Gallman (Cambridge: Cambridge University Press, 2000), 238.
26. White, *The Republic for Which It Stands,* 201–2.
27. J. R. Pole, *The Pursuit of Equality in American History* (Berkeley: University of California Press, 1978), 264.
28. Reynolds, *America, Empire of Liberty,* 274.
29. Ken Gormley, ed., *The Presidents and the Constitution: A Living History* (New York: New York University Press, 2016), 332.
30. Quoted in Brands, *American Colossus,* 479.
31. Edmund Morris, *The Rise of Theodore Roosevelt* (New York: Modern Library, 1979), 568.
32. Leuchtenburg, *The American President,* 63.
33. Hugh Rockoff, "Until It's Over, Over There: The U.S. Economy in World War I," NBER Working Paper No. 10580, National Bureau of Economic Research, January 2005.
34. Thomas Leonard, *Illiberal Reformers: Race, Eugenics and American Economics in the Progressive Era* (Princeton, NJ: Princeton University Press, 2016), 47–48.

35. Rockoff, "Until It's Over, Over There: The U.S. Economy in World War I."
36. Michael Edelstein, "War and the American Economy in the Twentieth Century," in *The Twentieth Century,* vol. 3 of *The Cambridge Economic History of the United States,* ed. Stanley Engerman and Robert Gallman (Cambridge: Cambridge University Press, 2000), 331–32.

Six. The Business of America Is Business

1. William Leuchtenburg, *The American President: From Teddy Roosevelt to Bill Clinton* (Oxford: Oxford University Press, 2015), 122.
2. Ibid., 130.
3. David M. Kennedy, *Freedom from Fear: The American People in Depression and War, 1929–1945* (New York: Oxford University Press, 1999), 30.
4. James Grant, *The Forgotten Depression: 1921: The Crash That Cured Itself* (New York: Simon & Schuster, 2013).
5. Liaquat Ahamed, *Lords of Finance: The Bankers Who Broke the World* (New York: Penguin Press, 2009), 271–74.
6. Kevin Phillips, *Wealth and Democracy: A Political History of the American Rich* (New York: Broadway Books, 2002), 58.
7. Robert J. Gordon, *The Rise and Fall of American Growth: The U.S. Standard of Living Since the Civil War* (Princeton, NJ: Princeton University Press, 2016), 167.
8. Charles R. Morris, *A Rabble of Dead Money: The Great Crash and the Global Depression, 1929–1939* (New York: Public Affairs, 2017), 35.
9. Kennedy, *Freedom from Fear,* 17.
10. Gordon, *The Rise and Fall of American Growth,* 160.
11. Ibid., 158.
12. Ibid., 132.
13. Anthony Mayo and Nitin Nohria, *In Their Time: The Greatest Business Leaders of the Twentieth Century* (Boston, MA: Harvard Business School Press, 2005), 91.
14. Louis Cain, ed., "Transportation," in *Economic Sectors,* vol. 4 of *Historical Statistics of the United States: Millennial Edition,* ed. Susan B. Carter et al. (New York: Cambridge University Press, 2006), 773.
15. Gordon, *The Rise and Fall of American Growth,* 123.
16. Adolf Berle and Gardiner Means, *The Modern Corporation and Private Property* (New York: Macmillan, 1932), 60.
17. Ibid., 35.
18. Ibid., 3.
19. Mayo and Nohria, *In Their Time,* 87.
20. Thomas K. McCraw, *American Business Since 1920: How It Worked* (Wheelan, IL: Harland Davidson, 2000), 21.
21. Oliver E. Williamson, *Markets and Hierarchies: Analysis and Antitrust Implications* (New York: Free Press, 1975).
22. Richard Tedlow, *The Rise of the American Business Corporation* (Chur, Switzerland: Harwood Academic Publishers, 1991), 57–59.
23. McCraw, *American Business Since 1920,* 30.
24. Ibid., 30–31.
25. Bhu Srinivasan, *Americana: A 400-Year History of American Capitalism* (New York: Penguin Press, 2017), 313.
26. Claude S. Fischer, *Made in America: A Social History of American Culture and Character* (Chicago: University of Chicago Press, 2010), 68.
27. Charles Rappleye, *Herbert Hoover in the White House: The Ordeal of the Presidency* (New York: Simon & Schuster, 2016), 42.
28. Ibid., 11.
29. Kennedy, *Freedom from Fear,* 11.

Seven. The Great Depression

1. Charles R. Morris, *A Rabble of Dead Money: The Great Crash and the Global Depression, 1929–1939* (New York: Public Affairs, 2017), 111–12.
2. Charles Rappleye, *Herbert Hoover in the White House: The Ordeal of the Presidency* (New York: Simon & Schuster, 2016), 103.

3. David M. Kennedy, *Freedom from Fear: The American People in Depression and War, 1929–1945* (New York: Oxford University Press, 1999), 35.

4. Ibid., 41.

5. Ibid., 40.

6. Ron Chernow, *The House of Morgan: An American Banking Dynasty and the Rise of Modern Finance* (New York: Touchstone, 1990), 302.

7. Ibid., 346.

8. Alan Greenspan, *The Map and the Territory 2.0: Risk, Human Nature, and the Future of Forecasting* (New York: Penguin Press, 2013), 73–87.

9. Alan Greenspan, "The Crisis," Brookings Papers on Economic Activity, Spring 2010.

10. Adam Cohen, *Nothing to Fear: FDR's Inner Circle and the Hundred Days That Created Modern America* (New York: Penguin Press, 2009), 1.

11. Harold Cole and Lee Ohanian, "New Deal Policies and the Persistence of the Great Depression: A General Equilibrium Analysis," *Journal of Political Economy* 112, no. 4 (August 2004): 779–816.

12. Burton Folsom Jr., *New Deal or Raw Deal? How FDR's Economic Legacy Has Damaged America* (New York: Threshold Editions, 2008), 2.

13. Liaquat Ahamed, *Lords of Finance: The Bankers Who Broke the World* (New York: Penguin Press, 2009), 131.

14. Ibid., 164.

15. "The Battle of Smoot-Hawley," *Economist*, December 18, 2008, https://www.economist.com/node/12798595.

16. Douglas A. Irwin, *Clashing over Commerce: A History of U.S. Trade Policy* (Chicago: University of Chicago Press, 2017), 386.

17. Kennedy, *Freedom from Fear*, 77.

18. Had there been only one bank all checks would clear the same bank. In such a clearing arrangement defaults would not occur. Four banks reduce the risk of financial contagion relative to twenty-five thousand banks.

19. Ahamed, *Lords of Finance*, 4.

20. Ibid., 173–74.

21. "Hooverville" was coined by Charles Michelson, the Democratic National Committee's publicity chief.

22. Chernow, *The House of Morgan*, 314.

23. Morris, *A Rabble of Dead Money*, 245.

24. Cohen, *Nothing to Fear*, 60–61.

25. Kennedy, *Freedom from Fear*, 121.

26. William Leuchtenburg, *The American President: From Teddy Roosevelt to Bill Clinton* (Oxford: Oxford University Press, 2015), 149.

27. Kennedy, *Freedom from Fear*, 153.

28. Ibid., 276–77.

29. Cohen, *Nothing to Fear*, 286.

30. Ahamed, *Lords of Finance*, 441.

31. Leuchtenburg, *The American President*, 181.

32. Robert Underhill, *The Rise and Fall of Franklin Delano Roosevelt* (New York: Algora Publishing, 2012), 46.

33. Cohen, *Nothing to Fear*, 47.

34. Michael Barone, *Our Country: The Shaping of America from Roosevelt to Reagan* (New York: Free Press, 1990), 31.

35. Kennedy, *Freedom from Fear*, 280.

36. John F. Cogan, *The High Cost of Good Intentions: A History of U.S. Federal Entitlement Programs* (Palo Alto, CA: Stanford University Press, 2017), 93.

37. Ibid., 139–60.

38. Ira Katznelson, *Fear Itself: The New Deal and the Origins of Our Time* (New York: W. W. Norton, 1994), 385–403.

39. Cole and Ohanian, "New Deal Policies and the Persistence of the Great Depression," 779–816.

40. Ibid.

41. Leuchtenburg, *The American President*, 157.

42. Folsom Jr., *New Deal or Raw Deal?*, 71.
43. Kennedy, *Freedom from Fear*, 197.
44. Barone, *Our Country*, 71.
45. Kennedy, *Freedom from Fear*, 351.
46. Ibid., 282.
47. Ibid., 283.
48. Ibid., 351.
49. Cole and Ohanian, "New Deal Policies and the Persistence of the Great Depression," 779–816.
50. Folsom Jr., *New Deal or Raw Deal?*, 242–44.
51. Kennedy, *Freedom from Fear*, 617.
52. Robert J. Gordon, *The Rise and Fall of American Growth: The U.S. Standard of Living Since the Civil War* (Princeton, NJ: Princeton University Press, 2016), 536.
53. Kennedy, *Freedom from Fear*, 621.
54. Ibid., 653.
55. Ibid., 646.
56. Ibid., 648.

Eight. The Golden Age of Growth: 1945–1970

1. Tony Judt, *Postwar: A History of Europe Since 1945* (London: Pimlico, 2007), 17.
2. Jeffry Frieden, *Global Capitalism: Its Fall and Rise in the Twentieth Century* (New York: W. W. Norton, 2006), 261.
3. Ian Kershaw, *To Hell and Back: Europe 1914–1949* (London: Allen Lane, 2015), 470.
4. Judt, *Postwar*, 16–17.
5. James Patterson, *Grand Expectations: The United States, 1945–1974* (New York: Oxford University Press, 1996), 139.
6. Kershaw, *To Hell and Back*, 488.
7. Patterson, *Grand Expectations*, 184.
8. Judt, *Postwar*, 94.
9. Frieden, *Global Capitalism*, 261.
10. William Leuchtenburg, *The American President: From Teddy Roosevelt to Bill Clinton* (Oxford: Oxford University Press, 2015), 330.
11. Anthony Mayo and Nitin Nohria, *In Their Time: The Greatest Business Leaders of the Twentieth Century* (Boston, MA: Harvard Business School Press, 2005), 160.
12. Jerome Karabel, *The Chosen: The Hidden History of Admission and Exclusion at Harvard, Yale and Princeton* (New York: Houghton Mifflin, 2005), 164.
13. Walter Isaacson, *The Innovators: How a Group of Hackers, Geniuses, and Geeks Created the Digital Revolution* (New York: Simon & Schuster, 2014), 220.
14. Leuchtenburg, *The American President*, 356.
15. Karabel, *The Chosen*, 263.
16. Price Fishback and Melissa Thomasson, eds., "Social Welfare: 1929 to the Present," in *Work and Welfare*, vol. 2 of *Historical Statistics of the United States: Millennial Edition*, ed. Susan B. Carter et al. (New York: Cambridge University Press, 2006), 715.
17. Robert J. Gordon, *The Rise and Fall of American Growth: The U.S. Standard of Living Since the Civil War* (Princeton, NJ: Princeton University Press, 2016), 466.
18. Patterson, *Grand Expectations*, 318.
19. Earl Swift, *The Big Roads: The Untold Story of the Engineers, Visionaries, and Trailblazers Who Created the American Superhighways* (Boston: Houghton Mifflin Harcourt, 2011), 6.
20. Gordon, *The Rise and Fall of American Growth*, 390.
21. Rick Wartzman, *The End of Loyalty: The Rise and Fall of Good Jobs in America* (New York: Public Affairs, 2017), 107.
22. Peter Drucker, "The New Society 1: Revolution by Mass Production," *Harper's Magazine*, September 1949, 21–30.
23. Robert Reich, "How Business Schools Can Help Reduce Inequality," *Harvard Business Review*, September 12, 2014.
24. Wartzman, *The End of Loyalty*, 111.
25. Ibid., 133.
26. Mayo and Nohria, *In Their Time*, 162–63.

27. Ibid., 165–70.
28. Ibid., 202–7.
29. Douglas A. Irwin, *Clashing over Commerce: A History of U.S. Trade Policy* (Chicago: University of Chicago Press, 2017), 535.
30. Mayo and Nohria, *In Their Time,* 199.
31. Geoffrey Jones, *Entrepreneurship and Multinationals: Global Business and the Making of the Modern World* (Cheltenham, UK: Edward Elgar, 2013), 77.
32. Patterson, *Grand Expectations,* 338.

Nine. Stagflation

1. William Leuchtenburg, *The American President: From Teddy Roosevelt to Bill Clinton* (Oxford: Oxford University Press, 2015), 577.
2. Steven F. Hayward, *The Age of Reagan: The Fall of the Old Liberal Order, 1964–1980* (New York: Forum, 2001), 321.
3. Mancur Olson, *The Rise and Decline of Nations* (New Haven, CT: Yale University Press), 299.
4. Leuchtenburg, *The American President,* 399.
5. Sebastian Mallaby, *The Man Who Knew: The Life and Times of Alan Greenspan* (New York: Penguin Press, 2016), 104–5.
6. Marc Levinson, *An Extraordinary Time: The End of the Postwar Boom and the Return of the Ordinary Economy* (New York: Basic Books, 2016), 261.
7. Ibid., 5.
8. John F. Cogan, *The High Cost of Good Intentions: A History of U.S. Federal Entitlement Programs* (Palo Alto, CA: Stanford University Press, 2017), 203.
9. Leuchtenburg, *The American President,* 495.
10. Cogan, *The High Cost of Good Intentions,* 231–65.
11. Ibid., 265.
12. Peter Lindert, "Twentieth-Century Foreign Trade and Trade Policy," in *The Twentieth Century,* vol. 3 of *The Cambridge Economic History of the United States,* ed. Stanley Engerman and Robert Gallman (Cambridge: Cambridge University Press, 2000), 432, 435.
13. Rick Wartzman, *The End of Loyalty: The Rise and Fall of Good Jobs in America* (New York: Public Affairs, 2017), 212–13.
14. Lindert, "Twentieth-Century Foreign Trade and Trade Policy," in *The Twentieth Century,* 419, 423.
15. Ibid., 428.
16. Thomas McCraw, *American Business Since 1920: How It Worked* (Wheelan, IL: Harlan Davidson, 2000), 98–112.
17. Michael C. Jensen, "The Modern Industrial Revolution, Exit, and the Failure of Internal Control Systems," *Journal of Finance* 48, no. 3 (July 1993): 847–48, 851.
18. Anthony Mayo and Nitin Nohria, *In Their Time: The Greatest Business Leaders of the Twentieth Century* (Boston, MA: Harvard Business School Press, 2005), 259.
19. Wartzman, *The End of Loyalty,* 290.
20. Mayo and Nohria, *In Their Time,* 213.
21. Neal R. Peirce and Jerry Hagstrom, *The Book of America: Inside Fifty States Today* (New York: W. W. Norton, 1983), 258–59.
22. Carol Heim, "Structural Changes: Regional and Urban," in *The Twentieth Century,* vol. 3 of *The Cambridge Economic History of the United States,* 155.
23. Mayo and Nohria, *In Their Time,* 271–78.
24. Ibid., 279.

Ten. The Age of Optimism

1. Daniel Yergin and Joseph Stanislaw, *The Commanding Heights: The Battle Between Government and the Marketplace That Is Remaking the Modern World* (New York: Simon & Schuster, 1998), 334.
2. William Leuchtenburg, *The American President: From Teddy Roosevelt to Bill Clinton* (Oxford: Oxford University Press, 2015), 592.
3. Anthony Mayo and Nitin Nohria, *In Their Time: The Greatest Business Leaders of the Twentieth Century* (Boston, MA: Harvard Business School Press, 2005), 292.

4. Naomi Lamoreaux, ed., "Business Organization," in *Economic Structure and Performance,* vol. 3 of *Historical Statistics of the United States: Millennial Edition,* ed. Susan B. Carter et al. (New York: Cambridge University Press, 2006), 491.

5. Mayo and Nohria, *In Their Time,* 307.

6. Gerald F. Davis, *Managed by the Markets: How Finance Re-Shaped America* (Oxford: Oxford University Press, 2009), 21.

7. Adrian Wooldridge, *Masters of Management: How the Business Gurus and Their Ideas Have Changed the World—for Better and for Worse* (New York: HarperBusiness, 2011), 30.

8. Michael Jensen and William H. Meckling, "Theory of the Firm: Managerial Behavior, Agency Costs and Ownership Structure," *Journal of Financial Economics* 3, no. 4 (October 1976): 305–60.

9. Michael Schuman, *The Miracle: The Epic Story of Asia's Quest for Wealth* (New York: Harper-Collins, 2009), 181–82; Wooldridge, *Masters of Management,* 432.

10. Walter Isaacson, *The Innovators: How a Group of Hackers, Geniuses, and Geeks Created the Digital Revolution* (New York: Simon & Schuster, 2014), 263.

11. Thomas McCraw, *American Business Since 1920: How It Worked* (Wheelan, IL: Harlan Davidson, 2000), 238–39.

12. Robert J. Gordon, *The Rise and Fall of American Growth: The U.S. Standard of Living Since the Civil War* (Princeton, NJ: Princeton University Press, 2016), 506.

13. Jerome Karabel, *The Chosen: The Hidden History of Admission and Exclusion at Harvard, Yale and Princeton* (New York: Houghton Mifflin, 2005), 444.

14. Alan Greenspan, *The Age of Turbulence: Adventures in a New World* (London: Allen Lane, 2007), 169.

Eleven. The Great Recession

1. Sebastian Mallaby, *The Man Who Knew: The Life and Times of Alan Greenspan* (New York: Penguin Press, 2016), 594.

2. Douglas A. Irwin, *Clashing over Commerce: A History of U.S. Trade Policy* (Chicago: University of Chicago Press, 2017), 666–67.

3. Alan Greenspan, *The Map and the Territory 2.0: Risk, Human Nature, and the Future of Forecasting* (New York: Penguin Press, 2013), 38.

4. Daniel Yergin and Joseph Stanislaw, *The Commanding Heights: The Battle Between Government and the Marketplace That Is Remaking the Modern World* (New York: Simon & Schuster, 1998), 168.

5. Mallaby, *The Man Who Knew,* 617.

6. Ibid., 466.

7. See Carmen M. Reinhardt and Kenneth S. Rogoff, *This Time Is Different: Eight Centuries of Financial Folly* (Princeton, NJ: Princeton University Press, 2011).

Twelve. America's Fading Dynamism

1. Deirdre Nansen McCloskey, *Bourgeois Equality: How Ideas, Not Capital or Institutions, Enriched the World* (Chicago: University of Chicago Press, 2016), 500.

2. Tyler Cowen, *The Complacent Class: The Self-Defeating Quest for the American Dream* (New York: St. Martin's Press, 2017). 25. Cowen's book has been an invaluable source of data and references for this chapter.

3. Oscar Handlin and Lilian Handlin, *Liberty in Expansion 1760–1850* (New York: Harper & Row, 1989), 13.

4. See Patrick Foulis, "The Sticky Superpower," *Economist,* October 3, 2016.

5. Chang-Tai Hsieh and Enrico Moretti, "Why Do Cities Matter? Local Growth and Aggregate Growth," NBER Working Paper No. 21154, National Bureau of Economic Research, May 2015; Cowen, *The Complacent Class,* 8.

6. Raj Chetty et al., "The Fading American Dream: Trends in Absolute Income Mobility Since 1940," NBER Working Paper No. 22910, National Bureau of Economic Research, March 2017.

7. Handlin and Handlin, *Liberty in Expansion,* 141.

8. Philip K. Howard, *The Rule of Nobody: Saving America from Dead Laws and Broken Government* (New York: W. W. Norton, 2014), 33.

9. Thomas Friedman and Michael Mandelbaum, *"That Used to Be Us": What Went Wrong with America and How It Can Come Back* (New York: Little, Brown, 2011), 26.
10. Howard, *The Rule of Nobody*, 13.
11. Robert J. Gordon, *The Rise and Fall of American Growth: The U.S. Standard of Living Since the Civil War* (Princeton, NJ: Princeton University Press, 2016), 585.
12. "Too Much of a Good Thing," *Economist*, March 26, 2016.
13. Adrian Wooldridge, "The Rise of the Superstars," *Economist*, Special Report, September 17, 2016.
14. Dan Andrews, Chiara Criscuolo, and Peter Gal, *Frontier Firms, Technology Diffusion and Public Policy: Micro Evidence from OECD Countries*, OECD Productivity Working Paper, 2015.
15. Gordon, *The Rise and Fall of American Growth*, 629.
16. Anne Case and Angus Deaton, "Rising Morbidity and Mortality in Mid-Life Among White Non-Hispanic Americans in the 21st Century," *Proceedings of the National Academy of the United States* 112, no. 49; Anne Case and Angus Deaton, "Mortality and Morbidity in the 21st Century," Brookings Institution, Brookings Paper on Economic Activity, March 23, 2017.
17. The 2017 Annual Report of the Board of Trustees of the Federal Old-Age and Survivors Insurance and Federal Disability Insurance Trust Funds, 199.
18. Howard, *The Rule of Nobody*, 8.
19. Ibid., 21.
20. "Rules for Fools," *Economist*, May 12, 2011.

Conclusion

1. Michael Haines, ed., "Population Characteristics," in *Population*, vol. 1 of *Historical Statistics of the United States: Millennial Edition*, ed. Susan B. Carter et al. (New York: Cambridge University Press, 2006), 21.
2. Susan Carter et al., eds., "Labor," in *Work and Welfare*, vol. 2 of *Historical Statistics of the United States: Millennial Edition*, 10.
3. Michael Haines, ed., "Vital Statistics," in *Population*, vol. 1 of *Historical Statistics of the United States: Millennial Edition*, 388.
4. Richard S. Tedlow, *Giants of Enterprise: Seven Business Innovators and the Empires They Built* (New York: HarperBusiness, 2001), 427.
5. Ibid., 200.
6. Peter Thiel, *Zero to One: Notes on Start-ups, or How to Build the Future* (New York: Crown Business, 2014), 34.
7. Ibid., 387.
8. Robert J. Gordon, *The Rise and Fall of American Growth: The U.S. Standard of Living Since the Civil War* (Princeton, NJ: Princeton University Press, 2016), 270–71.
9. Stanley Lebergott, *Pursuing Happiness: American Consumers in the Twentieth Century* (Princeton, NJ: Princeton University Press, 1993), 82.
10. Ibid., 98.
11. Gordon, *The Rise and Fall of American Growth*, 103.
12. Lebergott, *Pursuing Happiness*, 24.
13. Ibid., 112–13.
14. Ibid.
15. Carter et al., "Labor Force," in *Work and Welfare*, vol. 2 of *Historical Statistics of the United States: Millennial Edition*, 17–23.
16. Ibid., 20.
17. "Age Shall Not Wither Them," *Economist*, April 7, 2011.
18. "Researchers Find Risk-Taking Behavior Rises Until Age 50," University of Oregon, Media Relations, November 10, 2011, https://uonews.uoregon.edu/archive/news-release/2011/11/researchers-find-risk-taking-behavior-rises-until-age-50.

Appendix: Data and Methodology

1. Prominent among them Robert J. Gordon, Christina D. Romer, Robert E. Gallman, Paul David, Stanley L. Engerman, and John Kendrick.

2. Richard Sutch, ed., "National Income and Product," in *Economic Structure and Performance*, vol. 3 of *Historical Statistics of the United States: Millennial Edition*, ed. Susan B. Carter et al. (New York: Cambridge University Press, 2006).

3. *Historical Statistics* (2006), 3–27, 3–28.

4. *Historical Statistics*, series Dc662, 4–500.

5. *Historical Statistics*, table Ae-A, 1–654.

6. David R. Weir, "A Century of U.S. Unemployment, 1890–1990," in *Research in Economic History*, vol. 14, ed. Roger L. Ransom, Richard Sutch, and Susan B. Carter (Stamford CT: JAI Press, 1992).

7. Thomas Weiss, "Estimates of White and Nonwhite Gainful Workers in the United States by Age Group, Race, and Sex: Decennial Census Years, 1800–1900," *Historical Methods* 32 (1): 1999.

8. U.S. Department of the Treasury, *Statistical Appendix to the Annual Report of the Secretary of the Treasury* (1970 and 1971).

9. U.S. Department of Commerce, "Historical Statistics on Government Finance and Employment," in *Census of Governments, 1982*, vol. 6, 225–64.

10. Richard E. Sylla, John B. Legler, and John Joseph Wallis, *State and Local Government [United States]: Source and Uses of Funds, City and Country Data, Nineteenth Century*, computer file number 9728, Inter-University Consortium for Political and Social Research, 1993; John Joseph Wallis, "American Government Finance in the Long Run: 1790 to 1900," *Journal of Economic Perspectives* 14 (2000): 61–82.

11. Robert F. Martin, *National Income in the United States, 1799–1938* (New York: National Industrial Conference Board, 1939).

12. Marvin W. Towne and Wayne E. Rasmussen, "Farm Gross Product and Gross Investment During the Nineteenth Century," in *Studies in Income and Wealth*, vol. 24 (Washington, D.C.: National Bureau of Economic Research, 1960).

13. Weir, "A Century of U.S. Unemployment."

14. Weiss, "Estimates of White and Nonwhite Gainful Workers in the United States"; Weiss, "U.S. Labor Force Estimates and Economic Growth, 1800–1860," in *American Economic Growth and Standards of Living Before the Civil War*, ed. Robert E. Gallman and John Joseph Wallis (Chicago: National Bureau of Economic Research and University of Chicago Press, 1992).

15. John W. Kendrick, "Appendix B: Agriculture, Forestry, and Fisheries" in *Productivity Trends in the United States* (Princeton, NJ: National Bureau of Economic Research and Princeton University Press, 1961).

16. Witt Bowden, "Wages, Hours, and Productivity of Industrial Labor, 1909 to 1939," *Monthly Labor Review* 51, no. 3. U.S. Bureau of Labor Statistics, U.S. Department of Labor (September 1940).

17. Kendrick, "Appendix D: Manufacturing" in *Productivity Trends in the United States*.

18. "Technical Information About the BLS Multifactor Productivity Measures," U.S. Bureau of Labor Statistics, September 26, 2007, https://www.bls.gov/mfp/mprtech.pdf.

19. Raymond W. Goldsmith, "The Growth of Reproducible Wealth of the United States of America from 1805 to 1950," in International Association for Research in Income and Wealth, *Income and Wealth of the United States: Trends and Structure*, Income and Wealth Series II (Bowes and Bowes, 1952), 306; Raymond W. Goldsmith, *The National Wealth of the United States in the Postwar Period* (Princeton, NJ: Princeton University Press, 1962), appendix A and B.

20. "120 Years of American Education: A Statistical Portrait," U.S. Department of Education, January 1993, https://nces.ed.gov/pubs93/93442.pdf.

21. Robert A. Margo, *Wages and Labor Markets Before the Civil War* (Chicago: University of Chicago Press, 2000).

22. Stanley Lebergott, *Manpower in Economic Growth: The American Record Since 1800* (New York: McGraw-Hill, 1964).

INDEX

INDEX

INDEX